The Charlton Standard Catalogue of

Canadian Coins

58th EDITION
2004

W. K. CROSS
Publisher

The Charlton Press

TORONTO, ONTARIO α PALM HARBOR, FLORIDA

ABOUT PRICING IN THIS CATALOGUE

The purpose of this catalogue is to give the most accurate, up-to-date retail prices for all Canadian coins. To this end, we have from the very inception of this catalogue used a pricing panel of established experts who have submitted the most current market values from across Canada. These individual market results are drawn from both dealer and collector activity as well as recent auction results and are averaged to reflect the current marketplace for Canadian coins.

A necessary word of caution: no catalogue can or should propose to be a fixed price list. This catalogue then, should be considered as a guide, showing the most current retail prices possible for the collector and dealer alike.

The National Library of Canada has catalogued this publication as follows:

Canadian coins: a Charlton standard catalogue

Continues: Standard catalogue of Canadian coins, ISSN 0845-5708
Issues for winter 1981-   have title: Charlton standard catalogue
Canadian coins.
ISSN 0704-0424
ISBN 0-88968-278-X (58th edition)

    1. Coins, Canadian - Periodicals. 2. Coins - Prices - Periodicals.
I. Charlton Press II. Title: Charlton standard catalogue of Canadian coins

CJ1864.S82   737.4971   C82-031158-8

**Printed in Canada
in the Province of Quebec**

EDITORIAL

Editor	W. K. Cross
Editorial Assistant	Jean Dale
Graphic Technician	Davina Rowan
Photography	Scott Cornwell

SPECIAL MENTION

We would like to offer a special thanks to Sandy Campbell for his work, which lead to the pricing of the Pattern section of the 57th edition. Jim Charlton must be given special credit for all the work over the years which made this catalogue possible.

Phil Taylor, Susan Taylor and Cosme Saffioti, of the Royal Canadian Mint, in Ottawa, must be offered a special thank you for their assistance with the 58th edition.

We wish to thank the American Numismatic Association and Q. David Bowers, the author of the 'Official Grading Standards For U.S. Coins,' for allowing us to use parts of their work in our introduction.

PRICING PANEL FOR THE 58TH EDITION

The publisher would like to thank the following individuals and institutions for all their assistance and work that made the 58th edition possible:

Bob Armstrong	Alain Gallo	J. C. Levesque
Ted Bailey	Nick Gerbinksi	Guy Lestrade
Cameron Bevers	Andy Grecco	Peter McDonald
Sandy Campbell	Joe Iorio	Hugh A. Powell
Terry Campbell	Ian Laing	Michael Rogozinsky
J. E. Charlton	Serge Laramée	Charlie Taylor
Brian Cornwell	James Lawson	Sean Taylor
Bob Dowsett	Frank Leardi	Randy Weir

CONTRIBUTORS TO THE 58TH EDITION

David Cawdron	Morris Furball	Doug Shand
Jay Charland	Roger Grondin	Jack Shore
Louis Chevrier	Jeff Kennison	Ross Todd

Editorial Office
P.O. Box 820, Postal Station Willowdale B
North York, Ontario M2K 2R1
Tel.: (416) 488-1418 Fax: (416) 488-4656
Tel.: (800) 442-6042 Fax.: (800) 442-1542
www.charltonpress.com
email: chpress@charltonpress.com

TABLE OF CONTENTS

INTRODUCTION

The Charlton Standard Catalogue of Canadian Coins is an illustrated, descriptive price catalogue for the principal types of commercial and commemorative coins used in Canada over the years, including pre-Confederation regions. As a standard catalogue, it provides an accurate overview and introduction to Canadian numismatics and current market values. Each major variety of all issues of Canadian coins is listed, illustrated and priced. Several minor varieties that have a wide appeal to collectors, such as Arnprior dollars, are also included. Historical introductions provide important background information for each series, and relevant technical information is provided wherever available.

The new reader should find in this catalogue all the basic information needed to identify and evaluate individual coins as he or she embarks upon an old and widely enjoyed hobby. Continuing and expanding upon the completely revised and enlarged text introduced in the 32nd edition, readers will find herein more historical information, technical data and statistics than has ever before been compiled for a Canadian coin catalogue. A summary of the principal foreign coins used during the French and British regimes is included, as well as local, pre-decimal issues. The decimal series is complete for the provinces of British North America and Canada from its inception to the present, and also includes patterns, essais and test tokens.

This edition is just the latest in our continuing efforts to bring readers the best possible reference book for one of Canada's most popular and profitable pastimes. Welcome then to this new edition of the 'Charlton Standard Catalogue of Canadian Coins' and the exciting field of Canadian numismatics.

THE COLLECTING OF CANADIAN DECIMAL COINS
PAST AND PRESENT

Today, the majority of those collecting Canadian numismatic material specialize in the decimal coin series. The collecting popularity of decimal coins is a relatively recent phenomenon, however. When Canada's first coin club was formed in Montreal in 1862, there was little interest in either coins or paper money. Eighty years later this was still the case. Most collectors specialized in Canadian tokens, the private coppers that served for so long as a medium of exchange in the absence of official coins. Decimal coins were mostly collected by type. One or two examples of each design were sufficient, and there was little concern regarding the relative scarcity of the various dates and varieties.

The current preoccupation with collecting decimal coins by date and variety arose in the 1940's, under the influence of U.S. dealer Wayte Raymond. Shortly after World War II and on into the 1950's, Canadian pioneers J. Douglas Ferguson, Fred Bowman, Sheldon Carroll and Leslie Hill attempted to establish the relative rarities of the decimal coins issued up to that time.

In 1950 collectors in the Ottawa area joined with scattered groups and individuals to form the Canadian Numismatic Association. Its official publication, and annual conventions beginning in 1954, served to bridge the miles and facilitate the exchange of information and ideas.

Two years after the C.N.A. was formed, the Charlton Standard Catalogue made its appearance. Early editions were modest paperback pamphlets with line drawings, but they were a serious attempt to list and price Canadian coins, tokens, paper money and some medals. The first hard-cover edition of 128 pages appeared in 1960. By 1971 it had grown to 200 pages, and by 1978 so much additional numismatic information was available that it was decided the needs of collectors could best be met by splitting the catalogue into separate, specialized works.

The 27th (1979) Edition became the 'Standard Catalogue of Canadian Coins,' now issued yearly. This was followed by the annual edition of the 'Charlton Standard Catalogue of Canadian Government Paper Money,' the 'Standard Catalogue of Canadian Colonial Tokens,' and the 'Charlton Standard Catalogue of Canadian Bank Notes.' A new series, 'Canadian Commemorative Medals' is under development.

BUILDING A COLLECTION

Decimal coin collections can be formed in a variety of ways. Coins may come from pocket change, family hoards, the bank, the mint or from other collectors. In general, older coins no longer circulate and the excitement of searching through change for missing dates has been diminished by the withdrawal of most silver coins from circulation.

Collecting is a matter of individual taste. Some people collect by design type, others concentrate on one or two denominations or monarchs, while some brave souls try to collect the entire decimal series. Regardless of which path you choose, there is a variety of coin boards, envelopes and other supplies available to help house and organize your collection. For reasons of security many collectors keep their best coins in a bank vault.

Another decision that must be made when building a collection is the minimum state of preservation one will accept when buying coins. As a general rule, it is advisable to buy the best condition coins one can afford.

AGE - RARITY - DEMAND - CONDITION - VALUE

The value of a coin on the numismatic market is dictated by a complex mixture of factors. One feature that those unfamiliar with coins often mistakenly believe to be of great importance is age. That age is a minor contributor to value is illustrated by the fact that the 1969 Large Date variety 10 cents is worth far more than the 1870 10-cent piece, a coin nearly 100 years older!

Basically, a coin's value is determined by a combination of supply and demand. The 1870 50-cent piece does not command as high a premium as the 1921 coin of the same denomination because there are many more 1870s than 1921s available. On the other hand, the variety of the 1872H 50-cents with an "A" punched over the "V" in "VICTORIA" on the obverse sells for about the same as the variety with a normal "V" even though the coins from the blundered die are much rarer. The modest price difference reflects the slight difference in demand.

Finally, the state of preservation of a coin markedly influences its value. It is not unusual for an uncirculated (brand new) George V silver coin, for example, to sell for 50 times what a coin of the same date and denomination would bring in well-worn condition.

GRADING CANADIAN COINS

Canadian coins, as with coins of any other country, can be distinguished from each other by a simple comparison of their coin type, denomination, and date of issue. Coins of the same type, denomination and date can be further identified from each other by each coin's "condition" or state of preservation.

Coin conditions vary considerably. They range from the poorest state where the date and other details can barely be determined to the best states where details are as sharp and clear as the moment the coin was minted. Generally coin conditions are dvided into one or two categories, namely, circulated condition or uncirculated condition. Examples of circulated coins are those that you might find in pocket change. These coins have varying degrees of surface wear as a result of human handling or use as "money" in our world of commerce. Uncirculated coins (also called mint state coins) differ from circulated coins in that they must have absolutely no visible signs of wear on any part of the coin's surface. However uncirculated coins are not necessarily flawless. The majority will still have small marks, as opposed to wear, which are a result of contact with other coins received when they were distributed by the mint to our banking system in large bags.

Once a coin's condition is understood it can be assigned one of a number of circulated or uncirculated "grades" according to grading standards accepted by the coin industry in Canada. Early standards for grading Canadian coins that appeared in the first Charlton catalogue in 1952 used terms like Very Good and Extremely Fine to describe some of these grades. Since that time coin grading has been considerably refined. Today there are ten offically recognized grades for circulated coins and a further ten to designate all of the uncirculated grades, although only five of the latter are generally in use.

Since 1979 the Charlton Standard Catalogue has utilized a grading system similar to that accepted by the American Numismatic Association for United States coinage in 1977. Some of the following general text has been reproduced from "The Official ANA Grading Standards for

United States Coins". We wish to express our appreciation to the American Numismatic Association for allowing us to do so.

ADJECTIVAL AND NUMERICAL GRADING SYSTEMS

New coin collectors and investors are often confused when they read or hear about an adjectival grading scheme on the one hand and a numerical system on the other. There is no need for this confusion. Both systems use the same grade definitions. They simply refer to them by different labels.

Adjectival grading, as the name implies, uses adjectives to describe coin grades. This scheme has been in use since the earliest days of Canadian numismatics and is therefore the traditional grading nomenclature. The following adjectives represent most of the officially accepted grades (from poorest quality to best) in use today: About Good (AG), Good (G), Very Good (VG), Fine (F), Very Fine (VF), Choice Very Fine (Choice VF), Extremely Fine (EF), Choice Extremely Fine (Choice EF), About Uncirculated (AU), Choice About Uncirculated (Choice AU)), Typical Uncirculated (Unc. or BU), Select Uncirculated (Select Unc.), Choice Uncirculated (Choice Unc.), Gem Uncirculated (Gem Unc.) and Perfect Uncirculated (Perfect Unc.).

The numerical grading system is a modern day development by comparison. It was devised by Dr. William Sheldon in the late 1940's. Sheldon's numerical grading scale used numbers ranging from one to seventy. All circulated grades were assigned numbers in the range of 1 to 59 while the numbers from 60 to 70 were reserved for the uncirculated grades. His intent was to have a grading scheme that would inter-relate both coin grades and coin prices for each grade. He accomplished this by assigning specific numbers from these ranges to each of the traditionally used adjectival grades. A summary of these adjectival grades with his numerical designation follows:

About Good-3, Good-4, Very-Good 8, Fine-12, Very Fine-20, Choice Very Fine-30, Extremely Fine-40, Choice Extremely Fine-45, About Uncirculated-50, Choice About Uncirculated-55, Typical Uncirculated-60, Select Uncirculated-63, Choice Uncirculated-65, Gem Uncirculated-67, Perfect Uncirculated-70.

The basis of his actual number selection was the relative prices of early American copper coins in each of the various grades. For example, in the late 1940's, a typical uncirculated coin (MS-60) was determined to be about 7½ times the price of a typical Very Good (VG-8) example of the same kind and so on.

The numerical system has now been extended beyond early American copper coins to include most areas of North American numismatics. Sheldon's number assignments no longer have any relevance to current coin pricing as they once did. Today a typical MS-60 coin might easily be priced 50 to 100 times more than a typical VG-8 coin of the same kind! Unfortunately this only adds to the confusion of those graders who expect his number assignments to have some special pricing or other scientific meaning.

COIN GRADING AND HUMAN NATURE

Before actually trying to understand all of the rules relating to coin grading, it is equally important to appreciate the human elements that often surround the act of grading a coin. Inexperienced coin graders are often dismayed by the seemingly large number of grading arguments, some very heated, that arise within this industry. Why are there differences of opinion in the field of grading coins? There are numerous reasons, but the most common are as follows:

Grading coins can never be completely scientific in all areas. A great deal of human judgement is also involved. One may weigh a coin and also obtain its specific gravity by mechanical devices and the result will be factual if accurate equipment is used carefully. There are no scientific means available to measure the surface condition – the amount of wear – of a coin.

In grading coins, considerations such as striking, surface of the planchet, the presence of heavy toning (which may obscure certain surface characteristics), the design, and other factors each lend an influence. A panel containing a dozen of the foremost numismatic industry leaders justifiably could have some **slight** difference of opinion on the precise grade of some coins.

However, it is not **slight** differences which concern us here; it is serious or major differences. The term "overgrading" refers to describing a coin as a grade higher than it actually is. For example, if a coin in AU (About Uncirculated) grade is called Uncirculated, it is overgraded. If a coin in Very Fine grade is called Extremely Fine, it is overgraded.

What induces overgrading? Here are some of the factors:

Buyers Seeking Bargains. The desire to get a bargain is part of human nature. If a given Uncirculated coin actively traded at $100 is offered at $70, it will attract a lot of bargain seekers. These same buyers would reject an offering such as: "I am offering this stock which trades on the New York Stock Exchange for $100 for just $70 cash," or "I am offering $100 bills for $70 each."

In coins, as in any other walk of life, you get what you pay for. If a coin which has a standard value of $100 is offered for $70 there may be nothing wrong, but chances are the piece is overgraded.

False Assumptions. Buyers often assume falsely that any advertisement which appears in a numismatic publication has been approved by that publication. Actually, publishers cannot be expected to examine coins and approve of all listings offered. A person who has no numismatic knowledge or experience whatsoever can have letterheads and business cards printed and, assuming he has good financial and character references (but not necessarily numismatic expertise), run large and flashy advertisements. Months or years later it is often too late for the deceived buyer to get his money back. The solution to this is to learn how to grade coins and think for yourself. Examine the credentials of the seller. Is he truly an expert in his field? How do you know? What do collectors with more experience think of this seller? To what professional organizations does this dealer belong? It is usually foolish to rush and spend your hard-earned money with a coin seller who has no professional credentials and whose only attraction is that he is offering "bargains." Think for yourself!

The Profit Motive. Sellers seeking an unfair markup may overgrade. For purposes of illustration, let us assume that a given variety of coin is worth the following prices in these grades: AU $75, and Uncirculated $150. A legitimate dealer in the course of business would buy, for example, an AU coin at $50 or $60 and sell it retail for $75, thus making a profit of $15 to $25. However, there are sellers who are not satisfied with the normal way of doing business. They take shortcuts. They pay $50 or $60 for the same AU coin which is worth $75 retail, but rather than calling it AU they call it "Uncirculated" and sell it for $150. So, instead of making $15 to $25 they may make $90 to $100!

Inexperience or error on the part of the seller may lead to incorrect grading – both overgrading and undergrading.

GRADING CIRCULATED COINS

Once a coin enters circulation it begins to show signs of wear. As time goes on the coin becomes more and more worn until, after a period of many decades, only a few of the coin's original detailed features may be left. Some coins that have not entered circulation may still show signs of wear, usually through mishandling and poor storage. These too must be graded as circulated coins, as long as there is some visible sign of wear.

While numbers from 1 through 59 are continuous, it has been found practical to restrict their use to the limited number that follow. Hence, this text uses the following descriptions and their numerical equivalents.

Choice About Uncirculated-55. Abbreviation: AU-55. Only a small trace of wear is visible on the highest points of the coin. As is the case with other grades here, specific information is listed in the following text under the various types, for wear often occurs in different spots on different designs.

About Uncirculated-50. Abbreviation: AU-50. With traces of wear on nearly all of the highest areas. At least half of the original mint lustre is present.

Choice Extremely Fine-45. Abbreviation: EF-45. With light overall wear on the coin's highest points. All design details are very sharp. Mint lustre is usually seen only in protected areas of the coin's surface.

Extremely Fine-40. Abbreviation: EF-40. With only slight wear but more extensive than the preceeding, still with excellent overall sharpness. Traces of mint lustre may still show.

Choice Very Fine-30. Abbreviation: VF-30. With light even wear on the surface; design details on the highest points lightly worn, but with all lettering and major features sharp.

Very Fine-20. Abbreviation: VF-20. As preceeding but with moderate wear on highest parts.

Fine-12. Abbreviation: F-12. Moderate to considerable even wear. Entire design is bold. All lettering visible, but with some weaknesses.

Very Good-8. Abbreviation: VG-8. Well worn. Most fine details such as hair strands, leaf details, and so on are worn nearly smooth.

Good-4. Abbreviation: G-4. Heavily worn. Major designs visible, but with faintness in areas. Other major features visible in outline form without centre detail.

About Good-3. Abbreviation: AG-3. Very heavily worn with portions of the lettering, date and legends being worn smooth. The date is barely readable.

Note: The exact descriptions of circulated grades vary widely from issue to issue, so the preceeding commentary is only of a very general nature. It is essential to refer to a detailed grading guide when grading any coin.

HELPFUL TIPS WHEN GRADING CIRCULATED COINS

While circulated coins are graded primarily by the amount of wear shown on the coin's surfaces, it is sometimes difficult for beginner graders to appreciate just how much wear is allowable at each grade level. Several grading aids can help the beginner achieve a reasonable degree of grading accuracy and consistency from coin to coin:

(a) Standard photographs of coins of each coin type and grade are helpful for comparison grading. They indicate the approximate wear you can expect on a typical coin of that series and grade.

(b) Familiarize yourself with all of a coin's highest points of relief before trying to decide if the coin shows signs of wear or is strictly uncirculated.

(c) Circulated coins are more abundant in the commercial marketplace than uncirculated coins. This offers the novice grader ample opportunity to visually check with many graders for their interpretation of what constitutes each of the circulated grades. This is a more detailed form of comparison grading than (a).

Ask a recognized grading authority to criticize your grading ability and technique. Listen and learn from the professionals if you want to grade well.

GRADING UNCIRCULATED COINS

As the name implies, an uncirculated coin is one that has never been in circulation. Such coins must show absolutely no signs of wear to the naked eye. However the actual grade of the coin is determined by assessing three specific factors (none involving surface wear as with circulated coins) and furthermore can be influenced by still other considerations. Uncirculated coins are more difficult to grade than circulated coins. Some of the reasons are:

(a) **Three primary grading factors** - the grade of an uncirculated coin is determined by assessing the qualities of each of the coin's lustre, surface condition and fullness of strike. Furthermore these factors are interdependent. That is, if one factor is of truly exceptional quality it can "make up" for a deficiency in the quality of another factor.

(b) **Toning is not a grading factor** - unlike popular belief, the toning that might be present on a coin and which might add considerably to the coin's overall eye appeal is not to be considered one of the grading elements. Toning is an enhancing feature that might affect the coins final price but not its grade. Coins that are toned are best graded as if they were fully brilliant. Toning, if present, is described separately from the grade with such adjectives as "attractive rainbow toning" and so on.

(c) **Understand typical mintstate characteristics** - it is not possible to accurately grade an uncirculated coin unless the grader understands what qualities to expect for each of the factors of lustre, surfaces, and strike for a coin of that type. This is the main reason why graders of another country's coins can find so much difficulty in properly grading Canadian coins.

(d) **Understand the coinage metal** - the strike and surface quality of an uncirculated coin is partially dependent on the base metal used in the manufacture of a coin. Coin graders must understand that each of the metals of nickel, copper, gold and silver vary dramatically in the damage they will sustain when they come in contact with other hard objects. Gold coins are relatively soft and heavy. They damage easily. Nickel coins are very hard and often display mushy strikes.

(e) **Expect marks on normal uncirculated coins** - with the exception of certain special mint sets made in recent years for collectors. Uncirculated or normal production struck coins were produced on high speed presses, stored in bags together with other coins, run through counting machines, and in other ways handled without regard to numismatic posterity. As a result, it is the rule and not the exception for an Uncirculated coin to have bag marks and evidence of coin-to-coin contact, although the coin might not have had actual commercial circulation. The number of such marks will depend upon the coin's actual size and metal composition.

(f) **Striking and minting peculiarities** - certain early coins have mint-caused planchet or adjustment marks, a series of parallel striations. If these are visible to the naked eye they should be described adjectively in addition to the numerical or regular descriptive grade. For example: "MS-60 with adjustment marks," or "MS-65 with adjustment marks," or "Perfect Uncirculated with very light adjustment marks," or something similar.

If an Uncirculated coin exhibits weakness due to striking or die wear, or unusual (for the variety) die wear, this must be adjectively mentioned in addition to the grade. Examples are: "MS-60, lightly struck," or "Choice Uncirculated, lightly struck," and MS-70, lightly struck."

DEFINITIONS FOR UNCIRCULATED COINS

Uncirculated coins may be assigned one of a possible five grades that are officially in use within the numismatic industry. These are (with their numerical grade in brackets): Uncirculated (Mintstate-60), Select Uncirculated (MS-63), Choice Uncirculated (MS-65), Gem Uncirculated (MS-67) and Perfect Uncirculated (MS-70). The use of the remaining numbers in the range from 60 to 70 is not recommended. To do so might suggest or attach a degree of grading accuracy that is either unwarranted or unrecognizable to all but the most expert of graders. The definitions for each of the uncirculated grades are:

Perfect Uncirculated (MS-70). MS-70 is the finest quality available. Such a coin under 4X magnification will show no marks, lines or other evidence of handling or contact with other coins. The strike will be full and show all of the detail as intended by the engraver. The coin's lustre will be of the highest imaginable quality for a coin of that particular series or type.

A brilliant coin may be described as "MS-70, Brilliant" or "Perfect Brilliant Uncirculated." A lightly toned coin may be described as "MS-70, Toned" or "Perfect Toned Uncirculated." In the case of particularly attractive or unusual toning, additional adjectives may be used such as "Perfect Uncirculated with attractive iridescent peripheral toning."

Note for copper coins: To qualify as MS-70 or Perfect Uncirculated, a copper coin must have its full lustre and original natural surface colour, and may not be toned brown, olive or any other colour. Copper coins with toned surfaces which are otherwise perfect should be described as MS-67 as the following text indicates.

Gem Uncirculated (MS-67). MS-67 coins will appear as perfect coins to all but the most expert of graders. They are exceptional in all respects: superb surfaces, superb lustre and full strike or nearly so. If there are any negatives they will not be obvious at first glance but discovered only after extensive study and with 4X magnification.

Choice Uncirculated (MS-65). An MS-65 coin is easily distinguished from lower grades of uncirculated coins by its distinctive "quality" look. To the normal naked eye an MS-65 coin will appear "almost" perfect at first glance. Only under more detailed examination will minor flaws be discovered. The coin's lustre will usually be better than typically seen for uncirculated coins of this type. The strike will be at least typical for the series if not better. The surfaces will show only slight marks that will not at all be distracting to the overall appeal of the coin. Occasionally one of these factors may be of such high quality as to make up for another factor which is less than desirable; ie. superb lustre accommodating one extra slight bagmark.

Select Uncirculated (MS-63). An MS-63 coin is basically a nice example which does not meet the strict "quality" requirements of an MS-65. Many of the MS-63 coin's features will be attractive and at least typical of what you would expect of a new coin of this particular type. The surface marks generally are noticeable but their number and size are such that they are not major or bothersome distractions to the viewer. The lustre is generally attractive but may have a slight dullness or dull areas. The strike is most likely typical for the series. Often MS-63 coins are MS-65 coins that have slight "problems" such as "one mark too many" and so on. Very often one grading factor, with exceptional qualities not normally expected at this grade, will make up for weaker factors (eg. flawless surface makes up for dulled, less than typical lustre).

Typical Uncirculated (MS-60). An MS-60 coin will have a moderate number of bag marks of varying sizes depending on the softness of the coin's metal. The surfaces may have what is typically described as a "baggy" look. Also present may be minor edge nicks but none of a major concern. Unusually deep marks, however caused, must be described separately. The lustre may be impaired by dullness from cleaning and the like and consequently be considered less than typical for a new coin of this type. The strike may show clear evidence of weaknesses in one or more areas. Many of the coins "problems" will be distracting to anyone who thinks a "new" coin is in near-perfect condition.

SELECTION OF AN UNCIRCULATED GRADE

The definitions of the uncirculated grades at each end of the grading range (ie. MS-60 and MS-70) are straightforward. The MS-60 coin must show no signs of wear. The MS-70 coin must be perfect as defined earlier. Most graders have difficulty with the in-between uncirculated grades of MS-63, MS-65 and MS-67. This also seems to be the area where most grading conflicts exist. These difficulties arise because graders (a) are unfamiliar with a particular coin's typical mintstate characteristics which serve as a reference point, and (b) do not really appreciate that the factors of lustre, surfaces and strike can interrelate with each other, ie. that trade-offs can exist at each grade level. Graders of uncirculated coins must appreciate the following:

(a)   **Lustre qualities** - An uncirculated coin with excellent lustre can make an otherwise undesirable uncirculated coin desirable. That's because lustre, especially that which is 'alive' or 'blazing' can add considerably to a coin's overall eye appeal and divert attention away from other distracting problems with the coin. On the other hand, lustre that is dull or lifeless can have the opposite effect on the coin viewer and make the coin a very undesirable object.

(b)   **Surface condition** - An uncirculated coin is judged for the number, size and location of marks (as opposed to wear) on its surfaces. Coins that have fewer marks are more desirable than those that have many and look "baggy". Smaller marks are preferred to those that are large and very distracting. Marks, if they are to be present at all, are preferred to be hidden in unnoticeable places such as in the coin's detail rather than in open areas where they can be very distracting. Marks that are awkwardly located, such as on the nose of the monarch, are undesirable because they lower the aesthetic appeal of the coin.

(c)   **Strike qualities** - All uncirculated coins are judged for the quality of their strike relative to that typically seen on a mintstate coin of that particular series. Generally the fuller a coin's strike, the more desirable the coin. Strike qualities can vary considerably within the Canadian decimal series and even from date to date within a specific type series.

(d)   **Interrelationship of grading factors** - Particularly for the in-between grades of MS-63, MS-65 and MS-67, the three factors of lustre, surfaces and strike can occur in many combinations to still yield the same overall grade selection. The coin grader must therefore develop a "feel" for how one factor that might be of exceptional quality can make up for another that is slightly deficient from that typicaly expected.

HELPFUL HINTS FOR GRADING UNCIRCULATED COINS

Grading uncirculated coins is a more complex and demanding task than that required by circulated coins. To help achieve a reasonable degree of grading accuracy and grading consistency from uncirculated coin to uncirculated coin, graders should develop the following grading habits:

(a)   Always follow a fixed grading routine. Grading an uncirculated coin requires mental preparation, having the right equipment, studying the coin, analyzing the observed data, selecting a grade and checking your decision for reasonableness.

(b)   Study heavily toned coins carefully. Use good lighting and a strong magnifier. Toning can hide marks and other serious coin problems.

(c)   Examine coins under a wide range of lighting sources and angles at which the light strikes the coin's surfaces. Lighting can be very deceptive.

(d)   Do not attempt to grade too many coins at one sitting. For best results your eyes must be relaxed. Allow ample time to consider all factors.

(e)   Clearly understand the typical mintstate characteristics of the coin type that you are about to grade. This is your reference point to tell you what to expect so that you can then accurately select a grade.

SPLIT AND INTERMEDIATE GRADES

It is often the case that because of the peculiarities of striking or a coin's design, one side of the coin will grade differently from the other. In this situation, a diagonal mark is used to separate the two. For example, a coin with an AU-50 obverse and a Choice Extremely Fine-45 reverse can be described as AU-EF or alternatively 50/45. If, in the preceeding example, the grader chooses to select only one overall or composite grade to describe the coin, then the lower of the two grades must be chosen, ie. Choice Extremely Fine-45.

Most advanced collectors and dealers find the official grade designations to be sufficient to fairly describe the majority of coins that appear in the marketplace. However, some coins might more than meet the minimum requirements of one grade but not quite those of the next higher grade. The use of intermediate grades such as EF-42 or EF-43 to describe a nice example of an EF coin is not encouraged. Grading is not that precise and such finely split intermediate grades suggests a degree of accuracy that probably can not be verified by other numismatists. In this situation the best policy is to stick with the official designation of EF-40 and append adjectives to the grade such as in "a nice example of EF-40" and so on.

LIGHTING AND MAGNIFICATION

The same coin can have a different appearance depending upon the lighting conditions and also the amount of magnification used to examine it. For purposes of standardization, we recommend that a magnifying glass of four to eight power be used. This is sufficient to reveal all the differences and peculiarities necessary to grade the coin accurately. At the same time it is not too much magnification. Under extensive magnification — 10 power or more — even the finest coin may show many marks and imperfections in an exaggerated fashion. You may wish to keep a stronger magnifying glass on hand, however, for examination of minute die details.

It is also desirable to use a magnifying glass of sufficient width so that a fairly large amount of the coin's surface can be studied at one time.

Recommended for grading is a 100 watt incandescent light bulb approximately three feet (one metre) from the coin (or a 50 watt bulb at about half the distance, or other equivalents). Incandescent light furnishes a pinpoint light source and enables surface characteristics to be studied in more detail. Fluorescent light, which spreads illumination from a diffused origin, is apt to conceal minute differences. "Tensor" type lamps, popular at coin conventions, furnish a high intensity pinpoint light source and are satisfactory for grading.

To grade a coin, hold it between your fingertips (over a soft surface to prevent damage in the event of dropping) at an angle so that light from the bulb reflects from the coin's surface into your eye. Turn or rotate the coin horizontally so that different characteristics can be observed in better detail. You will want to examine the edge also.

Lamp wattages and magnifying intensities are less critical with circulated grades. They are very important, however, for Uncirculated and Proof coins where judgment is dependant upon relatively small differences in surface appearance.

NATURAL COLOURATION OF COINS

Knowledge of the natural colour which coinage metals acquire over a period of years is useful to the collector. To an extent, a coin's value is determined by the attractiveness of its colouration. Also, certain types of unnatural colour might indicate that a coin has been cleaned or otherwise treated.

The basic coinage metals used in Canada are alloys of copper, nickel, silver and gold. Copper tends to tone the most rapidly. Gold is the least chemically active and will tone only slightly and then only over a long period of years.

Copper. Copper is among the most chemically active of all coinage metals. When a copper coin is first struck, it emerges from the dies with a brilliant pale orange surface.

Once a freshly minted copper coin enters the atmosphere it immediately begins to oxidize. Over a period of years, especially if exposed to actively circulating air, if placed in contact with sulphites, the coin will acquire a glossy brown surface. In between the brilliant glossy brown stages it will be part red and part brown.

An Uncirculated coin with full original mint brilliance, usually slightly subdued in colouration, is typically described as Brilliant Uncirculated (our example here is for a typical Uncirculated or MS-60 coin); a Choice piece would be called Choice Brilliant Uncirculated, and so on. One which is part way between the brilliant and brown surface hues would be called Red and Brown Uncirculated. Specimens with brownish surfaces can be called Brown Uncirculated. Particularly valuable coins can have the colouration described in more detail. Generally, in any category of grading, the more explanation given, the more accurate the description.

Early copper coins with full original mint brilliance are more valuable than Red and Brown Uncirculated or Brown Uncirculated pieces. The more original mint brilliance present, the more valuable a coin will be. The same is true of Proofs.

Circulated copper coins are never fully brilliant, but are toned varying shades of brown.

Nickel. Uncirculated nickel coins when first minted are silver/gray in appearance, not as bright as silver but still with much brilliance. Over a period of time nickel coins tend to tone a hazy gray. Circulated nickel coins have a gray appearance.

Silver. When first minted, silver coins have a bright silvery-white surface. Over a period of time silver, a chemically active metal, tends to tone deep brown or black. Uncirculated and Proof silver pieces often exhibit very beautiful multi-coloured iridescent hues after a few years. The presence of attractive toning often increases a silver coin's value. Advanced collectors will often prefer attractive toned coins. Beginners sometimes think that "brilliant is best." Circulated silver coins will often have a dull gray appearance, sometimes with deep gray or black areas.

Gold. When first struck, gold coins are a bright yellow-orange colour. As gold coins are not pure gold but are alloyed with copper and traces of other substances, they do tend to tone over a period of time. Over a period of decades, a gold coin will normally acquire a deep orange colouration, sometimes with light brown or orange-brown toning "stains" or streaks in certain areas (resulting from improperly mixed copper traces in the alloy). Light toning does not affect the value of a gold coin.

Very old gold coins, particularly those in circulated grades, will sometimes show a red oxidation. Gold coins which have been recovered from treasure wrecks after centuries at the sea bottom will sometimes have a minutely porous surface because of the corrosive action of sea water. Such pieces sell for less than specimens which have not been so affected. Care must be taken to distinguish these from cast copies which often have a similar surface.

HANDLING AND STORAGE OF COINS

As a coin collector you are commissioned by posterity to handle each coin in your possession carefully and to preserve it in the condition in which it was received.

When examining a coin you should hold it by its edges and over a cloth pad or other soft surface. In this way if it accidentally falls no harm will be done. A coin should never be touched on either of its faces, obverse or reverse, for the oil and acid in one's skin will eventually leave fingerprints - if not soon, then years later. Also, one should avoid holding a coin near one's mouth while talking as small drops of moisture may land on the coin's surface and later cause what are commonly referred to as "flyspecks" - tiny pinpoints of oxidation.

Coins should be sorted in a dry location free of harmful fumes. The presence of sulphur in the atmosphere, a situation caused by certain types of coal combustion and also by industrial processes, sometimes will impart to silver coins in particular a yellowish or blackish toning. Dampness will result in oxidation or, in extreme instances, surface corrosion. Dampness can be best solved by moving coins to a drier location. If this is not possible, then a packet of silica gel (available in drugstores or photography supply stores) put in with the coins will serve to absorb moisture and may alleviate the problem. Also, the storage of coins in airtight containers will help.

The more a coin is exposed to freely circulating air, the more tendency it has to change colour or tone. Storage of coins in protective envelopes and hard plastic holders will usually help prevent this.

CLEANING COINS

Experienced numismatists will usually say that a coin is best left alone and not cleaned. However, most beginning collectors have the idea that "brilliant is best" and somehow feel that cleaning a coin will "improve" it. As the penchant for cleaning seems to be universal, and also because there are some instances in which cleaning can actually be beneficial, some important aspects are presented here.

All types of cleaning, "good" and "bad," result in the coin's surface being changed, even if only slightly. Even the most careful "dipping" of a coin will, if repeated time and time again, result in the coin acquiring a dullish and microscopically etched surface. It is probably true to state that no matter what one's intentions are, for every single coin actually improved in some way by cleaning, a dozen or more have been decreased in value. Generally, experienced numismatists agree that a coin should not be cleaned unless there are spots of oxidation, pitting which might worsen in time, or unsightly streaking or discolouration.

PROCESSING, POLISHING AND OTHER MISTREATMENT OF COINS

There have been many attempts to give a coin the appearance of being in a higher grade than it actually is. Numismatists refer to such treatments as "processing." Being different from cleaning (which can be "good" or "bad"), processing is never beneficial.

Types of processing include polishing and abrasion which removes metal from a coin's surface, etching and acid treatment, and "whizzing," the latter usually referring to abrading the surface of the coin with a stiff wire brush, often in a circular motion, to produce a series of minute tiny parallel scratches which to the unaided eye or under low magnification often appear to be like mint lustre. Under high magnification (in this instance a very strong magnifying glass should be used) the surface of a whizzed coin will show countless tiny scratches. Also, the artificial "mint lustre" will usually be in a uniform pattern throughout the coin's surfaces, whereas on an Uncirculated coin with true mint lustre the sheen of the lustre will be different on the higher parts than on the field. Some whizzed coins can be extremely deceptive. Comparing a whizzed coin with an untreated coin is the best way to gain experience in this regard.

Often one or more methods of treating a coin are combined. Sometimes a coin will be cleaned or polished and then by means of heat, fumes, or other treatment, an artificial toning will be applied. There are many variations.

When a coin has been polished, whizzed, artificially retoned, or in any other way changed from its original natural appearance and surface, it must be so stated in a description. For example, a coin which was Extremely Fine but whizzed to give it the artificial appearance of Uncirculated should be described as "Extremely Fine, whizzed." An AU coin, which has been recoloured should be described as "AU, recoloured." The simple "dipping" (without abrasion) of an already Uncirculated or Proof coin to brighten the surface does not have to be mentioned unless such dipping alters the appearance from when the coin was first struck (for example, in the instance of a copper or bronze coin in which dipping always produces an unnatural colour completely unlike the coin when it was first struck.)

COIN CERTIFICATION SERVICE

In recent years there has been an increase in the number of North American companies that offer third party professional coin grading services. Another service offered is that of an opinion as to whether a particular coin is genuine or counterfeit. Most of these companies operate along similar lines, that is, a coin is submitted by its owner for an independent grading and/or authentification assessment, an opinion is offered along with a certificate and a fee is charged on a per coin basis. These services are widely used by collectors and investors who recognize their grading skills are not at an expert's level. Many dealers in the United States also make use of such services because their clients often demand that the coins they buy have an official certificate with them. To date the most popular U.S. coin grading services appear to be: The Professional Coin Grading Service (PCGS) located in California, and The Numismatic Guaranty Corporation (NGC) located in New Jersey. All of these services specialize in U.S. coinage. In Canada the only such service is that offered by International Coin Certification Service (ICCS) in Toronto. ICCS specializes in all aspects of Canadian numismatics and includes amongst its senior consulting staff Bill Cross, Ingrid Smith, Scott Cornwell, Randy Weir and Brian Cornwell. Further information can be obtained from:

International Coin Certification Service
2010 Yonge Street, Suite 202
Toronto, Ontario, M4S 1Z9.
Canada
Tel.: (416) 488-8620
Fax.: (416) 488-6371

OBVERSE DESCRIPTIONS FOR VARIOUS SERIES

Victoria Laureated Head

G-4 - Braid worn through near ear.
VG-8 - No detail in braid around ear.
F-12 - Segments of braid beginning to merge into one another.
VF-20 - Braid is clear but not sharp.
EF-40 - Braid is slightly worn but generally sharp and clear.
AU-50 - Slight traces of wear on high points. Degree of mint lustre still present.
MS-60 - No traces of wear. High degree of lustre.
MS-63 - No traces of wear. Attractive lustre. Typical strike with minor surface marks.

Victoria Crowned Head

G-4 - Hair over ear worn through.
VG-8 - No details in the hair over ear.
F-12 - Strands of hair over ear beginning to run together.
VF-20 - Hair and jewels clear, but not sharp.
EF-40 - Hair over ear is sharp and clear. Jewels in diadem show sharply and clearly.
AU-50 - Slight traces of wear on high points. Degree of mint lustre still present.
MS-60 - No traces of wear. High degree of lustre.
MS-63 - No traces of wear. Attractive lustre. Typical strike with minor surface marks.

Edward VII

G-4 - Band of crown worn through.
VG-8 - Band of crown worn through at the highest point.
F-12 - Jewels in the band of crown blurred.
VF-20 - Band of the crown is still clear but no longer sharp.
EF-40 - Band of crown slightly worn but generally sharp and clear, including jewels.
AU-50 - Slight traces of wear on high points. Degree of mint lustre still present.
MS-60 - No traces of wear. High degree of lustre.
MS-63 - No traces of wear. Attractive lustre. Typical strike with minor surface marks.

George VI

VG-8 - No details in hair above ear.
F-12 - Only slight detail in hair above the ear.
VF-20 - Where not worn, the hair is clear but not sharp.
EF-40 - Slight wear in hair over ear.
AU-50 - Slight traces of wear on high points. Degree of mint lustre still present.
MS-60 - No traces of wear. High degree of lustre.
MS-63 - No traces of wear. Attractive lustre. Typical strike with minor surface marks.

George V

G-4 - Band of crown worn through.
VG-8 - Band of crown worn through at the highest point.
F-12 - Jewels in the band of crown blurred.
VF-20 - Band of the crown is still clear but no longer sharp.
EF-40 - Band of crown slightly worn but generally sharp and clear, including jewels.
AU-50 - Slight traces of wear on high points. Degree of mint lustre still present.
MS-60 - No traces of wear. High degree of lustre.
MS-63 - No traces of wear. Attractive lustre. Typical strike with minor surface marks.

Elizabeth II Young Head

F-12 - Leaves worn almost through. Shoulder fold indistinct.
VF-20 - Leaves are considerably worn; shoulder fold clear.
EF-40 - Laurel leaves on the band are somewhat worn.
AU-50 - Traces of wear on hair. Degree of mint lustre still present.
MS-60 - No traces of wear. High degree of lustre.
MS-63 - No traces of wear. Attractive lustre. Typical strike with minor surface marks.

THE MANUFACTURE OF CANADIAN COINS

The steps involved in the production of Canadian coins can be divided into the following: 1) production of a large three-dimensional model (for a new design); 2) the engraving of the dies and collar; 3) production of the blanks (planchets); and 4) the coining of them.

THE LARGE THREE-DIMENSIONAL MODEL

The design for a new coinage usually begins as a sketch. After the theme for the design is chosen, a suitable sketch is obtained in one of three ways. The most direct way is to generate the sketch "in house." This was done, for example, in the case of the 1977 Queen's Silver Jubilee silver dollar when Royal Canadian Mint engraver Walter Ott made an ink drawing of the throne of the Senate. On other occasions, such as for the 1937 coinage, a select group of outside artists is invited to submit designs. To date, this has been the method most frequently used by the Royal Canadian Mint. The final method is to have an open competition that any Canadian can enter. The designs for the 1951 commemorative 5-cent piece, the 1964 silver dollar, the twelve 1992 twenty-five cent pieces and the 125th Anniversary Dollar were the results of open competitions.

Once a suitable sketch is at hand, a three-dimensional plaster model of the design about 8 inches in diameter is made. This is sometimes produced by the original artist, but more often the modelling is done in the mint. Such models are usually made as a positive (i.e. the design elements are raised as on the final coin). A plastic, negative mould made from this model serves as the starting point for the next series of operations.

DIE PRODUCTION

The plastic, negative mould (design elements sunken) is placed in a device called a reducing machine. This machine works on the principle of the pantograph, reproducing on a reduced scale in three dimensions the design of the plastic model in metal. Generally the reduction proceeds in two steps. The first is to reproduce the plastic model as a brass block, making the design about 3 inches in diameter. This brass intermediate model then serves as the pattern for the machine during the reduction to coin scale. In the second reduction the design is engraved into a soft steel block. After the beads are added and other finishing touches applied, the steel block is hardened to become a reduction matrix.

From the reduction matrix one or more punches are made by placing it in a powerful press and impressing its design into soft steel blocks, which are later hardened. A punch has its design elements raised just as on the coins. The next step is to make the dies. Dies are made in the same way as punches, except it is a punch that is used to sink the design into soft steel blocks in the press. A single punch can produce thousands of dies before it must be retired.

The collar (the piece of metal that restrains the sideways expansion of the blank during striking and gives the coin its shape and edge design) is made at the Ottawa mint. For plain edge coins a hole is simply drilled in the centre of an appropriate piece of steel. If the collar is to be for a reeded edge coin, a smooth-edge hole is first drilled. Then the hole is given a serrated edge by the use of a small, hardened steel wheel.

If the design for the reverse is to be used for more than one year, the final digit or digits of the date are ground from a punch and a new matrix made from the modified punch. The missing digit(s) is then punched into the blank space in the matrix. From this matrix new punches are made.

Since 1945 dies for Canadian coinages have, with rare exceptions, been chromium plated. This extends the die life and gives the coins a superior finish.

THE PREPARATION OF THE BLANKS

At the present time Canadian coins are struck in bronze, nickel, silver, gold and platinum. The blanks for gold coins are obtained from an outside source. When blanks are produced in the Ottawa mint, as is the case with bronze and silver, the components of the metal alloys are mixed together in the melting pot and cast into bars. The bars are annealed (softened by heat treatment) and rolled to an exact thickness. The rolled metal is bent into the form of a large coil, which is then sent to the cutting room. In the cutting room the coils are fed into blanking presses, which punch blanks out of them. Following passage over a vibrating screen to remove defective (undersize) blanks, the good blanks are put through a machine which compresses their edges so as to produce raised rims. This facilitates coining by reducing the amount of metal that has to be displaced in the blank during striking. The rimmed blanks are next fed through a special furnace in which they are annealed. Finally, the cooled blanks are cleaned and dried, ready for the coining press.

Nickel is a difficult metal to work with, so both the Ottawa and the Winnipeg mints obtain this metal in strip or coil form. Winnipeg also obtains its blank bronze in this form.

COINING

Blanks are fed into the coining chamber of the press through a feed tube attached to a vibrating hopper of blanks contained above. A metal fork pushes a fresh blank over the hole in the collar and at the same time pushes away the coin just struck. The blank, being slightly smaller than the diameter of the hole in the collar, drops in and comes to rest on the bottom (obverse) die. The top die then descends and makes contact with the blank. This causes the blank to expand, filling the crevices of the dies and the collar to become a coin. Both dies rise, forcing the coin out of the collar so that it can be pushed away by the next blank being positioned. Struck coins are collected, examined, counted and bagged for issue.

TECHNICAL INFORMATION

This catalogue presents the most complete set of technical statistics ever assembled for the Canadian decimal series.

It is important to note that the artistic talent that goes into the production of a new coinage design does not end with the individual who did the original drawing. The designing, modelling and engraving of the master tools for a modern coinage also require great skill and, in some cases, each step may be the work of a different person. As far as possible, they are all listed.

Compositions are given as decimal fractions, adding up to 1.00; they can be converted to percentages by multiplying by 100. Weights are given in grams and can be converted into troy ounces by dividing by 31.1035. Diameters are given in millimetres and can be converted into inches by multiplying by .03937.

Canadian coins have been struck with both major die axis arrangements. In the medal arrangement (designated ↑↑) a coin held vertically between one's fingers with its obverse design right side up finishes with it reverse design right side up when it is rotated on its vertical axis. Dies in the coinage arrangement (↑↓) will result in the reverse being upside down when the coin is turned as previously described.

THE TREATMENT OF VARIETIES

A variety can be described as "any alteration in the design of a coin." A major variety is a coin of the same date, mint mark and denomination as another, but struck from a different set of dies, the finished coin having at least one major device added, removed or redesigned. In other words, a major variety is the result of an intentional change by the mint. A minor variety is one with all major devices the same as another, but with some easily recognizable variation. Minor varieties are thus the result of unintentional mint errors or other deviations.

Since this is a standard catalogue designed for general collectors, it is not possible to list minor varieties, nor to remark upon all the nuances of interest to the specialist. Following the format established in the 31st edition, the Charlton Standard Catalogue includes every major variety and several minor varieties that have a wide appeal to collectors. More specialized treatments will be available in the forthcoming The Charlton-Zoell Variety Catalogue.

MINTS, MINT MARKS AND OTHER LETTERS

Until 1908, all Canadian coins were produced in England. Most were coined at the Royal Mint in London and have no identifying mint mark. From time to time, however, the Royal Mint was so busy with other coinages that Canadian authorities were allowed to have their coins struck by a private mint in Birmingham. This mint, called Heaton's Mint until 1889 and The Mint, Birmingham thereafter, used a small "H" mint mark on all its Canadian issues except for the Prince Edward Island cent of 1871.

January 2, 1908 saw the opening of a mint in Ottawa, authorized under the Imperial Coinage Act of 1870. Until 1931 it was the Ottawa Branch of the Royal Mint. Its issues for the Dominion of Canada bear no mint mark, but those for elsewhere (British sovereigns and Newfoundland and Jamaica coinages) have a small "C" on the reverse. In 1931 the name of the Ottawa mint was changed to the Royal Canadian Mint and it came under the full control of the Canadian government as a branch of the Department of Finance. The status of the mint was altered in March, 1969 by the Government Organization Act, and it became a Crown Corporation effective April 1, 1969.

Today, Canada has three mints: the Ottawa mint, the Hull mint (established in 1965 for striking collectors coins) and the Winnipeg mint (opened in 1975).

The only recent occasion when Canadian coins were produced outside the country was in 1968. In that year part of the 10-cents issue was coined at the Philadelphia Mint in the United States. The Philadelphia Mint did not place a mint mark on these coins, but the Canadian and U.S. strikings can be distinguished by the shape of the grooves in the edge (see ten cent section).

In 1975 a branch mint was established in Winnipeg for the production of circulating coinage for the Canadian market, and to support sales initiative as supplier of coinage world wide. In 1997 Set production for the numismatic department was shifted to Winnipeg. In 1998, when Winnipeg again struck coins for the numismatic market, a small "W" was added to the obverse of the coins making Canada's first Mint Mark.

In 1999, in the Mint's continuing effort to reduce the production costs of the national coinage, a development breakthrough resulted in the Multi-Ply Plating process. This produced a significant reduction in the costs of coinage materials. During that year, to distinguish these coins from the previous nickel issues, a small "P" was added to the obverse, beneath the Queen's portrait. It was not until 2001 that four of the seven circulating coins (5¢ through to 50¢) carried the "P" mint mark. The one-cent, the Loon dollar and the Polar Bear two dollars did not carry the mint mark.

DESIGNER'S INITIALS

The following initials will be found on coins designed by these artists.

Debbie Adams	DA	Sir E. Bertram MacKennal	B.M
S. Armstrong-Hodgson	SAH	Terry Manning	TM
Germaine Arnaktauyok	GA	J.D. Mantha	JDM
Wade Stephen Baker	WB	John Mardon	JM
Tony Bianco	TB	Vincent McIndoe	VMc
Maurice Bissonnette	MB	Scott McKowen	SM
Patrick Brindley	B	Percy Metcalfe	P.M.
Huntley Brown	HB	Elliot John Morrison	EJM
Walter Burden	WB	Walter Ott	WO or WO monogram
Robert R. Carmichael	RRC	T. Humphrey Paget	H.P
Paul Cedarberg	PC	Donald D. Paterson	DDP
Harvey Chan	HC	Laura Paxton	LP
David J. Craig	DJC	Paul Pederson	PP
John Crosby	J.C.	Dora de Pédery-Hunt	DH
Donald H. Curley	D.C.	Friedrich Peter	FP
Sylvie Daigneault	SD	Benedetto Pistrucci	B.P
Haver Demirer	HD	William Wellesley Pole	WWP
George W. DeSaulles	DES	Henry C. Purdy	HCP
Daryl Ann Dorosz	DD	Karel Rohlicek	KR
Alf Gamble	AG	Walter Schluep	WS
Mrs. Mary Gillick	M.G	Cezar Serbanesco	CS
Pheobe Gilman	PG	Stewart Sherwood	SS
Christopher Gorey	CG	Thomas Shingles	TS or T.S.
Hector Grenville	HG	Karsten Smith	KS
Jean-Luc Grondin	JFG	Ian D. Sparkes	IDS
Emanuel Hahn	EH or H	Rita Swanson	RS
Adeline Halvorson	AH	Alan Syliboy	AS
Caren Heine	CH	Miyuki Tanobe	M.T.
Roger Hill	RH	Raymond Taylor	RT
Mark Hobson	MH	Michelle Thibodeau	MTT
Valentina Hotz-Entin	VH	Carola Tietz	CT
Brian Hughes	BH	Stephan Trenka	ST or ST monogram
Eric Hui	EH	Randy Trantau	R
John Jaciw	JJ	Kathy Vinish	KV
Peter Kiss	P.K.	Dinko Vodanovic	D.V
George E. Kruger-Gray	K.G. or KG	Donald F. Warkentine	DFW
Jean-Guy Lebel	JGL	Anny Wassel	AW
Pierre Leduc	PL	J. Franklin Wright	FW
Raymond Lee	RL	Leonard C. Wyon	L.C.W.

FRATERNAL AFFILIATION

Over the years, coin clubs have sprung up in many Canadian communities. In addition, both Canada and the United States have national organizations which hold annual conventions.

Coin clubs constitute one of the most attractive features of present-day collecting. They offer beginning collectors the opportunity for good fellowship and the encouragement and knowledge of more experienced collectors. The larger groups maintain lending libraries and publish a journal or newsletter on a regular basis. Memberships and other information can be obtained from:

The Canadian Numismatic Association
4936 Yonge Street, Suite 601
North York, Ontario
Canada M2N 6S3

The American Numismatic Association
818 N. Cascade Avenue
Colorado Springs, Colorado
U.S.A. 80903-3279

Ontario Numismatic Association
Post Office Box 33
Waterloo, Ontario
Canada N2J 3Z6.

FOREIGN COINS IN CANADA

Strictly speaking, Canada (rather, the areas that now form Canada) did not have a coinage struck for its specific use until the mid-19th century. After 1820, some provincial governments issued their own coppers, but this was without imperial government sanction until the 1850s. Thus, for some two centuries Canada relied on foreign coins to provide the lifeblood for her commerce.

The importance of foreign coins in our currency history has not been given the emphasis it deserves in Canadian catalogues. Certainly it is difficult to deal with this subject. None of the foreign coins that were once so important here can strictly be called Canadian. This includes the coins of the French regime, some of which have been listed in past catalogues. To simply list some French issues is both misleading and illogical. The Spanish-American dollar, for example, was a more important coin in our overall currency history than any French (or British) coin ever was. A more realistic listing must include coins of France, Great Britain, Spain and Spanish America, Portugal and the United States.

It has been decided to attempt to list the most important foreign coins that circulated in Canada, regardless of their country of origin. In order to qualify for listing a coin must have been specifically imported and in reasonable quantity. The many coins that filtered into North America in small quantities through trade cannot be listed.

NOTE: The prices listed below for broad types of coins, which may encompass several separate types and a span of many years, are for the most commonly encountered form of the coin only. Readers are advised to see specialized foreign catalogues for specific varieties, dates and prices.

COINS OF FRANCE

During the French regime (c. 1600-1760), French imperial coins were intermittently shipped to New France by the king or were imported by local merchants. Occasionally these were supplemented by general colonial coinages intended for circulation in France. But, as New France was just one of the recipients of the colonial issues, they cannot be considered to have been specifically for Canada. French coins became less important in Canada after 1760. The silver ecus and 1/2 ecus, however, remained in commercial use well into the next century.

Between 1680 and the early 1720's, French coins were subject to considerable variations in the rate at which they were to be officially current. We will not attempt to detail these changes or "reformations" for each coin. A single example is sufficient to make the point. One of the few French coins with its original value actually stated on it is the "mousquetaire" or 30-denier piece minted between 1710 and 1713. Its initial rate of 30 deniers was lowered to 27 deniers in 1714 and to 22 deniers the next year. It remained at that level until the wild inflation of John Law (1720-1721), when it soared to 60 deniers and quickly fell back to 45 deniers. In 1724 its rate was returned to 27 deniers and in 1732 it was lowered to 24 deniers. It continued at that level in New France until the Conquest.

By 1726 the French government realized the folly of frequent changes in the value of coins and generally the currency was stabilized.

MINT MARKS ON FRENCH COINS. Numerous mints produced French coins. Only for issues produced by a small number of mints will the listings by mint be separated. The following mint marks were employed on coins that circulated in quantity in New France and British Canada:

A - Paris	K - Bordeaux	S - Reims	& - Aix
B - Rouen	L - Bayonne	T - Nantes	AA - Metz
C - Caen	M - Toulouse	V - Troyes	BB - Strasbourg
D - Lyon	N - Montpellier	W - Lille	)(- Besancon
E - Tours	O - Riom	X - Amiens	a cow - Pau
G - Poitiers	P - Dijon	Y - Bourges	
H - LaRochelle	O - Perpignan	Z - Grenoble	
I - Limoges	R - Orleans	9 - Rennes	

COPPER COINS

DENIER. Along with the copper double and liard, the denier was one of the predominant coins in circulation in New France up to the early 1660's. The denier, although rated at 1 denier in France, circulated as a 2-denier piece in New France. The merchants saw a chance for a quick profit and imported these coins in large quantities. This resulted in an oversupply prompting the government at Quebec to ban the denier altogether in 1664.

Type and Denomination	VG	F	VF	EF
1610-1715, Denier, Louis XIII or XIV (6 types)	35.	75.	150.	300.

DOUBLE. In 1664 the Order of the Sovereign Council which demonetized the denier allowed the double to remain in circulation but reduced its value to 1 denier to curb its excessive importation. It had formerly circulated at 4 deniers in New France.

Type and Denomination	VG	F	VF	EF
1610-1715, Double, Louis XIII or XIV, (11 types)	30.	50.	125.	325.

LIARD. Until the Order of Sovereign Council of 1664, the liard passed in New France as a 6-denier piece. After 1664 its value was reduced to 2 deniers to discourage its excessive importation.

Type and Denomination	VG	F	VF	EF
1643-1774, Liard, Louis XIV or XV, (13 types)	40.	75.	130.	375.

½ SOL COINAGE OF 1710-1712. The first coinage of this denomination in copper took place in 1710-1712. When first issued it was rated at 6 deniers.

Type and Denomination	VG	F	VF	EF
1710-1712, ½ Sol, Louis XIV	125.	175.	250.	450.

COPPER COINAGE OF 1719-1724. This coinage consisted of a liard, a ½ sol and a double sol. The middle denomination (the half sol) was shipped to New France in large amounts in 1720.

Type and Denomination	VG	F	VF	EF
1719-1724, ½ Sol	25.	35.	75.	200.

Type and Denomination	VG	F	VF	EF
1719-1724, Sol	25.	50.	85.	250.

COLONIAL 9 DENIER COINAGE 1721-1722. This was a special colonial issue imported by a private trading company, the Company of the Indies. Following difficulties in circulating their new coins, the company attempted to have them transferred to the government of New France. This was not successful, so most of the coinage was returned to France in 1726 with only 8,000 plus pieces put into circulation in New France. These coins were also sent to other French colonies.

Type and Denomination	VG	F	VF	EF
1721B, 9 Deniers	325.	600.	950.	2,500.
1721H, 9 Deniers	125.	225.	450.	900.
1722H, 2 over 1	200.	250.	500.	1,000.
1722H, Normal Date	125.	200.	450.	900.
1722H, Brass		Extremely Rare		

BILLON SOLS MARQUES COINAGES

The most important coinages in circulation during the French regime were a group of billon (low grade silver) pieces collectively called sols (or sous) marques. They often constituted the smallest denomination coins because copper was generally unpopular with the colonists. There were no less than six coinages of sols marques; the coinages of 1709-1713 and 1738-1764 also had double sol denominations.

COUNTERSTAMPED DOUZAINS (1640). During the Middle Ages a new French coin called a gros tournois made its appearance. It was about the size of a 25-cent piece and made of good silver. By the first part of the 17th century this coin had become a billon piece called a douzain. The douzain or sol was rated at 12 deniers. In 1640 the French government called in all douzains and counterstamped them with a small fleur-de-lis in an oval to change their rating to 15 deniers. The term sol marque (marked sol) came from the fact that these coins were counterstamped. It later came to apply to all sols.

Type and Denomination	VG	F	VF	EF
Counterstamped Douzain (1640)	25.	50.	100.	—

COINAGE OF 1641. The next billon coin in the series was a new design dated 1641. It was initially rated at 15 deniers and supplemented the douzains counterstamped the year before. Its relation to these coins is clearly shown by its design (both obverse and reverse) containing a fleur-de-lis in an oval, in imitation of the counterstamp on the earlier issue.

Type and Denomination	VG	F	VF	EF
1641, 15 Deniers	125.	300.	600.	1,350.

COINAGE OF 1658. The douzain of 1658 was rated at 12 deniers in France but was given a rating of 20 deniers when it made its first appearance in New France in 1662. A 6-denier piece was also struck, but there is no reason to believe that denomination circulated in quantity in the colony.

Type and Denomination	VG	F	VF	EF
1658 Douzain	150.	300.	750.	1,650.

COINAGE OF 1692-1698. Beginning in 1692 and continuing through 1698, a new issue of sols marques was made. The designs were new, but instead of being struck on fresh blanks, many were struck over previous issues of sols. It is sometimes possible to detect parts of the undertypes on the overstruck coins. The new issue was rated at 15 deniers when it first came out.

Type and Denomination	VG	F	VF	EF
1692-1698, 15 Deniers, Billion, (4 types)	20.	35.	60.	125.

Note: Extremely fine prices are indications only. These coins are rarely found in this condition. If an example does appear for sale, it will more than likely trade at a much higher price.

"MOUSQUETAIRE" ISSUES OF 1709-1713. This issue consisted of a 15-denier piece and a 30-denier piece. The name mousquetaire is believed to have come from the cross on the reverse of the coins, which resembled the crosses on the cloaks of the legendary musketeers.

Type and Denomination	VG	F	VF	EF
1709-1713, 15 Deniers, Billion	175.	300.	575.	1,150.

Type and Denomination	VG	F	VF	EF
1709-1713, 30 Deniers, Billion	100.	175.	350.	750.

COINAGE OF 1738-1764. The final billon coinage used in New France was that of 1738-1764, consisting of a sol and double sol. The double sol has often been mistakenly referred to as "the" sou marque. First, there is no single sol marque; some six coinages are involved. Second, the sol or sou was by 1738 a coin about the size of our present small cent. The larger coin so often called a sou marque is in fact a double sol.

SOL (SOU) 1738-1754. This coin was rated at 12 deniers in both France and New France.

Type and Denomination	VG	F	VF	EF
1738-1754, Sol, (14 different mint marks)	50.	75.	150.	300.

Note: Extremely fine prices are indications only. These coins are rarely found in this condition. If an example does appear for sale, it will more than likely trade at a much higher price.

DOUBLE SOL (2 SOUS) 1738-1764. Although this type was struck until 1764, it is unlikely that any dated later than 1760 circulated in New France. This coin was rated at 24 deniers.

Large quantities of contemporary counterfeits were made of the double sol, particularly of the dates 1740, 1741, 1742, 1750, 1751, 1755 and 1760. Differences in the rendition of the crown are the easiest way to tell the genuine from the counterfeit.

Original

Typical Counterfeit

Type and Denomination	VG	F	VF	EF
1738-1760, Double sol, (29 different mint marks)	75.	100.	150.	300.
1740-1760, Double sol, counterfeit	40.	60.	100.	150.

SILVER COINS

½ ECU. The ½ ecu was not routinely imported into French America; nevertheless, it did circulate in some quantity during the British regime in the first third of the 19th century. It is assumed that these coins came primarily from issues of Louis XIV and XV.

Type and Denomination	VG	F	VF	EF
1645-1774, ½ Ecu, Louis XIV or XV, (more than 40 types)	50.	100.	200.	450.

ECU. The ecu, a large silver coin about the size of the Canadian silver dollar, was imported into French America in significant quantities. The ecu continued in use after the fall of New France, when it was called the French crown. Most types of ecu minted between 1640 and the 1750s probably circulated in Canada.

Type and Denomination	VG	F	VF	EF
1641-1643, Ecu, (60 Sols), Louis XIII		Very Rare		
1643-1715, Ecu, Louis XIII or XIV, (4 major bust varieties)	200.	375.	500.	900.
1715-1774, Ecu, Louis XIV or XV, (7 major bust varieties)	75.	150.	250.	500.

Colonial Coinage of 1670

In 1670 a special coinage of silver 5-sol and 15-sol pieces was produced for circulation in the French colonies in the New World. On the reverse was "GLORIAM REGNI TVI DICENT" meaning "They shall speak of the glory of Thy kingdom" and taken from the 145th Psalm of the Bible. Despite their fame, these coins barely qualify as "Canadian." Period documents suggest that they probably were intended for the West Indies rather than New France. Authorities in the West Indies were anxious to obtain a subsidiary silver coinage for payment of day labourers and artisans, who were being paid in goods. In New France these coins were not particularly wanted because they could not be used for buying goods in France; they were not legal tender there. In any case it is quite clear that these coins had a very limited circulation in French America.

Date and Denomination	Quantity Minted	VG	F	VF	EF
1670A, 5 Sols	200,000	1,300.	1,800.	2,400.	4,000.

Date and Denomination	Quantity Minted	VG	F	VF	EF
1670A, 15 Sols	40,000	15,000.	20,000.	30,000.	—

Reduced Silver Coinages of 1674 - 1709

In the late 17th and early 18th centuries the French government was in a rather precarious financial condition. As a money-raising scheme it struck seven coinages with reduced silver content (approximately .800 fine) at the same time as the regular .917 fine silver types were being produced. Most of the reduced fineness types were sent to New France in quantity.

4 SOLS ISSUES OF 1674-1677. By 1679 there were so many of these coins in circulation in New France that they were being used in payment by the bagful. An ordinance passed in that year lowered their value to 3 sols 6 deniers and placed strict limits on the quantity that could be used for any one payment.

Date and Denomination	VG	F	VF	EF
1674-1677, 4 Sols	25.	45.	80.	250.

4 SOLS ISSUES OF 1691-1700. This coin was the successor to the previous reduced silver 4-sol piece and was struck over it.

Date and Denomination	VG	F	VF	EF
1691-1700, 4 Sols, (2 Denier)	30.	50.	100.	200.

5 SOLS OF 1702-1709. The next reduced silver coinage used in New France was a piece of approximately the same weight as the old 4-sol pieces, but which was called a 5-sol piece instead.

Date and Denomination	VG	F	VF	EF
1702-1704, 5 Sols, (27 varieties)	15.	35.	65.	175.

10 SOLS OF 1702-1708. This 10-sol piece is from the same series as the 5-sols.

Date and Denomination	VG	F	VF	EF
1703-1708, 10 Sols, (17 varieties)	25.	50.	100.	250.

LIVRE OF 1720. In 1720, during the wild inflation brought about by the schemes of John Law, a special coin was produced in pure silver and issued at the over-valued rating of one livre. The Company of the Indies imported a quantity of these coins into French America in 1722.

Date and Denomination	Quantity Minted	VG	F	VF	EF
1720A, Livre	6,918,583	35.	125.	225.	450.

SMALL SILVER LOUIS OF 1720. In 1720 a new coin called a small silver louis (petit louis d'argent) was brought into Canada. Its initial rating was 60 sols, but this was soon reduced to 40 sols.

Date and Denomination	F	VF	EF	AU
1720, Small Silver Louis	30.	90.	250.	350.

GOLD COINS

THE GOLD LOUIS. The only French gold coin to see significant circulation in French North America was the gold louis (louis d'or). Louis d'or were regularly sent over and saw use even after the Conquest. Any of the types struck between the 1640s and the 1750s potentially circulated here in quantity.

Type of 1680   Type of 1723-1725

Type and Denomination	VG	F	VF	EF
− , Louis, Louis XIV, (8 portrait varieties)	350.	650.	950.	1,500.
1723-1725, Louis, Louis XV, (26 varieties)	400.	750.	1,000.	1,600.
1726-1739, Louis, Louis XV, (30 varieties)	275.	400.	600.	1,000.

COINS OF GREAT BRITAIN

For most of the British colonial period (c. 1760-1870) the British government was hardly better than the French government had been at supplying Imperial coins for use in Canada. British coinage was struck infrequently during the last half of the 18th century, and England and her colonies alike suffered from the lack of coin.

A major alteration took place in the British coinage in 1816. The silver coinage was reduced to a subsidiary status (along with the coppers) by lowering the amount of silver it contained to bring the bullion value of the coins below the face value. This left gold as the sole standard coinage and marks the beginning of the British gold standard. The coinage of silver was begun on a large scale and British coins gradually became more available. In 1825-1826 a serious attempt was made to establish Imperial coins as the principal coinage of the colonies and to drive out the Spanish-American coins. This attempt largely failed in British North America. Nevertheless, at various times some British coins did achieve a significant circulation here, particularly in Nova Scotia. That province came the closest to adopting sterling coinage; when it was decided to institute a decimal currency in 1859, the dollar was rated so as to allow the continued circulation of British coins. The 2-shilling piece (florin) became a 50-cent piece, the shilling became a 25-cent piece and so on. The halfpenny and shilling also saw much use in Upper and Lower Canada and later in the united Province of Canada.

COPPER COINS

Halfpenny

GEORGE II ISSUES OF 1740-1754. These coins, along with the George III halfpenny listed below, formed the most important part of the British North American copper currency until the War of 1812. After that time they were supplemented by the tokens issued by local merchants and others. But, until the first bank tokens, they were the only copper sanctioned by the British government.

Date and Denomination	VG	F	VF	EF	AU	UNC
George II, 1740-1754, ½d	4.	9.	35.	175.	275.	400.

GEORGE III ISSUES OF 1770-1775. The majority of the coins of this issue that circulated in both Great Britain and America were contemporary counterfeits. Issues of halfpennies during later reigns seem not to have circulated in quantity in British North America.

Genuine Issue

Typical Counterfeit

Date and Denomination	VG	F	VF	EF	AU	UNC
George III, 1770-1775, ½d, genuine	3.	8.	35.	110.	225.	350.
George III, 1770-1775, ½d, counterfeit	7.	30.	60.	225.	—	—

Penny

The penny was not a frequently used denomination in British North America. In 1832, however, a special shipment was made to Upper Canada. This is known to have consisted of coins dated 1831.

Date and Denomination	VG	F	VF	EF	AU	UNC
William IV, 1831, Penny	7.	15.	55.	200.	375.	650.

SILVER COINS

British silver coins became more important in circulation in some parts of British North America after about 1830. The intermediate denominations were the most common.

Six Pence

Type and Denomination	VG	F	VF	EF	AU	UNC
William IV, Six Pence	4.	8.	35.	115.	165.	225.
Victoria (Young Head) 1838-1866 Six Pence	4.	7.	20.	85.	140.	200.

Shilling

Type and Denomination	VG	F	VF	EF	AU	UNC
William IV, Shilling	4.	8.	35.	140.	225.	350.
Victoria (Young Head) 1838-1863 Shilling	4.	8.	30.	115.	175.	275.

Florin

This denomination probably saw use in Nova Scotia during the 1850s and 1860s. In 1861 the florin, shilling and sixpence were imported into British Columbia.

Type and Denomination	VG	F	VF	EF	AU	UNC
Victoria (Gothic Head) 1851-1887 Florin*	6.	15.	60.	175.	300.	450.

*On these coins the date is on the obverse in the form of a Roman numeral.

Halfcrown

Type and Denomination	VG	F	VF	EF	AU	UNC
George IV, Halfcrown	12.	25.	50.	200.	300.	450.
William IV, Halfcrown	14.	30.	75.	250.	350.	450.
Victoria (Young Head), Halfcrown	8.	18.	65.	175.	275.	400.

GOLD COINS

GEORGE III ½ GUINEA. The ½ guinea was usually rated at 10 shillings 6 pence in Great Britain.

Type and Denomination	VG	F	VF	EF	AU	UNC
George III, ½ Guinea, 1787-1800	85.	165.	225.	350.	500.	750.

GEORGE III GUINEA, 1761-1813. The guinea or 21-shilling piece was one of the principal gold coins to circulate in British North America.

Type of 1765-1773

Type and Denomination	VG	F	VF	EF	AU	UNC
George III, Guinea	175.	200.	275.	550.	750.	1,000.

½ SOVEREIGN. The ½ sovereign was the successor to the ½ guinea and probably saw enough circulation in British North America and the Dominion of Canada to warrant its inclusion in this listing.

Type and Denomination	F	VF	EF	AU	UNC
George III, ½ Sovereign	100.	200.	500.	600.	800.
George IV, ½ Sovereign	140.	300.	700.	900.	1,200.
William IV, ½ Sovereign	150.	400.	850.	1,100.	1,500.
Victoria (Young Head), ½ Sovereign	90.	150.	275.	400.	600.

SOVEREIGN. The sovereign was perhaps the most widely used gold coin in Canada. It was used extensively by banks and the government for redeeming paper money right up to the 20th century.

Type and Denomination	F	VF	EF	AU	UNC
George III, Sovereign	200.	350.	750.	1,000.	1,500.
George IV, Sovereign	225.	375.	1,000.	1,400.	1,750.
William IV, Sovereign	175.	300.	950.	1,400.	1,800.
Victoria (Shield), Sovereign	BV	BV	250.	300.	450.

COINS OF PORTUGAL

During the 18th and early 19th centuries, several types of gold coins issued by Portugal found their way into British North America and were used extensively here.

MOIDORE. This coin had a denomination of 4,000 reis in Portugal and bore on its reverse the Cross of Jerusalem. It was struck from the reign of Alfonso VI (1656-1683) to the reign of John V (1706-1750).

Type and Denomination	VG	F	VF	EF
Alfonso VI to John V, Moidore	275.	375.	600.	1,000.

6,400 REIS (1/2 JOE). This coin, with a formal denomination of 6,400 reis, was introduced in the 1720's, along with a 12,800 reis coin of similar design. The king of Portugal at the time was John (Joao) V and from his name on the coins, Johannes V, came the nickname "Joe" for the 12,800 reis coin and "1/2 Joe" for the 6,400 reis coin. The "1/2 Joe" was also applied to the 6,400 reis coins issued in subsequent reigns. The larger coin was not issued in later reigns and "Joe" was eventually used for the 6,400 reis denomination.

Type and Denomination	VG	F	VF	EF
John V to John VI, 1706 - 1826 "1/2 Joe" (6,400 reis)	350.	450.	650.	1,200.

12,800 REIS (JOE). This was a coin of 12,800 reis issued during the reign of John V (see above).

Type and Denomination	VG	F	VF	EF
John V, "Joe" 1724 - 1732 (12,800 reis)	1,000.	2,000.	3,000.	5,000.

COINS OF SPAIN, SPANISH AMERICA AND FORMER SPANISH COLONIES

This group of coins was more important in the currency history of what is now Canada for a longer period of time than any other foreign coinage. It was the Spanish-American dollar that served as the basis for the United States dollar, upon which in turn was based the decimal dollar of the Province of Canada in 1858.

COINS OF SPAIN

The Spanish metropolitan coinage is relatively unimportant compared to that of her New World colonies, with one exception: the pistareen. This was the nickname for a reduced standard 2-real piece minted only in Spain and which enjoyed wide circulation in British North America in the first half of the 19th century.

Type and Denomination	VG	F	VF	EF	AU
18th Century, Spanish Pistareen	25.	50.	75.	100.	150.

COINS OF SPANISH AMERICA

The coinage of Spain's colonies emanated from the following principal mints: Potosi in Bolivia, Santiago in Chile, Sante Fe do Bogota and Popayan in Colombia (Nueva Granada). Guatemala in Guatemala, Mexico City in Mexico and Lima and Cuzco in Peru. Minting of Spanish-American coins began in the early 16th century with the coins being of conventional round appearance. These were replaced about 1580 by the "cob" series: crude-appearing coins hand-struck on irregular blanks hewn from bars of refined bullion.

The cob series was finally superseded by round coins in 1732. The round gold issues bore the portrait of the reigning Spanish monarch from the first; however, the silver did not carry portraits until 1772. In the intervening 40 years the obverses featured the "two world" or "pillar" design, consisting of two crowned hemisphere between the crowned pillars of Hercules.

The Spanish-American series came to an end in the 1820's as Spain's colonies successfully revolted and became independent. Nevertheless, the Spanish-American coins had been minted in such great quantities that they continued to exert an important influence for decades. Probably the most important coinages for Canada are those struck under the rulers Charles III (1760-1788), Charles IV (1788-1808) and Ferdinand VII (1808-1821).

1 REAL

Type and Denomination	VG	F	VF	EF	AU
Philip V to Charles III, 1 Real, Pillar Type	10.	20.	50.	100.	250.
Charles III to Ferdinand VII, 1 Real, Bust Type	6.	12.	25.	75.	150.

2 REALES

Type and Denomination	VG	F	VF	EF	AU
Philip V to Charles III, 2 Reales, Pillar Type	15.	30.	75.	175.	325.
Charles III to Ferdinand VII, 2 Reales, Bust Type	7.	15.	30.	150.	250.

4 REALES

Type and Denomination	VG	F	VF	EF
Philip V to Charles III, 4 Reales, Pillar Type	150.	250.	450.	750.
Charles III to Ferdinand VII, 4 Reales, Bust Type	40.	60.	125.	500.

8 REALES. This is by far the most important foreign coin to circulate in Canada. It was known and appreciated all over the civilized world and was the principal end product of the vast amounts of silver mined in the New World. The 8-real piece had the nickname dollar (even though it was not a decimal coin) due to its similarity in size to the European thalers and daalders. It is the famous "piece-of-eight" of pirate lore. The first 8-real pieces were produced in 1556 at the Mexico City mint.

Type and Denomination	VG	F	VF	EF
Philip V to Charles III, 8 Reales (Dollar), Pillar Type	100.	150.	200.	500.
Charles III to Ferdinand VII, 8 Reales, Bust Type	35.	55.	80.	175.

GOLD COINS

2 ESCUDOS. This gold coin was popularly known as the Spanish pistole and, next to the doubloon (see below), was the most widely used Spanish-American gold coin in Canada.

Type and Denomination	VG	F	VF	EF
Charles III to Ferdinand VII, 2 Escudos	200.	400.	550.	1,000.

4 ESCUDOS

Type and Denomination	VG	F	VF	EF
Charles III to Ferdinand VII, 4 Escudos	450.	900.	1,300.	2,200.

8 ESCUDOS (DOUBLOON). The most important gold coin in Canada was the 8-escudo piece or doubloon. It circulated widely, but was especially popular in the Atlantic provinces. After the Spanish colonies gained their independence, these coins were called "Royal" doubloons (as opposed to "Patriot" doubloons discussed below).

Type and Denomination	VG	F	VF	EF
Charles III to Ferdinand VII, 8 Escudos (Doubloon)	600.	700.	1,000.	1,500.

COINS OF FORMER SPANISH COLONIES

By 1826 Spain had lost all her colonies in the New World. This ushered in new coinages on the existing standards by each of the former colonies. They were accepted and circulated alongside the coins of the Spanish-American series. Probably only two denominations are necessary in this listing — the silver dollar and the gold doubloon.

8 REALES (DOLLAR). The most important dollars of former Spanish colonies to circulate in Canada are undoubtedly those of Mexico.

Type and Denomination	VG	F	VF	EF	AU	UNC
1820s to 1840s, Mexican 8 Reales (Dollar)	20.	30.	50.	100.	150.	200.

8 ESCUDOS (DOUBLOON). In the case of the doubloon it is more difficult to single out any one former colony's coinage as being the most important for Canada. Therefore a general listing is given. Contemporary sources refer to such doubloons as "Patriot" doubloons to distinguish them for the "Royal" doubloons of the Spanish-American series. It is known that "Patriot" doubloons were specifically imported into such provinces as Nova Scotia.

Typical "Patriot" Doubloon from Chile

Type and Denomination	VG	F	VF	EF	AU	UNC
1817- 1830s, "Patriot" 8 Escudos (Doubloon)	350.	400.	600.	1,200.	2,500.	–

COINS OF THE UNITED STATES

It is to the United States coinage that we owe our present decimal currency system. By the 1850s trade links between British North America and the U.S. were so strong and her coinage so commonplace here that the proponents of a currency akin to that of the U.S. instead of Great Britain won out.

The U.S. coinage on a decimal basis began in the 1790s and it has circulated here to varying degrees ever since. A great influx of U.S. silver coins took place during the 1850s and 1860s, after the proportion of silver contained in the 5-, 10-, 25- and 50-cent pieces was reduced. Previous to that time, U.S. large cents came across the border in quantity and large numbers of half dollars were imported to help pay for work on such projects as the Rideau Canal. The larger denominations of U.S. gold coins were important in Canada almost up to the beginning of this century because they were widely imported by banks and the government for use in backing and redeeming paper money.

COPPER COINS

ONE CENT

Many varieties exist in the size of letters, placement of letters, and the size of date and number of stars.

Type and Denomination	VG	F	VF	EF	AU	UNC
1816-1836, Coronet Head	20.	35.	75.	150.	250.	400.
1837-1857, Braided Hair	18.	22.	30.	70.	150.	250.

SILVER COINS

HALF DIME – SEATED LIBERTY

Type and Denomination	VG	F	VF	EF	AU	UNC
1837-1838, No stars on obverse	55.	80.	150.	300.	550.	900.
1838-1859, Stars on obverse	15.	20.	30.	60.	175.	250.
1853-1855, Arrows at date	13.	15.	25.	60.	200.	275.
1860-1873, Legend on obverse	15.	20.	25.	50.	100.	200.

DIME – SEATED LIBERTY

Type and Denomination	VG	F	VF	EF	AU	UNC
1837-1838, No stars on obverse	45.	100.	400.	600.	900.	1,400.
1838-1853, Stars on obverse	15.	18.	25.	60.	160.	400.
1853-1855, Arrows at date	15.	16.	20.	60.	175.	425.
1856-1860, Stars on obverse	15.	16.	20.	50.	150.	400.
1860-1873, Legend on obverse	15.	16.	18.	40.	100.	250.
1873-1874, Arrows at date	15.	18.	60.	175.	400.	850.
1875-1891, No arrows, Legend on obverse	8.	10.	18.	40.	100.	200.

QUARTER DOLLAR – SEATED LIBERTY

Type and Denomination	VG	F	VF	EF	AU	UNC
1838-1853	25.	35.	60.	125.	300.	750.
1853, Rays around eagle	25.	30.	60.	225.	500.	1,400.
1854-1855, Arrow at date, no rays around eagle	25.	30.	45.	125.	300.	750.
1856-1865, No motto above eagle	22.	30.	40.	80.	200.	500.
1866-1873, Motto above eagle	40.	75.	125.	250.	400.	750.
1873-1874, Arrows at date	25.	45.	90.	300.	600.	1,100.
1875-1891, No arrows at date, motto above eagle	22.	35.	40.	65.	175.	375.

HALF DOLLAR - SEATED LIBERTY

Type and Denomination	VG	F	VF	EF	AU	UNC
1807-1836, many minor varieties	55.	60.	80.	130.	300.	750.
1836-1837, 50 "CENTS"	60.	75.	120.	200.	450.	1,150.
1838-1839, "HALF DOL."	60.	75.	125.	275.	650.	1,200.
1839-1853, No motto above eagle	40.	60.	70.	140.	250.	650.
1853, Arrows at date; Rays around eagle	35.	60.	125.	250.	750.	2,000.
1854-1855, Arrows at date; No rays around eagle	35.	55.	75.	150.	360.	750.
1856-1866, No motto above eagle	35.	50.	60.	125.	225.	600.
1866-1873, "IN GOD WE TRUST" above eagle	30.	45.	50.	100.	200.	575.
1873-1874, Arrows at date	40.	60.	120.	250.	600.	1,200.
1875-1891, No arrows at date	30.	45.	60.	125.	200.	500.

GOLD COINS

FIVE DOLLARS - HALF EAGLE

Type and Denomination	F	VF	EF	AU	UNC
1834-1838, Classic Head	350.	450.	700.	1,250.	4,000.
1839-1866, Coronet Head	250.	275.	300.	400.	1,750.
1866-1908	175.	200.	220.	250.	300.

TEN DOLLARS - EAGLE

Type and Denomination	F	VF	EF	AU	UNC
1838-1865, Coronet Head 2 Varieties	350.	400.	500.	750.	5,000.
1866-1907	270.	290.	300.	350.	450.

TWENTY DOLLARS – DOUBLE EAGLE

Type and Denomination	F	VF	EF	AU	UNC
1849-1866, Coronet Head 3 Varieties	600.	750.	875.	1,100.	3,000.
1866-1876	650.	700.	750.	850.	1,150.
1877-1907	500.	575.	600.	625.	675.

LOCAL PRE-DECIMAL COINS

Although it is sometimes stated that the first coins produced for local use in Canada were the 1858-1859 decimal coins for the Province of Canada, this is not the case. A small but important group of local coinages was produced prior to the adoption of decimal currency. These coinages were at first specially modified Spanish-American silver coins, but coppers were added to this group in the 1850s.

NEW FRANCE (FRENCH REGIME)

COUNTERSTAMPED SPANISH-AMERICAN COINS

During the last part of the 17th century, the quantity of Spanish-American silver coins in circulation in New France increased. This increase was due primarily to the illegal trade in furs which the colonists were carrying on with the Dutch and English. At that time such coins circulated at a value that depended upon their weight; the more worn the coin was, the lower it was valued compared to unworn pieces. Since many Spanish-American coins in New France had varying amounts of wear, their use in commerce was difficult. Colonial authorities were not anxious to see these coins used in preference to French coins, but the latter were so scarce that they relented. In the early 1680s treasury officials weighed a quantity of these coins and counterstamped each with a fleur-de-lis. Underweight coins also received a Roman numeral counterstamp (from I to IV) to indicate the amount by which the weight was deficient. The coins could then be compared to a table to determine the exact value at which they were current.

Unfortunately for collectors, no surviving examples of this interesting local issue are known.

NOVA SCOTIA, NEW BRUNSWICK, PRINCE EDWARD ISLAND

For the pre-decimal coinage of Colonial New Brunswick, Nova Scotia and Prince Edward Island, see the 'Charlton Standard Catalogue of Canadian Colonial Tokens.'

HISTORY OF CANADIAN DECIMAL COINS

The decimal coins which we take so much for granted today have a history that stretches back into the last century and beyond. During the 1700s, the single most important coin in North America was the Spanish-American dollar, a large silver coin produced in great quantities by mints in Mexico, Peru and other parts of the New World. The Spanish- American dollar was not a decimal coin; its formal denomination was 8 reales. It was nicknamed dollar in deference to its resemblance in size to German thalers and other large European coins of similar name. This Spanish-American coin was so important in the United States that when the U.S. adopted a decimal system of dollars and cents in the 1790s, their silver dollar was made with the same amount of silver as the Spanish-American dollar.

In British North America in the first half of the 19th century each colony used a system of accounting which consisted of pounds, shillings and pence. However, the coins actually in circulation were mostly Spanish-American and U.S. As trade with the United States increased in the 1840s and 1850s, the British North American colonies (provinces) were naturally drawn toward the adoption of a currency system more like that of the U.S. than Great Britain.

All through the 1850s British North America struggled with the problem of currency standards. The Province of Canada, under Francis Hincks, took the lead in fighting for a decimal system. Acts passed in 1851 and 1853 stipulated that public accounts be kept in dollars and cents, but no coins were issued under their provisions. An 1857 act provided a broader base for a decimal currency system. It directed that both government and private accounts be kept in dollars, cents and mils. A decimal coinage followed in 1858-1859, based upon a dollar equal to the U.S. gold dollar.

Other British North American provinces soon followed the Province of Canada's lead. New Brunswick and Nova Scotia adopted decimal systems in 1859-1860, Newfoundland followed suit in 1864 and Prince Edward Island went decimal in 1871. Thus, even before Confederation the use of decimal coins was firmly established.

NOVA SCOTIA

In the years immediately preceding the adoption of a decimal currency system in Nova Scotia in 1859, British coins formed an important part of the circulating currency, much more so than in the other British North American provinces. Consequently, the Nova Scotia government chose a decimal dollar equal to one-fifth of a pound sterling (i.e. $5 = £1), allowing British silver coins to conveniently fit into the new system and continue circulating. The British 2-shilling piece (florin) became a 50-cent piece, the shilling became a 25-cent piece and the sixpence became a 12 1/2-cent piece. The only coins the province needed to have specially produced were a cent, and to make change for the sixpence and half crown, a half cent.

HALF CENT
Victoria 1861 - 1864

The half cent was coined with the same diameter as the British farthing and utilized the same obverse. Pattern pieces incorporated the royal crown and a wreath of roses (see NS-1 to NS-3 and NS-5 in the chapter on Patterns). However, a local campaign in favour of the provincial flower, the mayflower, resulted in the adoption of a design using the royal crown surrounded by a wreath of both roses and mayflowers.

Designer and Modeller:
Obverse: Leonard C. Wyon
Reverse: Leonard C. Wyon
from a model by C. Hill
Composition: .95 copper, .04 tin, .01 zinc
Weight: 2.84 grams
Diameter: 20.65 mm
Edge: Plain
Die Axis: ↑↑

Date and Mint Mark	Quantity Minted	VG-8	F-12	VF-20	EF-40	AU-50	MS-60 Brown	MS-63 Red/Br
1861	400,000	7.	10.	15.	30.	75.	150.	450.
1864	400,000	7.	10.	15.	25.	65.	125.	325.

ONE CENT
Victoria 1861 - 1864

The cent was minted with the same diameter as the British halfpenny and used the same obverse. The reverse designs are similar to those used for the half cent, including pattern pieces with a wreath of roses (see NS-4 and NS-6 in the chapter on Patterns).

The circulation issues of this denomination have two distinct reverses. The first (1861) has much detail in the crown and a large rosebud at the lower right part of the wreath. On the second reverse (1861-1864) the crown has a narrower headband and generally less detail, the rosebud at the lower right is smaller, and the rosebud and certain other parts of the design come closer to the lettering and the raised line just inside the rim denticles.

MINTAGE FIGURES, 1861-1862. The mintage figures of 800,000 for 1861 and 1,000,000 for 1862 have puzzled collectors for many years since the 1862-dated coins are scarcer. The probable explanation is that some, perhaps most, cents struck in 1862 were from dies dated 1861. Therefore, the mintages for the two years have been combined.

Designer and Modeller:
 Obverse: Leonard C. Wyon
 Reverse: Leonard C. Wyon
  from a model by C. Hill
Engraver: Leonard C. Wyon
Composition: .95 copper, .04 tin,
  .01 zinc
Weight: 5.67 grams
Diameter: 25.53 mm
Edge: Plain
Die Axis: ↑↑

| Large Rosebud | | Small Rosebud | | | | | | |

Date and Mint Mark	Quantity Minted	VG-8	F-12	VF-20	EF-40	AU-50	MS-60 Brown	MS-63 Red/Br
1861 Large bud	1,800,000	4.	6.	9.	20.	55.	200.	425.
1861 Small bud	Incl. above	6.	8.	12.	30.	70.	250.	575.
1862	Incl. above	100.	125.	250.	450.	1,100.	3,000.	—
1864	800,000	5.	7.	10.	25.	60.	225.	625.

*Most of the cents issued in 1862 were dated 1861.

NEW BRUNSWICK

When New Brunswick adopted a decimal dollar in 1860, it chose the same rating for its dollar and ordered the same denominations as the Province of Canada: cents in bronze and 5-, 10- and 20-cent pieces in silver. The effective date for the decimal currency act was November 1, 1860 but, like Nova Scotia, New Brunswick had to wait until early 1862 before the first coins arrived from England. In the meantime, the government introduced other decimal coins as a temporary expedient. Thus, in late 1861 and early 1862 some 500,000 Province of Canada cents and a quantity of United States small denomination silver coins were put into circulation in the province.

HALF CENT
Victoria 1861

This denomination was not required by the province since its dollar and hence British coins went at a different rating than in the sister province of Nova Scotia. Nevertheless, the Royal Mint became confused and struck a half cent for New Brunswick. Over 200,000 of these coins came off the presses before the error was discovered. Most of the mintage was returned to the melting pot. The circulation strikes that survived are thought to have become mixed with the Nova Scotia half cents and sent to Halifax.

The obverse is that of the British farthing and the reverse is a royal crown and a rose/mayflower wreath very similar to that used for Nova Scotia.

Designer and Modeller:
    Obverse: Leonard C. Wyon
    Reverse: Leonard C. Wyon
      from a model by C. Hill
Engraver: Leonard C. Wyon
Composition: .95 copper, .04 tin,
          .01 zinc
Weight: 2.84 grams
Diameter: 20.65 mm
Edge: Plain
Die Axis: ↑↑

Date and Mint Mark	Quantity Minted	G-4	VG-8	F-12	VF-20	EF-40	AU-50	MS-60 Brown	MS-63 Red/Br
1861	222,800*	110.	150.	200.	350.	500.	700.	1,000.	2,000.

*most were melted prior to issue.

ONE CENT
Victoria 1861 - 1864

The New Brunswick 1-cent pieces have the British halfpenny obverse and a reverse similar to that used for the Nova Scotia cent.

For the 1864 issue two styles of 6 were used in the date: a figure with a round centre in its loop and a short top, and a figure with a more oval centre and a longer top.

Designer and Modeller:
    Obverse: Leonard C. Wyon
    Reverse: Leonard C. Wyon
      from a model by C. Hill
Engraver: Leonard C. Wyon
Composition: .95 copper, .04 tin,
          .01 zinc
Weight: 5.67 grams
Diameter: 25.53 mm
Edge: Plain
Die Axis: ↑↑

Short 6   Tall 6

Date and Mint Mark	Quantity Minted	G-4	VG-8	F-12	VF-20	EF-40	AU-50	MS-60 Brown	MS-63 Red/Br
1861	1,000,000	3.	5.	8.	15.	35.	75.	250.	450.
1864 Short 6	1,000,000	3.	5.	8.	15.	35.	85.	275.	550.
1864 Tall 6	Incl. above	5.	7.	10.	20.	45.	90.	350.	600.

FIVE CENTS
Victoria 1862 - 1864

The production of New Brunswick's first silver decimal coinage had to await the completion of the bronze coinage. Consequently, it could not commence until 1862. The 5-cent piece designs were basically those of the Province of Canada with an appropriately modified obverse legend.

Two styles of 6 were employed in dating the 1864 issue: a small 6 and a large 6.

Engraver: Obverse: Leonard C. Wyon
Composition: .925 silver, .075 copper
Weight: 1.16 grams
Diameter: 15.49 mm
Edge: Reeded
Die Axis: ↑↓

Small 6   Large 6

Date and Mint Mark	Quantity Minted	G-4	VG-8	F-12	VF-20	EF-40	AU-50	MS-60	MS-63
1862	100,000	50.	100.	200.	400.	850.	2,000.	3,250.	5,500.
1864 Small 6	100,000	60.	110.	225.	450.	900.	2,250.	3,750.	7,500.
1864 Large 6	Incl. above	110.	200.	350.	650.	1,300.	3,500.	5,500.	—

TEN CENTS
Victoria 1862 - 1864

The designs for the New Brunswick 10-cent piece were adapted from existing Province of Canada designs. The reverse was used without modification and the obverse involved changing the legend only.

The 1862 issue is usually collected as two varieties. One has a normal date and the other has an obviously double-punched 2.

Engraver: Obverse: Leonard C. Wyon
Composition: .925 silver, .075 copper
Weight: 2.32 grams
Diameter: 17.91 mm
Edge: Reeded
Die Axis: ↑↓

Normal Date

Double-punched 2

Date and Mint Mark	Quantity Minted	G-4	VG-8	F-12	VF-20	EF-40	AU-50	MS-60	MS-63
1862	150,000	55.	90.	175.	350.	700.	1,400.	2,250.	5,000.
1862 D-P 2	Incl. above	85.	150.	300.	600.	1,200.	2,500.	4,000.	8,500.
1864	150,000	55.	90.	175.	350.	800.	1,750.	3,500.	7,000.

TWENTY CENTS
Victoria 1862 - 1864

The New Brunswick 20-cent piece has an unusual reverse design once rejected for the Province of Canada (see PC-4 in the chapter on Patterns). The reverse adopted by the Province of Canada differs in style from that chosen by New Brunswick, while using the same elements. This stylistic difference, plus the fact a die for the New Brunswick 20-cent piece of 1862 was used to strike one side of George W. Wyon's obituary medalet, suggests that it was George Wyon and not Leonard Wyon who engraved this reverse. The obverse utilizes the Province of Canada 20 cents portrait with a special legend for New Brunswick.

Designer and Modeller:
Reverse: possibly Geo. W. Wyon
Engraver: Obverse: Leonard C. Wyon
Composition: .925 silver, .075 copper
Weight: 4.65 grams
Diameter: 23.27 mm
Edge: Reeded
Die Axis: ↑↓

Date and Mint Mark	Quantity Minted	G-4	VG-8	F-12	VF-20	EF-40	AU-50	MS-60	MS-63
1862	150,000	22.	30.	55.	90.	350.	700.	2,000.	6,000.
1864	150,000	22.	30.	55.	90.	400.	900.	2,400.	7,000.

PRINCE EDWARD ISLAND

ONE CENT
Victoria 1871

Prince Edward Island adopted a decimal currency system in 1871. Its dollar was given the same rating as those of the provinces of Canada and New Brunswick. The only coinage in the new system was bronze cents in 1871. The island entered Confederation two years later. The provincial government experienced considerable difficulty placing its cents in circulation. It took almost ten years to deplete the stock and the last of it was sold at a 10 percent discount.

The reverse was prepared specifically for the Prince Edward Island government, incorporating the seal of the island and a Latin phrase, "PARVA SUB INGENTI," meaning "The small beneath the great." The seal shows a large oak tree, representing England, sheltering three young oak trees, representing the three counties on the island.

Because of pressure to produce domestic coin, the Royal Mint in London made arrangements with Heaton's Mint in Birmingham to strike P.E.I. cents. For some unknown reason Heaton's familiar "H" mint mark is absent from the coins.

Designer and Modeller:
Obverse: Leonard C. Wyon, from a portrait model by William Theed
Reverse: Leonard C. Wyon
Composition: .95 copper, .04 tin, .01 zinc
Weight: 5.67 grams
Diameter: 25.40 mm
Edge: Plain
Die Axis: ↑↑

Date and Mint Mark	Quantity Minted	G-4	VG-8	F-12	VF-20	EF-40	AU-50	MS-60 Brown	MS-63 Red/Br
1871	2,000,000	2.	4.	6.	10.	25.	55.	110.	200.

NEWFOUNDLAND

Since Newfoundland remained separate from Canada until 1949, it has a much larger decimal coin series than the other pre-Confederation British colonies. The island adopted decimal currency in 1863, hoping to have coins on the new standard in circulation in 1864. The most important coin in Newfoundland had been the Spanish-American dollar or 8-real piece, so the government set its dollar equal in value to this coin. This made the new decimal cent equal to the British halfpenny and $4.80 equal to £1 sterling.

ONE CENT
Victoria 1865 - 1896

Beginning in 1864, several designs were considered for the Newfoundland cent. The first tendency was to use the same designs as New Brunswick. Pattern dies are known for an 1864 Newfoundland cent with the royal crown, rose/mayflower design (see NF-1 in the chapter on Patterns). This design was rejected in favour of a royal crown and wreath of pitcher plant (the provincial flower) and oak, with unusual broad, bold lettering and date. The obverse incorporated the British halfpenny portrait with the legend "VICTORIA QUEEN," also in the same bold type (see NF-6 in the chapter on Patterns). However, it was decided that this legend was inappropriate and the cents struck for circulation in 1865 use the British halfpenny obverse legend - "VICTORIA D:G:BRITT:REG:F:D:."

An interesting variation in die axes occurs on this denomination. For all dates except 1872 the dies are in the medal arrangement (↑↑) but on the 1872s they are coinage arrangement (↑↓). The most reasonable explanation for this difference is that the Heaton Mint, which struck the 1872 cents, did not receive specific instructions regarding which die arrangement to use and chose the same arrangement as for the silver. The error was corrected in 1876 when Heaton's next coined cents for Newfoundland.

Designer:
   Reverse: Horace Morehen
Engraver: Thomas J. Minton
Composition: .95 copper, .04 tin,
              .01 zinc
Weight: 5.67 grams
Diameter: 25.53 mm
Edge: Plain
Die Axis: ↑↑ (1865, 1873-1896);
        ↑↓ (1872)

Heaton Mint issues have an "H" mint mark
at the bottom of the wreath (1872, 1876).
London Mint strikings have no letter.

Date and Mint Mark	Quantity Minted	VG-8	F-12	VF-20	EF-40	AU-50	MS-60 Brown	MS-63 Red/Br
1865	240,000	7.	9.	20.	50.	125.	300.	700.
1872H	200,000	5.	7.	15.	35.	85.	135.	275.
1873	200,000	6.	10.	30.	80.	200.	600.	2,000.
1876H	200,000	6.	8.	17.	60.	175.	450.	1,000.

VARIETIES 1880. Three date varieties exist for 1880. The first has a narrow 0 in the date, while the second and third have a wide 0, in different positions. The positional differences between the second and third varieties are not felt to be important, so they are combined into one variety, the Wide 0.

1880 Narrow O   1880 Wide O

Date and Mint Mark	Quantity Minted	VG-8	F-12	VF-20	EF-40	AU-50	MS-60 Brown	MS-63 Red/Br
1880 Narrow 0	400,000	250.	400.	500.	900.	1,500.	2,500.	7,500.
1880 Wide 0	Incl. above	5.	7.	15.	50.	100.	225.	650.
1885	40,000	40.	90.	125.	275.	550.	1,000.	3,500.
1888	50,000	35.	80.	120.	300.	750.	1,500.	5,000.
1890	200,000	5.	7.	15.	50.	200.	500.	1,500.
1894	200,000	5.	7.	15.	50.	175.	300.	1,000.
1896	200,000	5.	7.	15.	45.	100.	200.	550.

Note: MS-60 cents are brown in colour, while MS-63 cents are red/brown. Higher mint state grades will require full red colour coins.

ONE CENT
Edward VII 1904 - 1909

The reverse design is a modification of the Victorian reverse, substituting the Imperial State crown for the St. Edward's crown. The obverses of most Edward VII denominations were those of the corresponding Dominion of Canada coinage; however, the Newfoundland cent has a distinctive design. The bust is very large and the letter size in the legend correspondingly small.

Designer and Modeller:
    Portrait: G. W. DeSaulles,
    (DES below bust)
Engraver: Reverse: W.H.J. Blakemore
        modifying existing coinage tools
Composition: .95 copper, .04 tin,
        .01 zinc
Weight: 5.67 grams
Diameter: 25.53 mm
Edge: Plain
Die Axis: ↑↑

The Mint, Birmingham issue (1904 only) has an "H" mint mark at the bottom of the wreath. Royal Mint strikings have no letter.

Date and Mint Mark	Quantity Minted	VG-8	F-12	VF-20	EF-40	AU-50	MS-60 Brown	MS-63 Red/Br
1904H	100,000	11.	20.	35.	80.	175.	500.	1,250.
1907	200,000	4.	6.	12.	40.	125.	300.	1,000.
1909	200,000	4.	6.	11.	30.	80.	150.	200.

ONE CENT
George V 1913 - 1936

The reverse for the cents of this reign is that established for the Edward VII series and the obverse is that of the Dominion of Canada cents.

Designer and Modeller:
    Portrait: Sir E.B. MacKennal,
    (B.M. on the truncation)
Composition: .95 copper, .04 tin,
        .01 zinc (1913-1920);
        .955 copper, .030 tin,
        .015 zinc (1926-1936)
Diameter: 25.53 mm (1913,1929-1936);
        25.40 mm (1917-1920)
Edge: Plain
Die Axis: ↑↑

Ottawa Mint issues (1917-1920) have a "C" mint mark at the bottom of the wreath, Royal Mint strikings have no letter.

Date and Mint Mark	Quantity Minted	VG-8	F-12	VF-20	EF-40	AU-50	MS-60 Brown	MS-63 Red/Br
1913	400,000	2.	3.	4.	9.	30.	60.	100.
1917C	702,350	2.	3.	4.	12.	35.	125.	350.
1919C	300,000	2.	3.	5.	15.	55.	250.	550.
1920C	302,184	2.	3.	7.	20.	100.	500.	1,250.
1929	300,000	2.	3.	4.	9.	30.	90.	175.
1936	300,000	2.	3.	4.	6.	15.	55.	110.

ONE CENT
George VI 1938 - 1947

In 1937 the Newfoundland government reviewed the question of converting to a small cent, similar to those used in Canada and the United States. The smaller coin was less expensive to produce and Newfoundlanders objected to the reverse design of the large cent, in which their provincial flower was forced into an unnatural configuration.

The reverse design adopted for the new coins was a very lifelike rendition of the pitcher plant in bloom. The plant is native to Newfoundland, and is one of the insectivores of the plant kingdom. The large leaves are pitcher-like receptacles, the inner surfaces being covered with downward-sloping bristles. Insects are attracted onto their leaves by a sweet sticky syrup at the bottom and the bristles help prevent their escape. The digestible portions of the insects are then absorbed by the plant.

During World War II, Newfoundland cents were coined at Ottawa rather than in England to avoid the risks of transatlantic shipping. In 1940 and 1942 the "C" mint mark was omitted in error.

Designer and Modeller:
    Portrait: Percy Metcalfe
    (P.M. below bust)
    Reverse: Walter J. Newman
Composition: .955 copper, .030 tin, .015 zinc
Weight: 3.24 grams
Diameter: 19.05 mm
Edge: Plain
Die Axis: ↑↑

Royal Canadian Mint issues (1940-47) have a "C" mint mark to the right of CENT on the reverse (except for the 1940 and 1942 issues, which have none). The Royal Mint issue (1938) has no mint mark.

Date and Mint Mark	Quantity Minted	VG-8	F-12	VF-20	EF-40	AU-50	MS-60 Brown	MS-63 Red/Br
1938	500,000	1.	2.	3.	4.	10.	30.	60.
1940	300,000	3.	5.	8.	20.	55.	125.	350.
1941C	827,662	1.	1.	1.	3.	10.	40.	125.
1942	1,996,889	1.	1.	2.	3.	15.	60.	200.
1943C	1,239,732	1.	1.	1.	3.	10.	25.	75.
1944C	1,328,776	2.	5.	20.	40.	125.	400.	1,250.
1947C	313,772	1.	2.	10.	25.	50.	110.	250.

FIVE CENTS
Victoria 1865 - 1896

Work on the coinage tools for the silver began later than for the cent, so there are no legend wording varieties for this denomination. The first pattern is a bronze striking of the adopted obverse (derived from the New Brunswick obverse by substitution of "NEWFOUNDLAND" for "NEW BRUNSWICK") and the Canada/New Brunswick reverse with a maple wreath and royal crown (see NF-2 in the chapter on Patterns). A later pattern, in silver, has an arabesque design similar to the adopted design, except the arches are thinner (see NF-8 in the chapter on Patterns).

Designer and Modeller:
Reverse: Leonard C. Wyon
Engraver: Obverse: Leonard C. Wyon
Composition: .925 silver, .075 copper
Weight: 1.18 grams
Diameter: 15.49 mm
Edge: Reeded
Die Axis: ↑↓

Heaton Mint issues have an "H" mint mark either on the obverse under the bust (1872-1876) or on the reverse under the date (1882). London Mint strikings have no letter.

Date, Mint Portrait	Quantity Minted	G-4	VG-8	F-12	VF-20	EF-40	AU-50	MS-60	MS-63
1865, NF1	80,000	22.	65.	110.	225.	450.	750.	1,600.	3,500.
1865, NF2	Incl. above	22.	65.	110.	225.	450.	750.	1,600.	3,500.
1870, NF1	40,000	60.	110.	225.	325.	750.	1,250.	2,250.	4,500.
1870, NF2	Incl. above	60.	110.	225.	325.	750.	1,250.	2,250.	4,500.
1872H, NF2	40,000	22.	55.	110.	190.	375.	650.	1,500.	3,000.
1873, NF1	40,000	70.	150.	275.	550.	1,600.	3,000.	–	–
1873, NF2	Incl. above	70.	150.	275.	550.	1,600.	3,000.	–	–
1873H, NF2	Incl. above	650.	1,500.	2,200.	4,000.	6,500.	9,000.	–	–
1876H, NF2	20,000	70.	190.	300.	450.	850.	1,250.	2,250.	3,500.
1880, NF2	40,000	33.	80.	135.	275.	475.	1,000.	2,250.	4,000.
1881, NF2	40,000	33.	65.	135.	225.	425.	1,000.	2,250.	5,500.
1882H, NF3	60,000	11.	33.	85.	135.	350.	900.	1,750.	4,000.
1885, NF2	16,000	135.	250.	375.	600.	1,400.	2,250.	3,750.	7,000.
1888, NF2	40,000	40.	80.	165.	300.	750.	1,750.	3,500.	6,500.
1888, NF3	Incl. above								
1890, NF3	160,000	8.	17.	33.	75.	190.	600.	1,750.	3,750.
1894, NF3	160,000	4.	13.	28.	55.	165.	450.	1,500.	4,000.
1896, NF3	400,000	3.	11.	17.	33.	100.	375.	1,500.	3,750.

VICTORIA OBVERSE PORTRAIT VARIETIES

NEWFOUNDLAND FIVE CENTS - NF

PORTRAIT: NF1

Two well defined strands of hair at top of brow, below top leaf of laurel crown. Dot before and after Newfoundland on obverse.

NF-1 will be found on the following dates: 1865; 1870; 1873

PORTRAIT: NF2

Two weakly defined strands of hair at top of brow, below top leaf of laurel crown. No dot before and after Newfoundland on obverse:

NF2 will be found on the following dates: 1865; 1870; 1872H; 1873; 1873H; 1876H; 1880; 1881; 1885; 1888

PORTRAIT: NF3

Three well defined strands of hair at top of brow, below top leaf of laurel crown. Dot after Newfoundland on obverse:

NF3 will be found on the following dates: 1882H; 1888; 1890; 1894; 1896

FIVE CENTS
Edward VII 1903 - 1908

The obverse for this denomination is that of the Dominion of Canada issues. The reverse, a new design by G.W. DeSaulles, is one of the last coinage designs he did before his death.

Designer and Modeller:
George W. DeSaulles,
(DES. below bust)
Composition: .925 silver, .075 copper
Weight: 1.18 grams
Diameter: 15.49 mm
Edge: Reeded
Die Axis:↑↓

The Mint, Birmingham issue of 1904 has an "H" mint mark below the oval at the bottom on the reverse. Royal Mint issues have no letter.

Date and Mint Mark	Quantity Minted	VG-8	F-12	VF-20	EF-40	AU-50	MS-60	MS-63
1903	100,000	6.	11.	35.	85.	225.	600.	1,750.
1904H	100,000	5.	8.	25.	60.	125.	200.	400.
1908	400,000	5.	8.	25.	60.	150.	350.	1,250.

FIVE CENTS
George V 1912 - 1929

The obverse is the same as for the Dominion of Canada issue and the reverse is the same as the Newfoundland Edward VII issue.

Designer and Modeller:
Portrait: Sir E.B. MacKennal,
(B.M. on the truncation)
Composition: .925 silver, .075 copper
Weight: 1.18 grams (1912);
1.17 grams (1917-1929)
Diameter: 15.49 mm (1912-1919);
15.69 mm (1929)
Edge: Reeded
Die Axis: ↑↑

The Ottawa Mint issues (1917-1919) have a "C" mint mark below the oval at the bottom on the reverse. Royal Mint strikings have no letter.

Date and Mint Mark	Quantity Minted	VG-8	F-12	VF-20	EF-40	AU-50	MS-60	MS-63
1912	300,000	2.	4.	10.	33.	65.	175.	325.
1917C	300,319	2.	4.	10.	55.	150.	475.	1,500.
1919C	100,844	9.	12.	35.	150.	650.	1,500.	4,500.
1929	300,000	2.	4.	8.	20.	70.	200.	450.

FIVE CENTS
George VI 1938 - 1947

While considering the replacement of the large cent, the Newfoundland government also contemplated dropping its "fish scale" silver 5-cent piece in favour of a nickel coin similar to Canada's. At that time, because of a strong conservative element, it was decided to change only the cent. The reverse design was continued from the previous reign and the obverse used the standard portrait for British colonial coinages.

Designer and Modeller:
Portrait: Percy Metcalfe,
(P.M. below bust)
Composition: .925 silver,
.075 copper (1938-1944);
.800 silver, .200 copper
(1945-1947)
Weight: 1.17 grams
Diameter: 15.69 mm (1938);
15.49 mm (1940-1947)
Edge: Reeded
Die Axis: ↑↑

Royal Canadian Mint issues (1940-47) have a "C" mint mark below the oval at the bottom on the reverse. The Royal Mint issue (1938) has no letter.

Date and Mint Mark	Quantity Minted	VG-8	F-12	VF-20	EF-40	AU-50	MS-60	MS-63
1938	100,000	1.	2.	4.	8.	25.	100.	350.
1940C	200,000	1.	2.	4.	8.	35.	150.	425.
1941C	612,641	1.	2.	4.	6.	12.	25.	55.
1942C	298,348	1.	2.	4.	7.	15.	30.	65.
1943C	351,666	1.	2.	4.	6.	12.	25.	55.
1944C	286,504	2.	4.	7.	11.	25.	60.	175.
1945C	203,828	1.	2.	4.	6.	12.	25.	55.

1946C - 1947C ISSUES. The 1946C issue is an anomaly. Published official mint reports, as well as unpublished mint accounting records, do not indicate any mintage of this denomination during 1946. It appears that this scarce issue was actually coined during 1947. The mintage figures given for the years 1946 and 1947 must be considered unofficial although they are believed to have come from a mint officer many years ago.

Date and Mint Mark	Quantity Minted	VG-8	F-12	VF-20	EF-40	AU-50	MS-60	MS-63
1946C	2,041	450.	550.	650.	800.	1,100.	1,750.	2,500.
1947C	38,400	4.	5.	9.	20.	50.	100.	175.

TEN CENTS
Victoria 1865 - 1896

Like the 5 cents, the 10 cents has a bronze pattern with the adopted obverse (derived from the New Brunswick obverse by substituting "NEWFOUNDLAND" for "NEW BRUNSWICK") and the Canada/New Brunswick reverse (see NF-3 in the chapter on Patterns). As well there is a silver pattern with very thin arches in the arabesque design on the reverse (see NF-9 in the chapter on Patterns).

Designer and Modeller:
Reverse: Leonard C. Wyon
Engraver: Obverse: Leonard C. Wyon
Composition: .925 silver, .075 copper
Weight: 2.36 grams
Diameter: 17.98 mm
Edge: Reeded
Die Axis: ↑↓

Heaton Mint issues have an "H" mint mark either on the obverse under the bust (1872-1876) or on the reverse under the date (1882). London Mint strikings have no letter.

Date, Mint Portrait	Quantity Minted	G-4	VG-8	F-12	VF-20	EF-40	AU-50	MS-60	MS-63
1865-ND1	80,000	13.	40.	65.	165.	400.	700.	1,750.	3,500.
1870-ND1	30,000	110.	250.	400.	700.	1,500.	2,000.	3,500.	7,000.
1870-ND2	Incl. above								

1871H NEWFOUNDLAND/CANADA MULE. A rare variety exists because an 1871H Dominion of Canada reverse die was muled, apparently accidentally, with an "H" Newfoundland obverse die. All known examples are in well-worn condition.

1871H Newfoundland/Canada Mule

1880 Second 8 over 7

Date, Mint Portrait	Quantity Minted	G-4	VG-8	F-12	VF-20	EF-40	AU-50	MS-60	MS-63
1871H Mule	40,000				Extremely Rare				
1872H-ND2	Incl. above	12.	33.	60.	135.	300.	550.	1,500.	3,000.
1873-ND1	20,000	33.	65.	135.	350.	850.	2,500.	–	–
1873-ND2	Incl. above	33.	65.	135.	350.	850.	2,500.	–	–
1876H-ND2	10,000	28.	65.	140.	325.	750.	1,400.	2,250.	4,000.
1880-ND2	10,000	33.	75.	150.	375.	850.	1,300.	3,000.	4,500.
1882H-ND3	20,000	22.	55.	110.	300.	900.	2,250.	4,000.	–
1885-ND2	8,000	60.	120.	250.	500.	1,250.	1,750.	3,500.	7,000.
1885-ND3	Incl. above	60.	120.	250.	500.	1,250.	1,750.	3,500.	7,000.
1888-ND3	30,000	22.	55.	110.	400.	2,000.	–	–	–
1890-ND3	100,000	7.	12.	28.	65.	225.	600.	2,250.	5,000.
1894-ND2	100,000	5.	11.	22.	60.	200.	500.	1,500.	4,000.
1896-ND3	230,000	5.	10.	20.	55.	165.	550.	1,750.	4,500.

Note: All examples of the 1880 issue are from dies in which the second 8 of the date is punched over a 7.

VICTORIA OBVERSE PORTRAIT VARIETIES

NEWFOUNDLAND TEN CENTS - ND

PORTRAIT: ND1
Two leaves at top of laurel crown; uppermost rising into legend band. Dot before and after Newfoundland on obverse.

ND1 will be found on the following dates: 1865; 1870; 1873

PORTRAIT: ND2
Three leaves at top of laurel crown; uppermost leaf well into legend band. Dot before but not after Newfoundland on obverse.

ND2 will be found on the following dates: 1870; 1872H; 1873; 1876H; 1880; 1885; 1894

PORTRAIT: ND3
Two leaves at top of laurel crown. Top leaf barely touches legend band. Dot before and after Newfoundland on obverse.

ND3 will be found on the following dates: 1882H; 1885; 1888; 1890; 1894; 1896

TEN CENTS
Edward VII 1903 - 1904

The obverse is that used for the Dominion of Canada issues. The reverse is a new design by G.W. DeSaulles.

Designer and Modeller:
G.W. DeSaulles, (DES. below bust)
Composition: .925 silver, .075 copper
Weight: 2.36 grams
Diameter: 17.96 mm
Edge: Reeded
Die Axis: ↑↓

The Mint, Birmingham issue of 1904 has an "H" mint mark below the oval at the bottom on the reverse. The Royal Mint issue (1903) has no letter.

Date and Mint Mark	Quantity Minted	G-4	VG-8	F-12	VF-20	EF-40	AU-50	MS-60	MS-63
1903	100,000	5.	13.	33.	100.	300.	650.	1,750.	4,000.
1904H	100,000	4.	7.	18.	45.	85.	175.	300.	600.

TEN CENTS
George V 1912 - 1919

The obverse is the same as for the Dominion of Canada issues. The reverse is a continuation of the Newfoundland Edward VII designs.

Designer and Modeller:
Portrait: Sir E.B. MacKennal,
(B.M. on the truncation)
Composition: .925 silver, .075 copper
Weight: 2.36 grams (1912-1917)
2.33 grams (1919)
Diameter: 17.96 mm (1912)
18.03 mm (1917-1919)
Edge: Reeded
Die Axis: ↑↑

Ottawa Mint issues (1917-1919) have a "C" mint mark below the oval at the bottom on the reverse. The Royal Mint issue (1912) has no letter.

Date and Mint Mark	Quantity Minted	G-4	VG-8	F-12	VF-20	EF-40	AU-50	MS-60	MS-63
1912	150,000	1.	2.	6.	18.	60.	135.	250.	450.
1917C	250,805	1.	2.	6.	22.	65.	300.	600.	2,500.
1919C	54,342	6.	12.	20.	35.	100.	200.	400.	600.

TEN CENTS
George VI 1938-1947

The obverse for this denomination used Percy Metcalfe's standard portrait of George VI fo. British colonial coinages and the existing Edward VII/George V reverse. The 1946C issue was probably coined in 1947 (see preceding comments on the 1946C 5 cents); the mintage figures for 1946 and 1947 must be considered unofficial.

Designer and Modeller:
  Portrait: Percy Metcalfe,
  (P.M. below bust)
Composition: .925 silver, .075 copper
  (1938-1944);
  .800 silver, .200 copper
  (1945-1947)
Weight: 2.33 grams
Diameter: 18.03 mm
Edge: Reeded
Die Axis: ↑↑

Royal Canadian Mint issues of 1941-47 have a "C" mint mark below the oval at the bottom on the reverse. The Royal Mint issue (1938) and the Royal Canadian Mint issue of 1940 have no letter.

Date and Mint Mark	Quantity Minted	VG-8	F-12	VF-20	EF-40	AU-50	MS-60	MS-63
1938	100,000	2.	3.	7.	13.	45.	150.	450.
1940	100,000	2.	3.	7.	13.	45.	150.	400.
1941C	483,630	1.	2.	4.	7.	22.	60.	150.
1942C	292,736	1.	2.	4.	7.	22.	75.	250.
1943C	104,706	1.	2.	4.	7.	22.	90.	400.
1944C	151,471	2.	4.	10.	30.	100.	450.	1,750.
1945C	175,833	1.	2.	4.	7.	22.	50.	300.
1946C	38,400	4.	8.	18.	30.	65.	100.	400.
1947C	61,988	2.	5.	9.	20.	50.	100.	400.

TWENTY CENTS
Victoria 1865 - 1900

The first pattern known for the Newfoundland 20-cent piece is a bronze striking with the adopted obverse (derived from the New Brunswick obverse) and a reverse from a die for the 1864 New Brunswick 20 cents (see NF-4 in the chapter on Patterns). Later patterns in silver have an arabesque design similar to that finally adopted. The first (see NF-10 in the chapter on Patterns) has very thin arches and corresponds to similar 5-cent and 10-cent patterns. The second stands alone and has arches more like the adopted design and a raised line just inside the denticles (see NF-13 in the chapter on Patterns).

This denomination proved popular with Newfoundlanders and was minted on a regular basis throughout the remainder of Victoria's reign. With the passing years, however, it became increasingly unpopular with Canadians (due to its similarity to their 25-cent piece) and was replaced with a 25-cent coin during World War I.

Designer: Reverse: Horace Morehen
Modeller: Reverse: Leonard C. Wyon
Engraver: Obverse: Leonard C. Wyon
Composition: .925 silver, .075 copper
Weight: 4.71 grams
Diameter: 23.19 mm
Edge: Reeded
Die Axis: ↑↓

Heaton Mint issues have an "H" mint mark on the obverse under the bust (1872-1876) or on the reverse under the date (1882). London Mint strikings have no letter.

Date, Mint Portrait	Quantity Minted	G-4	VG-8	F-12	VF-20	EF-40	AU-50	MS-60	MS-63
1865-NT1	100,000	10.	25.	45.	125.	400.	850.	2,000.	4,000.
1870-NT1	50,000	13.	35.	65.	175.	450.	1,000.	2,250.	4,000.
1872H-NT1	90,000	10.	20.	35.	90.	300.	750.	1,500.	3,000.
1873-NT1	40,000	11.	30.	65.	200.	850.	2,250.	–	–
1876H-NT1	50,000	23.	50.	90.	225.	700.	1,300.	2,500.	3,750.
1880-NT1	30,000	20.	45.	80.	200.	600.	1,500.	2,500.	6,500.
1881-NT1	60,000	8.	13.	40.	125.	500.	1,200.	2,000.	–
1882H-NT2	100,000	8.	12.	28.	75.	400.	900.	2,000.	7,500.
1885-NT1	40,000	10.	18.	50.	125.	550.	2,000.	–	–
1888-NT2	75,000	10.	13.	30.	100.	450.	1,250.	3,500.	8,000.
1890-NT2	100,000	8.	10.	25.	70.	400.	1,000.	2,500.	8,000.
1894-NT1	100,000	7.	10.	25.	65.	300.	750.	1,750.	3,500.
1894-NT2	Incl. above	7.	10.	25.	65.	300.	750.	1,750.	3,500.

VICTORIA OBVERSE PORTRAIT VARIETIES

NEWFOUNDLAND TWENTY CENTS - NT

PORTRAIT: NT1

Two leaves at top of laurel crown, with the rear leaf being very thin. Knot of hair at the back of the head touches the legend band. Prominent upper lip. Dot before and after Newfoundland on obverse.

NT1 will be found on the following dates:
1865; 1870; 1872H; 1873; 1876H; 1880;
1881; 1885; 1894; 1896

PORTRAIT: NT2

Two leaves at top of laurel crown; both distinctive and well into legend band. Knot of hair at the back of the head enters legend band. Repressed upper lip. Dot before and after Newfoundland on obverse.

NT2 will be found on the following dates:
1882H; 1888; 1890; 1894; 1896;
1899 (all varieties); 1900

VICTORIA 1865 - 1900, TWENTY CENTS CONTINUED.

1896	1896	1899	1899	1899
Small 96 (S)	Large 96 (L)	Small 99 (S)	Hooked 99 (H)	Large 99 (L)

Date, Mint Portrait	Quantity Minted	G-4	VG-8	F-12	VF-20	EF-40	AU-50	MS-60	MS-63
1896, S96-T1	125,000	6.	10.	20.	60.	300.	750.	2,500.	–
1896, S96-T2	Incl. above	6.	10.	20.	60.	300.	750.	2,500.	–
1896, L96-T1	Incl. above	6.	11.	25.	75.	450.	1,000.	–	–
1896, L96-T2	Incl. above	6.	11.	25.	75.	450.	1,000.	–	–
1899, S99-T2	125,000	6.	10.	17.	60.	275.	650.	2,000.	7,000.
1899, H99-T2	Incl. above	20.	35.	70.	150.	500.	1,250.	2,500.	7,500.
1899, L99-T2	Incl. above	6.	10.	17.	60.	275.	750.	2,250.	7,500.
1900-T2	125,000	6.	10.	15.	50.	175.	600.	1,750.	4,500.

TWENTY CENTS
Edward VII 1904

Coins of this denomination were required on only one occasion during Edward's short reign, making the 1904 issue a one-year type.

Designer and Modeller:
Portrait: G.W. DeSaulles,
(DES. below bust)
Reverse: W.H.J. Blakemore,
copying DeSaulles design for
the reverse of 5¢ and 10¢ pieces
Composition: .925 silver, .075 copper
Weight: 4.71 grams
Diameter: 23.19 mm
Edge: Reeded
Die Axis: ↑↓

This issue was coined by The Mint, Birmingham and bears an "H" mint mark below the oval at the bottom on the reverse.

Date and Mint Mark	Quantity Minted	G-4	VG-8	F-12	VF-20	EF-40	AU-50	MS-60	MS-63
1904H	75,000	10.	17.	45.	90.	400.	1,750.	4,000.	10,000.

TWENTY CENTS
George V 1912

Like its Edwardian predecessor, the George V 20 cents is a one-year type. The reverse established for the previous reign was reused.

Designer and Modeller:
    Portrait: Sir E.B. MacKennal,
    (B.M. on truncation)
Composition: .925 silver, .075 copper
Weight: 4.71 grams
Diameter: 23.19 mm
Edge: Reeded
Die Axis: ↑↑

Date and Mint Mark	Quantity Minted	VG-8	F-12	VF-20	EF-40	AU-50	MS-60	MS-63
1912	350,000	5.	8.	20.	70.	200.	500.	1,250.

TWENTY-FIVE CENTS
George V 1917 - 1919

The second time 20-cent pieces were required during George V's reign was toward the end of World War I. By that time, however, arrangements had been made for the Ottawa Mint to produce Newfoundland's coins. Canada took a dim view of the 20 cents because it circulated in Canada as well, and was confused with the Canadian 25 cents. The Canadian government convinced the Newfoundland government to drop the 20 cents and adopt a 25 cents, struck on the same standard as the corresponding Canadian coin. Indeed, the obverse of the new coin was identical to that for the Canadian 25 cents.

Designer and Modeller:
    Portrait: Sir E.B. MacKennal,
    (B.M. on truncation)
Engraver: Reverse: W.H.J. Blakemore,
    modifying the 20¢ reverse
Composition: .925 silver, .075 copper
Weight: 5.83 grams
Diameter: 23.62 mm
Edge: Reeded
Die Axis: ↑↑

This denomination was coined by the Ottawa Mint and bears a "C" mint mark below the oval at the bottom on the reverse.

Date and Mint Mark	Quantity Minted	VG-8	F-12	VF-20	EF-40	AU-50	MS-60	MS-63
1917C	464,779	5.	6.	11.	28.	70.	225.	450.
1919C	163,939	6.	7.	17.	45.	150.	550.	2,000.

FIFTY CENTS
Victoria 1870 -1900

The 50-cent piece was the last denomination to be added to the Victoria coinage, coming in 1870. Its laureate portrait is stylistically unlike anything used for the rest of the British North America series. This denomination became popular on the island and assumed even greater importance after the failure of the Commercial and Union Banks of Newfoundland during the financial crisis of 1894.

Designer and Modeller:
Leonard C. Wyon
Composition: .925 silver,
.075 copper
Weight: 11.78 grams
Diameter: 29.85 mm
Edge: Reeded
Die Axis: ↑↓

Heaton Mint issues have an "H" mint mark either on the obverse under the bust (1872-1876) or on the reverse under the date (1882). London Mint strikings have no letter.

Date, Mint Portrait	Quantity Minted	G-4	VG-8	F-12	VF-20	EF-40	AU-50	MS-60	MS-63
1870-NH1	50,000	13.	30.	55.	225.	1,250.	2,000.	7,500.	22,500.
1872H-NH1	48,000	13.	25.	40.	150.	600.	900.	3,000.	6,500.
1873-NH1	32,000	40.	75.	160.	425.	1,250.	4,000.	8,000.	–
1874-NH1	80,000	25.	50.	80.	225.	1,000.	3,500.	–	–
1876H-NH1	28,000	30.	55.	90.	275.	800.	1,500.	3,500.	7,000.

All examples of the 1880 issue are from dies in which the second 8 of the date is punched over a 7.

Date, Mint Portrait	Quantity Minted	G-4	VG-8	F-12	VF-20	EF-40	AU-50	MS-60	MS-63
1880-NH1	24,000	30.	60.	100.	375.	1,100.	2,500.	7,500.	20,000.
1881-NH1	50,000	20.	40.	65.	275.	1,000.	2,000.	5,000.	–
1882H-NH2	100,000	11.	25.	35.	150.	550.	1,250.	3,500.	9,000.
1885-NH1	40,000	15.	40.	65.	250.	1,000.	2,000.	5,000.	17,500.
1888-NH1	20,000	30.	75.	125.	400.	1,750.	5,000.	–	–
1894-NH1	40,000	9.	15.	35.	150.	650.	1,250.	4,500.	17,500.
1896, LW-NH1	60,000	9.	15.	30.	125.	650.	1,250.	3,500.	12,500.
1896, SW-NH2	Incl. above	9.	15.	30.	125.	650.	1,250.	3,500.	12,500.
1898, LW-NH1	79,607	9.	15.	25.	125.	500.	1,250.	5,000.	–
1898, SW-NH2	Incl. above	9.	15.	25.	125.	500.	1,250.	5,000.	–

VICTORIA OBVERSE PORTRAIT VARIETIES

NEWFOUNDLAND FIFTY CENTS - NH

PORTRAIT: NH1

Four leaves at top of laurel crown; the uppermost leaf enters the legend band between the 'E' and 'I' in DEI. Prominent upper lip. No dot after Newfoundland on obverse.

NH-1 will be found on the following dates: 1870; 1872H; 1873; 1874; 1876H; 1880; 1881; 1885; 1888; 1894; 1896 (all varieties); 1898 (all varieties)

PORTRAIT: NH2

Four leaves at top of laurel crown, with none entering the legend band. Repressed upper lip. No dot after Newfoundland on obverse.

NH2 will be found on the following dates: 1882H; 1896 (all varieties); 1898 (all varieties); 1899 (all varieties); 1900

VICTORIA 1870 - 1900, TWENTY CENTS CONTINUED.

Narrow 9s with thick sides
and oval centres

Wide 9s with thin sides
and round centres

Date, Mint Portrait	Quantity Minted	G-4	VG-8	F-12	VF-20	EF-40	AU-50	MS-60	MS-63
1899, N9-H2	150,000	9.	15.	25.	90.	300.	1,000.	4,500.	–
1899, W9-H2	Incl. above	9.	15.	35.	125.	425.	1,250.	5,000.	–
1900-H2	150,000	9.	15.	25.	90.	350.	1,000.	3,500.	

FIFTY CENTS
Edward VII 1904 - 1909

The obverse for this denomination is that of the Dominion of Canada issues.

Designer and Modeller:
Portrait: G.W. DeSaulles,
(DES. below bust)
Reverse: W.H.J. Blakemore,
copying DeSaulle's design
for 5¢ and 10¢ pieces
Composition: .925 silver,
.075 copper
Weight: 11.78 grams
Diameter: 29.85 mm
Edge: Reeded
Die Axis: ↑↓ ↑↑

The Mint, Birmingham issue (1904) has an
"H" mint mark below the oval at the bottom
on the reverse. Royal Mint issues have no
letter.

Date and Mint Mark	Quantity Minted	VG-8	F-12	VF-20	EF-40	AU-50	MS-60	MS-63
1904H	140,000	6.	10.	30.	70.	150.	350.	1,250.
1907	100,000	7.	11.	35.	90.	275.	500.	1,500.
1908	160,000	6.	10.	28.	65.	135.	325.	1,000.
1909	200,000	6.	11.	35.	90.	275.	500.	1,500.

FIFTY CENTS
George V 1911 - 1919

The obverse for the Newfoundland 50-cent piece is the same as that for the 1912-1936 Dominion of Canada coins. That legend contains "DEI GRA" (see Dominion of Canada George V one-cent section) indicating that the modification of the Canadian obverses was made during 1911, prior to commencing the production of the Newfoundland issue for the year. The reverse continued the Edwardian design.

In 1917-1919 nearly 1,000,000 50 cents were struck and many were used to replace the discontinued government "cash notes" for making relief payments to the poor. The need for silver for this purpose diminished in 1920, when a new issue of government paper money was made.

Designer: Portrait: Sir E.B. MacKennal,
(B.M. on truncation)
Composition: .925 silver, .075 copper
Weight: 11.78 grams (1911);
11.66 grams (1917-1919)
Diameter: 29.85 mm (1911)
29.72 mm (1917-1919)
Edge: Reeded
Die Axis: ↑↑

Ottawa Mint issues (1917-1919) have a "C" mint mark below the oval at the bottom on the reverse. The Royal Mint issue has no letter.

Date and Mint Mark	Quantity Minted	VG-8	F-12	VF-20	EF-40	AU-50	MS-60	MS-63
1911	200,000	6.	9.	17.	40.	110.	300.	800.
1917C	375,560	6.	9.	17.	40.	90.	200.	550.
1918C	294,824	6.	9.	17.	40.	90.	200.	550.
1919C	306,267	6.	9.	17.	40.	125.	450.	1,500.

TWO DOLLARS
Victoria 1865 - 1888

In the original planning for the Newfoundland coinage a gold dollar was considered. However, it was decided that such a coin would be so small it could be easily lost by the fishermen, so a 2-dollar denomination was chosen instead. The initial bronze pattern combines the adopted obverse (derived from the New Brunswick 10 cents obverse and identical to the Newfoundland 10 cents obverse) with the crown and maple wreath of the Canada/New Brunswick 10 cents reverse (see NF-5 in the chapter on Patterns). The adopted reverse has more conventional letters and the unusual feature of expressing the denomination three ways: 2 dollars, 200 cents, 100 pence, the last being the equivalent value in sterling (British money). Newfoundland was the only British colony with its own gold issue.

Designer and Modeller:
Reverse: Leonard C. Wyon
Engraver: Obverse: Leonard C. Wyon
Composition: .917 gold, .083 copper
Weight: 3.33 grams
Diameter: 17.98 mm
Edge: Reeded
Die Axis: ↑↓

The Heaton Mint issue (1882) has an "H" mint mark below the date on the reverse. London Mint strikings have no letter.

Date, Mint Portrait	Quantity Minted	VF-20	EF-40	AU-50	MS-60	MS-63
1865-NTD1	10,000	350.	500.	675.	2,000.	9,000.
1870-NTD1	10,000	400.	500.	775.	3,000.	15,000.
1870-NTD2	Incl. above	325.	450.	675.	2,500.	12,500.
1872-NTD2	6,000	425.	700.	1,000.	3,250.	12,500.
1880-NTD2	2,500	1,700.	2,350.	3,250.	7,500.	20,000.
1881-NTD2	10,000	350.	450.	550.	3,000.	10,000.
1882H-NTD3	25,000	300.	325.	375.	700.	3,500.
1885-NTD2	10,000	325.	350.	425.	900.	4,000.
1888-NTD2	25,000	300.	325.	375.	900.	4,000.
1888-NTD3	Incl. above					

VICTORIA OBVERSE PORTRAIT VARIETIES

NEWFOUNDLAND TWO DOLLAR - NTD

PORTRAIT: NTD1
Young head portrait. Dot before and after
Newfoundland on obverse.

NTD-1 will be found on the following dates:
1865; 1870

PORTRAIT: NTD2
Mature head portrait. Dot before
Newfoundland on obverse

NTD-2 will be found on the following dates:
1870; 1872; 1880; 1881; 1885; 1888

PORTRAIT: NTD3
Older portrait. Dot before and after
Newfoundland on obverse.

NTDD-3 will be found on the following dates:
1882H; 1888

PROVINCE OF CANADA

LARGE CENTS
Victoria 1858 - 1859

After the decision to adopt decimal coins was approved, a number of designs, sizes and compositions were considered for the cent. The first trials used a reverse design consisting of 19 maple leaves placed side by side, radiating from the centre (see PC-1 to PC-3 in the chapter on Patterns). However, a serpentine motif of 16 maple leaves was adopted and trial pieces were struck in a cupro-nickel alloy. Later, it was decided the new cents would be bronze.

The adopted obverse design shows a youthful, idealized bust of the queen wearing a laurel wreath in her hair. In fact, by the late 1850s the queen was quite pudgy and decidedly older looking than the coinage portraits suggested.

The government optimistically ordered approximately 10,000,000 1-cent pieces, which proved to be much more than the province could absorb. At the time both Canada East and Canada West were inundated with the copper tokens issued by banks and individuals. The bank tokens were heavier than the thin cents (which weighed 1/100 lb. avoirdupois) which slowed their public acceptance. The majority of the mintage remained unissued in the original boxes. In 1861 part of it was sent to the New Brunswick government to provide a temporary supply of decimal coins while the province awaited the arrival of its own issues, but the bulk of the stock went to the Bank of Upper Canada, the governments's bank. Until 1866, when it closed its doors, the Bank of Upper Canada experienced considerable difficulty in reducing its stock of cents, even when it offered to sell them at 20 percent below face value.

A stock of several million Province of Canada cents was inherited by the Dominion of Canada government in 1867 and it proceeded to issue them as Dominion currency.

Designer and Modeller:
  Leonard C. Wyon
Composition: .95 copper, .04 tin, .01 zinc
    (except for the rare brass)
Weight: 4.54 grams
Diameter: 25.4 mm
Edge: Plain
Die Axis: ↑↑, ↑↓

Date and Mint Mark	Quantity Minted	G-4	VG-8	F-12	VF-20	EF-40	AU-50	MS-60 Brown	MS-63 Red/Br
1858 Medal	421,000	50.	90.	125.	175.	250.	325.	500.	1,500.
1858 Coinage	Incl. above	50.	90.	125.	175.	250.	325.	500.	1,500.

VARIETIES 1859. Since the coining of cents did not begin until the latter part of 1858, production continued throughout most of 1859, with most coins bearing an 1859 date. The first 1859s were undoubtedly overdates, on which a special wide 9 punch was employed to alter the second 8 to a 9, produced from several 1858-dated dies.

The majority of the 1859 dies were not overdates: they were dated with a narrow 9 punch. Many such dies were made and numerous re-punching varieties exist. Only those most widely collected are listed here.

Double-punched Narrow 9 #1: Resembles and often designated "narrow 9 over 8." Actually it is a double-punched narrow 9, confused by the presence of a die defect causing a small "tail" at the lower left of the 9.

Double-punched Narrow 9 #2: Traces of the original 9 at the left.

A very rare variety of the plain, narrow 9 exists in brass, which can be identified by its distinctive yellow colour.

Overdate,
Wide 9 over 8

Plain, Narrow 9

Date and Mint Mark	Quantity Minted	G-4	VG-8	F-12	VF-20	EF-40	AU-50	MS-60 Brown	MS-63 Red/Br
1859 W9/8 Medal	9,579,000	25.	50.	70.	100.	150.	250.	500.	–
1859 W9/8 Coinage	Incl.	25.	50.	70.	100.	150.	250.	500.	–
1859 N9, bronze	Incl. above	2.	4.	5.	8.	12.	28.	65.	175.
1859 N9, brass	Incl. above	5,000.	6,000.	10,000.	–	–	–	–	–

Double-punched Narrow 9 #1
Resembles narrow 9 over 8

Double-punched Narrow 9 #2
Traces of original 9 at left

Date and Mint Mark	Quantity Minted	G-4	VG-8	F-12	VF-20	EF-40	AU-50	MS-60 Brown	MS-63 Red/Br
1859 D-P N9#1	Incl. above	200.	300.	400.	500.	800.	1,500.	2,500.	6,000.
1859 D-P N9#2	Incl. above	45.	80.	125.	175.	250.	500.	800.	–

FIVE CENTS
Victoria 1858

The 5-cent piece chosen by the Province of Canada was a small silver coin, half the weight of the 10-cent piece and similar to the United States half dime. The obverse depicts an idealized, youthful laureated Victoria and the reverse features a maple wreath of 21 leaves surmounted by St. Edward's crown.

The first dies bore small, widely spaced digits in the date. Later strikings carried larger digits punched over the small figures, making the digits closer together.

Designer and Modeller:
Leonard C. Wyon
Composition: .925 silver, .075 copper
Weight: 1.16 grams
Diameter: 15.5 mm
Edge: Reeded
Die Axis: ↑↓

1858 Small Date
Digits widely spaced

1858 Large Date over Small Date
Digits closely spaced

Date and Mint Mark	Quantity Minted	G-4	VG-8	F-12	VF-20	EF-40	AU-50	MS-60	MS-63
1858 SD	1,460,389	12.	25.	40.	70.	100.	175.	375.	850.
1858 LD/SD	Incl. above	100.	175.	250.	450.	750.	1,100.	1,750.	4,000.

TEN CENTS
Victoria 1858

In design, the Province of Canada 10-cent pieces resemble the 5-cent pieces. An interesting variety occurred through a dating blunder in which a 5 punch was used to repair a defective first 8. The top of the 5 can be seen rising above the first 8, as these numbers were punched simultaneously.

Designer and Modeller:
  Leonard C. Wyon
Composition: .925 silver, .075 copper
Weight: 2.32 grams
Diameter: 18.0 mm
Edge: Reeded
Die Axis: ↑↓

1858
First 8 and 5 punched simultaneously

Date and Mint Mark	Quantity Minted	G-4	VG-8	F-12	VF-20	EF-40	AU-50	MS-60	MS-63
1858	1,216,402	15.	30.	55.	100.	175.	250.	425.	1,250.
1858 8 over 5	Incl. above	450.	900.	1,250.	2,250.	4,000.	—	—	—

TWENTY CENTS
Victoria 1858

This unusual denomination was chosen as a bridge between the two systems. It apparently deferred to the pounds, shillings, pence basis of the Halifax currency system while naming the new issue in the dollar, cents, mils system. The relationship between the two systems meant 20 cents was equivalent to a shilling in Halifax currency, and it was assumed that consequently the new coin would be found useful. This assumption proved unfounded because there had been no coin representing a shilling in the old system; the British shilling coin was worth just over 20 percent more than a shilling in Halifax currency. Furthermore, the size and weight of the 20-cent piece led to confusion with both British shillings and U.S. 25-cent pieces. As one would expect, the government had difficulty introducing the 20-cent piece and by 1860 it was decided to replace it with a 25-cent coin as the opportunity arose.

The replacement of the 20-cent piece with a 25-cent coin came after Confederation. The Dominion government actively withdrew the 20-cent pieces and at various times from 1885 onward sent them back to the Royal Mint in London for melting and recoining as 25-cent pieces.

Designer and Modeller:
  Leonard C. Wyon
Composition: .925 silver, .075 copper
Weight: 4.65 grams
Diameter: 23.3 mm
Edge: Reeded
Die Axis: ↑↓

Date and Mint Mark	Quantity Minted	G-4	VG-8	F-12	VF-20	EF-40	AU-50	MS-60	MS-63
1858	730,392	45.	85.	110.	160.	325.	500.	1,100.	3,500.

CANADA

CIRCULATING COINAGE

ONE CENT
Victoria 1876 - 1901

The large cents produced in 1858-1859 for the Province of Canada were inherited by the Dominion of Canada government at the time of Confederation. It was decided to issue them as Dominion cents. Nearly ten years were required to use up the stock; the first cents struck for the Dominion came out in 1876. An 1876 pattern cent (see DC-1 in the chapter on Patterns) with the laureated obverse of 1858-1859 suggests that initially it was intended the Dominion cents be the same design as those of the Province of Canada. However, the obverse of the pieces actually issued bore a diademed head adapted from that used for the Jamaica halfpenny and the Prince Edward Island cent. The government also took the opportunity to increase the weight to 1/80th of an avoirdupois pound, the same as the British halfpenny.

Three varieties of the reverse, from independently engraved master tools, are known to exist: the Provincial Leaves reverse (1876-1882), the Large Leaves reverse (1884-1891), and the Small Leaves reverse (1891-1901). Only in 1891 are the two reverses employed for a single year's coinage (see below). Four varieties exist for the obverse. Their detailed description and listing by year follow on the next two pages.

Designer and Modeller:
　　Obverse: Leonard C. Wyon
　　Provincial and Large Leaves Reverse:
　　　　Leonard C. Wyon;
　　Small Leaves Reverse:
　　　　G.W. DeSaulles
Composition: .95 copper, .04 tin
　　　　　　　　.01 zinc
Weight: 5.67 grams
Diameter: 25.4 mm
Edge: Plain
Die Axis: ↑↑

Heaton Mint issues of 1876-1882 and The Mint, Birmingham issue of 1890 have an "H" mint mark on the reverse under the date. London Mint strikings have no letter.

Date, Mint Portrait	Quantity Minted	G-4	VG-8	F-12	VF-20	EF-40	AU-50	MS-60 Brown	MS-63 Red/Br
1876H-C1	4,000,000	2.	5.	6.	8.	15.	35.	100.	250.
1881H-C1	2,000,000	3.	7.	10.	15.	26.	50.	110.	300.
1882H-C1	4,000,000	2.	5.	6.	8.	13.	22.	60.	250.
1882H-C2	Incl. above	2.	5.	6.	8.	13.	22.	60.	250.
1884-C1	2,500,000	3.	6.	8.	12.	20.	35.	250.	500.
1884-C2	Incl. above	3.	6.	8.	12.	20.	35.	110.	250.
1886-C1	1,500,000	6.	12.	16.	24.	40.	95.	250.	600.
1886-C2	Incl. above	4.	8.	12.	20.	30.	65.	175.	400.
1887-C2	1,500,000	2.	6.	8.	11.	20.	35.	100.	275.
1888-C2	4,000,000	3.	6.	7.	9.	12.	20.	55.	150.
1890H-C3	1,000,000	5.	10.	17.	28.	50.	85.	175.	400.

VICTORIA OBVERSE PORTRAIT VARIETIES

CANADA ONE CENT - C

The portrait varieties of Victorian coins have been part of Canadian numismatics since James Haxby's series of articles first appeared in the Canadian Numismatic Journal, Vol. 13, Number 12, in December 1968. In these articles Jim introduced six different portraits appearing on Canadian and Newfoundland coins between 1858 and 1901.

Identification and pricing has always been a major problem. Identification of the varieties as the coin moves from the uncirculated state to extremely fine, and on down to poor, results in the major identification points as outlined by Haxby, becoming a blur and in most cases in the lower grades lost completely. Digital images and the ability to manipulate these images may solve the identification problem.

With the 58th edition we start to build pricing tables for the Victorian portrait varieties. The foundation of the pricing data will be the number of units graded and reported by ICCS in their Population Report of 2003. The Report, released in January 2003, counts the number of each denomination by date and variety graded by ICCS on an accumulative basis from April 1988 to December 2002. Needless to point out that as time moves on the rarity factors will harden and more faith be placed in the pricing model. The following table will illustrate the pricing rationale. We have selected the 1891 varieties to do this. The next report, due in January 2004, will produce a new set of numbers, giving more support to already known accumulative findings.

ICCS POPULATION COUNT BY OBVERSE PORTRAIT NUMBER

QUEEN VICTORIA LARGE CENTS

Date	Portrait	Circulated	Mint State	Total
1891, LLLD	C-2	47	18	65
	C-3	26	15	41
1891, LLSD	C-2	40	2	42
	C-3	40	4	44
1891, SLSD	C-2	23	2	25
	C-3	90	7	97

From the chart we are able to start drawing conclusions about rarity and thus pricing. It is obvious that the 1891 SLSD variety, with Portrait C-2 will have the highest rarity of the group. But another point surfaces, that an 1891 SLSD with a Portrait C-2 obverse in mint state, with only one graded in over three years, may be extremely rare.

PORTRAIT: C1
Rounded chin and nose.

C1 will be found on the following dates:
1876H; 1881H; 1882H; 1884; 1886

VICTORIA OBVERSE PORTRAIT VARIETIES

CANADA ONE CENT - C

PORTRAIT: C2

Doubling of chin and pointing of nose.

C2 will be found on the following dates:
1882H; 1884; 1886; 1887; 1888;
1891 (all varieties); 1892

PORTRAIT: C3

Strong doubling of chin coupled with
strong cheek accent lines. Nose has a
shilled look.

C3 will be found on the following dates:
1890H; 1891 (all varieties); 1892

PORTRAIT: C4

The chin is again rounded with the doubling
reduced dramatically. The cheek accents are
removed, with the nose lines less harsh.

C4 will be found on the following dates:
1892; 1893; 1894; 1895; 1896; 1897;
1898H; 1899; 1900; 1900H; 1901

VARIETIES 1891. Three major varieties of the 1891 cent are known. The first two have the Large Leaves reverse. The broad, flat leaves have very little detail and the bottom leaf runs into the rim denticles. The third variety has the Small Leaves reverse, which has slightly smaller leaves with much more detail. The bottom leaf ends well short of the rim denticles. The first variety has a large date; the second and third varieties have a small date.

Large Leaves, Large Date - leaves close to beads and vine; note broad figure "9."

Large Leaves, Small Date - leaves close to beads and vine; note narrow figure "9."

Small Leaves, Small Date - leaves far from beads and vine; note narrow figure "9."

Date, Mint Portrait	Quantity Minted	G-4	VG-8	F-12	VF-20	EF-40	AU-50	MS-60 Brown	MS-63 Red/Br
1891 LL-C2	1,452,500	5.	10.	15.	28.	50.	100.	175.	500.
1891 LL-C3	Incl. above	6.	12.	18.	30.	60.	120.	200.	550.
1891 LS-C2	Incl. above	50.	100.	125.	175.	275.	500.	1,000.	—
1891 LS-C3	Incl. above	50.	100.	125.	175.	275.	500.	1,000.	—
1891 SS-C2	Incl. above	50.	100.	140.	175.	225.	325.	450.	1,000.
1891 SS-C3	Incl. above	40.	70.	90.	135.	175.	250.	350.	800.
1892-C2	1,200,000	7.	12.	20.	30.	45.	80.	125.	300.
1892-C3	Incl. above	4.	8.	15.	20.	30.	65.	100.	225.
1892-C4	Incl. above	4.	8.	15.	20.	30.	65.	100.	225.
1893-C4	2,000,000	2.	6.	8.	10.	18.	30.	70.	200.
1894-C4	1,000,000	8.	15.	22.	33.	55.	100.	135.	300.
1895-C4	1,200,000	4.	8.	15.	20.	27.	65.	90.	225.
1896-C4	2,000,000	2.	5.	7.	10.	13.	25.	55.	175.
1897-C4	1,500,000	2.	6.	9.	15.	18.	40.	75.	175.
1898H-C4	1,000,000	4.	10.	17.	25.	30.	50.	150.	350.
1899-C4	2,400,000	3.	5.	6.	8.	12.	20.	60.	125.

The Birmingham Mint issues of 1898 and 1900 have an "H" mint mark on the reverse under the wreath at the bottom. London Mint strikings have no letter.

Date, Mint Portrait	Quantity Minted	G-4	VG-8	F-12	VF-20	EF-40	AU-50	MS-60 Brown	MS-63 Red/Br
1900-C4	1,000,000	5.	11.	18.	30.	45.	80.	150.	500.
1900H-C4	2,600,000	3.	5.	6.	8.	12.	25.	50.	110.
1901-C4	4,100,000	3.	5.	6.	8.	12.	25.	50.	110.

ONE CENT
Edward VII 1902-1910

The reverse of this denomination is a continuation of the Victorian design.

Designer and Modeller:
  Obverse: G.W. DeSalles
  (DES. below bust)
Composition: .95 copper, .04 tin, .01 zinc
Weight: 5.67 grams
Diameter: 25.4 mm
Edge: Plain
Die Axis: ↑↑

The Birmingham Mint issue of 1907 has an "H" mint mark on the reverse above the wreath, below the date. London Mint strikings (1902-1907) and Ottawa Mint strikings (1908-1910) have no letter.

Date and Mint Mark	Quantity Minted	VG-8	F-12	VF-20	EF-40	AU-50	MS-60 Brown	MS-63 Red/Br
1902	3,000,000	3.	4.	5.	10.	13.	35.	55.
1903	4,000,000	3.	4.	5.	10.	15.	40.	65.
1904	2,500,000	3.	4.	6.	12.	22.	55.	90.
1905	2,000,000	4.	7.	11.	14.	25.	70.	110.
1906	4,100,000	3.	4.	5.	12.	17.	65.	190.
1907	2,400,000	3.	5.	9.	16.	30.	60.	160.
1907H	800,000	15.	20.	30.	50.	100.	225.	450.
1908	2,401,506	3.	5.	7.	14.	22.	50.	100.
1909	3,973,339	2.	3.	4.	8.	15.	40.	100.
1910	5,146,487	2.	3.	4.	7.	15.	40.	100.

ONE CENT - LARGE
George V 1911 - 1920

"GODLESS" OBVERSE 1911. The obverse introduced in 1911 broke a tradition set by the coins of the previous two reigns in which the Latin phrase "DEI GRATIA" (or an abbreviation for it) was included in the monarch's titles. Omission of the phrase aroused public criticism during which the coins were labeled "Godless." The coinage tools were modified during the year and cents with "DEI GRA:" in the legend appeared in 1912. The reverse also marked a departure from the previous reigns in the inclusion of "CANADA" in the legend. It had formerly been part of the obverse legend on this denomination.

Designer and Modeller:
Portrait: Sir E.B. MacKennal,
(B.M. on truncation)
Reverse: W.H.J. Blakemore
Composition: .95 copper, .04 tin, .01 zinc
Weight: 5.67 grams
Diameter: 25.4 mm
Edge: Plain
Die Axis: ↑↑

Date and Mint Mark	Quantity Minted	VG-8	F-12	VF-20	EF-40	AU-50	MS-60 Brown	MS-63 Red/Br
1911	4,663,486	2.	3.	4.	6.	12.	30.	50.

MODIFIED OBVERSE LEGEND 1912-1936

Composition: .95 copper, .04 tin, .01 zinc (1912-1919); .955 copper, .030 tin, .015 zinc (1919-1920)

The physical specifications are as for the 1911 issue.

Date and Mint Mark	Quantity Minted	VG-8	F-12	VF-20	EF-40	AU-50	MS-60 Brown	MS-63 Red/Br
1912	5,107,642	1.	2.	3.	5.	13.	33.	60.
1913	5,735,405	1.	2.	3.	5.	15.	33.	65.
1914	3,405,958	1.	2.	3.	6.	18.	45.	100.
1915	4,932,134	1.	2.	3.	6.	15.	40.	80.
1916	11,022,367	1.	2.	3.	4.	9.	25.	70.
1917	11,899,254	1.	2.	3.	4.	7.	20.	55.
1918	12,970,798	1.	2.	3.	4.	7.	20.	55.
1919	11,279,634	1.	2.	3.	4.	7.	20.	45.
1920	6,762,247	1.	2.	3.	5.	10.	30.	75.

ONE CENT - SMALL
George V 1920 - 1936

As a matter of economy the Canadian government introduced in 1920 a small cent similar in size and composition to that of the United States. The large cents were not immediately withdrawn, but were allowed to circulate until the late 1930s. The small coins lacked rim denticles, the first instance of this in the Canadian decimal series. The obverse design was retained while a new reverse design, featuring two maple leaves, was used.

Designer: Portrait: Sir E.B. MacKennal,
(B.M. on truncation)
Reverse: Fred Lewis
Modeller: Portrait: Sir E.B. MacKennal
Reverse: W.H.J. Blakemore
Composition: .955 copper, .030 tin,
.015 zinc
Weight: 3.24 grams
Diameter: 19.05 mm
Edge: Plain
Die Axis: ↑↑

Date and Mint Mark	Quantity Minted	G-4	VG-8	F-12	VF-20	EF-40	AU-50	MS-60 Brown	MS-63 Red/Br
1920	15,483,923	–	.25	.50	1.00	2.00	6.00	20.00	40.
1921	7,601,627	–	.50	1.00	2.00	7.00	14.00	60.00	225.
1922	1,243,635	9.00	20.00	28.00	35.00	60.00	100.00	275.00	750.
1923	1,019,022	16.00	30.00	37.00	50.00	75.00	150.00	425.00	2,000.
1924	1,593,195	4.00	6.00	8.00	11.00	22.00	40.00	150.00	500.
1925	1,000,622	13.00	25.00	30.00	45.00	65.00	100.00	275.00	650.
1926	2,143,372	3.00	6.00	7.00	10.00	20.00	40.00	150.00	450.
1927	3,553,928	–	2.00	3.00	7.00	18.00	20.00	60.00	200.
1928	9,144,860	–	.25	.50	1.00	3.00	5.00	25.00	75.
1929	12,159,840	–	.25	.50	1.00	3.00	5.00	25.00	75.
1930	2,538,613	–	3.00	4.00	6.00	11.00	22.00	70.00	225.
1931	3,842,776	–	1.00	2.00	3.00	6.00	13.00	60.00	225.
1932	21,316,190	–	.20	.30	.75	3.00	5.00	20.00	50.
1933	12,079,310	–	.20	.30	.75	3.00	5.00	20.00	50.
1934	7,042,358	–	.25	.50	1.00	4.00	5.00	20.00	50.
1935	7,526,400	–	.25	.50	1.00	4.00	5.00	20.00	30.
1936	8,768,769	–	.25	.50	1.00	3.00	5.00	20.00	25.

COINAGE USING GEORGE V DIES 1936. In December,1936, the reigning British king, Edward VIII, abdicated in favour of his brother, who became George VI. This placed a great strain upon the Royal Mint in London. It was well along in the preparation of the tools for the British Commonwealth coinage obverses, including those for Canada. All this work had to be scrapped and new obverse tools made for George VI.

In 1937, during the delay involved in the preparation of new obverses in London, the Royal Canadian Mint was forced to strike from 1936 dies quantities of all denominations, except the 5-cent and 50-cent piece. The dies for the 1, 10, and 25 cent pieces are said to have been marked with a tiny dot on the reverse. This was to indicate that the coins were struck in a year different than that borne on the dies and with the bust of the late King.

The 1936 dot cent is an extreme rarity; only three, all in mint state, are at present known. Numerous circulated examples of this rarity have come to light over the years; however, none has been satisfactorily authenticated. It seems unlikely that any genuine 1936 dot cents ever circulated, despite the supposedly official mintage of almost 700,000 pieces.

1936 with raised dot below date
struck in 1937

Date and Mint Mark	Quantity Minted	F-12	VF-20	EF-40	AU-50	MS-60 Brown	MS-63 Red/Br
1936 Dot	Incl. in 1936		Heritage Belzberg Sale 2003 - $230,000 U.S.F.				

ONE CENT
George VI 1937 - 1952

COINAGE OF GEORGE VI. In the early part of 1937 the Royal Mint in London decided to speed up the production of the new coinage tools for Canadian coinages by having some of the work done by the Paris Mint. Included in this work was the reverse for the cent. The model was sent to Paris for conversion into master coinage tools.

The reverse of the new cent continued the trend toward modernization of the Canadian coinage designs begun in 1935 with the voyageur silver dollar.

"ET IND:IMP:" IN OBVERSE LEGEND 1937-1947. The initial obverse (1937-1947) bore a legend containing the Latin abbreviation "ET IND:IMP:," indicating the king was the Emperor of India.

Designer and Modeller:
Portrait: T.H. Paget (H.P. below bust)
Reverse: G.E. Kruger-Gray
(K G below right-hand maple leaf)
Composition: .955 copper, .030 tin,
.015 zinc (1937-1942);
.980 copper, .005 tin,
.015 zinc (1942-1952)
Weight: 3.24 grams
Diameter: 19.05 mm
Edge: Plain
Die Axis: ↑↑

Date and Mint Mark	Quantity Minted	VF-20	EF-40	AU-50	MS-60 Brown	MS-63 R/B	MS-65 Red
1937	10,090,231	—	1.	2.	3.	8.	100.
1938	18,365,608	—	1.	2.	3.	9.	100.
1939	21,600,319	—	1.	2.	3.	8.	50.
1940	85,740,532	—	1.	2.	3.	8.	60.
1941	56,336,011	—	1.	3.	8.	55.	375.
1942	76,113,708	—	1.	2.	7.	40.	500.
1943	89,111,969	—	1.	2.	4.	22.	400.
1944	44,131,216	—	1.	3.	8.	50.	1,250.
1945	77,268,591	—	1.	1.	3.	8.	600.
1946	56,662,071	—	1.	1.	3.	8.	100.
1947	31,093,901	—	1.	1.	3.	8.	70.

MAPLE LEAF TWIG ISSUE 1947. The granting of independence to India resulted in a dilemma for the Royal Canadian Mint in the early part of 1948. New obverse coinage tools with "ET IND: IMP:" omitted would not arrive for several months, yet there was a pressing need for all denominations of coins. The mint satisfied this demand by striking coins dated 1947 and bearing an obverse with outmoded titles. To differentiate this issue from the regular strikings of 1947, a tiny maple leaf was placed after the date.

1947 Maple Leaf Issue
struck in 1948

Date and Mint Mark	Quantity Minted	EF-40	AU-50	MS-60 Brown	MS-63 R/B	MS-65 Red
1947 ML	43,855,448	1.	2.	3.	6.	125.

MODIFIED OBVERSE LEGEND 1948-1952. Following the arrival of the master tools with the new obverse legend lacking "ET IND: IMP:" in 1948, the 1947 Maple Leaf coinage was suspended. For the remainder of the year coins were produced with the new obverse and the true date 1948. This obverse was employed for the rest of the reign.

The physical and chemical specifications are as for the 1937-1947 issues.

"A" Points to Denticle   "A" Points between Denticles

Date and Mint Mark	Quantity Minted	EF-40	AU-50	MS-60 Brown	MS-63 R/B	MS-65 Red
1948 'A' points	25,767,779	1.00	2.00	4.00	25.00	275.00
1948 'A' between	Incl. above	1.00	2.00	4.00	30.00	350.00
1949 'A' points	33,128,933	50.00	75.00	100.00	125.00	700.00
1949 'A' between	Incl. above	1.00	2.00	3.00	8.00	75.00
1950	60,444,992	.50	.75	2.00	7.00	90.00
1951	80,430,379	.35	.50	2.00	7.00	225.00
1952	67,631,736	.35	.50	2.00	6.00	125.00

Note: George VI small cents in VF-30 and lower, at present, are not collectable.

ONE CENT
Elizabeth II 1953 to date

The portrait model for the new Queen Elizabeth coinages was prepared in England by a sculptress, Mrs. Mary Gillick. The relief of this model was too high, with the result that the centre portion containing two lines on the shoulder (representing a fold in the Queen's gown) did not strike up well on the coins. This first obverse variety has been commonly termed the "no shoulder strap" variety by many collectors. Later in 1953, Royal Canadian Mint authorities decided to correct the defects in the obverse design. Thomas Shingles, the Mint's Chief Engraver, lowered the relief of the model, and strengthened the shoulder and hair detail. This modified obverse (often called the "shoulder strap" variety due to the resemblance of the lines to a strap) was introduced before the end of the year and became the standard obverse. By mistake the No Shoulder Fold obverse was used to produce some of the 1954 cents for the Proof-like sets and a small quantity of 1955 cents for circulation.

Many collectors have difficulty differentiating the two varieties on slightly worn cents. The best way is to note that the "Is" on the No Shoulder Fold variety are flared at the ends and that an imaginary line drawn up through the centre of the "I" in "DEI" goes between two rim denticles. On the Shoulder Fold variety the "I's" are nearly straight sided and a line drawn up through the "I" of "DEI" runs into a rim denticle.

The reverse was a continuation of the George VI reverse.

Designer and Modeller:
　　Portrait: Mrs. Mary Gillick
　　(M.G. on truncation)
Engraver: No Shoulder Fold Obverse:
　　Thomas Shingles, using the Gillick
　　portrait model;
　　Shoulder Fold Obverse:
　　Thomas Shingles, modifying
　　existing NSF coinage tools
Composition: .980 copper, .005 tin,
　　.015 zinc
Weight: 3.24 grams
Diameter: 19.05 mm
Edge: Plain
Die Axis: ↑↑

No Shoulder Fold Obverse
Note flared ends of "Is", and "I" in
DEI points between two rim denticles.

Shoulder Fold Obverse
Note straight-sided "Is", and "I"
in DEI points at a rim denticle.

Date and Mint Mark	Quantity Minted	F-12	VF-20	EF-40	AU-50	MS-60 Brown	MS-63 R/B	MS-64 Red	MS-65 Red
1953 NSF	67,806,016	–	–	1.	1.50	2.00	4.00	10.00	40.00
1953 SF	Incl. above	2.	3.	5.	9.00	20.00	75.00	100.00	300.00
1954 SF	22,181,760	–	–	1.	1.50	2.00	7.00	15.00	60.00
1955 SF	56,403,193	–	–	–	–	2.00	5.00	15.00	40.00
1955 NSF	Incl. above	200.	350.	500.	700.	1,000.	2,000.	–	–
1956	78,685,535	–	–	–	–	2.00	5.00	10.00	25.00
1957	100,601,792	–	–	–	–	2.00	4.00	8.00	20.00
1958	59,385,679	–	–	–	–	2.00	4.00	8.00	20.00
1959	83,615,343	–	–	–	–	1.50	3.00	7.00	15.00
1960	75,772,775	–	–	–	–	1.00	2.00	5.00	15.00
1961	139,598,404	–	–	–	–	1.00	2.00	5.00	15.00
1962	227,244,069	–	–	–	–	1.00	2.00	5.00	15.00
1963	279,076,334	–	–	–	–	1.00	2.00	5.00	15.00
1964	484,655,322	–	–	–	–	1.00	2.00	5.00	15.00

Note: Elizabeth II small cents except for 1953/54/55 grading EF-45 and lower, at present, are not collectable.

TIARA PORTRAIT AND MAPLE LEAF TWIG REVERSE 1965-1966. In 1964 the British government decided to introduce a more mature portrait of Queen Elizabeth for domestic and Commonwealth coinages. The new portrait model, by Arnold Machin, features the Queen wearing a tiara instead of a laurel wreath. A copy of the model was forwarded to Canada and was incorporated into the obverses for 1965.

Designer and Modeller:
 Obverse: Arnold Machin
 Reverse: G.E. Kruger-Gray
Composition: .980 copper, .005 tin, .015 zinc
Weight: 3.24 grams
Diameter: 19.05 mm
Edge: Plain
Die Axis: ↑↑

VARIETIES 1965. During 1965, difficulties were encountered in striking the cents, resulting in the introduction of a second variety obverse. The first variety has small beads at the rim and a flat field; the second variety has large rim beads and a field that slopes up at the rim. Another way to distinguish the two obverses is by the location of the "A" in "REGINA" relative to the rim beads: on the small beads obverse it points between two beads, whereas on the large beads obverse it points at a bead. In addition, two reverses differing in the style of 5 in the date were used in 1965. The obverses and reverses were employed in all possible combinations, creating four varieties for the year.

Small Beads Obverse	Large Beads Obverse
A of REGINA points between beads	A of REGINA points at bead

Pointed 5
Top right of 5 comes to a point

Blunt 5
Top right of 5 is nearly square

Date and Mint Mark	Quantity Minted	AU-50	MS-60 Brown	MS-63 R/B	MS-64 Red	MS-65 Red
1965 Variety 1 (SB,P5)	304,441,082	1.00	2.00	4.0	10.00	25.00
1965 Variety 2 (SB,B5)	Incl. above	–	1.00	2.00	5.00	10.00
1965 Variety 3 (LB, B5)	Incl. above	–	1.00	2.00	5.00	10.00
1965 Variety 4 (LB, P5)	Incl. above	15.00	25.00	50.00	100.00	200.00
1966	183,644,388	–	1.00	2.00	4.00	15.00

COMMEMORATIVE FOR CENTENNIAL OF CONFEDERATION 1967. Alex Colville's design of a rock dove was selected for the 1967 cent reverse, struck in commemoration of Canada's centennial of Confederation. The event was marked by a special design for each denomination coined for circulation, plus a special $20 gold piece for collectors only. The obverse of the cent is the same as that for the 1966 issue.

The physical and chemical specifications are as for the 1965 issue.

Date and Mint Mark	Quantity Minted	MS-60 Brown	MS-63 R/B	MS-64 Red	MS-65 Red
1967 Confederation Comm.	345,140,645	1.00	2.00	5.00	15.00

MAPLE LEAF TWIG REVERSE RESUMED; LARGE PORTRAIT 1968-1978

The physical and chemical specifications are as for the 1965 issue.

Date and Mint Mark	Quantity Minted	MS-60 Brown	MS-63 R/B	MS-64 Red	MS-65 Red
1968	329,695,772	.25	.50	2.00	5.00
1969	335,240,929	.25	.50	2.00	5.00
1970	344,145,010	.25	.50	2.00	5.00
1971	298,228,936	.25	.50	2.00	5.00
1972	451,304,591	.25	.50	2.00	5.00
1973	457,059,852	.25	.50	2.00	5.00
1974	692,058,489	.25	.50	2.00	5.00
1975	642,618,000	.25	.50	2.00	5.00
1976	701,122,890	.25	.50	2.00	5.00
1977	453,050,666	.25	.50	2.00	5.00
1978	911,170,647	.25	.50	2.00	5.00

MODIFIED TIARA PORTRAIT 1979. As part of a general standardization of the coinage, the portrait of the queen was made smaller beginning with the 1979 coinage. The purpose was to make the size of the portrait proportional to the diameter of the coin, regardless of the denomination.

Designer and Modeller:
    Obverse: Arnold Machin, Walter Ott
    Reverse: G.E. Kruger-Gray
Composition: .980 copper, .005 tin,
    .015 zinc
Weight: 3.24 grams
Diameter: 19.05 mm
Edge: Plain
Die Axis: ↑↑

Date and Mint Mark	Quantity Minted	MS-60 Brown	MS-63 R/B	MS-64 Red	MS-65 Red
1979	753,942,953	.25	.50	2.00	5.00

REDUCED WEIGHT 1980-1981. In 1978 the Mint struck pattern pieces, dated 1979, with a considerably reduced weight and a diameter of 16 mm. The mint was prompted by the rising price of copper which resulted in the 1-cent piece being coined at a loss. Unfortunately, the diameter of the pattern was the same as that for the tokens used by the Toronto Transit Commission and this was enough to result in the cancellation of plans for the new 16 mm cent. The mint struck cents of the old size and design during 1979. However, in 1980 it introduced a coin of the same design as before, but with a decreased diameter and thickness (hence a decreased weight).

Designer and Modeller:
    Obverse: Arnold Machin
    Reverse: G.E. Kruger-Gray
Composition: .980 copper, .005 tin,
    .015 zinc
Weight: 2.8 grams
Diameter: 19.00 mm, Round
Thickness: 1.38 mm
Edge: Plain
Die Axis: ↑↑

Date and Mint Mark	Quantity Minted	MS-60 Brown	MS-63 B/R	MS-64 Red	MS-65 Red
1980	911,800,000	.25	.50	2.00	5.00
1981	1,209,468,500	.25	.50	2.00	5.00

12-SIDED, TIARA PORTRAIT, MAPLE LEAF TWIG DESIGN 1982-1989. In December of 1981 the Ministry of Supplies and Services announced that the Royal Canadian Mint would be modifying Canada's one-cent coin. The design was changed from a round to a twelve-sided piece. Also the rim denticles were removed to be replaced with beads.

Blunt Five   Pointed Five

Designer and Modeller:
Obverse: Arnold Machin
Reverse: G.E. Kruger-Gray
Composition: .980 copper, .005 tin, .015 zinc
Weight: 2.5 grams
Diameter: 19.1 mm, 12-sided
Edge: Plain
Die Axis: ↑↑

Date and Mint Mark	Quantity Minted	MS-60 Brown	MS-63 R/B	MS-64 Red	MS-65 Red
1982	876,036,898	.10	.25	1.50	4.00
1983	975,510,000	.10	.25	1.50	4.00
1984	838,225,000	.10	.25	1.50	4.00
1985 BL5	771,772,500	.10	.25	1.50	4.00
1985 PT5	Incl. above	15.00	20.00	30.00	100.00
1986	788,285,000	.10	.25	1.50	4.00
1987	774,549,000	.10	.25	1.50	4.00
1988	482,676,752	.10	.25	1.50	4.00
1989	1,066,628,200	.10	.25	1.50	4.00

CROWNED PORTRAIT, MAPLE LEAF TWIG DESIGN 1990-1991. In line with changes in Great Britain and other commonwealth countries Canada in 1990 introduced a new portrait design for Canadian coins. Designed by Dora de Pédery-Hunt, this crowned portrait of Queen Elizabeth II is the first effigy of the queen designed by a Canadian. The diamond crown is completely circular, decorated with symbolic roses, shamrocks and thistles. It was made for George IV and worn by Queen Victoria for many of her formal portraits. Today it is worn by Queen Elizabeth for her opening of Parliament.

Designer and Modeller:
Obverse: Dora de Pédery-Hunt, Ago Aarand
Reverse: G.E. Kruger-Gray
Composition: .980 copper, .005 tin, .015 zinc
Weight: 2.5 grams
Diameter: 19.1 mm, 12-sided
Edge: Plain
Die Axis: ↑↑

Date and Mint Mark	Quantity Minted	MS-60 Brown	MS-63 R/B	MS-64 Red	MS-65 Red
1990	218,035,000	.10	.25	1.50	4.00
1991	831,001,000	.10	.25	1.50	4.00

COMMEMORATIVE FOR THE 125TH ANNIVERSARY 1867-1992. The reserve design was modified to include the bracket dates 1867-1992 for the 125th birthday of Canada.

Designer, modeller, chemical and physical specifications are as for the 1990 issues.

Date and Mint Mark	Quantity Minted		MS-60 Brown	MS-63 R/B	MS-64 Red	MS-65 Red
1992	673,512,000		.10	.25	1.50	4.00

MAPLE LEAF TWIG DESIGN RESUMED 1993-1995. In 1993 the practice of using a single date was resumed.

Designer, modeller, chemical and physical specifications are as for the 1990 issues.

Date and Mint Mark	Quantity Minted		MS-60 Brown	MS-63 R/B	MS-64 Red	MS-65 Red
1993	808,585,000		.10	.25	1.50	4.00
1994	639,516,000		.10	.25	1.50	4.00
1995	624,983,000		.10	.25	1.50	4.00
1996	445,746,000		.10	.25	1.50	4.00

CROWNED PORTRAIT, MAPLE LEAF TWIG DESIGN 1997-2002: In 1997 a decision was made to change the composition of the one cent coin from copper to copper plated zinc. The twelve sided design was not conducive to copper plating resulting in the reintroduction of the round design. The Winnipeg Mint Mark (W) is found only on coins from the "Oh Canada" and "Tiny Treasures" sets issued by the Numismatic Department of the Mint.

Designer, Modeller and Engraver:
Obverse: Dora de Pédery-Hunt
Ago Aarand
Reverse: G.E. Kruger-Gray
Composition: Copper plated zinc
Weight: 2.25 grams
Diameter: 19.05 mm, round
Edge: Plain
Die Axis: ↑↑

Date and Mint Mark	Quantity Minted		MS-60 Brown	MS-63 R/B	MS-64 Red	MS-65 Red
1997	549,868,000		.10	.25	1.50	4.00
1998	999,578,000		.10	.25	1.50	4.00
1999	1,089,625,000		.10	.25	1.50	4.00
2000	761,970,000		.10	.25	1.50	4.00
2001	918,495,000		.10	.25	1.50	4.00

ELIZABETH II GOLDEN JUBILEE 1952-2002. Issued to commemorate the 50th anniversary of the reign of Queen Elizabeth II. All circulating coinage carries the double dates 1952-2002 on the obverse.

In 2002 two varieties of composition were used to make the cent, one plated zinc the other plated steel. The official breakdown being 80% plated zinc, and 20% plated steel.

Designer, modeller, chemical and physical specifications are as for the 1997 and 1999P issues.

Date and Mint Mark	Quantity Minted	MS-60 Brown	MS-63 R/B	MS-64 Red	MS-65 Red
1952-2002	716,366,000	.10	.25	1.50	4.00
1952-2002P	114,212,000	.25	.50	3.00	8.00

CROWNED PORTRAIT, MAPLE LEAF TWIG DESIGN, MULTI-PLY PLATED STEEL 1999-2003: In a cost reduction move the Royal Canadian Mint developed a new multi-ply plated steel process which allows for the production of plated steel blanks. The acid based process electroplates a thin coating of nickel, then copper onto a steel core.

In early 1999, for testing purposes within the vending industry, and at their request to escape from the test tokens, the Mint issued sets of new multi-ply plated steel coinage, one cent through to the fifty cents. Naturally, samples found their way into collectors' hands resulting in a brisk trade. So that the demand would not get out-of-hand, resulting in failure of the testing procedures, the Mint issued for collectors a set of "P" coins. Both copper plated zinc and multi-ply plated steel one cent coins were issued in 2002.

Designer, Modeller and Engraver:
Obverse: Dora de Pédery-Hunt
Ago Aarand
Reverse: G. E. Kruger-Gray
Composition: .940 steel, .045 copper
.015 nickel
Weight: 2.35 grams
Diameter: 19.05
Thickness: 1.45 mm
Edge: Plain
Die Axis: ↑↑

Date and Mint Mark	Quantity Minted	MS-60 Brown	MS-63 R/B	MS-64 Red	MS-655 Red
1999P	Not issued for circulation	–	–	–	–
2000P	Not Issued for circulation	–	–	–	–
2001P	Not issued for circulation	–	–	–	–
2001P	Not issued for circulation	–	–	–	–
2003P	N/A	.10	.25	1.50	4.00
2004P	N/A	.10	.25	1.50	4.00

FIVE CENTS
Victoria 1870 - 1901

The first 5-cent pieces for the Dominion of Canada were introduced in 1870. The initial designs were identical to those used for the Province of Canada in 1858. During the reign of Queen Victoria, five obverse varieties, differing primarily in the facial features, were employed. Their detailed description and listing by year follows on the next page. Three varieties of the reverse are known: the Wide Rim reverse (1870), the Narrow Rim, 21 Leaves reverse (1870-1881, 1890-1901) and the Narrow Rim, 22 Leaves reverse (1882-1889).

Designer, Modeller and Engraver:
 Leonard C. Wyon
Composition: .925 silver, .075 copper
Weight: 1.16 grams
Diameter: 15.50 mm
Edge: Reeded
Die Axis: ↑↓

Heaton Mint issues of 1872-1883 have an "H" mint mark on the reverse under the wreath. London Mint strikings have no letter.

VARIETIES 1870. Before the coinage of 1870 was complete, new master tools for the 5-cent piece were introduced, with the result that two varieties were created for the year. The first has wide rims (including unusually long rim denticles) on the obverse and reverse and the second has more conventional narrow rims.

1870 Wide Rims (W)   1870 Narrow Rims (N)

Date, Mint Portrait	Quantity Minted	G-4	VG-8	F-12	VF-20	EF-40	AU-50	MS-60	MS-63
1870 W-F1	2,800,000	12.	28.	38.	75.	110.	165.	375.	1,500.
1870 N-F2	Incl. above	11.	30.	50.	85.	120.	175.	350.	1,000.
1871-F2	1,400,000	17.	30.	50.	90.	130.	200.	400.	1,250.
1872H-F2	2,000,000	9.	22.	35.	70.	110.	275.	550.	2,500.

VICTORIA OBVERSE PORTRAIT VARIETIES

FIVE CENTS – F

PORTRAIT: F1
The hair to the side of the ear has an
'S' curl to the braid.

F1 will be found on the following dates:
1870 W

PORTRAIT: F2
The hair to the side of the ear has a faint
'S' curl to the braid.

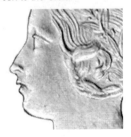

F2 will be found on the following dates:
1870 N; 1871; 1872H; 1874H S; 1874 L;
1875H S; 1875 L; 1880H; 1891; 1892;
1893; 1894; 1896; 1897 W; 1897 N;
1897 N/W; 1898; 1899; 1900 W; 1900 N;
1901

VICTORIA OBVERSE PORTRAIT VARIETIES

FIVE CENTS – F

PORTRAIT F3

The hair to the side of the ear curves up and is then flat to the ear.

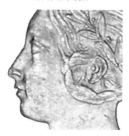

F-3 will be found on the following dates:
1880H; 1881H

PORTRAIT: F4

The braid to the side of the ear is flat and curves upward from the ear.

F4 will be found on the following date:
1882H

PORTRAIT: F5

The braid over the ear is very prominent with almost no visible strands.

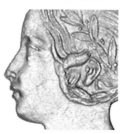

F5 will be found on the following dates:
1883H; 1884 N; 1884 F; 1885 S; 1885 5/5;
1885 L; 1886 S; 1886 L; 1887; 1888; 1889;
1890H; 1891; 1892

VARIETIES 1874H, 1875H and 1884. In 1874 and 1875 two sizes of digits were used for dating the dies. In addition to date sizes, the style of the 4 and 5 differ in their respective dates. The four of 1874 has either a plain 4 or a crosslet 4, while the five of 1875 has either a short top 5 or a long top 5.

In the 1884 'punch' variety we find a spacing difference between the 8 and the 4. Besides the punch spacing, the cross ends of the fours differ − a pointed end and a blunt end.

1874H Small Date (S)
(Plain 4)

1874H Large Date (L)
(Crosslet 4)

1875H Small Date (S)
Short top on 5

1875H Large Date (L)
Long top on 5

1884 Near 4, Pointed (N)   1884 Far 4, Blunt (F)

Date, Mint Portrait	Quantity Minted	G-4	VG-8	F-12	VF-20	EF-40	AU-50	MS-60	MS-63
1874H S-F2	800,000	15.	38.	75.	165.	250.	400.	700.	1,750.
1874H L-F2	Incl. above	12.	28.	65.	130.	225.	400.	850.	2,000.
1875H S-F2	1,000,000	100.	190.	325.	600.	900.	1,500.	3,000.	7,500.
1875H L-F2	Incl. above	175.	400.	650.	1,000.	2,000.	3,000.	6,000.	−
1880H-F2	3,000,000	12.	25.	40.	75.	150.	250.	750.	1,500.
1880H-F3	Incl. above	6.	12.	20.	45.	100.	175.	500.	1,000.
1881H-F3	1,500,000	7.	13.	25.	50.	110.	200.	550.	1,250.
1882H-F4	1,000,000	8.	20.	35.	65.	130.	250.	550.	1,250.
1883H-F5	600,000	17.	38.	75.	165.	325.	650.	1,500.	4,750.
1884 N-F5	200,000	100.	180.	300.	550.	1,250.	2,500.	5,000.	−
1884 F-F5	Incl. above	100.	180.	300.	550.	1,250.	2,500.	5,000.	−

VARIETIES 1885, 1886 and 1897. During the year 1885, two markedly different styles of 5 were used in the date. One is the small 5 seen on the 1875H issue; the other is the larger 5 used in the denomination "5 CENTS." There is also an overdate 5 over 5. In 1886 there is either a small 6 or a large 6 used. The uppermost part of the inner portion of the small 6 comes to a point, whereas that area on the large 6 is almost square. Again in 1897, different size punches were used, a wide 8 and a narrow 8 are found, along with a narrow over wide 8 variety.

1885 Small 5 (S)
Short top on 5

1885
Small 5 over
large 5

1885 Large 5 (L)
Large top on 5

1886 Small 6 (S) 1886 Large 6 (L)

1897 Wide 8 (W) 1897 Narrow 8 (N) 1897 Narrow over Wide 8 (N/W)

Date, Mint Portrait	Quantity Minted	G-4	VG-8	F-12	VF-20	EF-40	AU-50	MS-60	MS-63
1885 S-F5	1,000,000	10.	22.	40.	75.	200.	375.	1,000.	4,250.
1885 5/5-F5	Incl. above	40.	85.	160.	300.	700.	1,700.	4,750.	—
1885 L-F5	Incl. above	11.	22.	40.	80.	225.	400.	1,100.	4,250.
1886 S-F5	1,700,000	8.	17.	33.	50.	100.	225.	550.	1,750.
1886 L-F5	Incl. above	10.	20.	33.	55.	110.	250.	650.	2,000.
1887-F5	500,000	13.	33.	70.	100.	225.	325.	600.	1,750.
1888-F5	1,000,000	7.	12.	20.	40.	80.	125.	250.	750.
1889-F5	1,200,000	20.	45.	75.	165.	275.	375.	750.	2,500.
1890H-F5	1,000,000	8.	13.	25.	50.	100.	150.	300.	750.
1891-F2	1,800,000	6.	11.	15.	33.	65.	100.	250.	650.
1891-F5	Incl. above	6.	11.	15.	33.	65.	100.	250.	650.
1892-F2	860,000	7.	13.	22.	50.	100.	200.	500.	1,250.
1892-F5	Incl. above	15.	25.	45.	100.	200.	400.	800.	2,000.
1893-F2	1,700,000	6.	11.	15.	33.	65.	135.	300.	850.
1894-F2	500,000	12.	33.	55.	100.	225.	300.	600.	2,500.
1896-F2	1,500,000	7.	11.	17.	35.	65.	135.	300.	675.
1897 W-F2	1,319,280	6.	12.	20.	40.	80.	150.	300.	1,000.
1897 N-F2	Incl. above	6.	11.	17.	35.	65.	110.	250.	700.
1897 N/W-F2	Incl. above	10.	15.	40.	75.	150.	300.	600.	2,000.
1898-F2	580,400	10.	22.	33.	70.	135.	275.	500.	1,500.
1899-F2	3,000,000	6.	10.	13.	25.	65.	100.	225.	600.

VARIETIES 1900. Two sizes of date are seen on the 1900 issue. The large date has been referred to most often as the Round 0s variety and the small date as the Oval 0s variety, but there is a greater difference in the 9s. The large date has a Wide 9 as on the 1898 issue and the small date has a Narrow 9 as on the 1899 and 1901 issues.

1900 Large Date
Wide 0s and 9 (W)

1900 Small Date
Narrow 0s and 9 (N)

Date, Mint Portrait	Quantity Minted	G-4	VG-8	F-12	VF-20	EF-40	AU-50	MS-60	MS-63
1900 W-F2	1,800,000	15.	35.	65.	100.	225.	300.	500.	1,500.
1900 N-F2	Incl. above	7.	11.	13.	25.	65.	100.	225.	600.
1901-F2	2,000,000	6.	10.	13.	25.	65.	100.	225.	600.

FIVE CENTS
Edward VII 1902 - 1910

In 1902, the coronation year for Edward VII, the Royal Mint was extremely busy producing new coinage tools and striking the new coins and medals. One compromise this necessitated involved the reverse of the Canadian 5-cent piece. It had been intended to transfer both the word "CANADA" from the obverse to the reverse legend and to replace the old St. Edward's crown, showing depressed arches at the top, with the Imperial State crown, showing raised arches at the top. Instead, the mint had to settle for making the legend change only. The following year the crown was changed. The 1903H issue had a reverse with 21 leaves, but a modified design with 22 leaves was instituted for the London issue. The Mint, Birmingham issue has an "H" mint mark on the reverse under the wreath. The London Mint has no letter.

Designer and Modeller:
  Obverse: G.W. DeSaulles
  (DES under bust)
Engraver: Reverse: G.W. DeSaulles
Composition: .925 silver, .075 copper
Weight: 1.16 grams
Diameter: 15.50 mm
Edge: Reeded
Die Axis: ↑↓

MINT MARK VARIETIES 1902. Two sizes of "H" appear on the 1902 Heaton Mint issue of this denomination. One is a small, narrow "H" not seen on any other Canadian coins and the other is a large, wide "H" similar to that on the 1903H.

  1902 Large H   1902 Small H

Date and Mint Mark	Quantity Minted	VG-8	F-12	VF-20	EF-40	AU-50	MS-60	MS-63
1902	2,120,000	3.	4.	8.	17.	25.	55.	75.
1902H Large H	2,200,000	4.	5.	10.	20.	30.	65.	90.
1902H Small H	Incl. above	10.	18.	35.	65.	90.	140.	225.

IMPERIAL CROWN; 21 LEAVES IN REVERSE WREATH 1903 (The Mint, Birmingham Issue Only). The 1903 issue for The Mint, Birmingham was essentially the same as the 1902 coinage with the St. Edward's crown replaced by the Imperial State crown. This design was employed for only the one year and at the Birmingham Mint only.

Designer and Engraver:
  probably G.W. De Saulles

The physical and chemical specifications are as for the 1902 issue.

Date and Mint Mark	Quantity Minted	VG-8	F-12	VF-20	EF-40	AU-50	MS-60	MS-63
1903H	2,640,000	4.	5.	14.	28.	65.	175.	500.

IMPERIAL CROWN; 22 LEAVES IN REVERSE WREATH 1903 (London Mint - 1910). In a move unprecedented in Canadian coinage the Royal Mint produced a coin (the 5-cent piece) that bore a somewhat different design than that used by its sub-contractor, The Mint, Birmingham, in 1903. The 1903 London issue features a new wreath with 22 instead of 21 leaves.

Designer and Modeller:
  Obverse: G.W. De Saulles
  Reverse: W.H.J. Blakemore
Composition: .925 silver, .075 copper
Weight: 1.16 grams (1903-1910);
    1.17 grams (1910)
Diameter: 15.50 mm
Edge: Reeded
Die Axis: ↑↓ (1903-1907);
    ↑↑ (1908-1910)

Date and Mint Mark	Quantity Minted	VG-8	F-12	VF-20	EF-40	AU-50	MS-60	MS-63
1903	1,000,000	7.	12.	30.	60.	120.	250.	600.
1904	2,400,000	3.	5.	15.	40.	80.	275.	825.
1905	2,600,000	3.	4.	12.	25.	50.	135.	350.
1906	3,100,000	3.	4.	9.	20.	45.	125.	400.
1907	5,200,000	3.	4.	8.	15.	40.	90.	200.

1908
Small 8

1908
Large 8

VARIETIES OF 1908. In 1908, again different size punches were used, a small 8 and a large 8

Date and Mint Mark	Quantity Minted	VG-8	F-12	VF-20	EF-40	AU-50	MS-60	MS-63
1908 Small 8	1,197,780	10.	16.	35.	65.	100.	150.	250.
1908 Large 8	Incl. above	25.	40.	100.	200.	300.	500.	1,000.

VARIETIES 1909 AND 1910. In 1909 the existing reverse was modified to create a variety in which the maple leaves have sharp points along their edges, causing them to resemble holly leaves. Both the Maple Leaves and the Holly Leaves reverses saw use in 1909 and 1910.

Maple Leaves Reverse (1903-1910)   Holly Leaves Reverse (1909-1910)

Date and Mint Mark	Quantity Minted	VG-8	F-12	VF-20	EF-40	AU-50	MS-60	MS-63
1909 Maple	1,890,865	6.	9.	18.	45.	80.	300.	850.
1909 Holly	Incl. above	20.	30.	75.	150.	300.	1,100.	3,000.
1910 Maple	5,580,325	20.	30.	90.	200.	400.	1,250.	3,000.
1910 Holly	Incl. above	3.	4.	8.	15.	30.	75.	150.

FIVE CENTS - SILVER
George V 1911 - 1921

"GODLESS" OBVERSE 1911. The new obverse introduced in 1911 was criticized by the public because the Latin phrase "DEI GRATIA" (or an abbreviation for it), indicating that the King ruled by the grace of God, was omitted. The coinage tools were modified during the year and a new obverse with "DEI GRA:" included in the legend appeared on the 1912 issue. The Maple Leaves design reverse was that of the previous reign.

Designer and Modeller:
Portrait: Sir E.B. MacKennal
(B.M. on truncation)
Composition: .925 silver, .075 copper
Weight: 1.17 grams
Diameter: 15.50 mm
Edge: Reeded
Die Axis: ↑↑

Date and Mint Mark	Quantity Minted	VG-8	F-12	VF-20	EF-40	AU-50	MS-60	MS-63
1911	3,692,350	4.	5.	9.	18.	45.	90.	150.

MODIFIED OBVERSE LEGEND 1912-1921.

Composition: .925 silver, .075 copper
(1912-1919)
.800 silver, .200 copper
(1920-1921)

The physical specifications are as for the 1911 issue.

Date and Mint Mark	Quantity Minted	VG-8	F-12	VF-20	EF-40	AU-50	MS-60	MS-63
1912	5,863,170	4.	5.	7.	13.	33.	80.	325.
1913	5,588,048	4.	5.	6.	11.	20.	40.	75.
1914	4,202,179	4.	5.	6.	13.	33.	80.	250.
1915	1,172,258	17.	28.	45.	80.	190.	375.	800.
1916	2,481,675	5.	8.	12.	30.	60.	135.	350.
1917	5,521,373	3.	4.	5.	10.	22.	50.	110.
1918	6,052,289	3.	4.	5.	9.	20.	45.	100.
1919	7,835,400	3.	4.	5.	9.	20.	45.	100.
1920	10,649,851	3.	4.	5.	9.	20.	40.	75.

Note: Some 1920 5¢ are believed to have remained unissued and were returned to the melting pot in 1922.

FIVE CENTS 1921. During 1920-1921 plans moved forward for the replacement of the small silver 5-cents piece with a larger coin of pure nickel, the same size as the U.S. nickel. The enabling legislation was passed in May 1921 and thereafter no more circulating 5-cent pieces were coined in silver. The mint melted some 3,022,665 coins of this denomination. The presumed composition of this melt is almost all the 1921 mintage and a portion of the 1920 mintage, thus explaining the rarity of the 1921 date today. Only about 400 1921s are believed to have survived. A few are Specimen coins, issued to collectors in sets and the rest are thought to be circulation strikes sold to visitors to the Mint in the early months of 1921.

Designer and Modeller:
    Portrait: Sir E.B. MacKennal
    (B.M. on truncation)
Composition: .800 silver, .200 copper
Weight: 1.17 grams
Diameter: 15.50 mm
Edge: Reeded
Die Axis: ↑↑

Date and Mint Mark	Quantity Minted	G-4	VG-8	F-12	VF-20	EF-40	AU-50	MS-60	MS-63
1921	2,582,495*	1,900.	3,000.	3,500.	4,500.	5,500.	7,500.	11,000.	25,000.

*Almost all 1921 5¢ are believed to have remained unissued and were returned to the melting pot in 1922.

FIVE CENTS - NICKEL
George V 1922 - 1936

The new Canadian nickel 5-cent piece was introduced in 1922 after two years of planning. The silver coin it replaced was allowed to circulate also until the 1930s, when a more active withdrawal program was instituted.

Designer and Modeller:
    Portrait: Sir E.B. MacKennal
    (B.M. on truncation)
    Reverse: W.H.J. Blakemore
Composition: 1.00 nickel
Weight: 4.54 grams
Diameter: 21.21 mm
Edge: Plain
Die Axis: ↑↑

Date and Mint Mark	Quantity Minted	G-4	VG-8	F-12	VF-20	EF-40	AU-50	MS-60	MS-63
1922 Near Rim	4,763,186	—	—	1.	4.	15.	40.	65.	150.
1922 Far Rim	Incl. above	2.	4.	8.	15.	30.	80.	125.	300.
1923	2,475,201	—	—	3.	8.	22.	65.	150.	475.
1924	3,066,658	—	—	1.	4.	20.	50.	120.	375.
1925	200,050	50.	90.	140.	200.	400.	800.	1,750.	5,000.

VARIETIES 1922. See page 405 to 409 in the Variety Section for punch spacing.

VARIETIES 1926. It was the usual practice in the George V 5-cent series to complete the date at the matrix stage, eliminating the necessity to date every reverse die and thereby assuring that there would be no difference in the positioning of the date digits on a given year's coinage. A notable exception was 1926, when the reverse punch (bearing a 6 which nearly touched the maple leaf) was retired before the conclusion of the coinage. The second variety had the 6 slightly farther from the maple leaf.

1926 Near 6
the 6 almost touches the
maple leaf

1926 Far 6
the 6 is farther from the
maple leaf

Date and Mint Mark	Quantity Minted	G-4	VG-8	F-12	VF-20	EF-40	AU-50	MS-60	MS-63
1926 Near 6	933,577	2.	4.	8.	20.	80.	250.	550.	2,000.
1926 Far 6	Incl. above	80.	125.	225.	325.	700.	1,250.	2,000.	4,500.
1927	5,285,627	–	–	1.	4.	20.	45.	75.	225.
1928	4,588,725	–	–	1.	4.	20.	45.	75.	150.
1929	5,562,262	–	–	2.	4.	20.	45.	75.	250.
1930	3,685,991	–	–	1.	4.	20.	50.	125.	325.
1931	5,100,830	–	–	2.	6.	28.	60.	275.	900.
1932	3,198,566	–	–	2.	5.	25.	55.	165.	650.
1933	2,597,867	–	–	2.	7.	30.	80.	325.	1,000.
1934	3,827,303	–	–	2.	5.	25.	55.	165.	750.
1935	3,900,000	–	–	2.	5.	30.	60.	125.	325.
1936	4,400,450	–	–	1.	3.	15.	40.	70.	175.

FIVE CENTS
George VI 1937 - 1942

In 1937 Canada introduced new coinage designs for the lower denominations, in keeping with a trend towards modernization begun in 1935 with the silver dollar. The reverse of the 5-cent piece bore a beaver on a rock-studded mound of earth rising out of the water. At the left is a log on which the beaver has been chewing. The master tools for this reverse were produced at the Paris Mint because the Royal Mint in London was pressed for time.

Designer and Modeller:
   Portrait: G.E. Kruger-Gray
   (K.G. above water at left)
Composition: 1.00 nickel
Weight: 4.54 grams
Diameter: 21.21 mm
Edge: Plain
Die Axis: ↑↑

Date and Mint Mark	Quantity Minted	VF-20	EF-40	AU-50	MS-60	MS-63	MS-65
1937 Dot	4,593,263	2.	3.	6.	15.	30.	125.
1938	898,974	3.	12.	40.	90.	200.	1,500.
1939	5,661,123	2.	7.	20.	45.	75.	300.
1940	13,820,197	2.	5.	8.	20.	60.	375.
1941	8,681,785	2.	6.	10.	25.	75.	450.
1942 Nickel	6,847,544	2.	5.	8.	20.	50.	450.

Note: All 1937 5¢ have the dot after the date.

BEAVER DESIGN; TOMBAC COINAGE (12-sided) 1942. Nickel is an important component of stainless steel and other alloys needed for producing war materials, so World War II put a great strain upon Canada's nickel producers. By 1942 it was decided that nickel would have to be suspended as a coinage material for the duration of the war and experiments were initiated to find a substitute metal for the 5-cent piece. This led to the adoption of a 12-sided coin made of tombac, a kind of brass. The idea had come from the British 3-penny piece first issued in 1937. The tombac 5-cent was given its shape so that when tarnished it would still not be confused with 1-cent pieces.

Designer: Royal Canadian Mint staff, modifying existing designs
Engraver: Thomas Shingles, modifying Royal Mint coinage tools
Composition: .88 copper, .12 zinc
Weight: 4.54 grams
Diameter: c. 21.3 mm (opposite corners)
c. 20.0 mm (opposite sides)
Edge: Plain
Die Axis: ↑↑

Date and Mint Mark	Quantity Minted	VF-20	EF-40	AU-50	MS-60	MS-63	MS-65
1942 Tombac	3,396,234	2.	3.	4.	5.	20.	150.

TORCH & V DESIGN; TOMBAC COINAGE (12-sided) 1943-1944. In 1943 a new reverse design came into use for this denomination. Its purpose was to help promote the war effort. The idea for the design came from Churchill's famous "V" sign and the V denomination mark on the U.S. 5-cent pieces of 1883-1912. A novel feature was the use of an International Code message meaning, "We Win When We Work Willingly." It was placed along the rim on the reverse instead of denticles. The original master matrix was engraved entirely by hand by Royal Canadian Mint Chief Engraver Thomas Shingles. The obverse was the same as that for 1942, except rim denticles were added.

Designer, Engraver:
Obverse: Thomas Shingles, modifying existing design and tools
Reverse: Thomas Shingles (T.S. at lower right of V and torch)
Composition: .88 copper, .12 zinc
Weight: 4.54 grams
Diameter: c. 21.3 mm (opposite corners)
c. 20.9 mm (opposite sides)
Edge: Plain
Die Axis: ↑↑

Date and Mint Mark	Quantity Minted	VF-20	EF-40	AU-50	MS-60	MS-63	MS-65
1943	24,760,256	1.	2.	3.	5.	15.	100.
1944	8,000	ANA Sale 1999 $38,500. U.S.F.					

Note: 1. A 1943 5¢ Torch and V design struck on a nickel planchet was certified as an error coin by Numismatic Guarantee Corporation of America during 2001.
2. Most of the 1944 5¢ tombac remained unissued and were melted; only one is known to exist.

TORCH & V DESIGN; STEEL COINAGE (12-sided) 1944-1945. War demands for copper and zinc forced a suspension in the use of tombac for the 5-cent piece and the institution of plated steel. The steel was plated with nickel and then returned to the plating tank for a very thin plating of chromium. The chromium was hard and helped retard wear. Unfortunately it was necessary to plate the strips prior to the blanks being punched out. This resulted in the edges of the blanks (and hence the coins) being unplated and vulnerable to rusting.

Some collectors have noted steel 5-cent pieces which have a dull gray colour instead of the normal bluish-white colour. This is due to some of the strips being plated with nickel only and not nickel and chromium. Such coins do not ordinarily command a significant premium.

Composition: Steel with .0127 mm plating of nickel and .0003 mm plating of chromium

All other statistics are as for the 1943 coinage.

Date and Mint Mark	Quantity Minted	VF-20	EF-40	AU-50	MS-60	MS-63	MS-65
1944	11,532,784	–	1.	2.	4.	10.	40.
1945	18,893,216	–	1.	2.	4.	10.	40.

BEAVER DESIGN RESUMED; "ET IND:IMP:" IN OBVERSE LEGEND (12-sided) 1946-1947. After the end of World War II, the Mint returned to the issue of nickel 5-cent pieces of the beaver design. However, it was decided to retain the 12-sided shape, because it had become popular. The obverse was a continuation of that of 1943-1945.

Designer, Engraver:
Reverse: Thomas Shingles, modifying existing design and tools
Composition: 1.00 nickel
Weight: 4.54 grams
Diameter: c. 21.3 mm (opposite corners)
c. 20.9 mm (opposite sides)
Edge: Plain
Die Axis: ↑↑

Date and Mint Mark	Quantity Minted	VF-20	EF-40	AU-50	MS-60	MS-63	MS-65
1946	6,952,684	–	4.	8.	17.	45.	250.
1947	7,603,724	–	3.	6.	12.	25.	150.

MAPLE LEAF ISSUE 1947 (12-sided) . The granting of independence to India created a dilemma for the Royal Canadian Mint in the early part of 1948. The new obverse coinage tools (with "ET IND: IMP:" omitted) would not arrive for several months, yet there was a great need for all denominations of coins. Therefore, the mint struck coins dated 1947 and bearing the obverse with the outmoded titles. To differentiate this issue from the regular strikings of 1947, a tiny maple leaf was placed after the date.

1947 Maple Leaf issue, struck in 1948
The physical and chemical specifications are as for the 1946-1947 issues.

1947 Maple Leaf   1947 Dot

Date and Mint Mark	Quantity Minted	VF-20	EF-40	AU-50	MS-60	MS-63	MS-65
1947 ML	9,595,124	1.	3.	6.	12.	25.	125.
1947 Dot		35.	75.	200.	275.	450.	2,000.

MODIFIED OBVERSE LEGEND; BEAVER REVERSE (12-sided) 1948-1950. Following the arrival of the master tools with the new obverse legend lacking "ET IND: IMP:" in 1948, the 1947 Maple Leaf coinage was suspended from production. For the remainder of the year coins were produced with the new obverse and the true date, 1948.

Designer and Engraver:
Reverse: Thomas Shingles,
modifying existing design and tools
Composition: 1.00 nickel
Weight: 4.54 grams
Diameter: c. 21.3 mm (opposite corners)
c. 20.9 mm (opposite sides)
Edge: Plain
Die Axis: ↑↑

Date and Mint Mark	Quantity Minted	VF-20	EF-40	AU-50	MS-60	MS-63	MS-65
1948	1,810,789	2.	6.	11.	25.	45.	150.
1949	13,736,276	–	2.	4.	10.	25.	100.
1950	11,950,520	–	2.	4.	10.	25.	75.

COMMEMORATIVE FOR ISOLATION AND NAMING OF NICKEL 1951 (12-sided). In 1950 plans were made to strike a coin to commemorate the isolation and naming of the element nickel by the Swedish chemist A.F. Cronstedt in 1751. The three Canadian commemorative coins issued up to that time had been silver dollars, but the 5-cent piece was selected for use in 1951 because it was the only denomination struck in nickel. The design was chosen from entries submitted to the Mint in an open competition, the first of its type in Canada for a coinage that was actually issued. The winning design depicts a nickel refinery, with low buildings flanking a smoke stack in the centre. The obverse is the same as that for the 1948-1950 issues.

Some members of the public became confused and believed that the dates 1751-1951 should have read 1851-1951. This caused hoarding of these coins in the mistaken belief that they would become extremely valuable.

Designer and Modeller:
Reverse: Stephen Trenka
(ST monogram below the
building at the right)
Composition: 1.00 nickel
Weight: 4.54 grams
Diameter: c. 21.3 mm (opposite corners)
c. 20.9 mm (opposite sides)
Edge: Plain
Die Axis: ↑↑

Date and Mint Mark	Quantity Minted	VF-20	EF-40	AU-50	MS-60	MS-63	MS-65
1951 Comm.	12,642,641	.35	.50	1.00	3.00	12.00	125.00

BEAVER DESIGN RESUMED; STEEL COINAGE (12-sided) 1951-1952. The Korean War placed strong demand on nickel, forcing suspension of production of the commemorative nickel 5-cent piece before the end of 1951. In its place steel coins of the beaver design were struck. It was found during trials that the beaver design was not as easy to strike in steel as in nickel, so new, lower relief coinage tools were prepared for both obverse and reverse. By mistake, a High Relief obverse die was used to strike a small proportion of the 1951 steel coinage, resulting in two varieties for the year. Aside from the difference in relief the High and Low Relief obverses differ in the position of the last A of "GRATIA" relative to the rim denticles. On the High Relief variety the "A" points to a rim denticle; on the Low Relief variety it points between denticles. The entire 1952 issue was coined with the Low Relief obverse.

Modeller: Thomas Shingles, modifying existing models
Composition: Steel with .0127 mm plating of nickel and .0003 mm plating of chromium
Weight: 4.54 grams
Diameter: c. 21.3 mm (opposite corners) c. 20.9 mm (opposite sides)
Edge: Plain
Die Axis: ↑↑

A in GRATIA
points to a rim denticle

1951 High Relief
Obverse

A in GRATIA points
between rim denticles

1951 Low Relief
Obverse

Date and Mint Mark	Quantity Minted	VG-8	F-12	VF-20	EF-40	AU-50	MS-60	MS-63	MS-65
1951 High Relief	Incl. above	500.	600.	800.	1,400.	2,000.	3,500.	—	—
1951 Low Relief	Incl. above	—	—	.50	1.	2.	4.	12.	75.
1952	10,891,148	—	—	.50	1.	2.	4.	12.	75.

FIVE CENTS:
Elizabeth II 1953 to date

STEEL FIVE CENTS (12-sided) 1953-1954. Two obverse varieties, termed the No Shoulder Fold and Shoulder Fold obverses, saw use during 1953 (see 1-cent Elizabeth II, 1953 to date, for full explanation). On the 5-cent piece these varieties are best distinguished on worn coins by observing the styles of the letters in the obverse legends: they are more flared (particularly the I's) on the No Shoulder Fold variety. The reverses combined with the two obverses result in two mules, the 1953 NSF, near and the 1953 SF, far.

Designer and Modeller:
   Portrait: Mrs. Mary Gillick,
      (M.G. on truncation)
Engraver:
   No Shoulder Fold Obverse:
      Thomas Shingles, using the
      Gillick portrait model
   Shoulder Fold Obverse:
      Thomas Shingles, modifying
      existing NSF coinage tools
Composition: Steel with .0127 mm
   plating of nickel and .0003 mm
   plating of chromium
Weight: 4.54 grams
Diameter: c. 21.3 mm (opposite corners)
      c. 20.9 mm (opposite sides)
Edge: Plain
Die Axis: ↑↑

No Shoulder Fold Obverse
note flared ends of "I"s

No Shoulder Fold
Obverse

Far Maple Leaf

Shoulder Fold Obverse
note straight-sided "I"s

Shoulder Fold Obverse
note straigt-sided "I"s

Near Maple Leaf

Date and Mint Mark	Quantity Minted	VF-20	EF-40	AU-50	MS-60	MS-63	MS-64	MS-65
1953 NSF, far	16,635,552	—	1.	2.	5.	10.	25.	50.
1953 NSF, near	Incl. above	1,000.	1,250.	1,500.	1,750.	3,500.	—	—
1953 SF, near	Incl. above	—	2.	3.	6.	12.	30.	60.
1953 SF, far	Incl. above	550.	650.	1,000.	1,500.	—	—	
1954	6,998,662	—	2.	3.	6.	12.	30.	60.

NICKEL 12-SIDED COINAGE 1955-1962. The mint returned to nickel for the 5-cent piece in 1955. The reverse for the George VI coinage of 1946-1950 was continued.

Designers, modellers and physical specifications are as for the 1953 issues.
Composition: 1.00 nickel

Date and Mint Mark	Quantity Minted	AU-50	MS-60	MS-63	MS-64	MS-65
1955	5,355,028	2.50	5.00	10.00	25.00	50.00
1956	9,399,854	2.00	4.00	8.00	20.00	40.00
1957	7,387,703	1.75	3.50	7.50	18.00	35.00
1958	7,607,521	1.75	3.50	7.00	16.00	32.00
1959	11,552,523	1.25	2.50	5.00	10.00	20.00
1960	37,157,433	1.25	2.50	5.00	10.00	20.00
1961	47,889,051	1.25	2.50	5.00	10.00	20.00
1962	46,307,305	1.25	2.50	5.00	10.00	20.00

LAUREATED BUST; ROUND COINAGE 1963-1964. For strictly economic reasons the production of round 5-cent pieces was resumed in 1963 for the first time since 1942. It was cheaper to make round coins because the collars for the coining presses lasted longer.

1964 Extra
Water Line

Engraver: Thomas Shingles
Weight: 4.54 grams
Edge: Plain

Composition: 1.00 nickel
Diameter: 21.21 mm
Die Axis: ↑↑

Date and Mint Mark	Quantity Minted	VF-20	EF-40	AU-50	MS-60	MS-63	MS-64	MS-65
1963	43,970,320	–	–	–	.50	1.50	3.00	15.00
1964	78,075,068	–	–	–	.50	1.50	3.00	15.00
1964 XWL	Incl. above	20.00	25.00	30.00	45.00	75.00	400.00	–

TIARA PORTRAIT; BEAVER REVERSE 1965-1966. A new obverse with the Queen showing more mature facial features and wearing a tiara was introduced on all denominations in 1965.

Designer and Modeller:
Portrait: Arnold Machin

The physical and chemical specifications are as for the 1963-1964 issues.

1965 Small Beads
Attached Jewel

1965 Large Beads
Detached Jewel

Date and Mint Mark	Quantity Minted		MS-60	MS-63	MS-64	MS-65
1965 Small beads	84,876,018		.50	1.00	3.00	15.00
1965 Large beads	Incl. above		350.00	700.00	1,850.00	—
1966	27,976,648		.50	1.00	3.00	15.00

COMMEMORATIVE FOR CENTENNIAL OF CONFEDERATION 1967. A reverse design showing a hopping rabbit was selected for the 1967 5-cent piece. It was by Alex Colville, who also designed the reverses of the other Confederation commemoratives issued for circulation. The obverse was a continuation of the 1965-1966 design.

Designer: Reverse: Alex Colville
Modeller: Reverse: Myron Cook

The physical and chemical specifications are as for the 1963-1966 issues.

Date and Mint Mark	Quantity Minted		MS-60	MS-63	MS-64	MS-65
1967	36,876,574		.50	1.00	3.00	15.00

TIARA PORTRAIT; BEAVER REVERSE RESUMED 1968-1978. During 1977 a change in the matrix resulted in new punches and thus new dies creating a variety in the seven's for that year. The seven's vary in distance from Canada and are also different in type size.

Designer and Modeller:
 Obverse: Arnold Machin
 Reverse: G.E. Kruger-Gray
Composition: 1.00 nickel
Weight: 4.54 grams
Diameter: 21.21 mm
Edge: Plain
Die Axis: ↑↑

1977 High 7

1977 Low 7

Date and Mint Mark	Quantity Minted	MS-60	MS-63	MS-64	MS-65
1968	99,253,330	.50	1.00	3.00	7.50
1969	27,830,229	.50	1.00	3.00	7.50
1970	5,726,010	1.00	2.00	5.00	10.00
1971	27,312,609	.50	1.00	3.00	7.50
1972	62,417,387	.50	1.00	3.00	7.50
1973	53,507,435	.50	1.00	3.00	7.50
1974	94,704,645	.50	1.00	3.00	7.50
1975	138,882,000	.50	1.00	3.00	7.50
1976	55,140,213	.50	1.00	3.00	7.50
1977 High	89,120,791	.50	1.00	3.00	7.50
1977 Low	Incl. above	5.00	10.00	35.00	100.00
1978	137,079,273	.50	1.00	3.00	7.50

MODIFIED TIARA PORTRAIT; BEAVER REVERSE 1979-1989. Beginning on the 1979 coinage and as part of a general standardization of the coinage, the portrait of the Queen was made smaller. The purpose was to make the size of the portrait proportional to the diameter of the coin, regardless of the denomination.

Designer and Modeller:
  Obverse: Arnold Machin, Walter Ott
  Reverse: G.E. Kruger-Gray
Composition: 1.00 nickel (1979-1981)
  .75 copper, .25 nickel
  (1982-1989)
Weight: 4.54 grams
Diameter: 21.21 mm
Edge: Plain
Die Axis: ↑↑

Date and Mint Mark	Quantity Minted	MS-60	MS-63	MS-64	MS-65
1979	186,295,825	.50	1.00	3.00	7.50
1980	134,878,000	.50	1.00	3.00	7.50
1981	99,107,900	.50	1.00	3.00	7.50
1982	105,539,898	.50	1.00	3.00	7.50
1983	72,596,000	.50	1.00	3.00	7.50
1984	84,088,000	.50	1.00	3.00	7.50
1985	126,618,000	.50	1.00	3.00	7.50
1986	156,104,000	.50	1.00	3.00	7.50
1987	106,299,000	.50	1.00	3.00	7.50
1988	75,025,000	.50	1.00	3.00	7.50
1989	141,435,538	.50	1.00	3.00	7.50

CROWNED PORTRAIT; BEAVER REVERSE 1990-1991. A new obverse portrait of the Queen wearing a diamond diadem and jewellery was introduced on all denominations in 1990.

Designer and Modeller:
  Obverse: Dora de Pédery-Hunt
  Ago Aarand
  Reverse: G.E. Kruger-Gray
Composition: Cupro-nickel
  .75 copper, .25 nickel
Weight: 4.6 grams
Diameter: 21.2 mm
Edge: Plain
Die Axis: ↑↑

Date and Mint Mark	Quantity Minted	MS-60	MS-63	MS-64	MS-65
1990	42,537,000	.50	1.00	3.00	7.50
1991	10,931,000	.50	1.00	3.00	7.50

COMMEMORATIVE FOR THE 125TH ANNIVERSARY 1867-1992. The reverse design was modified to include the bracket dates 1867-1992 for the 125th birthday of Canada

Designer, modeller, chemical and physical specifications are as for the 1990 issues.

Date and Mint Mark	Quantity Minted	MS-60	MS-63	MS-64	MS-65
1992	53,732,000	.50	1.00	3.00	7.50

CROWNED PORTRAIT; BEAVER REVERSE 1993-2001. In 1993 the practice of using a single date was resumed. The transition from rim denticles to beads, which began in 1982 on the one cent piece, was carried out on the five cent piece in 1993. The Winnipeg Mint Mark (W) is found only on coins from the "Oh! Canada" and "Tiny Treasures" sets issued by the Numismatic Department of the Mint.

Designer, modeller, chemical and physical specifications are as for the 1990 issues.

5¢ 1996 Far 6

"6" Far from "D" in Canada

5¢ 1996 Near 6

"6" Near "D" in Canada

Date and Mint Mark	Quantity Minted	AU-50	MS-60	MS-63	MS-64	MS-65
1993	86,877,000	—	.50	1.00	3.00	7.50
1994	99,352,000	—	.50	1.00	3.00	7.50
1995	78,780,000	—	.50	1.00	3.00	7.50
1996 Far 6	36,686,000	1.00	2.00	5.00	12.50	25.00
1996 Near 6	Incl. above	1.00	2.00	5.00	12.50	25.00
1997	27,354,000	—	.50	1.00	3.00	7.50
1998	156,873,000	—	.50	1.00	3.00	7.50
1999	124,861,000	—	.50	1.00	3.00	7.50
2000	108,514,000	—	.50	1.00	3.00	7.50
2001	20,036,000	—	.50	1.00	3.00	7.50

CROWNED PORTRAIT; BEAVER REVERSE; MULTI-PLY PLATED STEEL 1999-2001. In 2000 the Royal Canadian Mint began issuing circulating 5-cent coins struck from their new multi-ply plated steel blanks. The process is acid based and electroplates a thin coating of nickel, then copper, then nickel again to a steel core.

Designer and Modeller:
Obverse: Dora de Pédery-Hunt
Ago Aarand
Reverse: G. E. Kruger-Gray
Composition: .945 steel, .035 copper, .02 nickel
Weight: 3.95 grams
Diameter: 21.10 mm
Thickness: 1.76 mm
Edge: Plain
Die Axis: ↑↑

Date and Mint Mark	Quantity Minted	MS-60	MS-63	MS-64	MS-65
1999P	Not issued for circulation	—	—	—	—
2000P	2,300,000 est.	2.00	3.00	6.00	12.00
2001P	146,650,000	.50	1.00	3.00	7.50

ELIZABETH II GOLDEN JUBILEE 1952-2002. To commemorate the 50th anniversary of the reign of Queen Elizabeth II, all circulating coinage carried the double date of her reign 1952-2002, on the obverse.

Designer, modeller, chemical and physical specifications are as for the 1999P issues.

Date and Mint Mark	Quantity Minted	MS-60	MS-63	MS-64	MS-65
1952-2002P	134,368,000	.50	1.00	3.00	7.50

CROWNED PORTRAIT; BEAVER REVERSE; MULTI-PLY PLATED STEEL 2003 TO DATE.

Designer, modeller, chemical and physical specifications are as for the 1999 issues.

Date and Mint Mark	Quantity Minted	MS-63	MS-64	MS-65
2003P	N/A	.25	.50	1.00
2004P	N/A	.25	.50	1.00

2003 P w/o Crown

TEN CENTS
Victoria 1870 - 1901

The initial designs for the Victoria 10-cent pieces issued by the Dominion government were identical to the 1858 Province of Canada issue. During the reign, six obverse varieties were used. They differed primarily in the features of the Queen's face. A detailed description and listing by year follow on the next pages. Two major varieties of the reverse exist; only in 1891 were both used for the same year's coinage (see below).

Designer, Modeller and Engraver:
Leonard C. Wyon
Composition: .925 silver, .075 copper
Weight: 2.33 grams
Diameter: 18.03 mm
Edge: Reeded
Die Axis: ↑↓

Heaton Mint issues of 1871-1883 and the Mint, Birmingham issue of 1890 have an "H" mint mark on the reverse under the wreath. London Mint strikings have no letter.

VARIETIES 1870. Two styles of 0 appear in the date of the 1870 issue. The Narrow 0 with sides of equal thickness is more common than the Wide 0, on which the right-hand side is thicker.

1870 Narrow "0" (N0)
Sides of equal thickness

1870 Wide "0" (W0)
Right side is thicker

Date, Mint Portrait	Quantity Minted	G-4	VG-8	F-12	VF-20	EF-40	AU-50	MS-60	MS-63
1870 N0-T1	1,600,000	15.	30.	60.	120.	200.	300.	500.	2,000.
1870 W0-T1	Incl. above	20.	50.	85.	175.	325.	400.	600.	2,250.
1871-T1	800,000	20.	45.	80.	175.	350.	450.	850.	4,000.
1871H-T1	1,870,000	25.	50.	85.	200.	375.	450.	700.	2,000.
1872H-T1	1,000,000	90.	165.	275.	500.	1,000.	1,350.	2,500.	5,000.

VICTORIA OBVERSE PORTRAIT VARIETIES

TEN CENTS – T

PORTRAIT: T1
The legend has large narrow letters.
The two top leaves of the laurel crown
are both well defined. The primary leaf
does not touch the 'I' in 'Dei'.

T1 will be found on the following dates:
1870 N0; 1870 W0; 1871; 1871H;
1872H; 1874H; 1875H; 1880H; 1881H

PORTRAIT: T2
The legend has large narrow letters. The two
top leaves in the laurel crown are well defined.
The primary leaf touches the lower pointed
serif of the 'I' in 'DEI'; the secondary leaf is fat.

T2 will be found on the following dates:
1880H; 1881H

PORTRAIT: T3
The legend has large narrow letters. The top
two leaves of the laurel crown are well defined
The primary leaf touches the lower serif of the
'I' in 'DEI'; and the secondary leaf is thin.

T3 will be found on the following dates:
1882H; 1883H

VICTORIA OBVERSE PORTRAIT VARIETIES

TEN CENTS – T

PORTRAIT: T4

The legend has small wide letters. Of the two top leaves of the laurel crown the primary leaf is fully outlined but weak in definition, the secondary leaf is cut with the top missing, only a small portion of it protruding from behind the primary.

T4 will be found on the following dates:
1884; 1885; 1886 (all varieties)

PORTRAIT: T5

The legend has large letters. Of the two top leaves of laurel crown, the primary leaf, which is ill-defined, is complete, the secondary leaf appears as only a small point.

T5 will be found on the following dates:
1885; 1886 (all varieties); 1887; 1888; 1889;
1890H; 1891 21 Lvs; 1891 22 Lvs; 1892;
1892 2/1; 1893 (all varieties); 1894; 1896; 1898

PORTRAIT: T6

The legend has large narrow letters. Of the top two leaves of the laurel crown, both the primary and the large secondary are well defined with the primary barely touching the 'I' in 'DEI'.

T6 will be found on the following dates:
1892; 1892 2/1; 1893 (all varieties); 1894;
1896; 1898; 1899 S9; 1899 L9; 1900; 1901

MINTAGE FIGURES 1874H AND 1875H. Through a clerical error part of the mintage of 1874H-dated coins was assigned to the next year's production figures. Therefore, the mintage figures for the two years, 600,000 and 1,000,000, respectively, have been combined.

Date, Mint Portrait	Quantity Minted	G-4	VG-8	F-12	VF-20	EF-40	AU-50	MS-60	MS-63
1874H-T1	1,600,000	17.	28.	45.	90.	200.	250.	475.	1,750.
1875H-T1	Incl. above	225.	450.	750.	1,250.	2,500.	4,000.	7,000.	15,000.
1880H-T1	1,500,000	15.	25.	50.	100.	165.	250.	425.	1,500.
1880H-T2	Incl. above	20.	35.	65.	125.	200.	325.	500.	2,000.
1881H-T1	950,000	20.	40.	75.	150.	300.	400.	650.	2,750.
1881H-T2	Incl. above	15.	30.	55.	110.	225.	300.	500.	2,000.
1882H-T3	1,000,000	15.	30.	55.	110.	225.	300.	600.	2,750.
1883H-T3	300,000	60.	100.	175.	375.	550.	750.	950.	2,250.
1884-T4	150,000	200.	400.	700.	1,250.	2,750.	5,000.	10,000.	25,000.
1885-T4	400,000	33.	75.	110.	400.	900.	2,000.	3,500.	9.000.
1885-T5	Incl. above				Very Rare				

VARIETIES 1886. For the 1886 coinage three distinctly different styles of 6 were used: a small 6, a

1886 Small 6	1886 Large, Pointed 6	1886 Large, Knobbed 6

large 6 with a point on its tail, and a large 6 with a large knob on its tail.

Date, Mint Portrait	Quantity Minted	G-4	VG-8	F-12	VF-20	EF-40	AU-50	MS-60	MS-63
1886 S6-T4	800,000				Very Rare				
1886 S6-T5	Incl. above	20.	35.	70.	175.	350.	850.	1,200.	5,000.
1886 Pt6-T4	Incl. above				Very Rare				
1886 Pt6-T5	Incl. above	75.	150.	225.	450.	650.	1,200.	2,250.	5,000.
1886 Kn6-T4	Incl. above	20.	45.	80.	190.	350.	850.	2,250.	5,000.
1886 Kn6-T5	Incl. above	20.	45.	80.	190.	350.	850.	2,250.	5,000.
1887-T5	350,000	28.	65.	135.	325.	650.	1,000.	2,000.	5,750.
1888-T5	500,000	12.	20.	45.	90.	175.	250.	450.	1,750.
1889-T5	600,000	500.	900.	1,750.	3,000.	5,500.	8,500.	20,000.	35,000.
1890H-T5	450,000	15.	30.	65.	135.	250.	350.	600.	2,000.

VARIETIES 1891, 1892 AND 1893. The two major reverse varieties seen on this denomination differ in the number of leaves in the wreath. The first (1870-1881 & 1891) has 21 leaves and the second (1882-1901) has 22 leaves. The 21-leaf reverse in 1891 occurs with small digits in the date, whereas the 22-leaf reverse in 1891 has a large date.

One 1891 large date die was carried over into 1892 and the 1 was overdated with a 2. Aside from the overpunching, the 1892 over 1 differs from the non-overdate 1892s in the style of the 9. The overdate has the large 9 of the 22 leaves, 1891 variety, and the non-overdates have the small 9 of the 21 leaves, 1891 variety.

Dating varieties continued into 1893. In that year one or two dies were dated with a large 9 and round-top 3, while the rest were dated with a medium 9 and a flat-top 3.

1891 - 21 Leaves, Small Date   1891 - 22 Leaves, Large Date

   1892 - 2 over 1, Large 9   1892 Normal Date, Small 9

   1893 Flat-top 3, Medium 9   1893 Round-top 3, Large 9

The 3 on this variety is often weakly struck.

Date, Mint Portrait	Quantity Minted	G-4	VG-8	F-12	VF-20	EF-40	AU-50	MS-60	MS-63
1891 21L-T5	800,000	18.	35.	75.	175.	350.	450.	700.	2,000.
1891 22L-T5	Incl. above	17.	33.	65.	150.	300.	375.	600.	2,000.
1892-T5	520,000	15.	30.	55.	100.	200.	325.	600.	1,750.
1892-T6	Incl. above	15.	30.	55.	100.	200.	325.	600.	1,750.
1892 2/1-T5	Incl. above	150.	250.	350.	600.	900.	1,500.	2,750.	–
1892 2/1-T6	Incl. above	150.	250.	350.	600.	900.	1,500.	2,750.	–
1893 F3-T5	500,000	25.	50.	120.	200.	400.	650.	1,250.	3,000.
1893 F3-T6	Incl. above	22.	45.	110.	190.	375.	600.	1,250.	3,000.
1893 R3-T5	Incl. above	600.	1,000.	2,000.	4,000.	6,500.	10,000.	–	–
1893 R3-T6	Incl. above	475.	800.	1,750.	3,500.	5,500.	8,500.	–	–
1894-T5	500,000	30.	60.	80.	200.	400.	500.	800.	2,750.
1894-T6	Incl. above	20.	40.	65.	150.	300.	375.	650.	2,200.
1896-T5	650,000	20.	40.	70.	100.	175.	300.	550.	1,750.
1896-T6	Incl. above	11.	22.	40.	75.	135.	250.	450.	1,250.
1898-T5	720,000	20.	40.	70.	100.	175.	325.	600.	2,000.
1898-T6	Incl. above	11.	22.	45.	75.	135.	250.	450.	1,250.

VARIETIES 1899. During the production of the 1899 10-cent pieces, two styles of 9 were used for dating the dies: a small, narrow 9 and a large, wide 9. The upper centre of the wide 9 is almost round, compared with the tall, rectangular centre of the narrow 9.

   1899 Small 9s   1899 Large 9s

Date, Mint Portrait	Quantity Minted	G-4	VG-8	F-12	VF-20	EF-40	AU-50	MS-60	MS-63
1899 S9-T6	1,200,000	8.	15.	33.	70.	150.	225.	325.	1,250.
1899 L9-T6	Incl. above	15.	33.	50.	100.	250.	350.	650.	2,000.
1900-T6	1,100,000	8.	13.	33.	65.	150.	200.	275.	1,100.
1901-T6	1,200,000	8.	13.	33.	65.	150.	200.	300.	1,250.

TEN CENTS
Edward VII 1902 - 1910

The reverse first employed for the 10-cent pieces of this reign was adapted from the 22-leaf Victorian reverse. The Imperial State crown replaced the St. Edward's crown at the top and the word "CANADA" was transferred from the obverse legend.

Designer and Modeller:
  Obverse: G.W. DeSaulles
  (DES. under the bust);
  Broad Leaves Reverse (1909-1910):
  W.H.J. Blakemore
Engraver: Victorian Leaves Reverse
  (1902-09): G.W. DeSaulles
Composition: .925 silver, .075 copper
Weight: 2.32 grams (1902-1910);
  2.33 grams (1910)
Diameter: 18.03 mm
Edge: Reeded
Die Axis: ↑↓ (1902-07);
  ↑↑ (1908-10)

The Mint, Birmingham issues (1902-1903) have an "H" mint mark on the reverse under the wreath. London Mint issues have no letter.

Date and Mint Mark	Quantity Minted	G-4	VG-8	F-12	VF-20	EF-40	AU-50	MS-60	MS-63
1902	720,000	6.	13.	28.	65.	140.	190.	550.	2,250.
1902H	1,100,000	5.	8.	20.	33.	75.	100.	175.	350.
1903	500,000	12.	25.	40.	110.	325.	700.	1,500.	3,250.
1903H	1,320,000	6.	11.	24.	60.	120.	190.	400.	1,250.
1904	1,000,000	11.	18.	40.	80.	165.	250.	450.	1,250.
1905	1,000,000	8.	15.	40.	100.	200.	350.	700.	1,750.
1906	1,700,000	5.	10.	22.	50.	110.	165.	350.	1,250.
1907	2,620,000	5.	10.	22.	45.	90.	165.	350.	850.
1908	776,666	10.	16.	35.	80.	175.	190.	275.	450.

VARIETIES 1909. In 1909 an entirely new model was prepared for this denomination. The variety thus created has been called the Broad Leaves variety because of its broad leaves with strong, detailed venation.

1909 Victoria Leaves   1909 Broad Leaves

VARIETIES 1909 (cont.)

Date and Mint Mark	Quantity Minted	G-4	VG-8	F-12	VF-20	EF-40	AU-50	MS-60	MS-63
1909 Victorian	1,697,200	6.	11.	35.	70.	165.	275.	550.	1,500.
1909 Broad	Incl. above	8.	16.	45.	90.	190.	350.	900.	2,500.
1910	4,468,331	4.	7.	16.	33.	70.	90.	200.	475.

TEN CENTS
George V 1911 - 1936

"GODLESS" OBVERSE 1911. The obverse combined with the 1911 reverse aroused criticism because it lacked reference to the king's ruling "by the grace of God." The coinage tools were modified during 1911 and a new legend containing the Latin abbreviation "DEI GRA." appeared on the 1912 and subsequent issues. The first reverse was a continuation of the Broad Leaves design introduced in 1909. It was replaced during 1913 (see below).

Designer and Modeller:
Portrait: Sir E.B. MacKennal
(B.M. on truncation);
Small Leaves Reverse:
W.H.J. Blakemore
Composition: .925 silver, .075 copper
Weight: 2.32 grams
Diameter: 18.03 mm
Edge: Reeded
Die Axis: ↑↑

Date and Mint Mark	Quantity Minted	G-4	VG-8	F-12	VF-20	EF-40	AU-50	MS-60	MS-63
1911	2,737,584	4.	10.	20.	35.	75.	110.	165.	275.

MODIFIED OBVERSE LEGEND 1912-1936

Composition: .925 silver, .075 copper
(1912-1919);
.800 silver, .200 copper
(1920-1936)
The physical specifications are as for the 1911 issue.

Date and Mint Mark	Quantity Minted	VG-8	F-12	VF-20	EF-40	AU-50	MS-60	MS-63
1912	2,234,557	3.	6.	13.	55.	120.	300.	850.

VARIETIES 1913. The reverse that replaced the Broad Leaves design during 1913 has smaller leaves with less venation. It is from a completely new model.

1913 Broad Leaves   1913 Small Leaves

Date and Mint Mark	Quantity Minted	G-4	VG-8	F-12	VF-20	EF-40	AU-50	MS-60	MS-63
1913 Small	3,613,937	–	3.	4.	12.	40.	100.	185.	550.
1913 Broad	Incl. above	100.	175.	325.	650.	1,750.	4,500.	7,000.	17,500.
1914	2,549,811	–	3.	4.	12.	40.	100.	185.	750.
1915	688,057	–	13.	22.	55.	175.	325.	500.	1,000.
1916	4,218,114	–	2.	3.	11.	30.	75.	125.	350.
1917	5,011,988	–	1.	3.	6.	22.	55.	80.	150.
1918	5,133,602	–	1.	3.	6.	20.	40.	75.	125.
1919	7,877,722	–	1.	3.	6.	20.	40.	75.	125.
1920	6,305,345	–	1.	3.	6.	22.	50.	80.	175.
1921	2,469,562	–	2.	4.	11.	33.	70.	110.	400.
1928	2,458,602	–	1.	3.	6.	25.	60.	90.	225.
1929	3,253,888	–	1.	3.	6.	25.	60.	90.	190.
1930	1,831,043	–	2.	3.	7.	28.	60.	90.	190.
1931	2,067,421	–	1.	2.	6.	25.	60.	90.	190.
1932	1,154,317	–	3.	5.	17.	40.	75.	120.	225.
1933	672,368	–	4.	7.	22.	60.	110.	200.	550.
1934	409,067	–	5.	12.	40.	110.	175.	350.	575.
1935	384,056	–	5.	13.	35.	100.	175.	350.	625.
1936	2,460,871	–	2.	3.	5.	120.	55.	70.	125.

COINAGE USING GEORGE V DIES 1936. Early in 1937, while the Royal Canadian Mint was awaiting the arrival of the master tools for the new coinage for George VI, an emergency coinage of 10-cent pieces dated 1936 and from George V dies is said to have taken place. To mark the special nature of the coinage the dies bore a small raised dot on the reverse under the wreath.

Although the mintage of the 1936 dot variety is claimed to be nearly 200,000, only five examples seem to survive today. All are specimen strikes, adding to the suspicion that circulation strikes were either never produced or were all melted. No genuine circulation strike has been confirmed.

The physical and chemical specifications are as for the 1911-1936 issues.	1936 With Raised Dot Below Date, struck in 1937

Date and Mint Mark	Quantity Minted	SPECIMEN
1936 Dot	191,237	Pittman Sale 1997 – $185,000

TEN CENTS
George VI 1937 - 1952

COINAGE OF GEORGE VI 1937-1952. The new reverse design introduced in 1937 was destined to become one of the most loved and most controversial of Canada's coinage designs. It features a "fishing schooner under sail," as the official proclamation states. Proud Nova Scotians, believing the ship represents the famous fishing and racing schooner "Bluenose" have continually pressed for official acknowledgment. It was not until March 15th, 2002 that the design was officially recognized to be that of the Bluenose. Available information indicates that the designer, Emanuel Hahn, used that ship as his primary model. The original master tools for the reverse were prepared at the Paris Mint. To improve the wearing qualities of the date, larger size digits were introduced in 1938.

BUST OF GEORGE VI OBVERSE; BLUENOSE REVERSE 1937-1947. The initial obverse bore a legend containing the Latin abbreviation "ET IND: IMP:" to indicate that the King was the Emperor of India.

Designer and Modeller:
Portrait: T.H. Paget (H.P. below bust);
Reverse: Emanuel Hahn
(H above waves at left)
Composition: .800 silver, .200 copper
Weight: 2.33 grams
Diameter: 18.03 mm
Edge: Reeded
Die Axis: ↑↑

Date and Mint Mark	Quantity Minted	F-12	VF-20	EF-40	AU-50	MS-60	MS-63	MS-65
1937	2,500,095	1.	3.	4.	8.	20.	35.	175.
1938	4,197,323	2.	4.	12.	33.	70.	120.	425.
1939	5,501,748	2.	3.	9.	28.	60.	100.	400.
1940	16,526,470	1.	2.	4.	10.	25.	45.	165.
1941	8,716,386	1.	4.	10.	28.	60.	120.	425.
1942	10,214,011	1.	2.	6.	20.	45.	70.	275.
1943	21,143,229	1.	2.	5.	11.	25.	45.	150.
1944	9,383,582	1.	2.	6.	15.	35.	60.	175.
1945	10,979,570	1.	2.	5.	11.	25.	40.	125.
1946	6,300,066	1.	3.	8.	18.	45.	70.	250.
1947	4,431,926	2.	4.	10.	22.	50.	80.	250.

NOTE: Lower grade silver coins, which do not have price listings are priced based on silver bullion on the day of purchase or sale. These lower grade coins do not have a numismatic premium at this time.

MAPLE LEAF ISSUE 1947. The granting of independance to India posed a problem for the Royal Canadian Mint in the early part of 1948. The new obverse coinage tools (with the Latin phrase "ET IND: IMP:" omitted to indicate that the king was no longer the Emperor of India) would not arrive for several months, yet there was a need for all denominations of coins. The mint satisfied the demand by striking coins dated 1947 bearing the obverse with the outmoded titles. To differentiate this issue from the regular strikings of 1947, a tiny maple leaf was placed after the date.

1947 Maple Leaf Issue
struck in 1948

Date and Mint Mark	Quantity Minted	F-12	VF-20	EF-40	AU-50	MS-60	MS-63	MS-65
1947 Maple Leaf	9,638,793	1.	2.	5.	9.	20.	28.	90.

MODIFIED OBVERSE LEGEND, BLUENOSE REVERSE 1948-1952. Following the arrival of the master tools with the obverse legend omitting "ET IND: IMP:" production of the 1947 Maple Leaf coinage was suspended. For the remainder of the year coins were produced with the new obverse and the true date, 1948. This obverse was employed for the rest of the reign.

Designer and Modeller:
Obverse: T.H. Paget
Reverse: Emanuel Hahn
Composition: .800 silver, .200 copper
Weight: 2.33 grams
Diameter: 18.03 mm
Edge: Reeded
Die Axis: ↑↑

Doubled Die 1951 10¢

Date and Mint Mark	Quantity Minted	F-12	VF-20	EF-40	AU-50	MS-60	MS-63	MS-65
1948	422,741	5.	12.	25.	40.	70.	100.	350.
1949	11,336,172	1.	2.	4.	7.	15.	22.	110.
1950	17,823,075	1.	2.	3.	6.	12.	20.	100.
1951	15,079,265	1.	1.	2.	5.	9.	17.	70.
1951 DD	Incl. above	2.	4.	8.	20.	50.	–	–
1952	10,474,455	1.	1.	2.	4.	8.	12.	55.

TEN CENTS
Elizabeth II 1953 to Date

LAUREATED PORTRAIT; BLUENOSE REVERSE 1953-1964. Two obverse varieties, termed the No Shoulder Fold and the Shoulder Fold obverses, saw use during 1953 (see 1-cent Elizabeth II 1953 to date for full explanation). On heavily circulated 10-cent pieces these varieties are most easily distinguished by observing the lettering styles in the legend. The No Shoulder Fold obverse has thicker letters with more flared ends (note the ls). The use of the George VI reverse was continued.

Designer and Modeller:
Portrait: Mrs. Mary Gillick
(M.G. on truncation)
Engraver: No Shoulder Fold Obverse:
Thomas Shingles, using the Gillick
portrait model;
Shoulder Fold Obverse:
Thomas Shingles, modifying existing
NSF coinage tools
Composition: .800 silver, .200 copper
Weight: 2.33 grams
Diameter: 18.03 mm
Edge: Reeded
Die Axis: ↑↑

No Shoulder Fold Obverse
1953, note the flared ends
of the letters.

Shoulder Fold Obverse
1953-1954, the ends of the
letters are not as flared.

Date and Mint Mark	Quantity Minted	EF-40	AU-50	MS-60	MS-63	MS-64	MS-65
1953 NSF	17,706,395	1.50	2.00	6.00	12.00	30.00	60.00
1953 SF	Incl. above	2.00	3.00	10.00	20.00	50.00	100.00
1954	4,493,150	3.00	5.00	15.00	30.00	75.00	150.00
1955	12,237,294	1.50	2.50	5.00	10.00	25.00	60.00
1956	16,732,844	1.50	2.50	5.00	10.00	25.00	50.00
1957	16,110,229	1.00	2.00	5.00	10.00	25.00	50.00
1958	10,621,236	1.00	2.00	5.00	10.00	25.00	50.00
1959	19,691,433	–	–	1.50	3.00	6.00	15.00
1960	45,466,835	–	–	1.50	3.00	6.00	15.00
1961	26,850,859	–	–	1.50	3.00	6.00	15.00
1962	41,864,335	–	–	1.50	3.00	6.00	15.00
1963	41,916,208	–	–	1.50	3.00	6.00	15.00
1964	49,518,549	–	–	1.50	3.00	6.00	15.00

TIARA PORTRAIT; BLUENOSE REVERSE 1965-1966. A new obverse with the Queen showing
more mature facial features and wearing a tiara was introduced on all denominations in 1965.

Designer and Modeller:
    Obverse: Arnold Machin
    Reverse: Emanuel Hahn
Composition: .800 silver, .200 copper
Weight: 2.33 grams
Diameter: 18.03 mm
Edge: Reeded
Die Axis: ↑↑

Date and Mint Mark	Quantity Minted	MS-60	MS-63	MS-64	MS-65
1965	55,965,392	1.00	3.00	7.50	15.00
1966	34,330,199	1.00	2.00	7.50	15.00

COMMEMORATIVE FOR CENTENNIAL OF CONFEDERATION 1967. A reverse design showing a mackerel was chosen as part of the group of commemorative designs for the centennial of Confederation. During the year, the rising price of silver forced a reduction in the silver content to .500 from .800. The two varieties are not distinguishable by eye. The obverse is the same as on the 1965-1966 issues.

Designer and Modeller:
　　Obverse: Arnold Machin
　　Reverse: Alex Colville, Myron Cook
Composition: .800 silver, .200 copper
　　　　　　　　　.500 silver, .500 copper
Weight: 2.33 grams
Diameter: 18.03 mm
Edge: Reeded
Die Axis: ↑↑

Date and Mint Mark	Quantity Minted	MS-60	MS-63	MS-64	MS-65
1967 .800 silver	32,309,135	1.00	3.00	7.50	15.00
1967 .500 silver	30,689,080	1.00	3.00	7.50	15.00

TIARA PORTRAIT; BLUENOSE REVERSE RESUMED 1968. During 1968 the use of silver in circulation coins was discontinued. Nickel was used in its place. The nickel coins are darker and are attracted to a magnet. In addition about half of the 1968 nickel 10-cent pieces were coined at the Philadelphia Mint in the United States because of the pressure of other work at the Royal Canadian Mint. The Philadelphia and Ottawa issues differ only in the number and shape of the grooves in the edge of the coins; the grooves have square bottoms on the Philadelphia coins and V-shaped bottoms on the Ottawa strikings.

Designer and Modeller:
　　Obverse: Arnold Machin
　　Reverse: Emanuel Hahn
Composition: .500 silver, .500 copper
　　　　　　　　　1.00 nickel
Weight: 2.33 gms silver, 2.07 gms nickel
Diameter: 18.03 mm
Thickness: 1.16 mm
Edge: Reeded
Die Axis: ↑↑

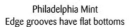

Philadelphia Mint　　　　　　　　　Royal Canadian Mint
Edge grooves have flat bottoms　　Edge grooves have V-shaped bottoms

Date and Mint Mark	Quantity Minted	MS-60	MS-63	MS-64	MS-65
1968 .500 silver	70,460,000	1.00	3.00	7.50	15.00
1968 Nickel, Philadelphia Mint	85,170,000	.50	1.50	3.00	7.50
1968 Nickel, Ottawa Mint	87,412,930	.50	1.50	3.00	7.50

NOTE: Lower grade silver coins, which do not have price listings, will have their value based on silver bullion on the day of purchase or sale. These lower grade coins do not have a numismatic premium at this time.

MODIFIED BLUENOSE REVERSE 1969. The 1969 Large Schooner-Large Date design is a rare variety. A small quantity was struck early in the year before it was discovered that the original designs had deteriorated so much that it was no longer useable. A completely new model with a noticeably smaller schooner and small date replaced the original master matrix in early 1969. The obverse is as on the 1965-1968 issues.

Designer and Modeller:
  Obverse: Arnold Machin
  Reverse: Emanuel Hahn
           Myron Cook
Composition: 1.00 nickel
Weight: 2.07 grams
Diameter: 18.03 mm
Edge: Reeded
Die Axis: ↑↑

NOTE: As of this edition only five examples of this extremely rare variety are known.

    1969 Large Date   1969 Small Date

Date and Mint Mark	Quantity Minted	VF-20	EF-40	AU-50	MS-60	MS-63	MS-64	MS-65
1969 Large Date	Incl. below	10,000.	15,000.	20,000.	–	–	–	–
1969 Small Date	55,833,929	–	–	–	.50	1.50	3.00	7.50

TIARA PORTRAIT, BLUENOSE REVERSE RESUMED 1968; 1970 - 1978.

Date and Mint Mark	Quantity Minted	MS-60	MS-63	MS-64	MS-65
1970	5,249,296	.50	1.50	3.00	7.50
1971	41,016,968	.50	1.50	3.00	7.50
1972	60,169,387	.50	1.50	3.00	7.50
1973	167,715,435	.50	1.50	3.00	7.50
1974	201,566,565	.50	1.50	3.00	7.50
1975	207,680,000	.50	1.50	3.00	7.50
1976	94,724,000	.50	1.50	3.00	7.50
1977	128,056,000	.50	1.50	3.00	7.50
1978	170,366,431	.50	1.50	3.00	7.50

MODIFIED TIARA PORTRAIT; BLUENOSE REVERSE 1979-1989. With the 1979 issue a general standardization of the coinage was started. The portrait of the Queen was reduced to make it proportional to the diameter of the coin, regardless of the denomination. In the general make over the type style came under review, with a finer style being selected.

Designer and Modeller:
  Obverse: Arnold Machin, Walter Ott
  Reverse: Emanuel Hahn,
Composition: 1.00 nickel
Weight: 2.07 grams
Diameter: 18.03 mm
Edge: Reeded
Die Axis: ↑↑

1980 Wide 0   1980 Narrow 0

Date and Mint Mark	Quantity Minted	MS-60	MS-63	MS-64	MS-65
1979	236,910,479	.50	1.50	3.00	7.50
1980 Wide	169,910,479	2.00	5.00	10.00	25.00
1980 Narrow	Incl. above	.50	1.50	3.00	7.50
1981	123,912,900	.50	1.50	3.00	7.50
1982	93,960,898	.50	1.50	3.00	7.50
1983	111,501,710	.50	1.50	3.00	7.50
1984	119,080,000	.50	1.50	3.00	7.50
1985	142,800,000	.50	1.50	3.00	7.50
1986	168,620,000	.50	1.50	3.00	7.50
1987	147,309,000	.50	1.50	3.00	7.50
1988	162,998,558	.50	1.50	3.00	7.50
1989	198,693,414	.50	1.50	3.00	7.50

CROWNED PORTRAIT; BLUENOSE REVERSE 1990-1991. A new obverse portrait of the Queen wearing a diamond diadem and jewellery was introduced on all denominations in 1990.

Designer and Modeller:
  Obverse: Dora de Pédery-Hunt
       Ago Aarand
  Reverse: Emanuel Hahn
Composition: Nickel
Weight: 2.07 grams
Diameter: 18.03 mm
Edge: Reeded
Die Axis: ↑↑

Date and Mint Mark	Quantity Minted	MS-60	MS-63	MS-64	MS-65
1990	65,023,000	.50	1.50	3.00	7.50
1991	50,397,000	.50	1.50	3.00	7.50

COMMEMORATIVE FOR THE 125TH ANNIVERSARY 1867-1992. The reverse design was modified to include the bracket dates 1867-1992 for the 125th birthday of Canada.

Designer, modeller, chemical and physical specifications are the same as for the 1990 issues.

Date and Mint Mark	Quantity Minted	MS-60	MS-63	MS-64	MS-65
1992	174,476,000	.50	1.50	3.00	7.50

CROWNED PORTRAIT; BLUENOSE REVERSE 1993-2000. In 1993 the practice of using a single date was resumed. The transition to beads from rim denticles which began in 1982 on the one-cent piece, was completed on the ten-cent piece in 1993. The Winnipeg Mint Mark (W) is found only on coins from the "Oh! Canada" and "Tiny Treasures" sets issued by the Numismatic department of the Mint and these are covered in the collector sets.

Designer, modeller and physical specifications are the same as for the 1990 issues.

Date and Mint Mark	Quantity Minted	MS-60	MS-63	MS-64	MS-65
1993	135,569,000	.50	1.50	3.00	7.50
1994	145,800,000	.50	1.50	3.00	7.50
1995	123,875,000	.50	1.50	3.00	7.50
1996	51,814,000	.50	1.50	3.00	7.50
1997	43,126,000	.50	1.50	3.00	7.50
1998	203,514,000	.50	1.50	3.00	7.50
1999	258,462,000	.50	1.50	3.00	7.50
2000	159,125,000	.50	1.50	3.00	7.50

CROWNED PORTRAIT; BLUENOSE REVERSE; MULTI-PLY PLATED STEEL 1999-2001. In 2001 the Royal Canadian Mint began issuing circulating coinage struck from their new multi-ply plated steel blanks. The process is acid based and electroplates a thin coating of nickel, then copper, then nickel again onto a steel core. Prior to 2001, "P" coinage was only issued to the vending industry for testing purposes. The scarce 2000P ten-cents originated from this source.

Designer and Modeller:
Obverse: Dora de Pédery-Hunt
        Ago Aarand
Reverse: Emanuel Hahn
Composition: Multi-Ply Plated steel;
        .920 steel, .055 copper,
        .025 nickel
Weight: 1.75 grams
Diameter: 18.03 mm
Thickness: 1.22 mm
Edge: Serrated
Die Axis: ↑↑

CROWNED PORTRAIT; BLUENOSE REVERSE; MULTI-PLY PLATED STEEL (cont.)

Date and Mint Mark	Quantity Minted	MS-60	MS-63	MS-64	MS-65
1999P	Not issued for circulation	–	–	–	–
2000P	Not issued for circulation	–	–	–	–
2001P	270,792,000	.50	1.50	3.00	7.50

INTERNATIONAL YEAR OF THE VOLUNTEER 2001. Issued for circulation in multi-ply plated steel to commemorate the 7.5 million Canadian volunteers who work towards making this country a better place for all. The Volunteer ten cents was also issued in sterling silver: see page 232.

Designers:
　　Obverse: Dora de Pédery-Hunt
　　Reverse: RCM Design
Modellers:
　　Obverse: Dora de Pédery-Hunt
　　Reverse: Stanley Witten

Chemical and physical specifications are the same as for the 1999P issue.

Date and Mint Mark	Quantity Minted	MS-60	MS-63	MS-64	MS-65
2001P	224,526,000	.50	1.50	3.00	7.50

ELIZABETH II GOLDEN JUBILEE 1952-2002. To commemorate the 50th anniversary of the reign of Queen Elizabeth II, all circulating coinage carried the double dates of her reign, 1952-2002, on the obverse. 2002 is also the year that the Royal Canadian Mint officially recognized the schooner that has graced the reverse of the Canadian ten cent coin since 1937 (except for 1967 and 2001) as the Bluenose.

Designers, modellers, chemical and physical specifications are the same as for the 1999P issue.

Date and Mint Mark	Quantity Minted	MS-60	MS-63	MS-64	MS-65
1952-2002P	251,278,000	.50	1.50	3.00	7.50

CROWNED PORTRAIT; BLUENOSE REVERSE 2003.

Designers, modellers, chemical and physical specifications are the same as for the 1999P issue.

Date and Mint Mark	Quantity Minted	MS-60	MS-63	MS-64	MS-65
2003P	N/A	.50	1.50	3.00	7.50
2004P	N/A	.50	1.50	3.00	7.50

TWENTY-FIVE CENTS
Victoria 1870 - 1901

The Province of Canada did not issue this denomination so new coinage tools were required for the Dominion of Canada issue. During Victoria's reign, five obverse and two reverse device varieties were employed. A detailed description of the obverse and listing by year follow on the next two pages. The basic design for the reverse is the same as all other silver denominations: crossed boughs of sweet maple, tied at the bottom by a ribbon and surmounted by St. Edward's crown.

Designer, Modeller and Engraver:
  Leonard C. Wyon
Composition: .925 silver, .075 copper
Weight: 5.81 grams
Diameter: 23.62 mm
Edge: Reeded
Die Axis: ↑↓

Heaton Mint issues of 1871-1883 and the Mint, Birmingham issue of 1890 have an "H" mint mark on the reverse under the wreath. London Mint strikings have no letter.

Date, Mint Portrait	Quantity Minted	G-4	VG-8	F-12	VF-20	EF-40	AU-50	MS-60	MS-63
1870-Q1	900,000	18.	33.	70.	165.	325.	450.	1,000.	3,000.
1870-Q2	Incl. above				Very Rare				
1871-Q1	400,000	30.	50.	100.	300.	550.	750.	1,500.	4,750.
1871-Q2	Incl. above	22.	38.	80.	225.	450.	650.	1,250.	4,000.
1871H-Q1	748,000	40.	60.	120.	325.	550.	750.	1,400.	3,000.
1871H-Q2	Incl. above	28.	45.	90.	275.	475.	675.	1,100.	2,500.
1872H-Q1	2,240,000				Very Rare				
1872H-Q2	Incl. above	11.	22.	30.	65.	175.	325.	900.	3,000.
1874H-Q2	1,600,000	11.	22.	30.	65.	175.	300.	550.	1,750.
1875H-Q2	1,000,000	300.	500.	1,100.	2,750.	5,000.	9,000.	–	–

VARIETIES 1880H AND 1885. Two styles of 0 were utilized for dating the dies for the 1880 issue of the denomination. Both the Narrow 0 and the Wide 0 occur alone, but in addition there is a scarce variety with the Narrow 0 punched over the Wide 0. The narrow over the wide O is difficult to identify in worn condition.

1880H Wide 0	Narrow 0 over wide 0	1880H Narrow 0

VICTORIA OBVERSE PORTRAIT VARIETIES

TWENTY-FIVE CENTS – Q

PORTRAIT: Q1
Two waves meet slightly below the crown
at top of brow.

Q1 is found on the following dates:
1870; 1871; 1871H; 1872H

PORTRAIT: Q2
A wave, which breaks into three, joins the
brow slightly below the crown.

Q2 will be found on the following dates:
1870; 1871; 1871H; 1872H; 1874H;
1875H; 1880H (all varieties); 1881H;
1885 (all varieties); 1886; 1886 6/3

PORTRAIT: Q3
A single wave of hair and crown meet at
top of brow.

Q3 will be found on the following date:
1882H.

VICTORIA OBVERSE PORTRAIT VARIETIES

TWENTY-FIVE CENTS – Q

PORTRAIT: Q4
Crown sits on a good strand of hair at top of brow.

Q4 will be found on the following dates:
1883H; 1886 6/6

PORTRAIT: Q5
No hair on brow beneath crown. Three waves to crown back from top of brow.

Q5 will be found on the following dates:
1886 N8; 1886 W8; 1887; 1888 N8;
1888 W8; 1889; 1890H; 1891; 1892;
1893; 1894; 1899; 1900; 1901

VARIETIES 1880H and 1885 (cont.)

 1885 Curved top 5

 1885 Re-engraved Straight top 5

Date, Mint Portrait	Quantity Minted	G-4	VG-8	F-12	VF-20	EF-40	AU-50	MS-60	MS-63
1880H W0-Q2	400,000	135.	275.	500.	900.	2,000.	3,000.	4,500.	–
1880H N/W-Q2	Incl. above	65.	135.	275.	550.	1,000.	1,350.	3,000.	10,000.
1880H N0-Q2	Incl. above	45.	85.	200.	500.	850.	1,100.	1,500.	4,500.
1881H-Q2	820,000	20.	40.	90.	200.	500.	750.	1,750.	5,000.
1882H-Q3	600,000	22.	45.	110.	225.	500.	850.	1,750.	4,500.
1883H-Q4	960,000	12.	33.	70.	150.	350.	500.	800.	2,250.
1885-Q2	192,000	120.	225.	425.	900.	2,000.	2,750.	5,000.	15,000.
1885 RED-Q2	Incl. above	120.	225.	425.	900.	2,000.	2,750.	5,000.	15,000.

1886 6/3

1886 6/6

1886 Narrow 8   1886 Wide 8

VARIETIES 1886.
A very interesting and long unrecognized overdate occurs on the 1886 25-cents. The overdate 1886/3 seems unlikely in view of the fact that the 1885 date came in between and the 1883 coins were all produced at The Mint, Birmingham with the H mint mark; however, in an article it is proved conclusively that the overdate here illustrated is indeed 6/3.

Another 1886 variety has surfaced which appears to be a repunched six. The six used for repunching is slightly smaller than the original 6.

Date, Mint Portrait	Quantity Minted	G-4	VG-8	F-12	VF-20	EF-40	AU-50	MS-60	MS-63
1886-Q2	540,000	22.	40.	85.	200.	550.	1,000.	1,750.	5,500.
1886, 6/3-Q2	Incl. above	30.	55.	135.	250.	650.	1,200.	2,000.	5,500.
1886, 6/6-Q4	Incl. above	40.	70.	175.	350.	800.	1,500.	–	–
1886, N8-Q5	Incl. above	22.	40.	85.	200.	550.	1,000.	1,750.	5,500.
1886, W8-Q5	Incl. above	22.	40.	85.	200.	550.	1,000.	1,750.	5,500.
1887-Q5	100,000	110.	225.	450.	900.	2,250.	4,000.	9,000.	–
1888, N8-Q5	400,000	13.	33.	65.	150.	350.	550.	900.	3,250.
1888, W8-Q5	Incl. above	13.	33.	65.	150.	350.	550.	900.	3,250.
1889-Q5	66,340	125.	225.	500.	1,100.	2,000.	3,000.	6,500.	25,000.
1890H-Q5	200,000	22.	45.	90.	250.	500.	800.	1,750.	4,000.
1891-Q5	120,000	65.	120.	275.	600.	1,000.	1,400.	2,000.	4,000.
1892-Q5	510,000	13.	30.	60.	135.	350.	500.	1,100.	3,750.
1893-Q5	100,000	90.	225.	375.	700.	1,200.	1,750.	2,250.	4,000.
1894-Q5	220,000	20.	50.	90.	250.	450.	650.	1,000.	2,000.
1899-Q5	415,580	11.	20.	40.	90.	275.	450.	800.	2,250.
1900-Q5	1,320,000	10.	18.	33.	85.	225.	300.	650.	2,000.
1901-Q5	640,000	10.	18.	33.	85.	225.	325.	700.	2,000.

TWENTY-FIVE CENTS
Edward VII 1902-1910

SMALL CROWN REVERSE 1902-1905. The initial reverse for the Edward VII coins of this denomination has an almost unaltered wreath from the Victorian issues coupled with a small Imperial State crown and a new legend containing "CANADA" (it was formerly on the obverse).

Designer and Modeller:
  Obverse: G.W. DeSaulles
  (DES. under the bust)
Engraver: Small Crown reverse:
  G.W. DeSaulles
Composition: .925 silver, .075 copper
Weight: 5.81 grams
Diameter: 23.62 mm
Edge: Reeded
Die Axis: ↑↓

The Mint, Birmingham issue of 1902 has an "H" mint mark on the reverse under the wreath. London Mint issues have no letter.

Date and Mint Mark	Quantity Minted	VG-8	F-12	VF-20	EF-40	AU-50	MS-60	MS-63
1902	464,000	20.	45.	110.	350.	500.	1,100.	3,250.
1902H	800,000	15.	28.	90.	200.	250.	325.	600.
1903	846,150	22.	45.	110.	350.	475.	1,100.	3,500.
1904	400,000	38.	85.	275.	700.	1,200.	2,500.	7,500.
1905	800,000	25.	50.	200.	600.	1,200.	2,500.	6,500.

LARGE CROWN REVERSE 1906-1910. The reverse for the 1906 coinage was modified to improve die life and impart a better overall appearance to the coins. The wreath was extensively retouched and a larger crown was placed at the top.

Engraver: Reverse: W.H.J. Blackmore
Weight: 5.81 grams (1906-1910);
  5.83 grams (1910)
Die Axis: ↑↓
  ↑↑ (1908-1910)

The other specifications are as for the 1902-1905 issues.

Small Crown

Large Crown

LARGE CROWN REVERSE 1906-1910.

Date and Mint Mark	Quantity Minted	VG-8	F-12	VF-20	EF-40	AU-50	MS-60	MS-63
1906 Sm. Cr.	Included	3,500.	5,500.	6,500.	7,500.	9,000.	12,000.	—
1906 Lg. Cr.	237,843	23.	40.	100.	325.	500.	750.	3,000.
1907	2,088,000	15.	30.	90.	275.	325.	600.	1,600.
1908	495,016	25.	55.	150.	400.	500.	500.	1,000.
1909	1,335,929	20.	45.	125.	400.	600.	1,100.	3,000.
1910	3,577,569	15.	30.	90.	200.	275.	400.	1,100.

TWENTY - FIVE CENTS
George V 1911 - 1936

"GODLESS" OBVERSE 1911. The obverse issued on the 1911 coins provoked public outcry because it lacked reference to the King's ruling "by the grace of God." The coinage tools were modified during the year and a new legend including the Latin abbreviation "DEI GRA:" appeared on the 1912 and subsequent issues. The reverse was a continuation of the Large Crown variety of Edward VII.

Designer and Modeller:
　　Portrait: Sir E.B. MacKennal
　　(B.M. on truncation)
Composition: .925 silver, .075 copper
Weight: 5.83 grams
Diameter: 23.62 mm
Edge: Reeded
Die Axis: ↑↑

Date and Mint Mark	Quantity Minted	VG-8	F-12	VF-20	EF-40	AU-50	MS-60	MS-63
1911	1,721,341	15.	33.	70.	165.	190.	375.	550.

MODIFIED OBVERSE LEGEND 1912-1936

Composition: .925 silver, .075 copper
　　　　　　　　(1912-1919)
　　　　　　　　.800 silver, .200 copper
　　　　　　　　(1920-1936)

The physical specifications are as for the 1911 issue.

Date and Mint Mark	Quantity Minted	VG-8	F-12	VF-20	EF-40	AU-50	MS-60	MS-63
1912	2,544,199	5.	9.	30.	75.	200.	550.	1,750.
1913	2,213,595	5.	9.	30.	75.	175.	475.	1,500.
1914	1,215,397	6.	11.	40.	110.	300.	900.	2,750.
1915	242,382	25.	60.	275.	700.	1,750.	3,250.	8,500.
1916	1,462,566	5.	9.	30.	70.	110.	275.	850.
1917	3,365,644	4.	7.	25.	40.	70.	175.	300.
1918	4,175,649	4.	7.	18.	35.	55.	125.	300.
1919	5,852,262*	4.	7.	18.	35.	55.	150.	300.
1920	1,975,278	5.	10.	25.	60.	100.	225.	525.
1921	597,337	20.	50.	150.	350.	800.	1,650.	4,750.
1927	468,096	40.	65.	190.	325.	575.	900.	2,000.
1928	2,114,178	4.	7.	28.	65.	80.	225.	500.

MODIFIED OBVERSE LEGEND 1912-1936 (cont.)

Date and Mint Mark	Quantity Minted	VG-8	F-12	VF-20	EF-40	AU-50	MS-60	MS-63
1929	2,690,562	4.	7.	28.	65.	80.	225.	500.
1930	968,748	4.	8.	33.	75.	110.	300.	675.
1931	537,815	4.	8.	40.	80.	120.	325.	725.
1932	537,994	6.	12.	40.	85.	135.	325.	900.
1933	421,282	6.	12.	50.	110.	135.	275.	400.
1934	384,350	6.	15.	55.	120.	175.	300.	675.
1935	537,772	6.	13.	40.	110.	150.	225.	375.
1936	1,125,779	4.	6.	20.	40.	55.	125.	300.

Note: *51,494 25¢ pieces, .925 fine and presumably all dated 1919, were melted in 1920.

COINAGE USING GEORGE V DIES 1936. Early in 1937, while the Royal Canadian Mint was awaiting the arrival of the master tools for the new coinage for George VI, an emergency issue of 25-cent pieces occurred to satisfy urgent demands for this denomination. To mark the special nature of the coinage the dies bore a small raised dot on the reverse under the wreath. That such an emergency issue even took place was generally not known until 1940, when collectors began noticing that some of the 25-cent pieces dated 1936 had a dot under the wreath. It was learned that supposedly 1- and 10-cent pieces were issued also, but no circulated examples of the two latter denominations have been proved genuine.

Physical specifications are as the 1911 issues
Chemical specifications are as the 1920 issues.

1936 With raised dot below
date struck in 1937.

Date and Mint Mark	Quantity Minted	VG-8	F-12	VF-20	EF-40	AU-50	MS-60	MS-63
1936 Dot	Incl. above	45.	100.	275.	500.	675.	1,250.	3,250.

TWENTY-FIVE CENTS
George VI 1937 - 1952

COINAGE OF GEORGE VI 1937-1952. The design chosen for the reverse of the new George VI coinage in 1937 was Emanuel Hahn's caribou head. This design was part of the government's program of modernizing the coinage. The original master tools were prepared at the Paris Mint because of a heavy work load at the Royal Mint in London at that time.

"ET IND: IMP:" IN OBVERSE LEGEND; CARIBOU REVERSE 1937-1947. The initial obverse bore a legend containing an abbreviation for the Latin phrase, "ET INDIAE IMPERATOR"' meaning "and Emperor of India," referring to the fact that the British monarch had held that position since Queen Victoria was made Empress of India in 1876.

Designer and Modeller:
  Portrait: T.H. Paget (H.P. below bust)
  Reverse: Emanuel Hahn (H in front
    of caribou's neck at bottom)
Composition: .800 silver, .200 copper
Weight: 5.83 grams
Diameter: 23.62 mm
Edge: Reeded
Die Axis: ↑↑

Date and Mint Mark	Quantity Minted	F-12	VF-20	EF-40	AU-50	MS-60	MS-63	MS-65
1937	2,689,813	2.	5.	7.	11.	25.	50.	250.
1938	3,149,245	2.	7.	11.	33.	90.	175.	750.
1939	3,532,495	2.	5.	10.	28.	80.	150.	600.
1940	9,583,650	2.	4.	6.	10.	30.	45.	225.
1941	6,654,672	2.	4.	6.	10.	35.	50.	200.
1942	6,935,871	2.	4.	6.	10.	35.	50.	250.
1943	13,559,575	2.	4.	6.	10.	30.	50.	275.
1944	7,216,237	2.	4.	6.	11.	40.	60.	250.
1945	5,296,495	2.	4.	6.	10.	28.	50.	250.
1946	2,210,810	2.	12.	22.	55.	80.	120.	300.
1947	1,524,554	2.	12.	22.	55.	70.	135.	325.

MAPLE LEAF ISSUE 1947. In early 1948 the Royal Canadian Mint was faced with a problem resulting from India's recent independence. The new obverse coinage tools, with the Latin abbreviation "ET IND: IMP." omitted to indicate that the King's titles had changed, would not arrive for several months, yet there was a great need for all denominations of coins. The mint satisfied the demand by striking coins dated 1947 and bearing outmoded titles on the obverse. To distinguish this issue from the regular strikings of 1947, a tiny maple leaf was placed after the date.

1947 Maple Leaf Issue
struck in 1948

Date and Mint Mark	Quantity Minted	F-12	VF-20	EF-40	AU-50	MS-60	MS-63	MS-65
1947 Maple Leaf	4,393,938	2.	4.	6.	10.	22.	45.	135.
1947 Dot		60.	90.	165.	225.	350.	700.	1,500.

MODIFIED OBVERSE LEGEND 1948-1952. Following the arrival of the master tools with the new obverse legend lacking "ET IND: IMP:" in 1948, production of the 1947 Maple Leaf coinage was suspended. For the remainder of the year coins were produced with the new obverse and the true date, 1948.

Designer and Modeller:
Portrait: T.H. Paget (H.P. below bust)
Reverse: Emanuel Hahn (H in front of caribou's neck at bottom)
Composition: .800 silver, .200 copper
Weight: 5.83 grams
Diameter: 23.62 mm
Edge: Reeded
Die Axis: ↑↑

Date and Mint Mark	Quantity Minted	F-12	VF-20	EF-40	AU-50	MS-60	MS-63	MS-65
1948	2,564,424	3.	6.	9.	22.	75.	150.	375.
1949	7,988,830	–	3.	4.	8.	18.	35.	200.
1950	9,673,335	–	3.	4.	6.	15.	25.	175.

VARIETIES 1951-1952. In an attempt to improve the appearance of the obverse of this denomination a fresh reduction was made to produce an obverse with a slightly larger, lower relief portrait. Both varieties were used in 1951 and 1952. Aside from the difference in relief and the size of the portrait, the two varieties can be distinguished by the lettering. The High Relief variety has a plain lettering style in the legend, and the first "A" in "GRATIA" points to a rim denticle. On the Low Relief variety the letters are more flared and the first "A" in "GRATIA" points between rim denticles.

High Relief Obverse

Low Relief Obverse

Date and Mint Mark	Quantity Minted	VF-20	EF-40	AU-50	MS-60	MS-63	MS-65
1951 Low Relief	8,290,719	30.	60.	90.	140.	175.	350.
1951 High Relief	Incl. above	3.	4.	6.	11.	20.	125.
1952 Low Relief	8,859,642	3.	4.	6.	11.	20.	125.
1952 High Relief	Incl. above	12.	20.	30.	55.	100.	250.

TWENTY-FIVE CENTS
Elizabeth II 1953 to Date

LAUREATED PORTRAIT 1953-1964. Two obverse varieties, called the No Shoulder Fold and Shoulder Fold obverses, saw use during 1953 (see 1-cent Elizabeth II, 1953 to date for full explanation). On the 25-cents these obverses are combined with reverses that are readily distinguishable. The No Shoulder Fold obverse comes with a Large Date reverse (carried over from George VI) and the Shoulder Fold was used with a Small Date reverse.

1953 No Shoulder Fold Obverse, Large Date Reverse

Designer and Modeller:
Portrait: Mrs. Mary Gillick
(M.G. on truncation);
Small Date Reverse: Thomas
Shingles, modifying existing models
Engraver: No Shoulder Fold Obverse:
Thomas Shingles, using the Gillick
portrait model;
Shoulder Fold Obverse:
Thomas Shingles, modifying existing
NSF coinage tools
Composition: .800 silver, .200 copper
Weight: 5.83 grams
Diameter: 23.62 mm (1953 large date);
23.88 mm (1953 small date/64)
Edge: Reeded
Die Axis: ↑↑

1953 Shoulder Fold Obverse
Small Date Reverse

Date and Mint Mark	Quantity Minted	VF-20	EF-40	AU-50	MS-60	MS-63	MS-64	MS-65
1953 LD, NSF	10,456,769	3.	8.	12.	30.	50.	80.	175.
1953 SD, SF	Incl. above	3.	4.	8.	20.	40.	100.	200.
1954	2,318,891	4.	11.	20.	40.	65.	175.	350.
1955	9,552,505	–	–	4.	10.	25.	75.	150.
1956	11,269,353	–	–	4.	6.	20.	65.	125.
1957	12,770,190	–	–	3.	5.	20.	55.	100.
1958	9,336,910	–	–	3.	5.	20.	50.	100.
1959	13,503,461	–	–	3.	5.	10.	30.	75.
1960	22,835,327	–	–	–	5.	10.	30.	75.
1961	18,164,368	–	–	–	5.	10.	30.	75.
1962	29,559,266	–	–	–	5.	10.	30.	75.
1963	21,180,642	–	–	–	5.	10.	30.	75.
1964	36,479,343	–	–	–	5.	10.	30.	75.

TIARA PORTRAIT; CARIBOU REVERSE 1965-1966. A new obverse with the Queen showing more mature facial features and wearing a tiara was introduced on all denominations in 1965.

Designer and Modeller:
Portrait: Arnold Machin

The physical and chemical specifications are as for the 1954-1964 issues.

Date and Mint Mark	Quantity Minted		MS-60	MS-63	MS-64	MS-65
1965	44,708,869		2.	6.	30.	100.
1966	25,388,892		2.	6.	30.	100.

COMMEMORATIVE FOR CENTENNIAL OF CONFEDERATION 1967. A reverse design featuring a walking wildcat (bobcat) was selected as part of the commemorative set of coins for this year. During the year, the rising price of silver entailed reducing the silver content from .800 to .500. The two varieties are not distinguishable by eye.

Designer: Reverse: Alex Colville
Modeller: Reverse: Myron Cook
Composition: .800 silver, .200 copper or
.500 silver, .500 copper
The other physical specifications are as for the 1954-1964 issues.

Date and Mint Mark	Quantity Minted		MS-60	MS-63	MS-64	MS-65
1967 .800 silver	48,855,500		2.	6.	30.	100.
1967 .500 silver	Incl. above		2.	6.	30.	100.

CARIBOU REVERSE RESUMED 1968-1972. During the 1968 coining it was necessary to discontinue the use of silver and substitute nickel for it. Nickel coins are darker in colour and are attracted to a magnet.

Designer and Modeller:
Portrait: Arnold Machin
Composition: 1968: .500 silver,
.500 copper
1968-1972: 1.00 nickel
Weight: Silver: 5.83 grams
Nickel: 5.07 grams
Diameter: 23.88 mm
Edge: Reeded
Die Axis: ↑↑

Date and Mint Mark	Quantity Minted		MS-60	MS-63	MS-64	MS-65
1968 .500 Silver	71,464,000		2.	8.	35.	75.
1968 Nickel	88,686,931		1.	2.	4.	10.
1969	133,037,929		1.	2.	4.	10.
1970	10,302,010		2.	4.	8.	20.
1971	48,170,428		1.	2.	4.	10.
1972	43,743,387		1.	2.	4.	10.

COMMEMORATING THE CENTENNIAL OF THE FOUNDING OF THE R.C.M.P. 1973. The special reverse on the 1973 25-cent piece commemorates the centennial of the founding of the North West Mounted Police, which later became the Royal Canadian Mounted Police. A new obverse with a smaller, more detailed portrait and fewer rim denticles placed farther from the rim was prepared for use with the commemorative reverse. However, a small quantity of coins was struck with the 1972 obverse, creating two varieties for the year. The quantity of the Large Bust variety struck for circulation is believed not to exceed 10,000.

Designer: Reverse: Paul Cedarberg
(PC behind horse)
Modeller: Small Bust Obverse:
Patrick Brindley, modifying the
existing Machin Portrait
Reverse: Walter Ott

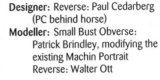

Chemical and physical specifications
as are for the 1968 nickel issue.

Small Bust   Large bust

Date and Mint Mark	Quantity Minted	VF-20	EF-40	AU-50	MS-60	MS-63	MS-64	MS-65
1973 Sm. Bust	135,958,589	–	–	–	1.	2.	4.	10.
1973 Lge. Bust	Incl. above	85.	100.	150.	200.	275.	350.	750.

TIARA PORTRAIT; CARIBOU REVERSE RESUMED; 1974-1978. With the return to the caribou reverse for the 25-cent piece in 1974, the use of the Large Portrait obverse was resumed.

The physical and chemical specifications
are as for the 1968 nickel issue.

Date and Mint Mark	Quantity Minted	MS-60	MS-63	MS-64	MS-65
1974	192,360,598	1.	2.	4.	8.
1975	252,259,000	1.	2.	4.	8.
1976	86,898,261	1.	2.	4.	8.
1977	99,634,555	1.	2.	4.	8.

1978 Far Canada
148 Small Denticles

1978 Near Canada
120 Large Denticles

Date and Mint Mark	Quantity Minted	MS-60	MS-63	MS-64	MS-65
1978 Small Denticles	174,475,408	4.	8.	16.	40.
1978 Large Denticles	Incl. above	1.	2.	4.	10.

CARIBOU REVERSE; MODIFIED DESIGN 1979-1989. Beginning with the 1979 issue and as part of a general standardization of the coinage, the portrait of the Queen was reduced. The intention was to make the size of the portrait proportional to the diameter of the coin, regardless of the denomination. This obverse is not the same as that employed in connection with the 1973 R.C.M.P. commemorative.

Designer, modeller, chemical and physical specifications are as for the 1968 nickel issue.

Date and Mint Mark	Quantity Minted	MS-60	MS-63	MS-64	MS-65
1979	131,042,905	1.	2.	4.	10.
1980	76,178,000	1.	2.	4.	10.
1981	131,583,900	1.	2.	4.	10.
1982	171,926,000	1.	2.	4.	10.
1983	13,162,000	2.	4.	8.	20.
1984	119,212,000	1.	2.	4.	10.
1985	158,734,000	1.	2.	4.	10.
1986	132,220,000	1.	2.	4.	10.
1987	53,408,000	1.	2.	4.	10.
1988	80,368,473	1.	2.	4.	10.
1989	19,624,307	2.	4.	8.	20.

CROWNED PORTRAIT; CARIBOU REVERSE 1990-1991. A new obverse portrait of the Queen wearing a diamond diadem and jewellery was introduced on all denominations in 1990.

Designer and Modeller:
    Obverse: Dora de Pédery-Hunt
            Ago Aarand
    Reverse: Emanuel Hahn
Composition: 1.00 nickel
Weight: 5.05 grams
Diameter: 23.88 mm
Edge: Reeded
Die Axis: ↑↑

Date and Mint Mark	Quantity Minted	MS-60	MS-63	MS-64	MS-65
1990	31,258,000	1.	2.	4.	10.
1991	459,000	8.	15.	30.	75

Note: A potential 1991 twenty-five cent variety exists. At present they are classified as wide and narrow rim varieties. The narrow rim is the scarcer. However, there are questions as to how these varieties came about, and if they are true varieties. One school has the varieties originating from the different treatment of the planchets, while the other is based on the use of two different reverse punches.

COMMEMORATIVE FOR 125TH ANNIVERSARY 1867-1992. The reverse design was modified to include the bracket dates 1867-1992 for the 125th birthday of Canada. No 1867 - 1992 dated quarters were issued for circulation. The double dated Caribou 25-cent coins can only be found in the uncirculated, specimen, or the seven-coin proof sets, issued by the Numismatic Department of the Mint.

Designer, modeller, chemical and physical specifications are as for the 1990 and 1991 issues.

Date and Mint Mark	Quantity Minted	MS-60	MS-63	MS-64	MS-65
1992	Not issued for circulation	—	—	—	—

125TH ANNIVERSARY OF CONFEDERATION 1867-1992. During each month of 1992 the Royal Canadian Mint issued a twenty-five cent coin bearing a unique design to represent one of the twelve provinces and territories. Each coin was launched at a special event organized in the capital city of the province or territory commemorated by the design. The designs for the thirteen coins issued to celebrate the 125th birthday (a one dollar coin was issued for Canada Day 1992) were chosen by a national contest.

Designer and Modeller:
Obverse: Dora de Pédery-Hunt
Ago Aarand
Reverse: See below

Chemical and physical specifications are as for the 1990 issue (except for the New Brunswick variety with die axis ↑↓)

The obverse and physical specifications are common to all twelve coins

New Brunswick	Northwest Territories	Newfoundland	Manitoba
January 9, 1992	February 6, 1992	March 5, 1992	April 7, 1992
Ronald Lambert	Beth McEachen	Christopher Newhook	Muriel Hope
Sheldon Beveridge	A. Aarand/C. Saffioti	Sheldon Beveridge	Ago Aarand

Yukon	Alberta	Prince Edward Island	Ontario
May 7, 1992	June 4, 1992	July 7, 1992	August 6, 1992
Libby Dulac	Mel Heath	Nigel Roe	Greg Salmela
William Woodruff	William Woodruff	Sheldon Beveridge	Susan Taylor

Nova Scotia	Quebec	Saskatchewan	British Columbia
September 9, 1992	October 1, 1992	November 5, 1992	November 9, 1992
Bruce Wood	Romualdas Bukauskas	Brian Cobb	Carla Egan
Terry Smith	Stanley Witten	Terry Smith	Sheldon Beveridge

Date and Mint Mark	Description	Quantity Minted	MS-60	MS-63	MS-64	MS-65
1992	New Brunswick, Medal	2,174,000	1.00	1.50	3.00	7.50
1992	New Brunswick, Coinage	Inc. above	75.00	100.00	150.00	450.00
1992	Northwest Territories	12,580,000	1.00	1.50	3.00	7.50
1992	Newfoundland	11,405,000	1.00	1.50	3.00	7.50
1992	Manitoba	11,349,000	1.00	1.50	3.00	7.50
1992	Yukon	10,388,000	1.00	1.50	3.00	7.50
1992	Alberta	12,133,000	1.00	1.50	3.00	7.50
1992	Prince Edward Island	13,001,000	1.00	1.50	3.00	7.50
1992	Ontario	14,263,000	1.00	1.50	3.00	7.50
1992	Nova Scotia	13,600,000	1.00	1.50	3.00	7.50
1992	Quebec	13,607,000	1.00	1.50	3.00	7.50
1992	Saskatchewan	14,165,000	1.00	1.50	3.00	7.50
1992	British Columbia	14,001,000	1.00	1.50	3.00	7.50

Note: For the brilliant uncirculated nickel map set and proof silver set please see page 239.

CROWNED PORTRAIT; CARIBOU REVERSE 1993-1999. In 1993 the practice of using a single date was resumed. The transition to beads from rim denticles, which began in 1982 on the one-cent piece, was completed in 1993 by the use of beads on the twenty-five cent coin. No circulating twenty-five cent coins were minted from 1997 to 1999. The numismatic department minted, 1997 through to 1999, caribou reverse twenty-five cent coins for use in the following numismatic sets: "Oh! Canada," "Tiny Treasures" and Specimen. The Winnipeg Mint 1998W twenty-five cent coins are only found in the "Oh! Canada" and "Tiny Treasures" sets, and were not issued for general circulation.

Designer, modeller, chemical and physical specifications are as for the 1990 issue.

Date and Mint Mark	Quantity Minted	MS-60	MS-63	MS-64	MS-65
1993	73,758,000	1.	1.50	3.00	7.50
1994	77,670,000	1.	1.50	3.00	7.50
1995	89,210,000	1.	1.50	3.00	7.50
1996	28,106,000	1.	1.50	3.00	7.50
1997	Not issued for circulation	—	—	—	—
1998	Not issued for circulation	—	—	—	—
1999	Not issued for circulation	—	—	—	—

MILLENNIUM 25-CENT COINS 1999: Struck to celebrate the millennium the following series of coins reflect development, milestones, discoveries, inventions and achievements in the past millennium which helped shape today's Canada.

Designers and Modellers:
Obverse: Dora de Pédery-Hunt
Ago Aarand
Reverse: See below

Chemical and physical specifications are as for the 1990 issue.

The obverse and physical specifications are common to all twelve coins

January	February	March	April
A Country Unfolds	Etched in Stone	The Log Drive	Our Northern Heritage
P. Ka-Kin Poon	L. Springer	M. Lavoie	Ken Ojnak Ashevac
Cosme Saffioti	José Osio	Stanley Witten	Sheldon Beveridge

May	June	July	August
The Voyageurs	From Coast to Coast	A Nation of People	The Pioneer Spirit
S. Minenok	G. Ho	M. H. Sarkany	A. Botelho
William Woodruff	William Woodruff	Stanley Witten	Cosme Saffioti

September	October	November	December
Canada Through a	A Tribute to	The Air Plane	This is Canada
Child's Eye	the First Nation	Opens the North	J. L. P. Provencher
C. Bertrand	J. E. Read	B. R. Bacon	Stanley Witten
Stanley Witten	Sheldon Beveridge	Stanley Witten	

MILLENNIUM 25-CENT COINS 1999 CONTINUED. During production of this series of 25 cent coins, die deteriation appeared to be a major problem for the Mint. Design and font styles used on these quarters played an important part in the life of the die.

Date and Mint Mark	Description	Quantity Minted	MS-60	MS-63	MS-64	MS-65
1999	January, A Country Unfolds	12,238,559	2.00	3.00	6.00	15.00
1999	February, Etched in Stone	13,985,195	1.00	1.50	3.00	7.50
1999	March, The Log Drive	15,157,061	1.00	1.50	3.00	7.50
1999	April, Our Northern Heritage	15,214,397	1.00	1.50	3.00	7.50
1999	May, The Voyageurs	14,906,187	1.00	1.50	3.00	7.50
1999	June, From Coast to Coast	19,821,722	1.00	1.50	3.00	7.50
1999	July, A Nation of People	16,537,018	1.00	1.50	3.00	7.50
1999	August, The Pioneer Spirit	17,621,561	1.00	1.50	3.00	7.50
1999	September, A Child's Eye	31,077,650	1.00	1.50	3.00	7.50
1999	October, First Nation	31,964,487	1.00	1.50	3.00	7.50
1999	November, The Air Plane	27,437,677	1.00	1.50	3.00	7.50
1999	December, This is Canada	42,927,482	1.00	1.50	3.00	7.50
1999	Total Issue	258,888,000	–	–	–	–

Note: For 1999 and 2000 Commemorative and Millennium souvenir sets see pages 240-242.

MILLENNIUM 25-CENT COINS 2000. The twelve-coin series for the year 2000 focused on the hopes and dreams of the future: Canadians' vision of our culture, exploration, science and technology for the third millennium.

Designers and Modellers:
Obverse: Dora de Pédery-Hunt
Reverse: See below

Chemical and physical specifications are as for the 1990 issue.

January	February	March	April
Pride	Ingenuity	Achievement	Health
Donald F. Warkentin	John Jaciw	Daryl Dorosz	Anny Wassef
José Osio	William Woodruff	Stanley Witten	Stanley Witten

 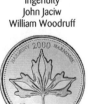

May	June	July	August
Natural Legacy	Harmony	Celebration	Family
Randy Trantau	Haver Demirer	Laura Paxton	Wade Stephen Baker
José Osio	José Osio	Stanley Witten	Susan Taylor

MILLENNIUM 25-CENT COINS 2000 CONTINUED

September	October	November	December
Wisdom	Creativity	Freedom	Community
Cezar Serbanescu	JErik (Kong Tat) Hui	Kathy Vinish	Michelle Thibodeau
Cosme Saffioti	Susan Taylor	William Woodruff	José Osio

Date and Mint Mark	Description	Quantity Minted	MS-60	MS-63	MS-64	MS-65
2000	January, Pride	50,749,102	1.00	1.50	3.00	7.50
2000	February, Ingenuity	35,812,988	1.00	1.50	3.00	7.50
2000	March, Achievement	35,135,154	1.00	1.50	3.00	7.50
2000	April, Health	34,663,619	1.00	1.50	3.00	7.50
2000	May, Natural Legacy	36,416,953	1.00	1.50	3.00	7.50
2000	June, Harmony	34,604,075	1.00	1.50	3.00	7.50
2000	July, Celebration	34,816,329	1.00	1.50	3.00	7.50
2000	August, Family	34,320,111	1.00	1.50	3.00	7.50
2000	September, Wisdom	33,993,016	1.00	1.50	3.00	7.50
2000	October, Creativity	35,102,206	1.00	1.50	3.00	7.50
2000	November, Freedom	33,251,352	1.00	1.50	3.00	7.50
2000	December, Community	34,378,898	1.00	1.50	3.00	7.50
2000	Total Issue	435,752,000	–	–	–	–

Note: For 1999 and 2000 Commemorative and Souvenir sets, please see pages 240-242.

CROWNED PORTRAIT; CARIBOU REVERSE RESUMED 2000-2001. 2001 was the last year for the use of pure nickel blanks in the production of 25-cent coins.

Designer, modeller and physical specifications are as for the 1990 issue.

Date and Mint Mark	Quantity Minted	MS-60	MS-63	MS-64	MS-65
2000	Not issued for circulation	–	–	–	–
2000W	Not issued for circulation	–	–	–	–
2001	8,409,000	1.00	1.50	3.00	7.50

CROWNED PORTRAIT; CARIBOU REVERSE; MULTI-PLY PLATED STEEL 1999-2001. In 2001 the Royal Canadian Mint began issuing circulating coinage struck from their new Multi-Ply Plated steel blanks. The process is acid based and electroplates a thin coating of nickel, then copper, then nickel again on to a steel core.

Designers and Modellers:
Obverse: Dora de Pédery-Hunt
Ago Aarand
Reverse: Emanuel Hahn
Composition: .940 steel, .038 copper, .022 nickel
Weight: 4.4 grams
Diameter: 23.58 mm
Thickness: 1.58 mm
Edge: Serrated
Die Axis: ↑↑

Date and Mint Mark	Quantity Minted	MS-60	MS-63	MS-64	MS-65
1999P	Not issued for circulation	–	–	–	–
2000P	Not issued for circulation	–	–	–	–
2001P	52,153,000	1.00	1.50	3.00	7.50

ELIZABETH II GOLDEN JUBILEE 1952-2002. To commemorate the 50th anniversary of the reign of Queen Elizabeth II, all circulating coinage carried the double dates of her reign 1952-2002, on the obverse.

Designers and Modellers:
Obverse: Dora de Pédery-Hunt, Ago Aarand
Reverse: Emanuel Hahn
Chemical and physical specifications are as for the 1999P issue.

Date and Mint Mark	Quantity Minted	MS-60	MS-63	MS-64	MS-65
1952-2002P	152,485,000	1.00	1.50	3.00	7.50

CROWNED PORTRAIT; CANADA DAY REVERSE 2002. The 2002 Canada Day twenty-five cents celebrates 135 years of National Pride. Presented to new Canadians at their citizenship ceremony during 'Celebrate Canada Day' week, this coin marks an important step for those who make Canada their home. The new 25 cent coins were issued for a three month period beginning July 2002 and ending September 2002.

Designers and Modellers:
    Obverse: Dora de Pédery-Hunt
        Ago Aarand
    Reverse: Judith Chariter
Chemical and physical specifications
are as for the 1999P issue.

Date and Mint Mark	Quantity Minted	MS-60	MS-63	MS-64	MS-65
1952-2002P	30,627	1.00	1.50	3.00	7.50

CROWNED PORTRAIT; CARIBOU REVERSE RESUMED 2003 TO DATE. In 2003 the caribou dated reverse was continued, with the planchet being multi-ply plated steel.

Designers and Modellers:
    Obverse: Dora de Pédery-Hunt
        Ago Aarand
    Reverse: Emmanuel Hahn
Chemical and physical specifications
are as for the 1999P issue.

Date and Mint Mark	Quantity Minted	MS-60	MS-63	MS-64	MS-65
2003P	N/A	1.00	1.50	3.00	7.50
2004P	N/A	1.00	1.50	3.00	7.50

FIFTY CENT
Victoria 1870 - 1901

Since the Province of Canada did not issue this denomination, new coinage tools had to be produced when the Dominion placed its first order for coins. For the obverse L.C. Wyon used the same portrait model as he did for the 25-cents: a crowned effigy of Victoria based on a model by William Theed. The reverse featured the St. Edward's crown atop crossed boughs of sweet maple, tied at the bottom by a ribbon. By the end of the reign four major obverses and two reverses had been utilized. A detailed description of the obverses and listing of these varieties by year follow on the next two pages.

Designer, Modeller and Engraver:
  Leonard C. Wyon
Composition: .925 silver,
  .075 copper
Weight: 11.62 grams
Diameter: 29.72 mm
Edge: Reeded
Die Axis: ↑↓

Heaton Mint issues of 1871-1881 and the Mint, Birmingham issue of 1890 have an "H" on the reverse under the wreath. London Mint strikings have no letter

VARIETIES 1870. The initial obverse for this denomination lacked the initial of the designer on the truncation of the queen's neck. The second obverse, also employed for the 1870 coinage, has the "L.C.W.," as well as a shamrock just behind the front cross in the Queen's tiara.

No shamrock behind front cross

1870 Without L.C.W.

Shamrock behind front cross

1870 L.C.W. on Truncation

VICTORIA OBVERSE PORTRAIT VARIETIES

FIFTY CENTS

PORTRAIT: H1
No shamrock behind first jewel of crown.
Without initials LCW.

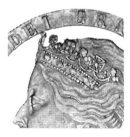

H1 will be found on the following date:
1870 No LCW

PORTRAIT: H2
With shamrock behind first jewel of crown.
Small space between poorly formed bow
and ribbon at the nape of the neck.

H2 will be found on the following dates:
1870 LCW; 1871; 1871H; 1872H;
1872H A/V

VICTORIA OBVERSE PORTRAIT VARIETIES

FIFTY CENTS

PORTRAIT: H3
With shamrock behind first jewel of crown.
Large space between crudely formed bow
and ribbon at the nape of the neck.

H3 will be found on the following dates:
1881H; 1888; 1890H; 1892

PORTRAIT: H4
With shamrock behind first jewel of crown.
No space between a well defined bow and
ribbon at the nape of the neck.

H4 will be found on the following dates:
1890H; 1892; 1894; 1898; 1899; 1900;
1901

IMPORTANT: In order to move the identification process forward we chose
the images illustrated as points of reference to establish the portrait varieties.
These are not the only reference points and may not be the best. If you have
any thoughts on identification points please write or email us.

Date, Mint Portrait	Quantity Minted	G-4	VG-8	F-12	VF-20	EF-40	AU-50	MS-60	MS-63
1870-H1	450,000	550.	1,000.	1,500.	3,000.	6,000.	10,000.	–	–
1870 LCW-H2	Incl. above	45.	80.	175.	350.	650.	2,000.	8,000.	25,000.
1871-H2	200,000	60.	110.	250.	500.	1,100.	3,000.	10,000.	30,000.
1871H-H2	45,000	100.	175.	350.	750.	2,000.	3,500.	11,000.	35,000.

VARIETIES 1872H. Numerous repunching varieties exist on the 1872H coinage, but the only one interesting enough to include in this catalogue involves a blundered obverse die. While repunching defective letters in the obverse legend the engraver inadvertently used an "A" punch to repair a defective "V" in "VICTORIA," converting the queen's name into "∀ICTORIA."

1872 Inverted A in VICTORIA

Date, Mint Portrait	Quantity Minted	G-4	VG-8	F-12	VF-20	EF-40	AU-50	MS-60	MS-63
1872H-H2	80,000	45.	80.	165.	375.	700.	2,000.	8,000.	25,000.
1872H A/V-H2	Incl. above	135.	275.	450.	1,000.	3,000.	6,000.	–	–
1881H-H3	150,000	55.	110.	175.	375.	900.	2,000.	9,000.	25,000.
1888-H3	60,000	150.	250.	500.	900.	1,750.	3,500.	12,000.	40,000.
1890H-H3	20,000				Very Rare				
1890H-H4	Inc. above	750.	1,200.	2,250.	3,500.	6,000.	9,000.	–	–
1892-H3	151,000				Very Rare				
1892-H4	Incl. above	50.	110.	225.	500.	1,000.	3,000.	12,500.	–
1894-H4	29,036	275.	500.	850.	1,500.	3,250.	6,000.	17,500.	–
1898-H4	100,000	45.	90.	200.	500.	1,000.	3,000.	12,500.	–
1899-H4	50,000	110.	190.	400.	800.	2,000.	4,500.	15,000.	–
1900-H4	118,000	40.	75.	150.	350.	750.	2,250.	8,000.	40,000.
1901-H4	80,000	50.	100.	175.	400.	850.	2,000.	9,000.	40,000.

FIFTY CENTS
Edward VII 1902 - 1910

The reverse of the Edward VII 50-cents followed the same design as the lower silver denominations: the word "CANADA" was made part of the legend, moved from it's former position at the bottom of the obverse, and the Imperial State crown replaced St. Edward's crown. The first reverse used the Victorian maple wreath almost untouched.

Designer and Modeller:
Obverse: G.W. DeSaulles
(DES. under the bust)
Engraver: Victorian Leaves Reverse:
G.W. DeSaulles
Edwardian Leaves Reverse:
W.H.J. Blakemore
Composition: .925 silver,
.075 copper
Weight: 11.62 grams (1902-1910)
11.66 grams (1910)
Diameter: 29.72 mm
Edge: Reeded
Die Axis: ↑↓ (1902-1907)
↑↑ (1908-1910)

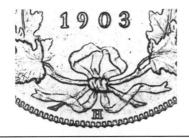

The Mint, Birmingham issue of 1903 has an "H" mint mark on the reverse under the wreath. London Mint issues (1902-1907) and Ottawa Mint issues (1908-1910) have no letter.

Date and Mint Mark	Quantity Minted	G-4	VG-8	F-12	VF-20	EF-40	AU-50	MS-60	MS-63
1902	120,000	13.	33.	70.	225.	550.	800.	2,000.	5,500.
1903H	140,000	22.	45.	70.	275.	650.	800.	2,000.	6,000.
1904	60,000	85.	200.	325.	750.	1,600.	2,400.	4,500.	15,000.
1905	40,000	110.	225.	425.	1,000.	2,400.	4,000.	7,500.	–
1906	350,000	12.	28.	65.	200.	550.	800.	2,000.	5,500.
1907	300,000	13.	25.	65.	200.	550.	800.	2,000.	6,000.
1908	128,119	22.	40.	125.	325.	700.	900.	1,500.	3,500.
1909	203,118	13.	30.	125.	375.	850.	1,400.	3,250.	12,500.

VARIETIES 1910. Because the Victorian Leaves variety 50-cent pieces being coined at the Ottawa Mint had almost no rim, it was requested that the parent Royal Mint in London make new reverse tools. In addition to a wider rim the new variety (Edwardian Leaves reverse) had several altered leaves and a different cross atop the crown. The most noticeable difference is the two outside leaves at the right side of the date. On the Victorian Leaves reverse these leaves have long points which nearly touch the denticles, but on the Edwardian Leaves reverse these leaves have shorter, more curved points farther from the denticles.

1910 Victorian
Leaves Reverse

1910 Edwardian
Leaves Reverse

Date and Mint Mark	Quantity Minted	G-4	VG-8	F-12	VF-20	EF-40	AU-50	MS-60	MS-63
1910 Victorian	649,521	14.	28.	85.	225.	650.	1,100.	2,500.	6,500.
1910 Edwardian	Incl. above	11.	20.	60.	175.	550.	800.	1,750.	–

FIFTY CENTS
George V 1911 - 1936

"GODLESS" OBVERSE 1911. Public outcry greeted the new George V coins issued in 1911 because the obverse legend lacked reference to the King's ruling "by the grace of God." The coinage tools were modified during the year and a new legend containing the Latin abbreviation "DEI GRA:" appeared on the 1912 and subsequent issues. The reverse was a continuation of the Edwardian Leaves variety of the previous reign.

Designer and Modeller:
Sir E.B. MacKennal
(B.M. on truncation)
Composition: .925 silver,
.075 copper
Weight: 11.66 grams
Diameter: 29.72 mm
Edge: Reeded
Die Axis: ↑↑

Date and Mint Mark	Quantity Minted	VG-8	F-12	VF-20	EF-40	AU-50	MS-60	MS-63
1911	209,972	20.	100.	375.	850.	1,250.	2,000.	4,500.

MODIFIED OBVERSE LEGEND 1912 - 1936.

Composition:
.925 silver, .075 copper
(1912-1919);
.800 silver, .200 copper
(1920-1936)

The physical specifications are as for the 1911 issue.

Wide Date 1920   Narrow Date 1920

Date and Mint Mark	Quantity Minted	VG-8	F-12	VF-20	EF-40	AU-50	MS-60	MS-63
1912	285,867	9.	40.	165.	375.	600.	1,750.	4,000.
1913	265,889	8.	40.	185.	400.	750.	2,500.	7,500.
1914	160,128	28.	90.	275.	750.	1,750.	4,500.	12,500.
1916	459,070	8.	35.	100.	250.	400.	1,250.	3,500.
1917	752,213	7.	25.	65.	200.	275.	700.	1,750.
1918	854,989	7.	25.	50.	150.	225.	650.	1,500.
1919	1,113,429	7.	25.	50.	150.	225.	650.	1,750.
1920 W0	584,429	10.	25.	50.	190.	275.	750.	1,750.
1920 N0	Incl. above	10.	25.	50.	190.	275.	750.	1,750.

Note: In 1920 144,200 fifty-cent pieces of .925 silver were melted. It is believed they were all dated 1919.

FIFTY CENTS 1921. This popular and very scarce coin was originally minted in considerable quantity. During the early and mid-1920s the demand for 50-cent pieces was very light; only 28,000 pieces were issued between 1921 and 1929. These are assumed to have been almost entirely 1920s. When a greater demand for this denomination arose later in 1929, the Master of the Ottawa Mint decided to melt the stock of 1920 and 1921 coins (amounting to some 480,392 pieces) and recoin the silver into 1929 coins. He took this decision because he feared that the public would suspect they were receiving counterfeits if a large quantity of coins with "old" dates were issued. It is believed that the 75 or so 1921s that have survived came from specimen sets sold to collectors or from circulation strikes sold to Mint visitors.

Composition:
.925 silver, .075 copper (1912-1919);
.800 silver, .200 copper (1920-1936)

Date and Mint Mark	Quantity Minted	G-4	VG-8	F-12	VF-20	EF-40	AU-50	MS-60	MS-63
1921	206,398	14,000.	22,500.	27,500.	32,500.	37,500.	50,000.	–	–
1929	228,328	–	10.	25.	50.	175.	300.	750.	1,750.
1931	57,581	–	20.	55.	135.	375.	800.	1,250.	3,000.
1932	19,213	125.	200.	300.	600.	1,500.	2,500.	5,000.	12,500.
1934	39,539	–	25.	55.	150.	400.	650.	1,000.	1,750.
1936	38,550	–	25.	55.	140.	350.	575.	800.	1,500.

Note: In 1929 480,392 pieces of this denomination, consisting of 1920 and 1921 dates, were melted.

FIFTY CENTS
George VI 1937 - 1952

"ET IND:IMP:" OBVERSE; SIMPLIFIED COAT-OF-ARMS REVERSE, 1937-1947. A stylized Canadian coat-of-arms designed by George Edward Kruger-Gray was selected for the George VI 50-cent piece, first issued in 1937. The initial obverse bore a legend containing an abbreviation for the Latin phrase, "ET INDIAE IMPERATOR," meaning "and Emperor of India," denoting that the King was emperor of that vast country.

Designer and Modeller:
Portrait: T.H. Paget
(H.P. below bust)
Reverse: G.E. Kruger-Gray
(K.G. flanking lower part of crown on shield)
Composition: .800 silver, .200 copper
Weight: 11.66 grams
Diameter: 29.72 mm
Edge: Reeded
Die Axis: ↑↑

1943
Near 3

1943
Far 3

Date and Mint Mark	Quantity Minted	F-12	VF-20	EF-40	AU-50	MS-60	MS-63	MS-65
1937	192,016	7.	12.	18.	20.	40.	100.	1,000.
1938	192,018	8.	25.	60.	75.	135.	500.	3,250.
1939	287,976	7.	18.	45.	55.	110.	300.	2,000.
1940	1,996,566	4.	7.	10.	17.	40.	100.	1,100.
1941	1,714,874	4.	7.	10.	17.	40.	100.	1,100.
1942	1,974,165	4.	7.	10.	17.	40.	100.	1,100.
1943 Near 3	3,109,583	8.	14.	20.	35.	70.	200.	2,500.
1943 Far 3	Incl. above	4.	7.	10.	17.	35.	100.	1,100.
1944	2,460,205	4.	7.	10.	17.	35.	100.	1,000.
1945	1,959,528	4.	6.	9.	17.	35.	100.	1,500.
1946	950,235	5.	9.	15.	25.	75.	150.	1,500.

VARIETIES 1947. There are two styles of 7 for the 1947 issue. The first is a tall figure with a tail curving to the left at the bottom (Straight 7), similar to that on the 1937 issue. The second (Curved 7) has a bottom that curves to the right.

1947 Straight 7

1947 Curved 7

Date and Mint Mark	Quantity Minted	F-12	VF-20	EF-40	AU-50	MS-60	MS-63	MS-65
1947 Straight 7	424,885	6.	9.	20.	55.	100.	250.	1,500.
1947 Curved 7	Incl. above	6.	9.	22.	60.	110.	325.	2,250.

MAPLE LEAF ISSUE 1947. With the granting of independence to India, the Royal Canadian Mint was faced with a dilemma in early 1948. The new obverse coinage tools with the Latin abbreviation "ET IND: IMP" omitted would not arrive for several months, yet there was a great need for all denominations of coins. The Mint satisfied the demand by striking coins dated 1947 and bearing an obverse with outmoded titles. To differentiate this issue from the regular strikings of 1947, a tiny maple leaf was placed after the date. Both styles of 7 (see above) were employed for the Maple Leaf coinage, creating four varieties of the 1947 date in all.

1947 Maple Leaf
Straight 7

1947 Maple Leaf
Curved 7

Date and Mint Mark	Quantity Minted	VG-8	F-12	VF-20	EF-40	AU-50	MS-60	MS-63	MS-65
1947 ML,S7	38,433	30.	40.	60.	100.	125.	250.	325.	1,000.
1947 ML,C7	Incl. above	1,500.	1,750.	2,250.	3,500.	4,500.	6,000.	15,000.	—

MODIFIED OBVERSE LEGEND 1948-1952. In 1948, following the arrival of the master tools with the new obverse legend, production of the 1947 Maple Leaf coinage was suspended. For the remainder of the year coins were produced with the new obverse and true date, 1948.

The physical and chemical specifications are as for the 1937-1947 issues.

Date and Mint Mark	Quantity Minted	VG-8	F-12	VF-20	EF-40	AU-50	MS-60	MS-63	MS-65
1948	37,784	75.	100.	140.	160.	200.	250.	400.	1,000.
1949	858,991	–	6.	9.	14.	18.	45.	150.	900.
1950	2,384,179	–	–	5.	6.	7.	16.	30.	400.
1951	2,421,730	–	–	5.	6.	7.	13.	25.	200.
1952	2,596,465	–	–	5.	6.	7.	12.	22.	200.

Note: Lower grade silver coins, which do not have price listings, are priced based on silver bullion on the day of purchase or sale. These lower grade coins do not have a numismatic premium at this time.

FIFTY CENTS
Elizabeth II 1953 to date

LAUREATED PORTRAIT; SIMPLIFIED COAT-OF-ARMS REVERSE 1953-1943. During 1953 two obverse varieties were employed. Known as No Shoulder Fold and Shoulder Fold varieties (see 1-cent Elizabeth II, 1953 to date for full description), they were combined with two major reverse varieties. The No Shoulder Fold obverse was used with both Small and Large Date reverses, though only a modest quantity of the latter were struck. The Small Date reverse was carried over from George VI issues. The Shoulder Fold obverse appeared only with the Large Date reverse.

Designer and Modeller: Portrait: Mrs. Mary Gillick, (M.G. on truncation);
    Large Date Reverse: Thomas Shingles, copying existing model
Engraver: No Shoulder Fold Obverse: Thomas Shingles, using the Gillick portrait model;
    Shoulder Fold Obverse: Thomas Shingles, modifying existing NSF coinage tools
Composition: .800 silver, .200 copper
Weight: 11.66 grams
Diameter: 29.72 mm
Edge: Reeded
Die Axis: ↑↑

No Shoulder Fold Obverse 1953
letters have pronounced flaring

Shoulder Fold Obverse
1953-1964

Letters have subdued
flaring

Small Date Reverse 1953

Large Date Reverse
1953-1964

Date and Mint Mark	Quantity Minted	VF-20	EF-40	AU-50	MS-60	MS-63	MS-64	MS-65
1953 SD, NSF	1,630,429	5.	6.	7.	10.	40.	60.	175.
1953 LD, NSF	Incl. above	7.	15.	60.	110.	175.	250.	750.
1953 LD, SF	Incl. above	5.	6.	7.	10.	25.	80.	250.
1954	506,305	6.	12.	20.	40.	80.	150.	300.

SIMPLIFIED COAT-OF-ARMS REVERSE 1955-1958. Continuing difficulties with the coat-of-arms reverse design resulted in the introduction of a major modification in 1955. The problem was the obverse portrait tended to draw away too much metal at the moment the coin was struck, leaving insufficient metal to completely fill the design on the reverse. Thus, the coins sometimes showed a weakness in the design at and around the crown and top of the shield. This problem was largely solved by a new reverse with a smaller version of the coat-of-arms.

Designer and Modeller:
Thomas Shingles, copying existing models

The physical and chemical specifications are as for the 1953-1954 issues.

Date and Mint Mark	Quantity Minted	VF-20	EF-40	AU-50	MS-60	MS-63	MS-64	MS-65
1955	753,511	6.	8.	10.	20.	50.	75.	250.
1956	1,379,499	5.	6.	7.	10.	25.	40.	200.
1957	2,171,689	5.	6.	7.	10.	20.	30.	125.
1958	2,957,266	5.	6.	7.	10.	20.	30.	125.

MODIFIED COAT-OF-ARMS REVERSE; LAUREATED OBVERSE 1959-1964. In 1959 the new Canadian coat-of-arms which had recieved government approval in 1957 was adapted for the 50-cent piece. One of the major changes compared to the previous design was the addition of a ribbon at the bottom bearing "A MARI USQUE AD MARE," meaning "from sea to sea" and making reference to the territorial extent of the country. The 1959 issue had horizontal lines in the bottom panel, indicating the colour incorrectly as blue. To indicate the correct colour, white, these lines were removed from the 1960 and subsequent issues. The obverse continued unchanged.

Designer and Modeller:
Reverse: Thomas Shingles
(TS flanking shield at bottom)
Composition: .800 silver,
.200 copper
Weight: 11.66 grams
Diameter: 29.72 mm
Edge: Reeded
Die Axis: ↑↑

Date and Mint Mark	Quantity Minted	MS-60	MS-63	MS-64	MS-65
1959	3,095,535	5.	12.	18.	70.
1960	3,488,897	5.	10.	15.	60.
1961	3,584,417	5.	10.	15.	60.
1962	5,208,030	5.	10.	15.	60.
1963	8,348,871	5.	10.	15.	60.
1964	9,377,676	5.	10.	15.	60.

TIARA PORTRAIT; MODIFIED COAT-OF-ARMS REVERSE 1965-1966. A new obverse with the Queen showing more mature facial features and wearing a tiara was introduced in 1965.

Designer and Modeller:
Portrait: Arnold Machin

The physical and chemical specifications are as for the 1959-1964 issues.

Date and Mint Mark	Quantity Minted	MS-60	MS-63	MS-64	MS-65
1965	12,629,974	5.	10.	15.	60.
1966	7,683,228	5.	10.	15.	60.

COMMEMORATIVE FOR CENTENNIAL OF CONFEDERATION 1967. A design for the reverse showing a howling wolf was chosen as part of the set of commemorative coins for this year. The obverse continued unchanged.

Designer: Reverse: Alex Colville
Modeller: Reverse: Myron Cook

The physical and chemical specifications are as for the 1959-1966 issues.

Date and Mint Mark	Quantity Minted	MS-60	MS-63	MS-64	MS-65
1967 Confederation Commemorative	4,211,395	4.	10.	20.	100.

MODIFIED COAT-OF-ARMS REVERSE RESUMED; REDUCED SIZE NICKEL COINAGE 1968-1976. When the coat-of-arms reverse design was resumed in 1968, the strikes were in nickel. In order to make the coins easier to strike in the harder metal the diameter was considerably reduced.

Designer and Modeller:
    Obverse: Arnold Machin
    Reverse: Thomas Shingles
Composition: 1.00 nickel
Weight: 8.10 grams
Diameter: 27.13 mm
Edge: Reeded
Die Axis: ↑↑

Date and Mint Mark	Quantity Minted	MS-60	MS-63	MS-64	MS-65
1968	3,966,932	2.	3.	5.	15.
1969	7,113,929	2.	3.	5.	15.
1970	2,429,516	2.	3.	5.	15.
1971	2,166,144	2.	3.	5.	15.
1972	2,515,632	2.	3.	5.	15.
1973	2,546,096	2.	3.	5.	15.
1974	3,436,650	2.	3.	5.	15.
1975	3,710,000	2.	3.	5.	15.
1976	2,646,000	2.	3.	5.	15.

COAT-OF-ARMS REVERSE; MODIFIED DESIGN 1977. The 1977 coinage featured pronounced changes on both sides. The obverse bears a smaller bust with increased hair detail, smaller lettering, and larger beads placed farther from the rim. The reverse shows a smaller coat-of-arms and for the first time beads instead of denticles at the rim.

Modeller: Obverse: Patrick Brindley, modifying the Machin portrait

Chemical and physical specifications are as for the 1968 issue.

Date and Mint Mark	Quantity Minted	MS-60	MS-63	MS-64	MS-65
1977	709,939	2.	4.	7.	20.

COAT-OF-ARMS REVERSE; MODIFIED DESIGN 1978-1989. In 1978 the Mint's attempts to settle upon standard designs continued. The beaded motif for the reverse was dropped and a design essentially the same as that for 1968-1976 was restored. Two minor varieties of the 1978 reverse are known. The 1978 obverse was a combination of the 1968-1976 and 1977 designs. The unmodified Machin portrait was restored, but the smaller lettering of 1977 was retained.

Designer and Modeller:
Obverse: Arnold Machin
Reverse: Thomas Shingles

Chemical and physical specifications are as for the 1968 issue.

1978 Square Jewels   1978 Round Jewels

1982 – 118 Large Beads   1982 – 120 Small Beads

COAT-OF-ARMS REVERSE; MODIFIED DESIGN 1978-1989 (cont).

Date and Mint Mark	Quantity Minted	MS-60	MS-63	MS-64	MS-65
1978 Square Jewels	3,341,892	2.	3.	5.	15.
1978 Round Jewels	Incl. above	5.	7.	11.	35.
1979	3,425,000	2.	3.	5.	15.
1980	1,943,155	2.	3.	5.	15.
1981	2,588,900	2.	3.	5.	15.
1982 Large Beads	2,884,572	2.	3.	5.	15.
1982 Small Beads	Incl. above	90.	135.	200.	400.
1983	1,177,000	2.	3.	5.	15.
1984	1,502,989	2.	3.	5.	15.
1985	2,188,374	2.	3.	5.	15.
1986	781,400	2.	3.	5.	15.
1987	373,000	3.	4.	6.	20.
1988	220,000	3.	4.	6.	20.
1989	266,419	3.	4.	6.	20.

CROWNED PORTRAIT; COAT-OF-ARMS REVERSE 1990-1991. A new obverse portrait of the Queen wearing a diamond diadem and jewellery was introduced on all denominations in 1990.

Designer and Modeller:
Obverse: Dora de Pédery-Hunt
             Ago Aarand
Reverse :   Thomas Shingles

Chemical and physical specifications are as for the 1968 issue.

Date and Mint Mark	Quantity Minted	MS-60	MS-63	MS-64	MS-65
1990	207,000	3.	4.	6.	20.
1991	490,000	3.	4.	10.	30.

COMMEMORATIVE FOR 125TH ANNIVERSARY 1867-1992. The reverse design was modified to include the bracket dates 1867-1992 for the 125th birthday of Canada.

Designers and modellers are as for the 1990 issue.

Chemical and physical specifications are as for the 1968 issue.

Date and Mint Mark	Quantity Minted	MS-60	MS-63	MS-64	MS-65
1992	248,000	3.	4.	6.	20.

COAT OF ARMS REVERSE RESUMED 1993-1996. In 1993 the practice of using a single date was resumed. Also, the transition to beads from rim denticles, which began in 1982 on the one cent coin, was completed in 1993 on the fifty cent piece.

Designers and modellers are as for the 1990 issue.

Chemical and physical specifications are as for the 1968 issue.

Date and Mint Mark	Quantity Minted	MS-60	MS-63	MS-64	MS-65
1993	393,000	2.	3.	5.	15.
1994	987,000	2.	3.	5.	15.
1995	626,000	2.	3.	5.	15.
1996	458,000	2.	3.	5.	15.

CROWNED PORTRAIT; REDESIGNED COAT OF ARMS REVERSE 1997-2000. A new coat of arms appeared for the first time in 1997. The new coin incorporates the motto "Desiderantes Meliorem Patriam" ("They desire a better country") on a ribbon behind the shield. The mantling depicts a series of overlapping stylized maple leaves. The arrangement of the English Rose, Scottish Thistle, Irish Shamrock and the French Fleur-de-lis has been modified and extends the width of the motto. The Winnipeg Mint Mark (W) is found only on coins from the "Oh! Canada" and "Tiny Treasures" sets issued by the Numismatic Department of the Mint.

Designer and Modeller:
Obverse: Dora de Pédery-Hunt
            Ago Aarand
Reverse: C. Bursey-Sabourin
            William Woodruff

Chemical and physical specifications are as for the 1968 issue.

Date and Mint Mark	Quantity Minted	MS-60	MS-63	MS-64	MS-65
1997	387,000	2.	3.	5.	15.
1998	308,000	2.	3.	5.	15.
1999	496,000	2.	3.	5.	15.
2000	559,000	2.	3.	5.	15.

CROWNED PORTRAIT; REDESIGNED COAT-OF-ARMS REVERSE; MULTI-PLY PLATED STEEL

1999-2001. In 2001 the Royal Canadian Mint began issuing circulating coinage struck from their new Multi-Ply Plated steel blanks. The process is acid based and electroplates a thin coating of nickel, then copper, then nickel again to a steel core.

Designers and modellers are as for the 1997 issue.

Composition: .9325 steel,
    .0475 copper,
    .0200 nickel
Weight: 6.9 grams
Diameter: 27.13 mm
Thickness: 1.95 mm
Edge: Serrated
Die Axis: ↑↑

Date and Mint Mark	Quantity Minted	MS-60	MS-63	MS-64	MS-65
1999P	Not issued for circulation	–	–	–	–
2000P	Not issued for circulation	–	–	–	–
2001P	389,000	1.	2.	5.	15.

Note: A 50-cent coin, dated 2000P, was incorporated into the cover of a desk clock and presented at the launch of the plating facilities in Winnipeg in 2000.

ELIZABETH II GOLDEN JUBILEE 1952-2002. To commemorate the 50th anniversary of the reign of Queen Elizabeth II, all circulating coinage carried the double dates of her reign, 1952-2002, on the obverse.

Designers and modellers are as for the 1997 issue.

Chemical and physical specifications are as for the 1999P issue.

Date and Mint Mark	Quantity Minted	MS-60	MS-63	MS-64	MS-65
1952-2002P	N/A	1.	2.	5.	15.

50TH ANNIVERSARY OF QUEEN ELIZABETH II ASCENSION TO THE THRONE, 2002. Using the obverse design of the 1953 Canadian Coronation Medallion, a new 50-cent circulating coin was issued to commemorate the golden jubilee of Her Majesty Queen Elizabeth II. The reverse design features Canada's Coat-of-Arms struck with the dual dates 1952-2002. This coin will also be found in the Golden Jubilee sets of 2002 (see page 363.)

Designers and Modellers:

Obverse:	Susan Taylor
Reverse:	C. Bursey-Sabourin
	William Woodruff

Chemical and physical specifications are as for the 1999P issue.

Date and Mint Mark	Quantity Minted	MS-60	MS-63	MS-64	MS-65
1952-2002P	1,440,000	1.	2.	5.	15.

CROWNED PORTRAIT; COAT-OF-ARMS REVERSE CONTINUED 2003 TO DATE. The use of the multi-ply plated steel planchets continued in 2003.

Designers and modellers are as for the 1997 issue.

Chemical and physical specifications are as for the 1999P issue.

Date and Mint Mark	Quantity Minted	MS-60	MS-63	MS-64	MS-66
2003P	N/A	1.	2.	5.	15.
2004P	N/A	1.	2.	5.	15.

ONE DOLLAR - SILVER
George V 1935 - 1936

SILVER JUBILEE COMMEMORATIVE 1935. Canada's first silver dollar for circulation, also the first commemorative coin, marked the 25th anniversary of the accession of King George V. The Bank of Canada $25 bill also commemorated the special event. The reverse of the silver dollar was a modern design by sculptor Emanuel Hahn, showing an Indian and a voyageur, a travelling agent for a fur company, paddling a canoe by an islet on which there are two wind-swept trees. In the canoe are bundles of goods; the bundle at the right has HB, representing the Hudson's Bay Company. The vertical lines in the background represent the northern lights. This modern design began a trend which produced the beautiful reverses for 1937.

The obverse was the commemorative side of the coin with the Latin legend indicating the King was in the 25th year of his reign. The portrait was by Percy Metcalfe and was never used for any other Canadian coinage, but had been used previously for the obverses of some New Zealand and Australian coinages.

Generally, the coins were issued in cardboard tubes of 20.

Designer and Modeller: Portrait: Percy Metcalfe;
　　　　Reverse: Emanuel Hahn (EH in water left end of canoe)
Composition: .800 silver, .200 copper
Weight: 23.33 grams
Diameter: 36.00 mm
Edge: Reeded
Die Axis:↑↑

Date and Mint Mark	Quantity Minted	VF-20	EF-40	AU-50	MS-60	MS-63	MS-64	MS-65
1935	428,707	35.	45.	55.	75.	125.	175.	350.

STANDARD OBVERSE 1936. In 1936 the issue of silver dollars continued, with the new reverse remaining unchanged. The obverse was the regular MacKennal design used for 1- to 50-cent pieces of 1912-1936. The tools for this obverse had already been prepared in 1911 for use on the 1911 dollar (see DC-6 in the chapter on Patterns).

Designer & Modeller: Portrait: Sir E.B. MacKennal (B.M. on trucation)

The physical and chemical specifications are as for the 1935 issue.

Date and Mint Mark	Quantity Minted	VF-20	EF-40	AU-50	MS-60	MS-63	MS-64	MS-65
1936	306,100	22.	28.	35.	60.	150.	275.	1,000.

ONE DOLLAR - SILVER
George VI 1937 - 1952

VOYAGEUR REVERSE 1937-1938. New reverse designs were under consideration for the 1937 issues; however, it was decided to retain the voyageur design, since it was already modern.

Designer and Modeller: Portrait: T.H. Paget (H.P. below bust)
Composition: .800 silver, .200 copper
Weight: 23.33 grams
Diameter: 36.00 mm
Edge: Reeded
Die Axis: ↑↑

Date and Mint Mark	Quantity Minted	VF-20	EF-40	AU-50	MS-60	MS-63	MS-64	MS-65
1937	241,002	17.	20.	26.	40.	100.	275.	3,000.
1938	90,304	65.	80.	95.	115.	275.	550.	3,000.

COMMEMORATIVE FOR ROYAL VISIT 1939. Canada's second commemorative coin was created when the reverse of the 1939 silver dollar was used to mark the visit of George VI and Queen Elizabeth to Canada. The design consists of the centre block of the Parliament buildings in Ottawa and the Latin phrase, "FIDE SVORVM REGNAT," meaning "He reigns by the faith of his people."

The usual means of issuing coins was through the Bank of Canada, but for this special coinage it was decided to make them available through the Post Office as well. Consequently, 369,500 of the original mintage of nearly 1.4 million were issued direct to the Post Office. This mintage proved to be larger than public demand and between 1939 and 1945 nearly 160,000 pieces were returned to the Mint and melted.

Designer and Modeller: Reverse: Emanuel Hahn (E H flanked the building in the original model, but was removed by order of Canadian government officials)

The physical and chemical specifications are as for the 1937-1938 issues.

Date and Mint Mark	Quantity Minted	VF-20	EF-40	AU-50	MS-60	MS-63	MS-64	MS-65
1939	1,363,816*	10.	12.	17.	20.	50.	150.	450.

* 158,084 pieces were returned to the Mint and melted between 1939 and 1945.

VOYAGEUR REVERSE RESUMED; "ET IND; IMP;" OBVERSE 1945-1947. Beginning with the 1945 silver dollar a more brilliant appearance was achieved. This resulted from the use of chromium-plated coinage dies. For previous issues unplated dies with a rougher surface had been used.

The chemical and physical specifications are as for the 1937-1939 issues.

Date and Mint Mark	Quantity Minted	VF-20	EF-40	AU-50	MS-60	MS-63	MS-64	MS-65
1945	38,391	175.	225.	250.	400.	750.	1,500.	3,250.
1946	93,055	40.	60.	80.	125.	400.	2,000.	4,000.

VARIETIES 1947. Two styles of 7 were used to date the 1947 dies; a tall figure with the lower tail pointing back to the right (Pointed 7); and a shorter 7 with the lower tail pointing almost straight down (Blunt 7).

1947 Pointed 7   1947 Blunt 7

Date and Mint Mark	Quantity Minted	VF-20	EF-40	AU-50	MS-60	MS-63	MS-64	MS-65
1947 Pointed 7	65,595	150.	175.	225.	425.	1,500.	3,500.	6,000.
1947 Pointed 7 Tripled	Incl.	175.	225.	300.	575.	–	–	–
1947 Pointed 7 Quad.	Incl.	225.	275.	350.	675.	–	–	–
1947 Blunt 7	Included	125.	150.	200.	225.	450.	2,000.	4,000.

MAPLE LEAF ISSUE 1947. In early 1948 the Royal Canadian Mint was faced with a problem. New obverse coinage tools with the Latin abbreviation "ET IND: IMP:" omitted to indicate that the King's titles had been changed to concur with India's recently granted independence would not arrive for several months. Yet, there was a great need for all denominations of coins. The Mint satisfied the demand by striking coins dated 1947 and bearing an obverse with outmoded titles. To differentiate this issue from the regular strikings of 1947, a tiny maple leaf was placed after the date. Only the Blunt 7 was employed for dating this issue.

1947 Maple Leaf Issue, struck in 1948

Date and Mint Mark	Quantity Minted	VF-20	EF-40	AU-50	MS-60	MS-63	MS-64	MS-65
1947 Maple Leaf	21,135	200.	250.	300.	400.	1,000.	2,500.	4,000.

Note: See page 396 and 397 of the Variety Section for the Doubled Die varieties of the 1947 Point and 1947 Maple Leaf dollars.

MODIFIED OBVERSE LEGEND; VOYAGEUR REVERSE 1948. Following the arrival in 1948 of the master tools with the new obverse legend, production of the 1947 Maple Leaf coinage was suspended. For the remainder of the year coins were produced with the new obverse and the true date, 1948.

Designer and Modeller: Portrait: T.H. Paget (H.P. below bust)
Composition: .800 silver, .200 copper
Weight: 23.33 grams
Diameter: 36.00 mm
Edge: Reeded
Die Axis: ↑↑

Date and Mint Mark	Quantity Minted	VF-20	EF-40	AU-50	MS-60	MS-63	MS-64	MS-65
1948	18,780	850.	1,000.	1,150.	1,300.	2,000.	4,000.	8,000.

COMMEMORATIVE FOR ENTRY OF NEWFOUNDLAND INTO CONFEDERATION 1949. On March 31, 1949 Newfoundland became the tenth province of the Dominion of Canada. This historic event was recognized on the Canadian coinage with a special reverse for the 1949 silver dollar. The design shows the ship Matthew in which it is thought John Cabot discovered Newfoundland in 1497. Below it is the Latin phrase, "FLOREAT TERRA NOVA," meaning "May the new found land flourish." The design was inspired by Newfoundland's commemorative postage stamp of 1947, based on a model of the ship by Ernest Maunder. The obverse continued unchanged from that of 1948.

The 1949 dollars were struck more carefully than those of previous years and were issued in plastic or cardboard tubes of 20 to protect them. Many of these coins remain in proof-like condition today. Thomas Shingles was the engraver, doing his work entirely by hand, without the aid of a "reducing" machine.

It was decided to strike these coins, dated 1949, as long as there was a demand for them. In 1950 some 40,718 pieces were coined. The 1949 and 1950 strikings have been combined to give the total production for the type.

Designer: Reverse: Thomas Shingles, based upon Ernest Maunder's
Model of the "Matthew" (T.S. above horizon at right)
Engraver: Reverse: Thomas Shingles

The physical and chemical specifications are as for the 1948 issues.

Date and Mint Mark	Quantity Minted	VF-20	EF-40	AU-50	MS-60	MS-63	MS-64	MS-65
1949	672,218	20.	30.	40.	45.	50.	60.	125.

VOYAGEUR REVERSE RESUMED 1950-1952; ARNPRIOR DOLLARS. During the year 1950 a technical problem arose that was to plague the Mint throughout the 1950's. At each end of the canoe are four (not three as is so often claimed) shallow water lines. In the process of polishing or repolishing the dies, parts of these lines tended to disappear, creating differences within a given year's coinage. Collectors have decided arbitrarily that a certain pattern of partial water lines at the right-hand end of the canoe should be collected separately and command a premium over dollars with perfect water lines or other partial lines configurations.

The so-called Arnprior configuration (see One Dollar, Queen Elizabeth II 1955 for more details) consists of 2 1/2 (often incorrectly called 1 1/2) water lines at the right. Any trace of the bottom water line disqualifies a coin from being an Arnprior. One should also beware of coins that have had part of the water lines fraudulently removed.

1950 Normal
4 Water Lines at Right

1950 Arnprior
2½ Water Lines at Right

Date and Mint Mark	Quantity Minted	VF-20	EF-40	AU-50	MS-60	MS-63	MS-64	MS-65
1950	261,002	15.	20.	25.	35.	75.	100.	200.
1950 SWL	Incl. above	30.	40.	60.	100.	300.	600.	1,200.
1950 Arn.	Incl. above	16.	20.	30.	50.	150.	400.	1,200.
1951	416,395	8.	10.	12.	15.	35.	100.	300.
1951 Arn.	Incl. above	45.	60.	80.	225.	450.	1,000.	3,000.

VARIETIES 1952. In 1952 a modified reverse, with no water lines at all, was put into use. In addition to removing the water lines, this reverse differs from the Water Lines variety in having a remodeled (larger) islet tip at the right end of the canoe. This variety is fundamentally different from the Arnpriors in that it is was deliberately, not accidentally created. The Water Lines variety was also used in 1952.

1952 Water Lines Variety

1952 No Water Lines Variety

Date and Mint Mark	Quantity Minted	VF-20	EF-40	AU-50	MS-60	MS-63	MS-64	MS-65
1952 WL	406,148	8.	10.	12.	15.	50.	150.	450.
1952 SWL	Incl. above	15.	18.	25.	60.	200.	600.	1,200.
1952 No Lines	Incl. above	12.	15.	18.	25.	60.	200.	800.

ONE DOLLAR - SILVER
Elizabeth II 1953 - 1967

LAUREATED PORTRAIT; VOYAGEUR REVERSE 1953-1957. As was true of all the lower denominations, the 1953 silver dollars came with two obverses, called the No Shoulder Fold and Shoulder Fold varieties (see one cent, Queen Elizabeth II, 1953 to date for full explanation). On this denomination these obverses are combined with different reverses. The No Shoulder Fold variety appears with the Wire Edge reverse, the Water Lines reverse of 1950-1952, and the Shoulder Fold obverse with the Wide Border reverse.

No Shoulder Fold Obverse 1953
letters have pronounced flaring

Shoulder Fold Obverse 1953-1964
letters have subdued flaring

Designer and Modeller: Portrait: Mrs. Mary Gillick (M.G. on truncation)
Engraver: No Shoulder Fold Obverse: Thomas Shingles, using the Gillick portrait
Shoulder Fold Obverse: Thomas Shingles, modifying existing NSF coinage tools
Composition: .800 silver, .200 copper
Weight: 23.33 grams
Diameter: 36.00 mm
Edge: Reeded
Die Axis: ↑↑

Date and Mint Mark	Quantity Minted	VF-20	EF-40	AU-50	MS-60	MS-63	MS-64	MS-65
1953 NSF	1,074,578	5.	7.	8.	12.	30.	125.	375.
1953 SF	Incl. bove	5.	7.	9.	15.	30.	125.	375.
1954	246,606	11.	15.	18.	25.	60.	175.	500.

ARNPRIOR DOLLAR 1955. In December,1955 the Mint made up an order of 2,000 silver dollars for a firm in Arnprior, Ontario. These coins had 2 1/2 water lines at the right of the canoe, similar to the configuration which occured on some of the 1950 - 1951 dollars. It was the 1955 dollars that first attracted the attention of collectors, but the term Arnprior has been applied to any dollar with a similar configuration of defective water lines. Confirmation of the 1955 Arnprior by collectors is the die break on the obverse legend, the joining of the "T"and "I" of GRATIA. Aprnprior dollars without this die break will command a slightly lower price. See the 1950-1951 silver dollars issues for additional comments.

| 1955 Normal | 1955 Arnprior | Obverse die break between |
| 4 Water Lines | 2½ Water Lines | "T" and "I" of GRATIA |

Date and Mint Mark	Quantity Minted	VF-20	EF-40	AU-50	MS-60	MS-63	MS-64	MS-65
1955	268,105	11.	15.	18.	25.	60.	175.	500.
1955 Arn.	Incl. above	50.	65.	75.	85.	150.	325.	750.
1955 Arn. w/die break	Incl. above	100.	125.	145.	165.	325.	650.	1,500.
1956	209,092	15.	20.	25.	35.	100.	300.	850.

ONE WATER LINE DOLLAR 1957. Part of the 1957 issue was struck from dies that retained only one of the long water lines at the right end of the canoe. This difference arose in the same way as the Arnprior dollars (see 1950-1951 issues for commentary) and is of questionable importance.

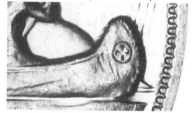

| 1957 Normal (4) Water Lines at Right | 1957 One Water Line at Right |

Date and Mint Mark	Quantity Minted	EF-40	AU-50	MS-60	MS-63	MS-64	MS-65
1957 Normal Water Lines	496,389	7.	9.	12.	25.	75.	300.
1957 One Water Line	Incl. above	7.	9.	15.	50.	150.	400.

BRITISH COLUMBIA COMMEMORATIVE 1958. The reverse of the 1958 dollar commemorates the centenary of the Caribou gold rush and the establishment of British Columbia as a crown colony. The design shows a totem pole section with mountains in the background. The top element in the totem is a raven, used by some Indians to symbolize death. As a result, it was rumoured that those Indians disliked the dollars, causing them to be called "death dollars." The obverse was the same as that on the 1954-1957 issues.

Designer and Modeller: Reverse: Stephan Trenka (ST on right-hand of lower base of totem pole)
Composition: .800 silver, .200 copper
Weight: 23.33 grams
Diameter: 36.00 mm
Edge: Reeded
Die Axis: ↑↑

Date and Mint Mark	Quantity Minted	EF-40	AU-50	MS-60	MS-63	MS-64	MS-65
1958	3,039,630	6.	7.	10.	15.	75.	200.

VOYAGEUR REVERSE RESUMED 1959-1963. During this period minor changes were made in the reverse details, the description of which is not listed in this standard catalogue. The obverse was continued from the previous year.

Date and Mint Mark	Quantity Minted	EF-40	AU-50	MS-60	MS-63	MS-64	MS-65
1959	1,443,502	6.	7.	10.	15.	75.	250.
1960	1,420,486	6.	7.	10.	15.	75.	250.
1961	1,262,231	6.	7.	10.	15.	100.	300.
1962	1,884,789	6.	7.	10.	15.	100.	300.
1963	4,179,981	6.	7.	10.	15.	75.	250.

CONFEDERATION MEETINGS COMMEMORATIVE 1964. The reverse of the 1964 silver dollar carried a special design marking the centennial of the 1864 meetings in Charlottetown, P.E.I. and Quebec City, Quebec which prepared the way for Confederation in 1867. The design depicts, conjoined within a circle, the French fleur-de-lis, the Irish shamrock, the Scottish thistle and the English rose. The obverse coupled with the commemorative reverse was a reworking of the Shoulder Fold variety.

Designer: Reverse: Dinko Vodanovic (D.V. near the Q of Quebec)
Modeller: Reverse: Thomas Shingles (T.S. near the C of Quebec)
  Obverse: Myron Cook, modifying existing model

The physical and chemical specifications are as for the 1958-1963 issues.

Date and Mint Mark	Quantity Minted	EF-40	AU-50	MS-60	MS-63	MS-64	MS-65
1964	7,296,832	6.	7.	10.	15.	75.	200.

TIARA PORTRAIT; VOYAGEUR REVERSE 1965-1966. A new obverse with the Queen showing more mature facial features and wearing a tiara was introduced on all denominations in 1965. The first obverse for the dollar had to be replaced because it gave such poor die life. The difficulty was caused by a flat field (Small Beads variety). A single trial die (Medium Beads variety) established that an obverse with the field sloping up at the edge was preferable, so new master tools were prepared (Large Beads variety) and those dies became the standard variety. In addition two reverses, bearing slightly different 5s were employed, creating five varieties in all for 1965. Through an error a small quantity of 1966 dollars were struck with the outmoded Small Beads obverse.

Designer: Portrait: Arnold Machin

The physical and chemical specifications are as for the 1958-1964 issues.

TYPE 1 and 2

Small Beads Obverse
1965-1966, rear jewel in
tiara is well attached

TYPE 3 and 4

Large Beads Obverse
rear jewel in tiara is well
attached

TYPE 5

Medium Beads Obverse
1965, rear jewel in tiara is
nearly detached

1965 Pointed 5 (at bottom)   1965 Blunt 5 (at bottom)

Date and Mint Mark	Quantity Minted	EF-40	AU-50	MS-60	MS-63	MS-64	MS-65
1965 SB, P5; T-1	10,768,569	6.	7.	10.	13.	100.	300.
1965 SB, B5; T-2, Medal	Incl.	6.	7.	10.	13.	100.	300.
1965 SB; T-2, Coinage	Incl.			Very rare			
1965 LB, B5; T-3	Incl. above	6.	7.	10.	13.	60.	150.
1965 LB, P5; T-4	Incl. above	6.	7.	10.	13.	60.	150.
1965 MB, B5; T-5	Incl. above	10.	12.	15.	40.	150.	600.
1966 LB	9,912,178	6.	7.	10.	13.	60.	150.
1966 SB	Incl. above	–	–	3,000.	3,500.	4,000.	5,000.

COMMEMORATIVE FOR CENTENNIAL OF CONFEDERATION 1967. A design for the reverse showing a Canada goose in flight was chosen as part of the set of commemorative coins for this year. The obverse was the Large Beads variety of 1965-1966.

Designer: Reverse: Alex Colville
Modeller: Reverse: Myron Cook
Composition: .800 silver, .200 copper
Weight: 23.33 grams
Diameter: 36.00 mm
Edge: Reeded
Die Axis: ↑↑

Date and Mint Mark	Quantity Minted	EF-40	AU-50	MS-60	MS-63	MS-64	MS-65
1967, Medal	6,767,496	7.	8.	10.	15.	100.	300.
1967, Coinage	Incl. above			Very rare			

Note: In 1967 141,741 pieces were melted.

ONE DOLLAR - NICKEL
Elizabeth II 1968 - 1987

VOYAGEUR REVERSE RESUMED; REDUCED SIZE COINAGE 1968-1969. When the voyageur reverse design was resumed in 1968, the strikes were in nickel. In order to make coining easier for the harder metal the diameter was reduced considerably.

Engraver: Myron Cook, using existing models
Composition: 1.00 nickel
Weight: 15.62 grams
Diameter: 32.13 mm
Edge: Reeded
Die Axis: ↑↑

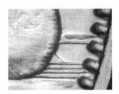

| Island | Small Island | No Island |

Date and Mint Mark	Quantity Minted	MS-60	MS-63	MS-64	MS-65
1968	5,579,714	2.	3.	5.	20.
1968 Small Island	Incl. above	6.	12.	18.	50.
1968 No Island	Incl. above	6.	12.	18.	50.
1969	4,809,313	2.	3.	5.	20.

Note: For the 1968 Double Die Waterline variety P.L. Dollar see page 344.

MANITOBA CENTENNIAL COMMEMORATIVE 1970. The year 1970 saw Canada's first commemorative nickel dollar, with a special reverse featuring a prairie crocus in recognition of the centenary of Manitoba's entry into Confederation. The obverse continued unchanged from the 1968-1969 issues.

Designer:
Reverse: Raymond Taylor
(RT to right of crocus plant)
Modeller: Reverse: Walter Ott

The physical and chemical specifications are as for the 1968-1969 issues.

Date and Mint Mark	Quantity Minted	MS-60	MS-63	MS-64	MS-65
1970	4,140,058	2.	3.	5.	20.

BRITISH COLUMBIA CENTENNIAL COMMEMORATIVE 1971. The nickel dollar for 1971 commemorates the entry in 1871 of British Columbia into Confederation. Its design is based on the arms of the province, with a shield at the bottom and dogwood blossoms at the top. The obverse was the same as on previous nickel issues.

Designer and Modeller:
Obverse: Arnold Machin
Reverse: Thomas Shingles
(TS at bottom of shield)
Composition: 1.00 nickel
Weight: 15.62 grams
Diameter: 32.13 mm
Edg: Reeded
Die Axis: ↑↑

Date and Mint Mark	Quantity Minted	MS-60	MS-63	MS-64	MS-65
1971	4,260,781	2.	3.	5.	20.

VOYAGEUR REVERSE RESUMED 1972. In 1972 the standard voyageur reverse was resumed. The obverse and reverse are the same as for the 1968-1969 issues. The physical and chemical specifications are as for the 1968-1969 issues.

Date and Mint Mark	Quantity Minted	MS-60	MS-63	MS-64	MS-65
1972	2,193,000	2.	3.	5.	20.

P.E.I. CENTENNIAL COMMEMORATIVE 1973. The special reverse on the nickel dollar of 1973 marks the 100th anniversary of the entry of Prince Edward Island into Confederation. The design depicts the provincial legislature building. A new obverse with a smaller, more detailed portrait, and fewer rim beads placed farther from the rim is brought into use with this reverse.

Designer and Modeller:
Obverse: Arnold Machin
Patrick Brindley
Reverse: Terry Manning
(TM at left of building)
Reverse: Walter Ott
(WO at right of building)
Composition: 1.00 nickel
Weight: 15.62 grams
Diameter: 32.13 mm
Edge: Reeded
Die Axis: ↑↑

Date and Mint Mark	Quantity Minted	MS-60	MS-63	MS-64	MS-65
1973	3,196,452	2.	3.	5.	20.

WINNIPEG COMMEMORATIVE 1974. The 1974 issue of nickel dollars commemorates the centenary of the city of Winnipeg, Manitoba. The design consists of a large 100; in the first 0 is a view of Main Street in 1874 and in the second 0 is a view of the same location 100 years later. For the first time the special collectors issue of silver dollars for that year had the same design.

Designer and Modeller:
Obverse: Arnold Machin
Patrick Brindley
Reverse: Paul Pederson
(PP above the date)
Patrick Brindley
(B below Winnipeg)
Composition: 1.00 nickel
Weight: 15.62 grams
Diameter: 32.13 mm
Edge: Reeded
Die Axis: ↑↑

1974 Single Yoke   1974 Double Yoke

Date and Mint Mark	Quantity Minted	MS-60	MS-63	MS-64	MS-65
1974 Single Yoke	2,799,363	2.	3.	5.	20.
1974 Double Yoke	Incl. above	75.	125.	175.	600.

VOYAGEUR REVERSE RESUMED 1975-1976. The designs employed for the voyageur dollars of 1975-1976 were essentially continuations of previous designs, except for some minor variations on the obverse. The physical and chemical specifications are as for the 1974 issues.

Date and Mint Mark	Quantity Minted	MS-60	MS-63	MS-64	MS-65
1975	3,256,000	2.	3.	5.	20.
1976	2,101,000	2.	3.	5.	20.

MODIFIED REVERSE 1977. A major alteration was made in the reverse of the 1977 dollar. A new model was prepared in which the size of the device was reduced and the legend was in small lettering, much farther from the rim. The rim denticles were replaced with beads.

Designer and Modeller:
Obverse: Arnold Machin
Patrick Brindley
Reverse: E. Hahn
Terry Smith
Composition: 1.00 nickel
Weight: 15.62 grams
Diameter: 32.13 mm
Edge: Reeded
Die Axis: ↑↑

Date and Mint Mark	Quantity Minted	MS-60	MS-63	MS-64	MS-65
1977	1,393,745	2.	3.	5.	20.

MODIFIED DESIGNS 1978-1981. Continued major changes occurred in the nickel dollar coinage in 1978. In a reversal of design policy, the Mint returned to designs more like those used prior to 1977. On the obverse the unmodified Machin portrait was restored, but the beads were farther from the rim than on the 1968-1972 issues. The reverse had a design similar to that of 1975-1976, complete with rim denticles instead of beads, but the northern lights were rendered as raised lines, as they were for the 1977 issue.

Designer and Modeller:
Obverse: Arnold Machin
Reverse: E. Hahn
Composition: 1.00 Nickel
Weight: 15.62 grams
Diameter: 32.13 mm
Edge: Reeded
Die Axis: ↑↑

Date and Mint Mark	Quantity Minted	MS-60	MS-63	MS-64	MS-65
1978	2,948,488	2.	3.	5.	20.
1979	1,884,789	2.	3.	5.	20.
1980	2,544,000	2.	3.	5.	20.
1981	2,778,900	2.	3.	5.	20.

CONSTITUTION COMMEMORATIVE DOLLAR 1982. On June 10, 1982, a one dollar pure nickel circulating coin was struck to commemorate the new Canadian Constitution. The obverse of the coin depicts the effigy of Queen Elizabeth II and the year 1982. The reverse features a faithful reproduction of the celebrated painting of the Fathers of Confederation. It commemorates the Constitution with the inscription "1867 CONFEDERATION" above the painting and "CONSTITUTION 1982" beneath it. This is the first time a commemorative and a voyageur dollar were issued in the same year for circulation. For the collector's edition of this dollar please see page 270.

Two varieties of the 1982 Constitution dollar are known: one with a coinage die axis, the other where the coin was struck on an under weight planchet. The thin planchet variety is the result of purchases of blanks from a private producer. Most of the latter were recovered by the Mint's quality control.

Designer and Modeller:
Obverse: Arnold Machin,
RCM Staff
Reverse: Ago Aarand,
RCM Staff
Composition: 1.00 Nickel
Weight: 15.62 grams
Diameter: 32.13 mm
Edge: Reeded
Die Axis: ↑↑, ↑↓

Date and Mint Mark	Quantity Minted	MS-60	MS-63	MS-64	MS-65
1982 Constitution, Medal	11,812,000	2.	3.	5.	20.
1982 Constitution, Coinage	Incl. above			Very rare	
1982 Constitution, Coinage, thin planchet	Incl. above			Very rare	

VOYAGEUR REVERSE; MODIFIED DESIGN 1982-1983. The modified designs of 1978 were continued for 1982 and 1983.

Date and Mint Mark	Quantity Minted	MS-60	MS-63	MS-64	MS-65
1982	1,544,398	2.	3.	5.	20.
1983	2,267,525	2.	3.	5.	20.

JACQUES CARTIER COMMEMORATIVE DOLLAR 1984. The four hundred and fiftieth year of Jacques Cartier's landing at Gaspe, Quebec was honoured on July 24, 1984 by the issuing of a commemorative nickel dollar. Again, as in 1982 a commemorative and a voyageur design were issued for circulation in the same year. For the collector's edition of this dollar please see page 271.

Designer and Modeller:
Obverse: Arnold Machin, RCM Staff
Reverse: Hector Greville, Victor Cote
Composition: 1.00 nickel
Weight: 15.62 grams
Diameter: 32.13 mm
Edge: Reeded
Die Axis: ↑↑

Date and Mint Mark	Quantity Minted	MS-60	MS-63	MS-64	MS-65
1984 Jacques Cartier	6,141,503	2.	3.	5.	20.

VOYAGEUR REVERSE; MODIFIED DESIGN 1984-1987. The modified designs of 1978 were continued between 1984 and 1987. The 1987 issue of the nickel dollar appeared only in uncirculated sets sold by the numismatic department of the Mint (see page 346).

Date and Mint Mark	Quantity Minted	MS-60	MS-63	MS-64	MS-65
1984	1,223,486	3.	5.	8.	25.
1985	3,104,592	2.	3.	5.	20.
1986	3,089,225	2.	3.	5.	20.
1987	Not issued for circulation	—	—	—	—

ONE DOLLAR - NICKEL/BRONZE
Elizabeth II 1987 to date

TIARA PORTRAIT; LOON REVERSE (11-sided) 1987-1989. The increased costs associated with the production of the one dollar bank note lead the Bank of Canada to request from the Mint a high denomination coin that would circulate, eventually replacing the paper note. The previous silver and nickel dollar issues did not. The new loon reverse is of reduced size, eleven-sided and new composition allowing the coin to be easily distinguishable from other circulating denominations. And of course, being lighter in weight it facilitated the use of pocket change. In 1987 two different sizes of dollar coins were issued, the Voyageur and the Loon. See page 273 for the proof loon dollar.

Designer and Modeller:
Obverse: Arnold Machin
Reverse: Robert R. Carmichael
Modeller: Reverse: Terrence Smith
Composition: .915 nickel,
.085 bronze
Weight: 7.00 grams
Diameter: 26.72 mm (1987)
26.50 mm (1988/89)
Thickness: 1.95 mm (1987)
1.75 (1988/89)
Edge: Plain
Die Axis: ↑↑

Date and Mint Mark	Quantity Minted	MS-60	MS-63	MS-64	MS-65
1987	205,405,000	2.	3.	5.	20.
1988	138,893,539	2.	3.	5.	20.
1989	184,773,902	2.	3.	5.	20.

CROWNED PORTRAIT; LOON REVERSE 1990-1991. A new obverse portrait of the Queen wearing a diamond diadem and jewellery was introduced on all denominations in 1990.

Designer and Modeller:
Obverse: Dora de Pédery-Hunt
Ago Aarand
Reverse: Robert R. Carmichael
Terrence Smith
Composition: .915 nickel,
.085 bronze
Weight: 7.00 grams
Diameter: 26.50 mm, 11 sided
Thickness: 1.75 mm
Edge: Plain
Die Axis: ↑↑

Date and Mint Mark	Quantity Minted	MS-60	MS-63	MS-64	MS-65
1990	68,402,000	2.	3.	5.	20.
1991	23,156,000	2.	3.	5.	20.

COMMEMORATIVE FOR 125TH ANNIVERSARY 1867-1992. The reverse design was modified to include the bracket dates 1867-1992 for the 125th birthday of Canada.

Designer, modeller and physical specifications are as for the 1990 issues.

Date and Mint Mark	Quantity Minted	MS-60	MS-63	MS-64	MS-65
1992	4,242,085	2.	3.	5.	20.

125TH ANNIVERSARY OF CONFEDERATION 1867-1992. Issued as part of the "Canada 125" coin program celebrating Canada's 125th birthday. The design features the centre block of the Parliament Buildings and three children seated on the ground. One child holds a Canadian flag while another points to the Peace Tower clock which reads 1:25. For the collector's issue see page 276.

Designer and Modeller:
Obverse: Dora de Pédery-Hunt
Ago Aarand
Reverse: Rita Swanson
Ago Aarand
Composition: Nickel electroplated with bronze
Weight: 7.00 grams
Diameter: 26.50 mm, 11 sided
Edge: Plain
Die Axis: ↑↑

Date and Mint Mark	Quantity Minted	MS-60	MS-63	MS-64	MS-65
1992	23,010,915	2.	3.	5.	20.

LOON REVERSE RESUMED 1993-1994. In 1993 the practice of using the current date was resumed.

Designer, modeller and physical specifications are as for the 1990 issues.

Date and Mint Mark	Quantity Minted	MS-60	MS-63	MS-64	MS-65
1993	33,662,000	2.	3.	5.	20.
1994	40,406,000	2.	3.	5.	20.

CROWNED PORTRAIT; REMEMBRANCE REVERSE 1994. The National War Memorial in Ottawa, unveiled by King George VI in May of 1939, commemorates the Canadians who died in WWI. The National War Memorial was rededicated in 1982 for WWII and the Korean War. For the collector's issue see page 278.

Designer and Modeller:
Obverse: Dora de Pédery-Hunt
          Ago Aarand
Reverse: RCM Staff
Composition: Nickel - bronze
Weight: 7.00 grams
Diameter: 26.50 mm, 11-sided
Thickness: 1.95 mm
Edge: Plain
Die Axis: ↑↑

Date and Mint Mark	Quantity Minted	MS-60	MS-63	MS-64	MS-65
1994	15,000,000	2.	3.	5.	20.

CROWNED PORTRAIT; PEACEKEEPING REVERSE 1995. Commemorating Canada's commitment to world peace and the 50th anniversary of the founding of the United Nations. The reverse depicts the Peacekeeping Monument in Ottawa, unveiled in 1992. For the collector's issue see page 278.

Designer and Modeller:
Obverse: Dora de Pédery-Hunt
          Ago Aarand
Reverse: J. K. Harman
          R. G. Henriquez
          C. H. Oberlander
          Susan Taylor
Composition: Nickel - bronze
Weight: 7.00 grams
Diameter: 26.50 mm, 11-sided
Thickness: 1.95 mm
Edge: Plain
Die Axis: ↑↑

Date and Mint Mark	Quantity Minted	MS-60	MS-63	MS-64	MS-65
1995	Included in 1995 Loon mintage	2.	3.	5.	20.

CROWNED PORTRAIT; LOON REVERSE CONTINUED 1995-2001. From 1997 to 2001 the One Dollar Loon coins were not issued for general circulation. They were found in the collectors sets for these years. The 1997 tenth anniversary Flying Loon was issued only in the collectors sets for that year (see page 281).

Designer, modeller and physical specifications are as for the 1990 issues.

Date and Mint Mark	Quantity Minted	MS-60	MS-63	MS-64	MS-65
1995	41,813,100	2.	3.	5.	10.
1996	17,101,000	2.	3.	5.	10.
1997	Not issued for circulation	–	–	–	–
1997 FL	Not issued for circulation	–	–	–	–
1998	Not issued for circulation	–	–	–	–
1998W	Not issued for circulation	–	–	–	–
1999	Not issued for circulation	–	–	–	–
2000	Not issued for circulation	–	–	–	–
2000W	Not issued for circulation	–	–	–	–
2001	Not issued for circulation	–	–	–	–

CROWNED PORTRAIT; ELIZABETH II, GOLDEN JUBILEE 1952-2002. Issued to commemorate the 50th anniversary of the reign of Queen Elizabeth II, all circulating coinage carried the double dates of her reign 1952-2002. The Family of Loons and the Centre Ice Loon reverses were issued only in the collectors sets for 2002 (see page 285 and 286).

Designer, modeller and physical specifications are as for the 1990 issues.

Date and Mint Mark	Quantity Minted	MS-60	MS-63	MS-64	MS-65
1952-2002	2,302,000	2.	3.	5.	10.

CROWNED PORTRAIT; LOON REVERSE CONTINUED 2003 TO DATE.

Designer, modeller and physical specifications are as for the 1990 issues.

Date and Mint Mark	Quantity Minted	MS-60	MS-63	MS-64	MS-65
2003	N/A	2.	3.	5.	10.
2004	N/A	2.	3.	5.	10.

TWO DOLLAR CIRCULATING COINS

TWO DOLLAR BI-METALLIC
Elizabeth II 1996 to 1999

CROWNED PORTRAIT; POLAR BEAR REVERSE 1996-1999. On February 19, 1996, Canada's new two dollar coin was officially launched. The lifespan of a coin is over twenty years, while that of a bank note is only a year. The economies are obvious. The new coin is bi-metallic with a nickel outer ring and an aluminum bronze core. The reverse features a polar bear along the edge of a floe, and the obverse features the effigy of Her Majesty Queen Elizabeth II. See the Collector section on page 288 for collector issues of the two dollar coin. The Winnipeg Mint Mark (W) is found only on coins from the "Oh! Canada" and "Tiny Treasures" sets issued by the Numismatic Department of the Mint.

Designer and Modeller:
Obverse: Dora de Pédery-Hunt
Ago Aarand
Reverse: Brent Townsend
Ago Aarand
Composition:
Outer Ring: .99 nickel
Inner Core: .92 copper,
.06 aluminum,
.02 nickel
Weight: 7.3 grams
Diameter:
Outer Ring: 28 mm
Inner Core: 16.8 mm
Thickness: 1.80 mm
Edge: Interrupted serration
Die Axis: ↑↑

Date and Mint Mark	Quantity Minted	MS-60	MS-63	MS-64	MS-65
1996	375,483,000	3.00	5.00	7.50	25.00
1997	16,942,000	3.00	5.00	7.50	25.00
1998	5,309,000	3.00	5.00	7.50	25.00
1998W	Not issued for circulation	—	—	—	—
1999	Not issued for circulation	—	—	—	—

CROWNED PORTRAIT; NUNAVUT REVERSE 1999. This two dollar coin was issued on May 27, 1999, to commemorate the creation of a third territory in Canada, Nunavut.

Designer and Modeller:
Obverse: Dora de Pédery-Hunt
Reverse: G. Arnaktavyok
José Osio
Specifications: Same as 1996

Date and Mint Mark	Quantity Minted	MS-60	MS-63	MS-64	MS-65
1999	25,130,000	3.00	5.00	7.50	25.00

CROWNED PORTRAIT; POLAR BEAR AND CUBS REVERSE 2000. Issued to commemorate 2000 Millennium, the Path of Knowledge $2.00 coin was launched July 1, 2000 at a citizenship ceremony at Downsview, Toronto. The coin is inscribed with knowledge - Le Savoir reflecting the experience, wisdom and knowledge that is passed down from generation to generation.

Designer and Modeller:
  Obverse: Dora de Pédery-Hunt
  Reverse: Tony Bianco
Specifications: Same as 1996

Date and Mint Mark	Quantity Minted	MS-60	MS-63	MS-64	MS-65
2000	29,847,000	3.00	4.00	7.50	25.00

CROWNED PORTRAIT; POLAR BEAR REVERSE CONTINUED 2000-2001.

Designers, Modellers and Physical specifications are as for the 1996 issues.

Date and Mint Mark	Quantity Minted	MS-60	MS-63	MS-64	MS-65
2000	Not Issued for circulation	–	–	–	–
2000W	Not issued for circulation	–	–	–	–
2001	11,910,000	3.00	7.00	7.50	25.00

ELIZABETH II GOLDEN JUBILEE 1952-2002. Issued to commemorate the 50th anniversary of the reign of Queen Elizabeth II, all circulating coinage carried the double dates of her reign 1952-2002.

Designers, modellers and physical specifications same as for 1996 issue.

Date and Mint Mark	Quantity Minted	MS-60	MS-63	MS-64	MS-65
1952-2002	27,008,000	3.00	5.00	7.50	25.00

CROWNED PORTRAIT; POLAR BEAR REVERSE CONTINUED 2003 TO DATE.

Designers, modellers and physical specifications are as for the 1966 issued.

Date and Mint Mark	Quantity Minted	MS-60	MS-63	MS-64	MS-65
2003	N/A	4.00	5.00	7.50	25.00
2004	N/A	4.00	5.00	7.50	25.00

OTTAWA MINT SOVEREIGNS

The British £1 pieces (sovereigns) coined at the Ottawa Mint between 1908 and 1919 occupy a controversial position in Canadian numismatics. Some argue that these pieces are Canadian and must be collected as part of the Canadian series, while others claim that they are British and are separate from the decimal series of the Dominion of Canada.

From the time of the opening of the Ottawa Mint it was the intention of the Dominion government to mint decimal gold coins; however, the fact that the Ottawa Mint was a branch of the Royal Mint in London meant it was obligated to mint sovereigns on request. And while sovereigns were legal tender in Canada, so were gold coins of the United States. Neither type of gold circulated to any significant degree in Canada in the 20th century. Most companies who requested the Ottawa Mint to strike sovereigns did so because they wanted the coins for export purposes. Finally, the fact that some sovereigns were coined at the Ottawa Mint does not automatically make them Canadian, any more than other coinages (e.g. Newfoundland or Jamaica) produced there.

ONE POUND (SOVEREIGNS)
Edward VII 1908 - 1910

As with all other branch mint sovereigns of the period, the Edward VII Canadian sovereigns are identical to the corresponding London mint issues except for the branch mint mark. The 1908 strikes were Specimen coins only and the tiny mintage was merely to establish the series.

Designer and Modeller:
  Portrait: G.W. DeSalles
  (DES below bust)
  Reverse: Benedetto Pistrucci
  (B.P. below ground line at right)
Composition: .917 gold,
  .083 copper
Weight: 7.99 grams
Diameter: 22.05 mm
Edge: Reeded
Die Axis: ↑↑

The "C" mint mark (for Canada) is on the ground line above the centre of the date.

Date and Mint Mark	Quantity Minted	VF-20	EF-40	AU-50	MS-60	MS-63	MS-64
1908C	636	3,000.	3,500.	4,000.	4,500.	5,000.	6,000.
1909C	16,273	300.	350.	475.	725.	3,000.	6,000.
1910C	28,012	275.	325.	400.	750.	4,000.	10,000.

ONE POUND (SOVEREIGNS)
George V 1911 - 1919

The mintages for the Ottawa mint sovereigns of George V continued the modest trend set in the previous reign. The total of all sovereigns from Ottawa barely equalled the yearly mintage at London or one of the Australian branch mints.

The 1916C issue is rare, with about fifty or so pieces known. The rarity of this issue is probably because most of the mintage was melted, although this is by no means an established fact. Until the last few years the 1916 London issue was also rare, but thousands of them were released from a British bank.

The reverse of the George V sovereigns is the same as that for Edward VII.

Designer and Modeller:
Portrait: E.B. Mackennal
(B.M. on truncation)
Composition: .917 gold, .083 copper
Weight: 7.99 grams
Diameter: 22.05 mm
Edge: Reeded
Die Axis: ↑↑

Date and Mint Mark	Quantity Minted	VF-20	EF-40	AU-50	MS-60	MS-63	MS-64
1911C	256,946	150.	155.	165.	185.	300.	850.
1913C	3,715	700.	900.	1,100.	2,000.	4,500.	–
1914C	14,891	350.	450.	550.	850.	1,700.	3,500.
1916C	6,111	16,500.	18,500.	22,500.	25,000.	30,000.	–
1917C	58,845	150.	155.	165.	350.	1,000.	3,000.
1918C	106,516	150.	155.	165.	350.	1,500.	3,000.
1919C	135,889	150.	155.	165.	350.	1,250.	3,000.

FIVE DOLLARS – GOLD
George V 1912 - 1914

From the first year of operation of the Ottawa Mint it was planned that gold should be coined in dollar denominations as well as British sovereigns. However, the preparations proceeded slowly and it was not until 1911 that final designs were decided upon (see DC-7 and DC-8 in the chapter on patterns) for the $5 and $10 coins. Originally it had been planned to strike denominations of $2.50, $5, $10 and $20, but sometime in 1911 these plans were modified to include only the two middle denominations.

Coins for circulation were first issued in 1912. Their production was halted in 1914, when Canada adopted new wartime legislation to restrict the flow of gold. At that time notes issued by the Dominion government ceased to be redeemable in gold. This redeemability was not restored until 1926.

The design for the reverse features the old Canadian coat-of-arms superimposed upon two boughs of maple.

Designer: Portrait: Sir E. B. Mackennal
        (B.M. on truncation)
        Reverse: W.H.J. Blakemore
Composition: .900 gold, .100 copper
Weight: 8.36 grams
Diameter: 21.59 mm
Edge: Reeded
Die Axis: ↑↑

Date and Mint Mark	Quantity Minted	VF-20	EF-40	AU-50	MS-60	MS-63	MS-64
1912	165,680	200.	250.	300.	400.	1,000.	2,500.
1913	98,832	200.	250.	300.	425.	1,100.	4,500.
1914	31,122	400.	500.	650.	900.	4,500.	9,000.

TEN DOLLARS – GOLD
George V 1912 - 1914

The designs of this denomination are the same as those of the $5 except for the change in value.

Designer: Portrait: Sir E. B. Mackennal
        (B.M. on truncation)
        Reverse: W.H.J. Blakemore
Composition: .900 gold, .100 copper
Weight: 16.72 grams
Diameter: 26.92 mm
Edge: Reeded
Die Axis: ↑↑

Date and Mint Mark	Quantity Minted	VF-20	EF-40	AU-50	MS-60	MS-63	MS-64
1912	74,759	400.	500.	600.	900.	3,250.	9,000.
1913	149,232	400.	500.	600.	950.	4,500.	12,500.
1914	140,068	550.	700.	800.	1,150.	4,000.	15,000.

SPECIMEN COINS OF CANADA

The sets of Specimen coins produced between 1858 and 1980 are among the most spectacular items in Canadian numismatics and are keenly sought after by collectors. These coins were beautifully struck and represent Canadian coinage at its finest.

The finish imparted to specimen coins has varied over the years. During the Victorian period, it consisted of frosted, raised elements with bright, mirror fields. In the reigns of Edward VII and George V an overall satin (sometimes called matte) finish was in vogue. The 1937 coins of George VI came with both finishes. Between 1938 and the mid-1940s the specimen coins tended to have an overall polished appearance.

Specimen sets were often issued in official cases. These cases are sometimes encountered without coins and so are numbered, described and priced as separate entities in the listings that follow.

This is the first major review of the Specimen section in over ten years. It is hoped the new listings are more friendly to the collector in the new format. Our next task is to strengthen the description of each entry, that is we hope to list Proof or Specimen quality for each entry in our listing. However, before this can be accomplished, modern definitions of these qualities must be derived. We solicit any help with these definitions which you may wish to give. Please write using the address given at the front of this catalogue.

These prices are only an indication, specimen coins being very rare with only a few examples known, and the final price will be set between the buyer and seller.

PROVINCE OF NEWFOUNDLAND

ONE CENT 1864 - 1947

Date and Mint Mark	Description	SP-63 Brown	SP-65 Brown	SP-65 Red
1864	Plain, NF-18	3,500.	5,000.	10,000.
1872H	Plain	400.	1,200.	2,500.
1873	Plain	3,000.	6,000.	12,500.
1880, Oval 0	Plain	3,000.	5,000.	10,000.
1885	Plain	3,000.	5,000.	10,000.
1894	Plain	1,200.	3,000.	7,500.
1896	Plain	1,200.	3,000.	7,500.
1904H	Plain	6,000.	10,000.	15,000.
1917C	Plain	750.	2,000.	4,000.
1919C	Plain	1,250.	2,000.	5,000.
1929C	Plain	1,250.	2,000.	4,000.
1938	Plain	750.	2,000.	5,000.
1940	Plain	750.	2,000.	5,000.
1947	Plain	1,500.	3,000.	6,500

PROVINCE OF NEWFOUNDLAND

FIVE CENTS 1865 - 1940

Date and Mint Mark	Description	SP-63	SP-65	SP-67
1865	Plain	4,500.	12,500.	25,000.
1870	Plain	4,500.	12,500.	25,000.
1870	Reeded	4,500.	12,500.	25,000.
1873	Reeded	12,500.	30,000.	50,000.
1880	Reeded	6,500.	15,000.	30,000.
1881	Reeded	6,500.	15,000.	30,000.
1882H	Reeded	2,000.	4,500.	12,500.
1885	Reeded	8,000.	20,000.	40,000.
1888	Reeded	8,000.	20,000.	40,000.
1890	Reeded	5,000.	12,000.	25,000.
1894	Reeded	5,000.	12,000.	25,000.
1896	Reeded	5,000.	12,000.	25,000.
1903	Reeded	2,000.	4,500.	10,000.
1904H	Reeded	1,250.	3,000.	7,500.
1912	Reeded	1,500.	6,000.	15,000.
1917C	Reeded	1,500.	6,000.	15,000.
1919C	Reeded	1,500.	6,000.	15,000.
1938	Reeded	1,250.	2,500.	7,500.
1940C	Reeded	1,250.	6,000.	10,000.

TEN CENTS 1864 - 1946

Date and Mint Mark	Description	SP-63	SP-65	SP-67
1865	Plain	5,000.	15,000.	30,000.
1870	Plain	10,000.	30,000.	50,000.
1870	Reeded	10,000.	30,000.	50,000.
1873	Reeded	10,000.	30,000.	50,000.
1880	Reeded	7,500.	17,500.	35,000.
1882H	Reeded	3,000.	5,500.	12,500.
1885	Reeded	7,500.	20,000.	40,000.
1888	Reeded	7,500.	20,000.	40,000.
1890	Reeded	5,000.	15,000.	30,000.
1894	Reeded	5,000.	15,000.	30,000.
1896	Reeded	5,000.	15,000.	30,000.
1903	Reeded	2,500.	5,000.	12,500.
1904H	Reeded	1,500.	4,000.	10,000.
1912	Reeded	1,750.	7,000.	17,500.
1917C	Reeded	1,750.	7,000.	17,500.
1919C	Reeded	1,750.	7,000.	17,500.
1938	Reeded	2,000.	4,500.	9,000.
1940	Reeded	1,500.	7,000.	11,500.
1946C	Reeded	750.	1,750.	3,500.

PROVINCE OF NEWFOUNDLAND

TWENTY CENTS 1865 - 1912

Date and Mint Mark	Description	SP-63	SP-65	SP-67
1865	Plain	6,500.	17,500.	35,000.
1865	Reeded	9,000.	25,000.	45,000.
1870	Plain	6,500.	17,500.	30,000.
1870	Reeded	6,500.	17,500.	30,000.
1873	Reeded	10,000.	30,000.	50,000.
1880	Reeded	7,500.	20,000.	40,000.
1881	Reeded	7,500.	20,000.	40,000.
1882H	Reeded	3,500.	10,000.	20,000.
1885	Reeded	10,000.	30,000.	50,000.
1888	Reeded	9,000.	27,500.	50,000.
1890	Reeded	6,500.	17,500.	35,000.
1894	Reeded	6,500.	17,500.	35,000.
1896, L6	Reeded	6,500.	17,500.	35,000.
1900	Reeded	6,500.	17,500.	35,000.
1904H	Reeded	1,500.	5,000.	10,000.
1912	Reeded	2,000.	8,000.	20,000.

TWENTY-FIVE CENTS 1917 - 1919

Date and Mint Mark	Description	SP-63	SP-65	SP-67
1917C	Reeded	2,000.	8,000.	20,000.
1919C	Reeded	2,000.	8,000.	20,000.

FIFTY CENTS 1870 - 1919

Date and Mint Mark	Description	SP-60	SP-63	SP-65
1870	Plain	15,000.	50,000.	100,000.
1870	Reeded	15,000.	50,000.	100,000.
1873	Reeded	20,000.	75,000.	150,000.
1874	Reeded	20,000.	75,000.	150,000.
1880	Reeded	20,000.	75,000.	150,000.
1881	Reeded	–	–	150,000.
1882H	Reeded	7,500.	15,000.	45,000.
1885	Reeded	20,000.	75,000.	150,000.
1888	Reeded	20,000.	75,000.	150,000.
1896	Reeded	15,000.	50,000.	100,000.
1904H	Reeded, Satin	–	–	35,000.
1904H	Reeded, Matte	4,500.	10,000.	25,000.
1917C	Reeded	3,000.	5,000.	10,000.
1919C	Reeded	3,000.	5,000.	10,000.

PROVINCE OF NEWFOUNDLAND

TWO DOLLARS 1865 - 1885

Date and Mint Mark	Description	SP-63	SP-64	SP-65
1865	Plain	30,000.	40,000.	75,000.
1870	Reeded	40,000.	60,000.	100,000.
1872	Reeded	25,000.	35,000.	65,000.
1880	Reeded	75,000.	115,000.	175,000.
1882H	Reeded	17,500.	25,000.	60,000.
1885	Reeded	40,000.	60,000.	100,000.

SPECIMEN SETS

Date and Mint Mark	Description	Average Grade	Price Indication
1865, Double Set	10 Coins w/box 1¢ - $2	SP-65	250,000.
1870	5 Coin, n/box 5¢ - $2	SP-65	200,000.
1880	6 Coin, n/box 1¢ - $2	SP-65	300,000.
1882H	5 Coin, n/box 5¢ - $2	SP-66	150,000.
1885	6 Coin, n/box 1¢ - $2	SP-65	250,000.
1888	4 Coin, n/box 5¢ - 50¢	SP-65	150,000.
1896	5 Coin, n/box 1¢ - 50¢	SP-65	100,000.
1904H	5 Coin, n/box 1¢ - 50¢	SP-67	85,000.
1912	3 Coin, n/box 5¢ - 20¢	SP-64	13,000.
1917C	6 Coin, n/box 1¢ - 50¢	SP-64	15,000.
1919C	6 Coin, n/box 1¢ - 50¢	SP-64	15,000.
1938C	3 Coin, n/box 1¢ - 10¢	SP-65	9,000.
1940C	3 Coin, n/box 1¢ - 10¢	SP-65	15,000.

CASES

Charlton Number	Intended Contents	Exterior Colour and Dimensions	Interior Colours	Price For Empty Case
1	Newfoundland 1864(1¢);1865 (others) 1¢, 5¢, 10¢, 20¢, $2 1¢, 5¢, 10¢, 20¢, $2		Details unknown. Possibly same as case #1	$2,000.

PROVINCE OF PRINCE EDWARD ISLAND

ONE CENT 1871

Date	Denom.	Description	SP-60 Brown	SP-63 Red/Brown	SP-65 Red
1871	1¢	Coinage axis	1,000.	2,500.	6,000.
1871	1¢	Medal axis	1,000.	2,500.	6,000.

PROVINCE OF NOVA SCOTIA

SPECIMEN COINAGE OF 1861

Date	Denom.	Description	SP-60 Brown	SP-63 Red/Brown	SP-65 Red
1861	½¢	Mirror	800.	2,000.	5,000.
1861	1¢	Large Rosebud, Mirror	1,000.	2,500.	6,000.

PROVINCE OF NEW BRUNSWICK

COPPER COINAGE OF 1861 AND 1862

Date	Denom.	Description	SP-60 Brown	SP-63 Red/Brown	SP-65 Red
1861	½¢	Plain, Mirror	1,500.	3,000.	6,000.
1861	1¢	Plain, Mirror	1,500.	3,000.	6,000.
1862	1¢	Plain, Mirror	2,500.	5,000.	10,000.

SILVER COINAGE OF 1862 AND 1864

Date	Denom.	Description	SP-60	SP-63	SP-65
1862	5¢	Plain	2,500.	7,500.	15,000.
1862	10¢	Plain, Normal Date	2,500.	7,500.	20,000.
1862	20¢	Plain	2,000.	7,500.	20,000.
1864	10¢	Plain	3,500.	10,000.	20,000.

CASES

Charlton Number	Intended Contents	Exterior Colour and Dimensions	Interior Colours	Price for Empty Case
2	New Brunswick, 1862 1¢, 5¢, 10¢, 20¢ 1¢, 5¢, 10¢, 20¢		Details unknown. Possibly same as case #1.	$1,750.
3	New Brunswick, 1862 1¢, 5¢, 10¢, 20¢		Details unknown.	$1,250.

PROVINCE OF CANADA — CANADA

ONE CENT 1858 - 1965

Date and Mint Mark	Description	SP-63 Brown	SP-65 Brown	SP-65 Red
1858	Plain	1,750.	3,000.	6,000.
1859/9	Plain, DP N-9	2,500.	4,000.	7,000.
1859	Plain, Bronze	2,500.	4,000.	7,000.
1876	Plain	3,000.	5,000.	8,000.
1876H	Plain, Copper	2,500.	4,000.	7,000.
1876H	Plain, Nickel	4,000.	7,500.	—
1881H	Plain	2,500.	4,000.	8,000.
1882H	Plain	2,500.	4,000.	8,000.
1898H	Plain	3,000.	6,000.	12,000.
1908	Plain	150.	350.	700.
1911	Plain	200.	400.	1,000.
1921	Plain	3,000.	5,000.	10,000.
1922	Plain	2,500.	4,500.	9,000.
1923	Plain	3,000.	5,000.	10,000.
1924	Plain	2,500.	4,500.	9,000.
1925	Plain	2,500.	4,500.	9,000.
1926	Plain	2,500.	4,500.	9,000.
1927	Plain	2,500.	4,500.	9,000.
1928	Plain	2,000.	4,000.	8,000.
1929	Plain	1,750.	3,500.	7,000.
1930	Plain	2,500.	4,500.	9,000.
1931	Plain	2,500.	4,500.	9,000.
1934	Plain	5,000.	10,000.	15,000.
1936, Dot	Plain	125,000.	200,000.	250,000.
1937	Plain, Mirror	100.	200.	400.
1937	Plain, Matte	30.	100.	200.
1938	Plain	2,500.	4,000.	7,000.
1944	Plain	2,500.	4,000.	7,000.
1945	Plain	450.	750.	1,500.
1946	Plain	100.	200.	300.
1947	Plain	125.	250.	400.
1947, ML	Plain	100.	200.	300.
1948	Plain	125.	225.	500.
1949	Plain	125.	200.	450.
1950	Plain	75.	150.	250.
1951	Plain	75.	150.	300.
1952	Plain	100.	200.	350.
1953, NSF	Plain	125.	250.	500.
1964	Plain	25.	50.	100.
1965	Plain	25.	50.	100.

PROVINCE OF CANADA – CANADA

FIVE CENTS 1858 - 1965

Date and Mint Mark	Description	SP-63	SP-65	SP-67
1858SD	Plain	1,200.	4,000.	10,000.
1858SD	Reeded	1,500.	4,500.	12,500.
1858LD	Plain	3,000.	7,500.	15,000.
1858LD	Reeded	4,000.	10,000.	17,500.
1870WR	Plain	3,000.	12,500.	20,000.
1870WR	Reeded	3,000.	12,500.	20,000.
1870NR	Plain	3,000.	12,500.	20,000.
1870NR	Reeded	3,000.	15,000.	20,000.
1872H	Reeded	5,000.	15,000.	25,000.
1874H, Crosslet 4	Reeded	3,500.	15,000.	25,000.
1875H, LD	Reeded	12,500.	30,000.	60,000.
1875H, SD	Reeded	15,000.	35,000.	70,000.
1880H	Reeded	3,500.	15,000.	25,000.
1881H	Reeded	3,500.	15,000.	25,000.
1882H	Reeded	4,500.	17,500.	30,000.
1885, Lg 5	Reeded	15,000.	30,000.	50,000.
1886, Sm 6	Reeded	15,000.	30,000.	50,000.
1902H	Reeded	3,500.	6,500.	17,500.
1905	Reeded	3,000.	6,000.	12,500.
1908, L8	Reeded	200.	750.	2,000.
1911	Reeded	300.	1,000.	3,000.
1921	Reeded	30,000.	60,000.	100,000.
1922	Plain	600.	1,200.	3,500.
1923	Plain	4,500.	12,000.	20,000.
1924	Plain	1,500.	5,000.	12,500.
1925	Plain	3,500.	10,000.	20,000.
1926, N6	Plain	3,000.	7,500.	20,000.
1927	Plain	2,000.	5,000.	15,000.
1928	Plain	2,500.	5,500.	17,500.
1929	Plain	1,500.	4,000.	10,000.
1930	Plain	2,500.	5,000.	15,000.
1931	Plain	2,500.	5,000.	15,000.
1932	Plain	10,000.	20,000.	50,000.
1934	Plain	2,500.	5,000.	15,000.
1936	Plain	3,000.	7,500.	20,000.
1937	Plain, Mirror	80.	150.	300.
1937	Plain, Matte	50.	125.	200.
1938	Plain	7,500.	15,000.	20,000.
1942	Plain, Nickel	–	20,000.	–
1942	Plain, Tombac	250.	1,000.	2,000.
1943	Plain, Tombac	200.	800.	1,750.
1944	Plain	200.	600.	1,500.
1945	Plain	450.	1,500.	3,000.
1946	Plain	150.	250.	500.
1947	Plain	200.	500.	1,000.
1947, ML	Plain	125.	300.	750.
1948	Plain	175.	350.	1,000.
1949	Plain	175.	300.	750.
1950	Plain	90.	250.	500.
1951, HR	Plain	1,750.	3,500.	8,500.
1951, Comm.	Plain	100.	350.	1,000.
1952	Plain	125.	300.	750.
1953, NSF	Plain	100.	250.	600.
1964	Plain	50.	100.	200.
1965	Plain	50.	100.	200.

PROVINCE OF CANADA — CANADA

TEN CENTS 1858 - 1965

Date and Mint Mark	Description	SP-63	SP-65	SP-67
1858	Plain	2,500.	6,500.	15,000.
1858	Reeded	3,000.	7,000.	17,500.
1870, Nar 0	Plain	4,500.	15,000.	25,000.
1870, Nar 0	Reeded	4,500.	15,000.	25,000.
1871	Reeded	7,500.	15,000.	25,000.
1872H	Reeded	7,500.	15,000.	25,000.
1875H	Reeded	15,000.	40,000.	100,000.
1880H	Reeded	4,000.	15,000.	25,000.
1881H	Reeded	5,000.	17,500.	30,000.
1882H	Reeded	4,500.	15,000.	25,000.
1885	Reeded	10,000.	25,000.	50,000.
1886, Lg 6	Reeded	11,000.	30,000.	60,000.
1888	Reeded	7,500.	20,000.	50,000.
1890H	Reeded	9,000.	18,000.	27,500.
1892	Reeded	7,500.	20,000.	50,000.
1894	Reeded	7,500.	20,000.	50,000.
1902H	Reeded	4,000.	10,000.	20,000.
1903H	Reeded	7,500.	15,000.	25,000.
1903	Reeded	7,500.	15,000.	25,000.
1908	Reeded	400.	1,000.	2,500.
1911	Reeded	650.	1,250.	3,500.
1913, SL	Reeded	7,500.	15,000.	25,000.
1921	Reeded	3,500.	10,000.	20,000.
1928	Reeded	2,000.	5,500.	12,500.
1929	Reeded	2,000.	5,500.	10,000.
1930	Reeded	3,500.	7,500.	15,000.
1931	Reeded	3,500.	7,500.	15,000.
1932	Reeded	5,000.	15,000.	25,000.
1934	Reeded	4,500.	10,000.	20,000.
1936, Dot	Reeded	125,000.	175,000.	225,000.
1937	Reeded, Mirror	80.	150.	300.
1937	Reeded, Matte	70.	125.	250.
1938	Reeded	2,500.	5,000.	7,500.
1939	Reeded, Mirror	2,000.	4,500.	7,500.
1944	Reeded	2,250.	4,500.	7,500.
1945	Reeded	300.	1,000.	2,000.
1946	Reeded	300.	600.	1,500.
1947	Reeded	300.	850.	1,700.
1947, ML	Reeded	150.	350.	750.
1948	Reeded	200.	400.	900.
1949	Reeded	350.	600.	1,500.
1950	Reeded	100.	300.	700.
1951	Reeded	100.	400.	800.
1952	Reeded	100.	400.	800.
1953, NSF	Reeded	100.	250.	400.
1964	Reeded	50.	100.	200.
1965	Reeded	50.	100.	200.

TWENTY CENTS 1858 - 1871

Date and Mint Mark	Description	SP-63	SP-65	SP-67
1858	Plain	3,000.	9,000.	25,000.
1858	Reeded	3,500.	10,000.	25,000.
1871	Plain	10,000.	15,000.	35,000.
1871	Reeded	10,000.	15,000.	35,000.

PROVINCE OF CANADA – CANADA

TWENTY-FIVE CENTS 1870 - 1965

Date and Mint Mark	Description	SP-63	SP-65	SP-67
1870	Reeded	6,000.	15,000.	30,000.
1870	Plain	6,000.	15,000.	30,000.
1871	Reeded	9,000.	20,000.	40,000.
1872H	Reeded	7,500.	25,000.	50,000.
1875H	Reeded	22,500.	45,000.	100,000.
1880H, Wide 0	Reeded	8,500.	25,000.	50,000.
1880H, Nar 0	Reeded	7,500.	25,000.	50,000.
1881H	Reeded	8,500.	25,000.	50,000.
1882H	Reeded	6,500.	25,000.	50,000.
1883H	Reeded	7,000.	17,500.	37,500.
1885	Reeded	15,000.	35,000.	75,000.
1886, 6/3	Reeded	15,000.	35,000.	75,000.
1888	Reeded	10,000.	25,000.	50,000.
1889	Reeded	25,000.	35,000.	75,000.
1892	Reeded	25,000.	35,000.	75,000.
1900	Reeded	9,000.	25,000.	40,000.
1902H	Reeded	4,500.	12,500.	25,000.
1903	Reeded	8,000.	17,500.	30,000.
1908	Reeded	650.	1,500.	3,500.
1911	Reeded	900.	2,000.	4,000.
1921	Reeded	7,500.	20,000.	40,000.
1927	Reeded	7,500.	20,000.	40,000.
1928	Reeded	3,000.	10,000.	20,000.
1929	Reeded	3,000.	8,000.	17,000.
1930	Reeded	3,000.	11,000.	20,000.
1931	Reeded	3,000.	11,000.	20,000.
1934	Reeded	8,000.	15,000.	25,000.
1936, Dot	Reeded	12,500.	30,000.	75,000.
1937	Reeded, Mirror	200.	500.	1,000.
1937	Reeded, Matte	100.	225.	450.
1938	Reeded	3,000.	5,000.	7,500.
1939	Reeded, Mirror	3,000.	5,000.	7,500.
1944	Reeded	3,000.	5,000.	10,000.
1945	Reeded	500.	1,500.	3,000.
1946	Reeded	400.	1,000.	2,500.
1947	Reeded	400.	1,250.	2,500.
1947, ML	Reeded	250.	600.	1,500.
1948	Reeded	350.	750.	2,000.
1949	Reeded	500.	1,000.	2,000.
1950	Reeded	150.	450.	1,000.
1951, HR	Reeded	125.	300.	750.
1952	Reeded	125.	300.	750.
1953, NSF	Reeded	150.	350.	700.
1964	Reeded	75.	150.	300.
1965	Reeded	75.	150.	300.

PROVINCE OF CANADA — CANADA

FIFTY CENTS 1870 - 1965

Date and Mint Mark	Description	SP-63	SP-65	SP-67
1870, LCW	Plain	20,000.	60,000.	100,000.
1870, LCW	Reeded	22,500.	65,000.	100,000.
1870, No LCW	Plain	50,000.	100,000.	200,000.
1871	Reeded	30,000.	60,000.	100,000.
1871H	Reeded	30,000.	60,000.	100,000.
1872H	Reeded, Mirror	30,000.	75,000.	135,000.
1872H	Reeded, Semi Matte	25,000.	60,000.	100,000.
1881H	Reeded	17,500.	35,000.	65,000.
1888	Reeded	25,000.	60,000.	100,000.
1908	Reeded	1,500.	3,000.	7,500.
1911	Reeded	3,000.	6,500.	12,500.
1921	Reeded	80,000.	150,000.	250,000.
1929	Reeded	6,500.	15,000.	30,000.
1931	Reeded	7,500.	17,500.	35,000.
1932	Reeded	12,500.	30,000.	60,000.
1934	Reeded	7,500.	20,000.	40,000.
1936	Reeded	10,000.	20,000.	35,000.
1937	Reeded, Mirror	400.	1,000.	2,000.
1937	Reeded, Matte	125.	300.	900.
1938	Reeded	2,500.	7,500.	12,500.
1944	Reeded	4,000.	12,000.	20,000.
1945	Reeded	1,000.	2,500.	7,500.
1946	Reeded	1,250.	3,000.	5,500.
1947, S7	Reeded	1,100.	3,000.	5,500.
1947, C7	Reeded	1,500.	3,500.	7,000.
1947, ML C7	Reeded	3,000.	4,000.	6,000.
1948	Reeded, Convex	750.	2,250.	6,000.
1948	Reeded, Concave	650.	1,750.	5,000.
1949	Reeded	650.	1,750.	3,500.
1950	Reeded	300.	750.	1,500.
1951	Reeded	300.	750.	1,500.
1952	Reeded	300.	750.	1,500.
1953, NSF SD	Reeded	250.	650.	1,500.
1953, NSF LD	Reeded	900.	2,000.	3,500.
1964	Reeded	150.	300.	500.
1965	Reeded	150.	300.	500.

PROVINCE OF CANADA – CANADA

ONE DOLLAR 1935 - 1966

Date and Mint Mark	Description	SP-63	SP-65	SP-67
1935	Satin Specimen	2,500.	10,000.	22,500.
1935	Matte Proof	4,500.	12,500.	25,000.
1936	Satin Specimen	2,500.	10,000.	25,000.
1936	Matte Proof	5,000.	12,500.	25,000.
1937	Mirror Proof	1,000.	2,000.	3,500.
1937	Matte Specimen	175.	400.	1,000.
1938	Mirror/Matte Proof	7,500.	17,500.	30,000.
1939	Mirror Specimen	800.	2,500.	6,000.
1939	Matte Specimen	500.	1,500.	4,000.
1945	Mirror Specimen	1,750.	5,000.	15,000.
1946	Mirror Specimen	1,500.	5,000.	10,500.
1947, BL	Satin Specimen	3,000.	9,500.	22,500.
1947, BL	Mirror Specimen	4,000.	10,000.	22,500.
1947, PT	Mirror Specimen	3,000.	9,000.	21,500.
1947, ML	Mirror Specimen	2,000.	6,000.	15,000.
1948	Mirror Specimen	3,500.	7,500.	20,000.
1948	Mirror Proof	3,500.	7,500.	20,000.
1949	Mirror Specimen	250.	1,000.	2,500.
1949	Mirror Proof	2,500.	6,500.	15,000.
1950	Mirror Specimen	600.	2,000.	3,500.
1950	Matte, one known	–	20,000.	–
1950, Arn	Mirror Specimen	2,000.	5,500.	12,500.
1951	Mirror Specimen	750.	1,750.	3,000.
1952, WL	Mirror Specimen	1,500.	3,500.	7,500.
1953, NSF	Mirror Specimen	1,000.	2,000.	3,500.
1964	Mirror Specimen	200.	450.	1,250.
1965, Ty 2	Mirror Specimen	200.	400.	1,000.
1966, LB	Mirror Specimen	200.	500.	1,500.

GOLD COINAGE 1908 - 1912

Date and Mint Mark	Description	SP-63	SP-65	SP-67	SP-68
1908C	Sovereign	5,000.	7,500.	25,000.	40,000.
1911C	Sovereign	6,500.	12,500.	25,000.	35,000.
1912	Five Dollars	10,000.	17,500.	27,500.	40,000.
1912	Ten Dollars	12,500.	20,000.	32,500.	55,000.

PROVINCE OF CANADA – CANADA

SPECIMEN SETS

Date and Mint Mark	Description	Average Grade	Price Indication
1858	4 Coin, Plain	SP-64	17,500.
1858	4 Coin, Reeded	SP-64	20,000.
1870	4 Coin, Plain w/box	SP-64	70,000.
1870	4 Coin, Reeded w/box	SP-64	70,000.
1875H	3 Coin	SP-66	175,000.
1880H	3 Coin, Wide 0	SP-67	100,000.
1880H	3 Coin, Narrow 0	SP-67	100,000.
1881H	5 Coin	SP-64	65,000.
1902H	3 Coin	SP-67	65,000.
1908	5 Coin	SP-64	4,500.
1911	5 Coin, 1¢ - 50¢	SP-64	8,000.
1911/12	3 Coin, Gold	SP-67	90,000.
1921	5 Coin	SP-65	250,000.
1929	5 Coin	SP-66	55,000.
1930	4 Coin	SP-66	40,000.
1931	5 Coin, Case #8	SP-66	70,000.
1934	5 Coin	SP-65	60,000.
1936, Dot	6 Coin	SP-66	650,000.
1937	6 Coin, Mirror	SP-65	3,500.
1937	12 Coin, Mirror	SP-65	10,000.
1937	6 Coin, Matte	SP-66	1,250.
1938	6 Coin	SP-65	50,000.
1944	5 Coin	SP-65	25,000.
1945	6 Coin	SP-65	13,500.
1946	6 Coin	SP-65	11,000.
1947	6 Coin, Point	SP-65	16,000.
1947	6 Coin, Blunt	SP-65	17,500.
1947, ML	6 Coin, Straight 7	SP-65	13,500.
1947, ML	6 Coin, Curved 7	SP-65	13,500.
1948	6 Coin, Concave	SP-65	12,000.
1948	6 Coin, Convex	SP-65	12,000.
1949	6 Coin	SP-66	15,000.
1950	6 Coin, Mirror	SP-66	4,500.
1950	6 Coin, Arnprior	SP-65	8,500.
1951	7 Coin, Low relief	SP-66	4,500.
1951	7 Coin, High relief	SP-66	10,000.
1952	6 Coin, WL	SP-66	4,000.
1952	6 Coin, NWL	SP-60	3,000.
1953, NS	6 Coin	SP-66	4,000.
1964	6 Coin	SP-67	2,000.
1965	6 Coin	SP-67	2,000.

Note: Average grade means the average condition in which these sets are found.

CASED SPECIMEN SET 1970

Cased Specimen Set 1970

In 1968 the Royal Canadian Mint began a feasibility study of the possibility of offering for sale six-coin specimen sets to the public. The 1967 specimen set was extremely successful and opened the way for expanded offerings. Trial cases were prepared and specimen coins of the years 1968 and 1969 were struck.

In 1970 the Royal Canadian Mint issued specimen sets to provide Prime Minister Pierre Trudeau with special sets for presentation purposes during his trip to China that year. A quantity of specimen sets in narrow cases were made up. After Trudeau's trip, some of these sets were sold to the public for $13. each. The total quantity of 1970 specimen sets issued in Canada is believed to be less than 1,000 and the only way 1970 specimen coins were available was in these sets. When the Mint made specimen sets available to the public starting in 1971, they were housed in a larger, eight-coin case. These sets are listed under prestige sets 1971-1980 on page 340.

Date and Mint Mark	Description	SP-65
1970	Specimen set in black case	$700.

CASES FOR SPECIMEN COINAGE

CASE FOUR

Charlton Number	Intended Contents	Exterior Colour and Dimensions	Interior Colours	Price for Empty Case
4	1858 1¢, 5¢, 10¢, 20¢ 1¢, 5¢, 10¢, 20¢	Black 7.5 x 11.5 cm	u: white l: dark blue	$2,500.

CASE FIVE

Charlton Number	Intended Contents	Exterior Colour and Dimensions	Interior Colours	Price for Empty Case
5	1870 5¢, 10¢, 25¢, 50¢	Dark brown 6.5 x 10.5 cm	u: white l: dark blue	$1,750.

CASE SIX

Struck to commemorate the opening of the Royal Canadian Mint in Ottawa in 1908. This is the first set of specimen coins offered to the general public. The issue price was $2.00. Coins had a matte finish. Impressed red leather strips were mailed separately to customers who possibly were initially sent sets housed in box 6a.

Charlton Number	Intended Contents	Exterior Colour and Dimensions	Interior Colours	Price for Empty Case
6	1908 1¢, 5¢, 10¢, 25¢, 50¢	Maroon, 5.3 x 15.5 cm	u:purple,impressed in gold lettering: "First Coinage in Canada/1908/Ottawa" l:purple	$250.
6a	1908 1¢, 5¢, 10¢, 25¢, 50¢	Red, 5.3 x 15.5 cm	u & l:purple	$250.
6b	1908 1¢, 5¢, 10¢, 25¢, 50¢	Red, 5.3 x 15.5 cm top impressed in gold lettering: "First Coinage in Canada/1908/Royal Mint Ottawa"	u & l: purple	$350.
6c	1908 1¢, 5¢, 10¢, 25¢, 50¢	Red, 5.3 X 15.5 cm	u:purple with affixed red leather strip impressed in gold lettering: "First Coinage of Canadian Mint/Ottawa/1908" l:purple	$250.

CASE SEVEN

As in 1908 the George V Coronation of 1911 prompted the Mint to again offer sets to the general public. The sets issued were:

1911 Set: 5 coins all dated 1911
1¢, 5¢, 10¢, 25¢, 50¢
Issue Price: $2.00

1911-12 Set: 8 coins, 6 dated 1911,
1¢, 5¢, 10¢, 25¢, 50¢, £1
2 dated 1912, $5, $10
Issue Price: $24.00

Case for 9 coins, one cent to ten dollars, never issued.
Case 7

Case for 6 coins, one cent to the dollar, never issued.
Case 7a

CASE SEVEN (cont.)

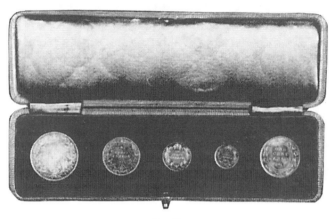

Case 7b

Charlton Number	Intended Contents	Exterior Colour and Dimensions	Interior Colours	Price for Empty Case
7	1911 1¢, 5¢, 10¢, 25¢, 50¢, $1, £1, $5, $10	Red, 8.9 x 19.7 cm top impressed in gold lettering: "Specimen Coins/Silver and Bronze/ Ottawa Mint/1911"	u & l:purple	$1,000.
7a	1911 1¢, 5¢, 10¢, 25¢, 50¢, $1	Red, 5.3 x 19.7 cm top impressed in gold lettering: "Specimen Coins/Silver and Bronze/ Ottawa Mint/1911"	u & l:purple	$750.00
7b	1911 1¢, 5¢, 10¢, 25¢, 50¢	As case #7a	As case #7a	$500.00
7c	1911 1¢, 5¢, 10¢, 25¢, 50¢ £1 and 1912 $5,$10 1911	Red, 8.9 x 19.7 cm top impressed in gold lettering: "Specimen Coins/Ottawa Mint/ 1911-12"	u & l:purple	$1,000.00

CASE EIGHT

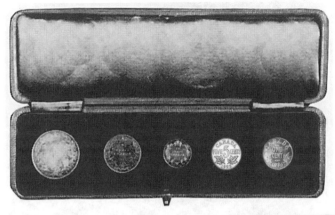

Charlton Number	Intended Contents	Exterior Colour and Dimensions	Interior Colours	Price for Empty Case
8	1931 1¢ (small), 5¢ (nickel), 10¢, 25¢, 50¢	Red, 5.3 x 19.7 cm top impressed in gold lettering: "Specimen Coins/Silver and Bronze/ Ottawa Mint	u & l: purple	$750.

CASE NINE

Case #9 1937

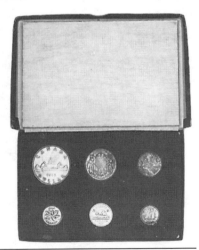

Charlton Number	Intended Contents	Exterior Colour and Dimensions	Interior Colours	Price for Empty Case
9	1937 1¢, 5¢, 10¢, 25¢, 50¢, $1	Red cardboard 10.2 x 15.3 cm with horizontal ridges, crowns and scepters and in black lettering: "Royal Canadian Mint/ 1937/Ottawa, Canada"	u:coarse white cloth	$75.

CASE NINE (cont.)

Case 9a or b

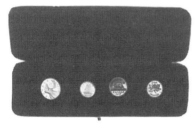

Case 9a

Case 9b

Charlton Number	Intended Contents	Exterior Colour and Dimensions	Interior Colours	Price for Empty Case
9a	1937 1¢, 5¢, 10¢, 25¢	As case #7a except date covered by paper Union Jack.	As case #7a	$400.
9b	1937 1¢, 5¢, 10¢, 25¢, 50¢, $1	As case #7a, except the inscription is covered by a blue leather strip upon which is impressed in gold a view of the centre section of the Royal Canadian Mint surrounded on the sides and bottom by a ribbon "1937" is below. On the ribbon is "Royal Canadian Mint"	As case #7a	$275.

CASE NINE (cont.)

Case 9c

Charlton Number	Intended Contents	Exterior Colour and Dimensions	Interior Colours	Price for Empty Case
9c	1937 Double Set 1¢, 5¢, 10¢, 25¢, 50¢, $1	Red, 8.9 x 19.7 cm lettering as above on a paper label	u & l, purple	$1,000.

CASE TEN

Charlton Number	Intended Contents	Exterior Colour and Dimensions	Interior Colours	Price for Empty Case
10	1938-1953 1¢, 5¢, 10¢, 25¢, 50¢, $1	As case #9b, except for the absence of "1937"	As case #9b	$300.

CASE ELEVEN

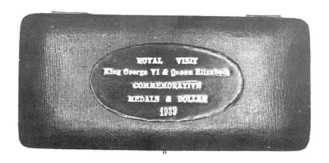

Charlton Number	Intended Contents	Exterior Colour and Dimensions	Interior Colours	Price for Empty Case
11	1939 54mm medal, $1 54mm medal	As case #7, except the inscription is covered by an oval blue patch impressed in gold lettering: "Royal Visit/King George VI & Queen Elizabeth/ Commemorative/Medals & Dollar/1939"	As case #9a	$500.

CASE TWELVE

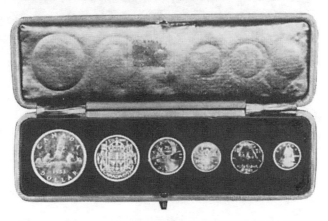

Charlton Number	Intended Contents	Exterior Colour and Dimensions	Interior Colours	Price for Empty Case
12	1953 1¢, 5¢, 10¢, 25¢, 50¢, $1	Red, top impressed in gold with a view of the centre section of the Royal Canadian Mint surrounded on the sides and bottom by a ribbon bearing "Royal Canadian Mint"	u & l:purple	$300.

CASE THIRTEEN

Charlton Number	Intended Contents	Exterior Colour and Dimensions	Interior Colours	Price for Empty Case
13	1953 1¢, 5¢, 10¢, 25¢, 50¢, $1	Large size, Red, top impressed in gold with a view of the centre section of the Royal Canadian Mint surrounded on the sides and bottom by a ribbon bearing "Royal Canadian Mint"	u & l:purple	$300.

PATTERNS, TRIAL PIECES AND OFFICIAL FABRICATIONS

A PATTERN is a piece submitted as a design sample by engravers when a new coinage is contemplated. If the design is adopted for regular coinage with the same date, the piece ceases to be a pattern. If the design is adopted with a later date, the piece remains a pattern. Patterns are usually struck as proofs.

A TRIAL PIECE or ESSAY is from dies already accepted for regular coinage. It may bear a date or mint mark other than on the coins issued for circulation or it may be in a different metal.

AN OFFICIAL FABRICATION is a piece that was created for some special purpose unconnected with design proposals or experiments on coinage design or metals. For example, the New Brunswick pieces bearing the dates 1870, 1871 and 1875 were obviously not connected with an attempt to revive a separate coinage for that province after Confederation.

The best listing of patterns, trial pieces and official fabrications has been by Fred Bowman in his book Canadian Patterns. The present listing is greatly revised compared to Bowmans and new numbers are used. However, Bowmans original numbers are also included for those pieces which were listed in his book.

PROVINCE OF NOVA SCOTIA

Charlton   Bowman   **PATTERNS**

NS-1   –

Price Range
$2,000. - $5,000.
PR63 to 65

Half cent 1860. Reverse – crown surrounded by wreath of roses; date below wreath. (The illustration is from a matrix. It is uncertain whether patterns bearing this date were actually produced.)

NS-2   –

Price Range
$2,000. - $5,000.
PR63 to 65

One cent 1860. Reverse – crown surrounded by wreath of roses; date below wreath. (The illustration is from a matrix. It is uncertain whether patterns bearing this date were actually produced.)

PROVINCE OF NOVA SCOTIA

Charlton	Bowman	PATTERNS

NS-3   **B-11**

Price Range
$2,000. - $5,000.
PR63 to 65

Half cent 1861, bronze. Proof; dies ↑↓; wt. 2.85g; dia. 20.65mm. Obverse - large bust of Victoria by James Wyon. Reverse - pattern design as on NS-1. (National Currency Collection)

NS-4   **B-7**

Price Range
$2,000. - $5,000.
PR63 to 65

One cent 1861, bronze. Proof; dies ↑↑; wt. 4.69g; dia. 25.4mm. Obverse - large bust of Victoria by James Wyon. Reverse - pattern design as on NS-2. (National Currency Collection)

NS-5   **B-13**

Price Range
$2,500. - $6,000.
PR63 to 65

Half cent 1861, bronze. Proof; dies ↑↓. Obverse - adopted (small bust) design by L.C. Wyon. Reverse - pattern design as NS-3. (National Currency Collection)

NS-6   **B-8**

Price Range
$2,500. - $6,000.
PR63 to 65

One cent 1861, bronze. Not a proof; dies ↑↑; wt. 5.59g; dia. 25.4mm. Obverse - adopted (small bust) design by L.C. Wyon. Reverse - pattern design as NS-4. (National Currency Collection)

NS-7   **B-12**

Price Range
$2,500. - $6,000.
PR63 to 65

Half cent 1861, bronze. Proof; dies ↑↑; wt. 2.78g; dia. 20.65mm. Obverse - pattern design as on NS-3. Reverse - adopted design (crown and date surrounded by a wreath of mayflowers and roses). (New Netherlands Coin Sale 1960)

PROVINCE OF NOVA SCOTIA

Charlton	Bowman	PATTERNS

NS-8 **B-10**

Price Range
$2,000. - $4,500.
PR63 to 65

One cent 1861, bronze. Proof; dies ↑↑; wt. 5.65g; dia. 25.4mm and dies ↑↓; wt. 5.74g; dia. 25.4mm. Obverse - pattern design as on NS-4. Reverse - adopted design (1861), large rose bud variety. (National Currency Collection)

NS-8a **B-10**

Price Range
$2,000. - $4,500.
PR63 to 65

One cent 1861, bronze. Proof; dies ↑↑; wt. 5.80g; dia. 25.4mm. As NS-8, except the reverse is the small rose bud variety (adopted design for 1861-1864).

NS-9 **B-14**

Price Range
$3,500. - $7,500.
PR63 to 65

Half cent 186-, bronze. Proof. As NS-5, except for the incomplete date.

NS-10 **B-9**

Price Range
$3,500. - $7,500.
PR63 to 65

One cent 186-, bronze. Dies ↑↑; wt. 5.78g; dia. 25.4mm. As NS-6, except for the incomplete date.

PROVINCE OF NEW BRUNSWICK

Charlton	Bowman	
		PATTERNS

NB-1   **B-15**

Price Range
$3,000. - $6,000.
PR63 to 65

One cent 1861, bronze; proof; dies ↑↑; wt. 5.64g; dia. 25.4mm ; obverse - large bust design by James Wyon as on NS-6, etc. reverse - adopted design. (National Currency Collection)

NB-2   **B-20**

Price Range
$20,000. - $35,000.
PR63 to 65

Ten cents 1862, silver; reeded edge; proof; dies ↑↑; wt. 2.34g; dia. 18.0mm; obverse - adopted design; reverse - legend and date surrounded by arabesque design somewhat similar to that used for Newfoundland. The arabesque reverse on this piece was also used for a pattern 10-cent piece for Hong Kong. (National Currency Collection)

TRIAL PIECES

NB-3   —

Price Range
$5,000. - $10,000.
PR63 to 65

One cent 1862, bronze; proof. As adopted design, except for the date. Struck to make the date uniform for the 1862 proof sets.

OFFICIAL FABRICATIONS

NB-4   **B-23**

Price Range
$2,500. - $5,000.
PR63 to 65

Twenty cents 1862, silver; plain edge; proof; dies ↑↑; wt. 5.6g; dia. 22.0 mm; obverse - plain, except for the legend G.W. WYON/OBIT/MARCH 27TH 1862/AETAT/26YEARS. Reverse - adopted design. This is an obituary medalet for George W. Wyon, who was resident engraver at the Royal Mint. The fact that this reverse was chosen for the piece suggests that it was engraved by George Wyon. (National Currency Collection)

PROVINCE OF NEW BRUNSWICK

The following six pieces (NB-5 to NB-10) obviously have nothing to do with contemplated designs for New Brunswick, since they bear dates after Confederation. It is believed they were struck for exhibition purposes where only the type was considered important.

Charlton   Bowman   **OFFICIAL FABRICATIONS**

NB-5   B-18

Price Range
$25,000. - $40,000.
PR63 to 65

Five cents 1870, silver; plain edge; proof; dies ↑↑; wt. 1.7g; dia. 15.5 mm; obverse - adopted design; reverse - adopted design for the Dominion of Canada (wire rim variety). (National Currency Collection)

NB-6   B-21

Price Range
$20,000. - $35,000.
PR63 to 65

Ten cents 1870, silver; reeded edge; proof; dies ↑↑; wt. 2.3g; dia. 18.03 mm; plain edge; proof; dies ↑↑, wt. 2.32g; dia. 18.03 mm; obverse - adopted design; reverse - adopted design for the Dominion of Canada and New Brunswick. (National Currency Collection, reeded edge; Norweb Collection, plain edge)

NB-7   B-22

Price Range
$30,000. - $50,000.
PR63 to 65

Ten cents 1871, silver; reeded edge; proof; dies ↑↑; wt. 2.32g; dia. 18.03 mm; plain edge; wt. 2.3g; dia. 18.03 mm. As NB-6, except for the date. (National Currency Collection)

NB-8   B-24

Price Range
$12,500. - $35,000.
PR63 to 65

Twenty cents 1871, silver; reeded edge; proof; dies ↑↑; wt. 5.90g; dia. 22.5mm; plain edge; proof; wt. 4.7g; dia. 23.27 mm. As the adopted design, except for the date. (National Currency Collection)

NB-9   B-19

Price Range
$35,000. - $55,000.
PR63 to 65

Five cents 1875, silver; reeded edge; proof; dies ↑↑, wt. 1.16g; dia. 15.5; obverse - adopted design; reverse - adopted design for the Dominion of Canada. (National Currency Collection)

NB-10   —

Price Range
$35,000. - $55,000.
PR63 to 65

Five cents 1875H, silver; reeded edge; proof; dies ↑↑. As NB9, except for the H mint mark.

PROVINCE OF NEWFOUNDLAND

The following five patterns (NF-1 to NF-5) are the result of a directive given by the master of the Royal Mint, Thomas Graham, in which he stated that the designs for the reverses of the Newfoundland coins should be those of New Brunswick. This was later altered.

Charlton   Bowman

NF-1   —

Price Range
$2,000. - 5,000.
PR63 to 65

PATTERNS

One cent 1864; reverse - similar to the design adopted for the New Brunswick cent. Unknown at present as a struck piece, but may exist.

NF-2   B-28

Price Range
$25,000. - $40,000.
PR63 to 65

Five cents 1864, bronze; plain edge; proof; dies ↑↓; wt. 1.40g; dia. 15.5 mm; obverse - adopted design; reverse - crown and wreath design adopted for New Brunswick. (W.W.C. Wilson Sale 1925)

NF-3   B-29

Price Range
$25,000. - $40,000.
PR63 to 65

Ten cents 1864, bronze; plain edge; proof; obverse - adopted design; reverse - crown and wreath design adopted for New Brunswick. (British Museum)

NF-4   B-32

Price Range
$25,000. - $40,000.
PR63 to 65

Twenty cents 1864, bronze; indented corded edge; proof; dies ↑↓; wt. 6.2g; dia. 22.95 mm; obverse - adopted design; reverse - crown and wreath design adopted for New Brunswick. (National Currency Collection)

NF-5   B-31

Price Range
$50,000. - $75,000.
PR63 to 65

Two dollars 1864, bronze; plain edge; proof; dies ↑↓; wt. 2.4g; dia. 17.1 mm; obverse - adopted design; reverse - crown and wreath for New Brunswick. 10 cents with the legend "TWO/DOLLARS/1864" in the centre. (National Currency Collection)

PROVINCE OF NEWFOUNDLAND

Charlton **Bowman** **PATTERNS**

NF-6 **B-25**

Price Range
$3,500. - $7,500.
PR63 to 65

One cent, bronze; not a proof; dies ↑↑; wt. 5.69 grams; dia. 25.4 mm; obverse - similar to adopted design, except the legend reads VICTORIA QUEEN. Reverse - similar to adopted design, except one leaf is missing from the top of each side of the wreath. (National Currency Collection)

NF-7 **B-27**

Price Range
$4,000. - $10,000.
PR63 to 65

One cent 1865, bronze; proof; dies ↑↓; wt. 5.45 grams; dia. 25.4 mm; obverse - adopted design for Nova Scotia and New Brunswick. Reverse - pattern design as for NF-6, except for the date. (National Currency Collection)

NF-8 —

Price Range
$4,000. - $10,000.
PR63 to 65

Five cents 1865, silver; plain edge; proof; dies ↑↓; wt. 0.9 grams; dia. 15.5 mm; obverse - adopted design; reverse - similar to the adopted design, except the arches are thinner. (National Currency Collection)

NF-9 —

Price Range
$5,000. - $12,500.
PR63 to 65

Ten cents 1865, silver; plain edge; proof; dies ↑↓; obverse - adopted design; reverse - similar to the adopted design, except the arches are much thinner. (National Currency Collection)

PROVINCE OF NEWFOUNDLAND

Charlton	Bowman	PATTERNS

NF-10 —

Price Range
$5,000. - $17,500.
PR63 to 65

Twenty cents 1865, silver; plain edge; proof; dies ↑↓; wt. 4.6 grams; dia. 23.19mm; obverse - adopted design; reverse - similar to the adopted design, except the arches are much thinner. (National Currency Collection)

NF-11 —

Price Range
$4,000. - $10,000.
PR63 to 65

Five cents 1865, silver; plain edge; proof; dies ↑↓; wt. 1.10 grams; dia. 15.5mm; obverse - adopted design; reverse - as the adopted design, except the arches and dots have raised edges. (National Currency Collection)

NF-12 —

Price Range
$5,000. - $12,500.
PR63 to 65

Ten cents 1865, silver; plain edge; proof; dies ↑↓; wt. 2.3 grams; dia. 18.03 mm; obverse - adopted design; reverse - as the adopted design, except the arches and dots have raised edges. (National Currency Collection)

NF-13 —

Price Range
$5,000. - $17,500.
PR63 to 65

Twenty cents 1865, silver; plain edge; proof; dies ↑↓; wt. 4.5 grams; dia. 23.19 mm; obverse - adopted design; reverse - similar to the adopted design, except for some details of the arches and the presence of a raised line just inside the rim denticles. (National Currency Collection)

PROVINCE OF NEWFOUNDLAND

Charlton	Bowman		
		PATTERNS	

NF-14   **B-33**

Price Range
$75,000. - $175,000.
PR63 to 65

Two dollars 1865, gold; plain edge; proof; dies ↑↑; wt. 3.3 grams; dia. 17.6 mm; obverse - adopted design; reverse - similar to the adopted design, except the legend and date are in block type. (National Currency Collection)

NF-15   **B-34**

Price Range
$75,000. - $175,000.
PR63 to 65

Two dollars 1865, gold; plain edge; proof; dies ↑↓; wt. 3.36 grams; dia. 17.98 mm; obverse - small bust of Victoria (from the 5 cents) in beaded circle with the legend VICTORIA D:G REG:/NEWFOUNDLAND. Reverse - pattern design as on NF-14.

NF-16   **B-35**

Price Range
$25,000. - $75,000.
PR63 to 65

Fifty cents 1870, bronze; plain edge; proof; dies ↑↑; wt. 9.4 grams; dia. 29.6 mm; obverse - adopted design; reverse - as the adopted design, except the denticles are longer and touch the device. (National Currency Collection)

NF-17   —

Price Range
$75,000. - $175,000.
PR63 to 65

Two dollars 1870, gold; plain edge; proof; obverse - pattern designs as on NF-15; reverse - adopted design.

PROVINCE OF NEWFOUNDLAND

Charlton	Bowman
NF-18	**B-26**

TRIAL PIECES

Price Range
$3,500. - $7,500.
PR63 to 65

One cent 1864, bronze; proof; dies ↑↑; wt. 5.6 grams; dia. 25.4 mm. As the adopted design, except for the date. This is the piece that is believed to have been included in the specimen sets of 1864-1865. Proofs of the adopted design of the cent dated 1865 seem not to have been produced. (National Currency Collection)

NF-19 —

Price Range
$60,000. - $150,000.
PR63 to 65

Fifty cents 1882, silver; reeded edge; proof. As the adopted design, except for the absence of the H mint mark. (British Museum)

NF-20 —

Price Range
None
Mint Error

Ten cents 1945 C, nickel. Struck on a thin blank; not a proof. This piece is rather weakly struck because of the thinness of the blank, suggesting that it is nothing more than a mint error. (National Currency Collection)

NF-21 —

Price Range
$25,000. - $40,000.
PR63 to 65

Twenty cents 1865, bronze; plain edge; proof; dies ↑↑; wt. 5.16g, dia. 23.1 mm as adopted design. (Norweb Collection)

PROVINCE OF BRITISH COLUMBIA

Charlton   Bowman   **PATTERNS**

BC-1   B-37

Price Range
$40,000. - $70,000.
PR63 to 65

Ten dollars 1862, silver; dies ↑↓; wt. 11.2g; dia. 27.0mm; obverse - crown and legend; reverse - wreath, denomination and date. (National Currency Collection)

BC-1a   B-37

Price Range
$50,000. - $80,000.
PR63 to 65

Ten dollars 1862, silver; reeded edge; dies ↑↑. Design as above. (Brand Sale 1983)

BC-2   B-36

Price Range
$55,000. - $85,000.
PR63 to 65

Twenty dollars 1862, silver; dies ↑↓; obverse - crown and legend; reverse - wreath, denomination and date. (Brand Sale 1983).

BC-2a   B-36

Price Range
$60,000. - $90,000.
PR63 to 65

Twenty dollars 1862, silver; reeded edge; dies ↑↑; wt. 23.6g; dia. 34.0mm. Design as above. (National Currency Collection)

BC-3   B-37

Price Range
$400,000. - $750,000.
PR63 to 65

Ten dollars 1862, gold. Design as BC-1. (B.C. Provincial Archives)

BC-4   B-36

Price Range
$375,000. - $1,000,000.
PR63 to 65

Twenty dollars 1862, gold. Design as BC-2. (B.C. Provincial Archives)

Note: The ten and twenty dollar gold patterns of British Columbia were designed by George Albert Ferdinand Kuner (1819-1906)

PROVINCE OF CANADA

Charlton	Bowman	TRIAL PIECES

PC-1 **B-4**

Price Range
$15,000. - $20,000.
PR63 to 65

One cent 1858, bronze; not a proof; wt. 5.7g; dia. 23.7mm; uniface - obverse blank; reverse - wreath of maple leaves and seed pods with beaded circle containing ONE/CENT/1858. (National Currency Collection)

PC-2 **B-4**

Price Range
$15,000. - $20,000.
PR63 to 65

One cent 1858, bronze; proof; wt. 4.0 - 5.4g; dia. 23.7mm; uniface - obverse blank; reverse - similar to PC-1 except the date is more closely spaced and the device is farther from the inner beaded circle. (National Currency Collection)

PC-3 **B-3**

Price Range
$20,000. - $30,000.
PR63 to 65

One cent 1858, bronze; proof; dies ↑↓; wt. 3.88g; dia. 23.7mm; obverse - adopted legend with diademed bust of Victoria. Reverse - pattern design as on PC-2. (Wayte Raymond Sale 1928)

PC-4 **B-6**

Price Range
$10,000. - $35,000.
PR63 to 65

Twenty cents 1858, silver; plain edge; proof; dies ↑↑; wt. 4.50g; dia. 23.7mm; dies ↑↓; wt. 4.03g; dia. 23.27mm; obverse - adopted design; reverse - adopted design for New Brunswick. (National Currency Collection)

PROVINCE OF CANADA

Charlton	Bowman
PC-5	**B-5**

PATTERNS

Price Range
$25,000. - $35,000.
PR63 to 65

One cent 1859 (in Roman numerals), bronze; proof; obverse - adopted design; reverse - Britannia reverse for a pattern British halfpenny. (Parsons Collection 1936. The Norweb Collection contains an example struck in copper-nickel; wt. 5.63g; dia. 25.4mm.)

Charlton	Bowman
PC-6	—

TRIAL PIECES

Price Range
$15,000. - $25,000.
PR63 to 65

One cent 1858, cupro-nickel; dies ↑↑; wt. 9.11g; dia. 25.4mm. Adopted design; struck from proof dies on an unpolished blank of double thickness. (National Currency Collection)

PC-7 —

Price Range
$5,000. - $15,000.
PR63 to 65

One cent 1858, cupro-nickel; proof; dies ↑↑; wt. 4.42g; dia. 25.4mm. Adopted design; normal thickness. (National Currency Collection)

CANADA

Charlton   Bowman

DC-1   B-38

Price Range
$12,500. - $20,000.
PR63 to 65

One cent 1876H, bronze; proof; dies ↑↑; dia. 25.45mm; obverse - adopted laureated head design for the Province of Canada. Reverse - adopted design. The existence of this pattern suggests that the government of the Dominion of Canada initially considered using the Province of Canada laureated obverse for its new cent. (National Currency Collection)

DC-2   —

Price Range
$7,500. - $15,000.
PR63 to 65

Ten cents (no date), bronze; reeded edge; proof; wt. 2.1g; dia. 17.85mm; obverse - adopted design (Haxby Obv. 6); reverse - plain, except for a B engraved on the piece after it was struck. Probably unique. (National Currency Collection)

DC-3   —

Price Range
$40,000. - $80,000.
PR63 to 65

Fifty cents 1870, bronze; plain edge; proof; dies ↑↑; wt. 9.2g; dia. 29.72mm; obverse - no L.C.W. on the truncation, but otherwise very similar to Haxby Obv. 2. Reverse - slight differences in some leaves compared to the adopted design. (National Currency Collection)

DC-4   —

Price Range
$65,000. - $175,000.
PR63 to 65

Images as above

As DC-3, but silver. Dies ↑↓; wt. 11.2g; dia. 29.72mm.

CANADA

Charlton   Bowman

DC-5   —

Price Range
$25,000. - $40,000.
PR63 to 65

One cent 1911, bronze; dies ↑↑; wt. 5.6g; dia. 25.4mm; specimen. As the adopted design for 1912-1920, except for the date; i.e. the obverse legend has DEI GRA:. (Royal Mint Collection)

DC-6   B-40

Price Range
$1,000,000.
PR63 to 65

One dollar 1911, silver; reeded edge; specimen; dies ↑↑; obverse - the standard MacKennal design later adopted for the 1936 dollar. Reverse - crown, wreath, legend and date.

In the Dominion of Canada Currency Act of 1910, which received royal assent on May 4, 1910, provision was made for the striking of a Canadian silver dollar. The schedule appended to the act specified a coin of 360 grains weight and a standard fineness of .925 silver. The Dominion Government, having decided to add a silver dollar to the coinage, purchased a new coining-press from Taylor and Challen of Birmingham, England, for the express purpose of striking coins of this size. A pair of dies for the new coin was prepared by the Die and Medal Department of the Royal Mint, London, and at least two specimens were struck. When cases were prepared for the specimen sets of the first Canadian coinage of George V, a space was left for the dollar. Later, however, the Dominion authorities decided against the issue of a silver dollar at that time, although no reason was given for this decision.

Only two specimens of the 1911 silver dollar are known to exist; one is in the National Currency Collection and the other was sold at auction in 2003 for $690,000 U.S.F., at the Heritage Belzberg Sale.

CANADA

Charlton   Bowman   **PATTERNS**

DC-6a   —

Price Range
$250,000.
PR63 to 65

One dollar 1911, lead. As DC-6, except for the metal. Probably unique. This piece was only recently discovered by the numismatic world, having been in storage in Ottawa since 1911. It is believed to be a sample piece struck at the Ottawa mint to be used for gaining approval to proceed with the production of coins for circulation. (National Currency Collection)

DC-7   B-41

Price Range
$100,000. - $250,000.
PR63 to 65

Five dollars 1911, gold; reeded edge specimen; dies ↑↑; dia. 21.6mm. As the adopted design for 1912-1914, except for the date. (Royal Mint Collection)

DC-8   B-42

Price Range
$100,000. - $250,000.
PR63 to 65

Ten dollars, 1911, gold; reeded edge specimen; dies ↑↑; dia. 26.9mm. As the adopted design for 1912-1914, except for the date. (Royal Mint Collection)

In 1926 Dominion notes (the treasury notes issued by the government of the Dominion of Canada) were made redeemable in gold for the first time since 1914. Since the time of the production of the gold $5 and $10 of 1912-1914, it had been concluded that the coat-of-arms borne on their reverses was incorrect. Therefore, new reverses were engraved in the event that a gold coinage would again have to be struck. Bronze patterns were produced to have samples of the designs. A few of these, probably made for the designer, G.E. Kruger-Gray, have the obverse design machined off, SPECIMEN punched in instead, and the entire piece acid-etched.

CANADA

Charlton	Bowman			**PATTERNS**

DC-9 —

Price Range
$25,000. - $40,000.
PR63 to 65

Five dollars 1928, bronze; reeded edge; dies ↑↑; wt. 4.2g; dia. 21.6mm; obverse - as the adopted design for the 1912-1914 issues. Reverse - modified Canadian arms by G.E. Kruger-Gray. (National Currency Collection)

DC-10 —

Price Range
$27,500. - $50,000.
PR63 to 65

Ten dollars 1928, bronze; reeded edge; dies ↑↑; wt. 8.49g; dia. 26.92mm; obverse - as the adopted design for the 1912-1914 issues. Reverse - modified Canadian arms by G.E. Kruger-Gray. (National Currency Collection)

DC-11 —

Price Range
$15,000. - $30,000.
PR63 to 65

Five dollars 1928, bronze; reeded edge; wt. 3.7g; dia. 21.6mm; obverse - planed off flat just inside the denticles after striking; SPECIMEN has been punched in by hand. Reverse - pattern design as on DC-9. The entire piece has been acid-etched (officially) giving it a light brown colour. (National Currency Collection)

DC-12 —

Price Range
$15,000. - $35,000.
PR63 to 65

Ten dollars 1928, bronze; reeded edge; wt. 7.2g; dia. 26.92mm; obverse - planed off flat just inside denticles after striking; SPECIMEN has been punched in by hand. Reverse - pattern design as on DC-10. The entire piece has been etched as for DC-11. (National Currency Collection)

CANADA

Charlton   Bowman

DC-13   —

Price Range
$10,000. - $15,000.
PR63 to 65

One dollar 1964, tin; plain edge, struck on a thick planchet; not a proof; wt. 26.9g; dia. 35.5mm; obverse - blank, except for small symbol ∫. Reverse - similar to the adopted design, except for being higher in relief and having thin rounded rim denticles instead of wide square ones. Unique. This unusual piece is a matrix trial. (National Currency Collection)

DC-14   —

Price Range
$17,500. - $22,500.
PR63 to 65

One dollar 1967, silver; reeded edge; not a specimen. Similar to the adopted design, except the fields on both sides are flat instead of concave and the rim beads differ slightly in size and position.

DC-15   —

Price Range
$5,000.
PR63 to 65

Fifty cents (no date), white metal. Trial impression of portrait of Victoria only; as on Haxby Obv.2, 1870-1972. (National Currency Collection)

DC-16   —

Price Range
$40,000. - $60,000.
PR63 to 65

Five cents 1875, silver; reeded edge; proof; dies ↑↓; wt. 1.20g; dia. 15.45mm. As the adopted design, except for the absence of the H mint mark. (National Currency Collection)

CANADA

Charlton	Bowman
DC-17	—

Price Range
$3,500. - $7,500.
PR63 to 65

One cent 1876H, cupro-nickel; proof; dies ↑↓; wt. 5.81g; dia. 25.4mm. As the adopted design. These pieces are believed to have been struck for exhibition purposes, without regard to the fact that there was no currency issue corresponding exactly to them. (American Numismatic Society)

DC-18 —

Price Range
$3,500. - $7,500.
PR63 to 65

One cent 1876, bronze; proof; dies ↑↑; wt. 5.6g; dia. 25.4mm. As the adopted design, except for the absence of the H mint mark. (National Currency Collection)

The five brass pieces listed below (DC-19 to DC-23) were produced at the Paris mint. It is there that the original matrices for these denominations were engraved as the Royal Mint was too busy producing coins for Great Britain.

DC-19 —

Price Range
$4,000. - $6,000.
PR63 to 65

One cent 1937, brass; specimen; dies ↑↓; wt. 3.1g; dia. 19.05mm. As the adopted design. Slightly thicker than normal. (National Currency Collection)

DC-20 —

Price Range
$3,500. - $5,500.
PR63 to 65

Five cents 1937, brass; specimen; dies ↑↓; wt. 4.98g; dia. 21.5mm. As the adopted design. Slightly thicker than normal. (National Currency Collection)

CANADA

Charlton	Bowman	TRIAL PIECES

DC-21 —

Price Range
$3,500. - $5,500.
PR63 to 65

Ten cents 1937, brass; reeded edge; specimen; dies ↑↓; wt. 2.46g; dia. 18.03mm. As the adopted design. Slightly thicker than normal. (National Currency Collection)

DC-22 —

Price Range
$3,500. - $5,500.
PR63 to 65

Twenty-five cents 1937, brass; reeded edge; specimen; dies ↑↓; wt. 6.1g; dia. 23.9mm. As the adopted design. Slightly thicker than normal. (National Currency Collection)

DC-23 —

Price Range
$5,000. - $8,500.
PR63 to 65

Fifty cents 1937, brass; reeded edge; specimen; dies ↑↓; wt. 14.9g; dia. 30.0mm. As the adopted design. Thicker than normal. (National Currency Collection)

DC-24 —

Price Range
$6,500. - $10,000.
PR63 to 65

Twenty-five cents 1937, bronze; reeded edge; dies ↑↑; wt. 5.5g; dia. 23.62mm. As the adopted design. Normal thickness. (National Currency Collection)

CANADA

Charlton   **Bowman**   **TRIAL PIECES**

DC-25   —

Price Range
$7,500. - $10,000.
PR63 to 65

Five cents 1942, nickel; not a specimen; dies ↑↑; wt. 5.5g; dia. 23.62mm. As the 12-sided design adopted for the tombac pieces. (National Currency Collection)

DC-26   —

One cent 1943, copper-plated steel; not a specimen; dies ↑↑; wt. 3.0g; dia. 19.05mm. As the adopted design. (National Currency Collection)

DC-26a   —   One cent 1943, steel; not a specimen; dies ↑↑; wt 3.1g; dia. 19.05mm. As the adopted design. (National Currency Collection)

DC-27   —   Five cents 1943, steel; specimen. As the design adopted for the tombac pieces. (Piece seen, but composition not confirmed.)

DC-28   —   Five cents 1944, tombac. As the design adopted for the chrome-plated steel pieces. (Piece seen, but composition not confirmed.)

DC-29   —

Price Range
$5,000. - $7,500.
PR63 to 65

Five cents 1951, chrome-plated steel; specimen; dies ↑↑; wt. 4.6g; dia. 21.3mm. As the commemorative design struck in nickel. (National Currency Collection)

Note: Where the only known examples are in institutional collections the prices are not shown.

CANADA

Charlton	Bowman	
		TRIAL PIECES

DC-30 —

Price Range
$2,500. - $5,000.
PR63 to 65

Five cents 1952, composition unknown; specimen; dies ↑↑; wt. 3.80g; dia. 21.3mm. As the adopted designs. (National Currency Collection)

DC-31 —

Price Range
$7,500.
PR63 to 65

Fifty cents 1959, tin; uniface on thick, oversize blank; obverse - blank except for the engraved inscription (added after the piece was struck) FIRST TRIAL/Oct 27th/1958. Reverse - as the adopted design, except lacks rim denticles. Unique. (National Currency Collection)

DC-32 —

Price Range
$1,500. - $2,500.
PR63 to 65

One cent 1966, nickel; dies ↑↑; wt. 3.50g; dia. 19.05mm. As the adopted designs.

DC-33 —

Price Range
$1,500. - $2,000.
PR63 to 65

Ten cents 1967, nickel; dies ↑↑; wt. 2.07g; dia. 18.03mm. As the adopted designs.

CANADA

Charlton   Bowman

DC-34   —

Price Range
$1,500. - $2,000.
PR63 to 65

TRIAL PIECES

Twenty-five cents 1967, nickel; dies ↑↑; wt. 5.07g; dia. 23.62mm. As the adopted designs.

Charlton   Bowman

DC-50   —

Price Range
$7,500. - $30,000.
PR63 to 65

OFFICIAL FABRICATION

Twenty cents 1871, silver; reeded edge; proof; dies ↑↓; wt. 4.62g; dia. 23.3mm; plain edge; proof; dies ↑↑; wt. 4.70g; dia. 23.3mm. As the adopted design for the Province of Canada, except for the date. This piece does not represent a proposed 20 cents for the Dominion of Canada. It is believed to have been struck for exhibition to show the Province of Canada 20 cents. Only the type was important; no concern was given to using a date corresponding to the coins actually issued for circulation. (National Currency Collection)

CANADA — TEST TOKENS

On occasion the mint has produced special tokens for vending machine testing or other purposes. These tokens are usually the diameter of standard Canadian coins, but they may or may not have the same composition and other physical properties as the coins to which they correspond.

ONE CENT TEST TOKENS

ROUND COPPER TOKEN; THREE MAPLE LEAVES WITH BEADS; FULL WEIGHT;1976.

Weight: 3.24 grams
Diameter: 19.05 mm
Thickness: 1.42 mm
Edge: Plain
Die Axis: ↑↓

TT-1.1A   English/English legends

ROUND COPPER TOKEN; REDUCED SIZE AND WEIGHT; 1977. The Royal Canadian Mint issued a one-cent test token on December 15, 1977; however, because it was almost identical in diameter to those used by the Toronto Transit Commission, it was withdrawn.

Weight: 1.87 grams
Diameter: 16.0 mm
Thickness: 1.35 mm
Edge: Plain
Die Axis: ↑↑

TT-1.2   Obverse and reverse design only

Cat. No.	Date	Description	Price Range
TT-1.1A	1976	Round copper, full weight	75.-125.
TT-1.2	1977	Round copper, reduced weight	75.-125.

CANADA — TEST TOKENS

ROUND COPPER TOKEN; THREE MAPLE LEAVES WITH BEADS; REDUCED WEIGHT; 1979. In August 1979 another test token was introduced. This time the weight of the copper planchet was reduced.

Weight: 2.80 grams
Diameter: 19.05 mm
Thickness: 1.38 mm
Edge: Plain
Die Axis: ↑→

TT-1.3A   English/English legends "TEST TOKEN ROYAL CANADIAN MINT"

Weight: 2.80 grams
Diameter: 19.05 mm
Thickness: 1.38 mm
Edge: Plain
Die Axis: ↑↑

TT-1.3B   French/French legends "EPREUVE MONNAIE ROYALE CANADIENNE"

Weight: 2.80 grams
Diameter: 19.05 mm
Thickness: 1.38 mm
Edge: Plain
Die Axis: ↑↑

TT-1.3C   English/French legends "TEST TOKEN ROYAL CANADIAN MINT /
EPREUVE MONNAIE ROYALE CANADIENNE"

Cat. No.	Date	Description	Price Range
TT-1.3A	1979	With Beads, English/English	150.-200.
TT-1.3B	1979	With Beads, French/French	150.-200.
TT-1.3C	1979	With Beads, English/French	30.-50.

CANADA – TEST TOKENS

ROUND COPPER TOKEN; THREE MAPLE LEAVES WITHOUT BEADS; 1979

Photograph not available	**Weight:** 2.50 grams **Diameter:** 19.05 mm **Thickness:** 1.38 mm **Edge:** Plain **Die Axis:** ↑↑

TT-1.4A English/English legends "TEST TOKEN ROYAL CANADIAN MINT"

Weight: 2.50 grams
Diameter: 19.05 mm
Thickness: 1.38 mm
Edge: Plain
Die Axis: ↑↑

TT-1.4B French/French legends "EPREUVE/MONNAIE ROYALE CANADIENNE"

Photograph not available	**Weight:** 2.50 grams **Diameter:** 19.05 mm **Thickness:** 1.38 mm **Edge:** Plain **Die Axis:** ↑↑

TT-1.4C English/French legends "TEST TOKEN ROYAL CANADIAN MINT /
EPREUVE MONNAIE ROYALE CANADIENNE"

Cat No.	Date	Description	Price Range
TT-1.4A	1979	Without beads, English/English	Rare
TT-1.4B	1979	Without beads, French/French	150.-200.
TT-1.4C	1979	Without beads, English/French	Rare

ROUND COPPER-ZINC TOKEN; THREE MAPLE LEAVES WITH BEADS; 1979.

Weight: 2.70 grams
Diameter: 19.20 mm
Thickness: 1.30 mm
Edge: Plain
Die Axis: ↑↑

TT-1.5A English/English legends "TEST TOKEN ROYAL CANADIAN MINT

Weight: 2.68 grams
Diameter: 19.05 mm
Thickness: 1.85 mm
Edge: Plain
Die Axis: ↑↑

TT-1.5B English/French legends "TEST TOKEN ROYAL CANADIAN MINT"/
"EPREUVE MONNAIE ROYALE CANADIENNE"

Cat. No.	Date	Description	Price Range
TT-1.5A	1979	With Beads English/English	150.-200.
TT-1.5B	1979	With Beads English/French	150.-200.

7-SIDED COPPER TOKEN; THREE MAPLE LEAVES; CIRCA 1980

Weight: 2.3 grams
Diameter: 18.7 mm
Thickness: 1.3 mm
Edge: Plain
Die Axis: ↑↑

TT-1.6   English/French legends "TEST TOKEN ROYAL CANADIAN MINT" / "EPREUVE MONNAIE ROYALE CANADIENNE"

Cat. No.	Date	Description	Price Range
TT-1.6	c.1980	7-sided, English/French	175.-225.

11-SIDED COPPER TOKEN; THREE MAPLE LEAVES - SHARP CORNERS; 1981. The 11-sided Mark I test token was issued on July 12, 1981, but due to it's sharp corners it wasrejected.

Weight: 2.60 grams
Diameter: Across corners: 18.95 mm
               Across flat: 18.40 mm
Thickness: 1.50 mm
Edge: Plain
Die Axis: ↑↑

TT-1.7A   English/English legends "TEST TOKEN ROYAL CANADIAN MINT"

Technical specifications are the same as TT-1.6A

TT-1.7B   French/French legends "EPREUVE/MONNAIE ROYALE CANADIENNE"

Technical specifications are the same as TT-1.6A

TT-1.7C   English/French legends "TEST TOKEN ROYAL CANADIAN MINT / EPREUVE MONNAIE ROYALE CANADIENNE"

Cat. No.	Date	Description	Price Range
TT-1.7A	1981	11-sided, Square Corners, English/English	175.-225.
TT-1.7B	1981	11-sided, Square Corners, French/French	175.-225.
TT-1.7C	1981	11-sided, Square Corners, English/French	75.-125

12-SIDED COPPER TOKEN; THREE MAPLE LEAVES - ROUNDED CORNERS; 1981. This 12-sided test token (mark II) was a success, and a new one cent coin went into production spring 1982.

Weight: 2.50 grams
Diameter: Across corners: 19.10 mm
Across flat: 18.80 mm
Thickness: 1.45 mm
Edge: Plain
Die Axis: ↑↑

TT-1.8A   English/English legends "TEST TOKEN ROYAL CANADIAN MINT" / "TEST TOKEN ROYAL CANADIAN MINT"

Technical specifications are the same as TT-1.8A

TT-1.8B   French/French legends "EPREUVE MONNAIE ROYALE CANADIENNE" / "EPREUVE MONNAIE ROYALE CANADIENNE"

Technical specifications are the same as TT-1.8A

TT-1.8C   English/French legends "TEST TOKEN ROYAL CANADIAN MINT" / "EPREUVE MONNAIE ROYALE CANADIENNE"

Cat. No.	Date	Description	Price Range
TT-1.8A	1981	12-sided, Round Corners, English/English	175.-225.
TT-1.8B	1981	12-sided, Round Corners, French/French	175.-225.
TT-1.8C	1981	12-sided, Round Corners, English/French	75.-125.

FIVE CENT TEST TOKENS

ROUND NICKEL TOKEN; THREE MAPLE LEAVES WITH BEADS; 1976

Weight: 4.30 grams
Diameter: 21.9 mm
Thickness: 1.71 mm
Edge: Plain
Die Axis: ↑↑

TT-5.1A   English/English legends "TEST TOKEN - ROYAL CANADIAN MINT"

Technical specifications are the same as TT-5.1A

TT-5.1B   French/French legends "EPREUVE/MONNAIE ROYALE CANADIENNE"

Technical specifications are the same as TT-5.1A

TT-5.1C   English/French legends "TEST TOKEN ROYAL CANADIAN MINT / EPREUVE MONNAIE ROYALE CANADIENNE"

Cat. No.	Date	Description	Price Range
TT-5.1A	1976	Beads, English/English	75.-125.
TT-5.1B	1976	Beads, French/French	75.-125.
TT-5.1C	1976	Beads, English/French	75.-125.

ROUND TEST TOKENS; VARIOUS COMPOSITION; DATES UNKNOWN. The letters or numbers given in quotation marks, for example "S", is punched into the test token. The different composition test tokens are not priced due to lack of market activity.

Photographs not available at press time

TT-5.2 to 5.6 English/French legends "TEST TOKEN ROYAL CANADIAN MINT / EPREUVE MONNAIE ROYALE CANADIENNE"

Edge: Plain   **Die Axis:** ↑↑

Cat. No.	Composition	Identification Letter (s)	Weight Grams	Diameter mm	Thickness mm
TT-5.2	Stainless Steel	"430" Incused	3.50 g	21.1 mm	1.3 mm
TT-5.3	Stainless Steel	"304" Incused	4.10 g	21.1 mm	1.7 mm
TT-5.4	Nickel bonded Steel 6%	"NBS" Incused	4.09 g	21.2 mm	1.7 mm
TT-5.5	Steel	"S" Incused	4.00 g	21.1 mm	1.8 mm
TT-5.6	Nickel	"T" Incused	4.07 g	21.1 mm	1.8 mm

TEN CENT TEST TOKENS

ROUND NICKEL TOKEN; BOUQUET OF FLOWERS AND FLEUR-DE-LIS; 1965.

Weight: 2.09 grams
Diameter: 17.8 mm
Thickness: 1.2 mm
Edge: Reeded
Die Axis: ↑↑

TT-10.1A   Legend "R.C.M. TEN TOKENS 1965"

Technical specifications are the
same as TT-10.1A

TT-10.1B   Legend "TEN TOKENS 1965"

ROUND NICKEL TOKEN; THREE MAPLE LEAVES; 1976.

Weight: 1.75 grams
Diameter: 17.95 mm
Thickness: 1.2 mm
Edge: Reeded
Die Axis: ↑↑

TT-10.2   Legend "TEST TOKEN/ROYAL CANADIAN MINT / EPREUVE/MONNAIE
ROYAL CANADIENNE" "TWENTY FIVE TOKENS/1965/CANADA"

Cat. No.	Date	Description	Price Range
TT-10.1A	1965	With RCM	40.-60.
TT-10.1B	1965	Without RCM	40.-60.
TT-10.2	1976	Round, nickel	75.-125.

ROUND TEST TOKENS; VARIOUS COMPOSITION; DATES UNKNOWN. The letters or numbers given in quotation marks, for example "S", is punched on the test token. The different composition test tokens are not priced due to lack of market activity.

TT-10.3 to 10.8 English/French legends "TEST TOKEN ROYAL CANADIAN MINT /
EPREUVE MONNAIE ROYALE CANADIENNE"

Photographs not available at press time

Edge: Reeded   **Die Axis:** ↑↑

Cat. No.	Composition	Identification Letter (s)	Weight Grams	Diameter mm	Thickness mm
TT-10.3	Stainless Steel	"430" Incused	1.92 g	17.9 mm	1.0 mm
TT-10.4	Stainless Steel	"304" Incused	1.98 g	17.9 mm	1.0 mm
TT-10.5	Nickel Bonded Steel 6.3%	"NBS" Incused	1.78 g	17.9 mm	1.0 mm
TT-10.6	Steel	"S" Incused	2.00 g	17.9 mm	1.0 mm
TT-10.7	Nickel	"T" Incused	2.00 g	17.9 mm	1.0 mm
TT-10.8	Nickel Bonded Steel 6%	"NBS" Incused	1.80 g	17.9 mm	1.0 mm

TWENTY-FIVE CENT TEST TOKENS

ROUND NICKEL TOKEN; THREE CANADA GEESE; 1965. Struck to provide an example of the quality of coins produced by the Royal Canadian Mint and to provide a piece for adjusting vending machines for nickel coins.

Weight: 5.01 grams
Diameter: 23.7 mm
Thickness: 1.6 mm
Edge: Reeded
Die Axis: ↑↑

TT-25.1A   Legend "TWENTY FIVE TOKENS/1965/R.C.M."

Weight: 5.01 grams
Diameter: 23.7 mm
Thickness: 1.6 mm
Edge: Reeded
Die Axis: ↑↑

TT-25.1B   Legend "TWENTY FIVE TOKENS/1965"

ROUND COPPER TOKEN; THREE CANADA GEESE; 1965.

Weight: 5.16 grams
Diameter: 23.7 mm
Thickness: 1.6 mm
Edge: Plain
Die Axis: ↑↑

TT-25.2A   Legend "TWENTY FIVE TOKENS/1965"

Cat. No.	Date	Description	Price Range
TT-25.1A	1965	With RCM	65.-85.
TT-25.1B	1965	Without RCM	65.-85.
TT-25.2A	1965	Without RCM	65.-85.

ROUND CUPRO-NICKEL TOKEN; CONJOINED BUSTS OF KING GEORGE VI AND QUEEN ELIZABETH / THREE CANADA GEESE; 1965.

Weight: 5.02 grams
Diameter: 23.7 mm
Thickness: 1.3 mm
Edge: Reeded
Die Axis: ↑↑; ↑↓

TT-25.3A; TT-25.3B   Legend Rev.: "TWENTY FIVE TOKENS/1965/CANADA"

Cat. No.	Date	Description	Price Range
TT-25.3A	1965	Royal Visit Obverse ↑↑	175.-225.
TT-25.3B	1965	Royal Visit Obverse ↑↓	175.-225.

ROUND STAINLESS STEEL 304; THREE CANADA GEESE; 1965 (1977). Struck in 1977 as a test token to support a tender to suppy circulating coinage to the Government of Bangladesh. These coins are not magnetic.

Weight: 5.82 grams
Diameter: 23.6 mm
Thickness: 1.7 mm
Edge: Plain
Die Axis: ↑↑

TT-25.4   Legend Obv.: "TWENTY FIVE TOKENS/1965/R.C:M."
Legend Rev.: "TWENTY FIVE TOKENS/1965/CANADA"

Cat. No.	Date	Description	Price Range
TT-25.4	(1977)	304 Stainless Steel	175.-225.

ROUND, VARIOUS COMPOSITION TEST TOKENS; THREE MAPLE LEAVES, 1983. The following test tokens are round. Letters are used to identify the test tokens' composition. The different composition test tokens are not priced because of lack of market activity, however a price indication may be in the $150.00 to $250.00 range.

Photograph not available at press time

TT-25.5 to 25.17   English/French legends "TEST TOKEN/ROYAL CANADIAN MINT" / "EPREUVE/MONNAIE ROYALE CANADIENNE"

Edge: Plain   **Die Axis:** ↑↑

Cat. No.	Composition	Identification Letter(s)	Weight Grams	Diameter mm	Thickness mm
TT-25.5	Aluminum	"T" Raised	1.47	23.9	1.65
TT-25.6	Brass	"H" Raised	5.25	23.8	1.70
TT-25.7	Copper	"O" Raised	5.02	23.8	1.65
TT-25.8	Copper	"V" Raised	4.72	23.8	1.55
TT-25.9	Copper-Nickel	"I" Raised	5.08	23.8	1.65
TT-25.10	Copper-Nickel	"U" Raised	5.11	23.8	1.70
TT-25.11	Nickel	"T" Incused	4.53	23.8	1.30
TT-25.12	Nickel	"W" Raised	5.16	23.9	1.65
TT-25.13	Nickel Bonded Steel 6%	"NBS" Incused	4.50	23.9	1.10
TT-25.14	Nickel Bonded Steel 6.3%	"Sherritt" Incused	4.79	23.9	1.40
TT-25.15	Stainless Steel	"304" Incused	4.07	23.8	1.10
TT-25.16	Stainless Steel	"430" Incused	4.24	23.4	1.10
TT-25.17	Steel	"S" Incused	4.55	23.8	1.10

12-SIDED ALUMINUM TOKEN, THREE MAPLE LEAVES, 1983.

Weight: 1.78 grams
Diameter: 24.0 mm
Thickness: 1.30 mm
Edge: Plain
Die Axis: ↑↑

TT-25.18   English/French legends "TEST TOKEN/ROYAL CANADIAN MINT" / "EPREUVE/MONNAIE ROYALE CANADIENNE"

Cat. No.	Date	Description	Price Range
TT-25.18	1983	"M" Raised, Aluminum	200.

ROUND, UNKNOWN COMPOSITION TEST TOKEN, THREE MAPLE LEAVES, DATE UNKNOWN.
This test token is magnetic and may have been used to test multy-ply plated blanks.

Weight: 4.5 grams
Diameter: 23.7 mm
Thickness: 1.20 mm
Edge: Reeded
Die Axis: ↑↑

TT-25.18   English/French legends "TEST TOKEN/ROYAL CANADIAN MINT" / "EPREUVE/MONNAIE ROYALE CANADIENNE"

Cat. No.	Date	Description	Price Range
TT-25.19	Unknown	Magmetic	200.-250.

FIFTY CENT TEST TOKENS

ROUND BRONZE TOKEN; 1907. Struck to adjust the coining presses prior to the first production of Canadian coins at the new Ottawa branch of the Royal Mint.

Weight: N/A
Diameter: 30.6 mm
Thickness: 2.0 mm
Edge: Reeded
Die Axis: ↑↑

TT-50.1   Legend "OTTAWA MINT/TRIAL RUN/NOVEMBER/1907"

ROUND NICKEL TOKEN; STANDING RAM; 1965. Struck to provide an example of the quality of coins produced at the Royal Canadian Mint.

Weight: N/A
Diameter: N/A
Thickness: N/A
Edge: Reeded
Die Axis: ↑↑

TT-50.2   Legend "50 TOKENS/R.C. MINT/1965"

ROUND BRASS TOKEN; STANDING RAM; 1965

Weight: N/A
Diameter: N/A
Thickness: N/A
Edge: Reeded
Die Axis: ↑↑

TT-50.3   Legend "50 TOKENS/R.C. MINT/1965"

Cat. No.	Date	Description	Price Range
TT-50.1	1907	Round, bronze	1,750.-2,000.
TT-50.2	1965	Round, nickel	450.-750.
TT-50.3	1965	Round, brass	450.-750.

ONE DOLLAR TEST TOKENS

ROUND TOKEN (VARIOUS COMPOSITIONS); THREE MAPLE LEAVES; 1983

Legends and the individual specifications listed above the table are common to all round 1983 tokens. Each token is counterstamped with the composition's initials such as "N.B.S." for Nickel Bonded Steel.

TT-100.0   Legend "TEST TOKEN/ROYAL CANADIAN MINT/COUNTER STAMP" EPREUVE/MONNAIEROYALE CANADIENNE/COUNTER STAMP"

Diameter: 32.8mm   **Edge:** Plain   **Die Axis:** ↑↑

Cat. No.	Composition	Identification Letter (s)	Weight Grams	Thickness mm	Price
TT-100.1	Nickel Bonded Steel	"N.B.S."	13.2 gms	2.31 mm	350.00
TT-100.2	Nickel Plated Zinc	"NI.PL.ZN."	10.4 gms	2.11 mm	350.00
TT-100.3	Unknown	"C.B.R."	12.4 gms	2.13 mm	350.00
TT-100.4	Stainless Steel	"S.S."	10.2 gms	1.92 mm	350.00
TT-100.5	Bronze	"BR"	12.8 gms	2.13 mm	350.00
TT-100.6	Nickel	"NI"	14.0 gms	2.25 mm	350.00
TT-100.7	Gold Plated Nickel	"AV.PL.NI"	14.0 gms	2.32 mm	350.00
TT-100.8	Copper Nickel	"CO.NI"	12.4 gms	2.00 mm	350.00
TT-100.9	Unknown	"92/8"	13.0 gms	2.11 mm	350.00
TT-100.10	Aluminum	"AL 5454"	4.0 gms	2.13 mm	350.00

11-SIDED TOKEN (COMPOSITION UNKNOWN); THREE MAPLE LEAVES; 1984

Weight: 7.0 grams
Diameter: 26.5 mm
Thickness: 1.43 mm
Edge: Plain
Die Axis: ↑↓

TT-100.11   Legend "TEST TOKEN/ROYAL CANADIAN MINT/EPREUVE/ MONNAIE ROYALE CANADIENNE"

11-SIDED GOLD PLATE ON NICKEL TOKEN; THREE MAPLE LEAVES;1985. This is the blank International Nickel submitted to the Royal Canadian Mint upon tendering for the "Loon" contract.

Weight: 7.09 grams
Diameter: 26.5 mm
Thickness: 1.80 mm
Edge: Plain
Die Axis: ↑↑

TT-100.12   Legend "TEST/ROYAL CANADIAN MINT/EPREUVE/ MONNAIE ROYALE CANADIENNE"

11-SIDED BRONZE PLATE ON NICKEL TOKEN; THREE MAPLE LEAVES; 1985. The Sherritt Gordon blank was chosen to produce blanks for the 1987 "Loon" dollar.

Weight: 7.09 grams
Diameter: 26.5 mm
Thickness: 1.80 mm
Edge: Plain
Die Axis: ↑↑

TT-100.13 Legend "TEST/ROYAL CANADIAN MINT/EPREUVE/
MONNAIE ROYALE CANADIENNE"

Cat. No.	Date	Description	Price Range
TT-100.11	1984	Unknown composition, wide rims	75.-125.
TT-100.12	1985	Gold plated on nickel, narrow rims	175.-225.
TT-100.13	1985	Nickel brass, narrow rims	175.-225.

Note: There is no known visual method of distinguishing TT-100.12 and TT-100.13 from each other.

TWO DOLLAR TEST TOKEN

During the preparation period for the two dollar coin, which would soon replace the two dollar bank note, between 1994 and 1995, the Royal Canadian Mint tested many different sizes, shapes and compositions of two dollar blanks. Table One contains a listing of bi-metal planchets, while Table Two lists tri-metal planchets. These test tokens are not priced because of the lack of market activity.

Weight: 9.34 grams
Diameter: 24.61 mm
Thickness: 2.46 mm
Edge: Reeded
Die Axis: ↑↑

TT-200.6   Legend "TEST TOKEN/ROYAL CANADIAN MINT/EPREUVE/
MONNAIE ROYALE CANADIENNE

Single Metal Two Dollar Test Tokens

Cat. No.	Description	Diameter	Weight	Edge	Composition
TT-200.1	2-sided	22.5 mm	4 gms	Scalloped smooth	Copper-zinc
TT-200.2	6-sided	22.5 mm	4 gms	Scalloped smooth	Copper-zinc
TT-200.3	12-sided	22.5 mm	4 gms	Scalloped smooth	Stainless steel
TT-200.4	6-sided	22.5 mm	4 gms	Scalloped smooth	Copper-nickel
TT-200.5	Round	22.5 mm	7.5 gms	Reeded	Copper-zinc
TT-200.6	Round	24.6 mm	9.3 gms	Reeded	Copper-zinc
TT-200.7	7-sided	22.5 mm	5.8 gms	Plain	Copper-zinc

TT-200.12 English/English legends   TT-200-12 English/French Legend

Bi-Metallic Two Dollar Test Tokens

Cat. No.	Description	Diameter	Weight	Edge	Composition
TT-200.8	Round	22.5 mm	5 g	Interrupted reeded	Aluminum-bronze ring Nickel centre
TT-200.9	Round	25.25 mm	6.2 g	Interrupted reeded	Nickel ring Copper-tin-zinc centre
TT-200.10	Round	25.25 mm	6.2 g	Interrupted reeded	Nickel ring Aluminum-bronze centre
TT-200.11	Round	27.1 mm	7.7 g	Plain	Ring unknown centre
TT-200.12	7-sided	28 mm	7.7 g	Smooth	Copper-nickel ring Aluminum-bronze centre
TT-200.13	8-sided	28 mm	8.5 g	Smooth	Copper-nickel ring Aluminum-bronze centre
TT-200.14	9-sided	28 mm	8.5 g	Smooth	Copper-nickel ring Aluminum-bronze centre

Tri-Metallic Two Dollar Test Tokens

Cat. No.	Description	Diameter	Weight	Edge	Composition
TT-200.15	11-sided	29 mm	9.6 g	N/A	Aluminum-bronze ring Aluminum-bronze centre Copper-nickel inner ring
TT-200.16	11-sided	29 mm	9.6 g	N/A	Copper-nickel outer ring Copper-nickel centre Aluminum-bronze inner ring

ROUND BI-METALLIC TOKEN; THREE MAPLE LEAVES; 1996. Bi-metallic test tokens were made available to the public for the first time in 1996.

Weight: 7.30 grams
Diameter: 28 mm
Thickness: 1.7 mm
Edge: Interrupted serration
Die Axis: ↑↑

TT-200.17 Legend "TEST TOKEN/ROYAL CANADIAN MINT/EPREUVE/
              MONNAIE ROYALE CANADIENNE"

Cat. No.	Date	Description	Price Range
TT-200.17	1996	Round bi-metallic	75.-100.

TEST TOKEN SETS

TTS-1   1984: 4 coin set

Cat. No.	Date	Description	Price Range
TTS-1	1973	Round one cent	150.-250.
	1984	12-sided one cent	
	1984	Round dollar	
	Undated	11-sided test token	

TTS-2   1986: 3 coin set

Cat. No.	Date	Description	Price Range
TTS-2	1985	Round dollar	350.-450.
		Gold plate on nickel test token	
		Bronze plate on nickel test token	

Note: For the 1999 Legal Tender "Test Token" set of Multi-Ply Plated Steel coinage see page 336.

COLLECTOR COINS

From the 19th century onward, mints have often struck small quantities of special coins for collectors in addition to those produced for general circulation. In the Canadian context these collector coins have been of several different qualities and finishes, depending upon the particular period and the mint that produced them. Three terms can be correctly applied to Canadian collectors coins, and it is important for the reader to understand them.

PROOF: The highest quality of collector coins, generally with frosted relief and highly polished mirror fields. The Olympic Proof coins were the first Canadian Proofs produced in this century. The only other 20th century Canadian Proof coins have been the $100 gold pieces and the proof sets of circulating coins which were introduced in 1981.

SPECIMEN: A general term applying to any specially produced collectors coin. Most often it is used in connection with the best quality Canadian collector coins struck between 1858 and 1972. Specimen coins are usually double struck, with very sharp details and square edges, but are not of the same superlative quality as Proofs. Before 1973, the Royal Canadian Mint did not have the equipment sufficient to strike Proof coins.

PROOF-LIKE: A term originated in 1953 by J.E. Charlton to describe special silver dollars and sets that were obviously superior to circulation strikes, but whose surfaces were not as bright as those of other collector coins (Specimens) being struck at that time. It was commonly assumed that Proof-like coins were simply circulation strikes that had been carefully handled to avoid abrasions. This is not the case; these coins are struck using selected dies and blanks and on slower moving presses than for circulation coins. Because of their superior finish, the Proof-like coins are sometimes mistakenly classed as Specimens or Proofs. It should be noted that Proof-like coins are not as sharply struck, and the higher denominations often have a slight roughness at the queen's shoulder as a result. Proofs and Specimens are usually double struck under much greater pressure which results in a flawless surface, sharp wire edge and better detail.

IMPORTANT PRICING NOTE: Proof, Specimen and Proof-like coins were manufactured under special conditions so as to ensure the highest quality product available from the Mint. Unlike ordinary production or business strike coins which are expected to have slight marks, these special coins were intended to be mark free. We have, therefore, shown prices for these coins only in MS-65 condition. Coins or sets that meet the requirements of the MS-65 grade for special strike coins may show very slight hairlines but only detectable after considerable study of the coin. Generally special strike coins that show any visible marks, nicks, or busyness in terms of hairlines (from mishandling or cleaning attempts) will not meet the MS-65 grade and must be priced much lower. Those coins that are MS-67 and MS-70 will likely command higher prices from buyers interested in coins of this perfection.

NUMISMATIC THREE CENTS

150TH ANNIVERSARY OF CANADA'S FIRST POSTAGE STAMP 2001. Sir Sandford Fleming's (1851) Three Pence Beaver was Canada's first postage stamp and a symbol of the transfer of postal authority from Britain to Canada. Canada's first three cent coin was issued by Canada Post as part of the Three Pence Beaver coin, medallion and stamp set.

Designers:
    Obverse: Dora de Pédery-Hunt
    Reverse: Sir Sandford Fleming
Modellers:
    Obverse: Dora de Pédery-Hunt
    Reverse: Cosme Saffioti
Composition: .925 silver, .075 copper, 24-karat gold covered
Weight: 5.3 grams
Diameter: 21.2 mm
Thickness: 1.9 mm
Edge: Plain
Die Axis: ↑↑

Case of Issue: Maroon leatherette case with buff insert, encapsulated coin, brown printed sleeve, COA

Date	Description	Issue Price	Mintage	PR-65
2001	3 Cent Beaver	39.95	59,573	35.00

NUMISMATIC FIVE CENTS

COMMEMORATING THE LES VOLTIGEURS de QUEBEC 2000. Since 1862 the first French-Canadian Regiment served with dignity and honour. The reverse of the 5-cent proof sterling silver coin features a baton, drums and sash the Regimental Insignia of Les Voltigeurs de Québec.

Designers:
    Obverse: Dora de Pédery-Hunt
    Reverse: RCM Staff
Modellers:
    Obverse: Dora de Pédery-Hunt
    Reverse: RCM Staff
Composition: .925 silver, .075 copper
Weight: 5.3 grams
Diameter: 21.2 mm
Thickness: 1.9 mm
Edge: Plain
Die Axis: ↑↑

Case of Issue: Black leatherette clam case; green insert and sleeve; encapsulated coin

Date	Description	Issue Price	Mintage	PR-65
2000	Les Voltigeurs de Québec	16.95	34,024	16.00

ROYAL MILITARY COLLEGE OF CANADA COMMEMORATIVE 2001. The second sterling silver commemorative five-cent coin was issued to honour the Royal Military Colleges in Canada that train our officers for the Armed Forces.

Designer:
    Obverse: Dora de Pédery-Hunt
    Reverse: Gerald T. Locklin
Modeller:
    Obverse: Dora de Pédery-Hunt
    Reverse: Susan Taylor
Specifications: Same as for 2000

Case of Issue: Black leatherette clam case; green insert, encapsulated coin; multicoloured sleeve

Date	Description	Issue Price	Mintage	PR-65
2001	Royal Military College	16.95	25,834	16.00

85TH ANNIVERSARY OF THE BATTLE FOR VIMY RIDGE 2002. On April 9th, 1917, the Canadian Army launched an assault on a small hill in France during World War I. Six days later the Canadians took Vimy Ridge, which was the turning point in the war.
    This is the last in the three-coin military series.

Designer:
    Obverse: Dora de Pédery-Hunt
    Reverse: S. A. Allward
Modeller:
    Obverse: Dora de Pédery-Hunt
    Reverse: Susan Taylor
Specifications: Same as for 2000

Case of Issue: Black leatherette clam case; maroon insert; encapsulated coin; multicoloured sleeve.

Date	Description	Issue Price	Mintage	PR-65
2002	Vimy Ridge	16.95	22,646	18.00

NUMISMATIC TEN CENTS

500TH ANNIVERSARY OF CABOTO'S FIRST TRANSATLANTIC VOYAGE 1997. Giovanni Caboto sailed from Bristol, England, in 1497, sighting "Newfoundland" weeks later. He is credited with opening North America for settlement. The 'Matthew' is depicted in full sail approaching the rocky coast of Newfoundland.

Designer: Obverse: Dora de Pédery-Hunt   **Modeller:** Obverse: Dora de Pédery-Hunt
         Reverse: Donald H. Curley   Reverse: Stanley Witten
Composition: .925 silver, .075 copper   **Thickness:** 1.2 mm
Weight: 2.4 grams   **Edge:** Reeded
Diameter: 18.0 mm   **Die Axis:** ↑↑
Case of Issue: Clear plastic case with black insert, white sleeve.

Date	Description	Issue Price	Mintage	PR-65
1997	Matthew, 500th Anniversary	10.95	49,848	26.00

100TH ANNIVERSARY OF THE BIRTH OF THE CREDIT UNION IN QUEBEC 2000. In 1900 Alphonse Desjardins founded Canada's Savings and Credit Union in Lévis, Quebec. His house "Maison Desjardins", illustrated on the ten cent coin, was the site of the first Caisse Populaire.

Designer: Obverse: Dora de Pédery-Hunt   **Modeller:** Obverse: Dora de Pédery-Hunt
         Reverse: William Woodruff   Reverse: William Woodruff
Specifications: Same as for 1997
Case of Issue: Green printed card folder with encapsulated coin

Date	Description	Issue Price	Mintage	PR-65
2000	Site of First Caisse Populaire	14.95	69,791	12.00

INTERNATIONAL YEAR OF THE VOLUNTEERS 2001. Celebrating the contributions of millions of Canadians who volunteered their time and energy towards making this country and our provinces better places for all.

Designers: Obverse: Dora de Pédery-Hunt   **Modellers:** Obverse: Dora de Pédery-Hunt
            Reverse: R.C.M. Design   Reverse: Stan Witten
Specifications: Same as for 1997
Case of Issue: Multicoloured printed card folder with encapsulated coin

Date	Description	Issue Price	Mintage	PR-65
2001	International Year of Volunteers	14.95	40,634	15.00

NUMISMATIC TWENTY-FIVE CENTS

125TH ANNIVERSARY OF CANADA SILVER PROOF SET 1992. Issued by the Royal Canadian Mint, in silver, the twelve different designs represent a familiar scene from each of the twelve provinces and territories of Canada. This is the first issue of sterling silver twenty-five cent coins since 1919. For illustrations and more information on these issues see page 123 for the companion circulating issue.

Designers and Modellers: See page 123
Composition: .925 silver, .075 copper
Weight: 5.9 grams
Diameter: 23.9 mm
Thickness: 1.7 mm
Edge: Reeded
Die Axis: ↑↑

Case of Issue: (A) Royal blue flocked single coin case
(B) Royal blue flocked case, 13 coins. Twelve 25¢ coins; one $1.00 coin

Date	Description	Issue Price	Mintage	PR-65
1992	New Brunswick	9.95	Total	8.00
1992	Northwest Territories	9.95	mintage	8.00
1992	Newfoundland	9.95	of silver	8.00
1992	Manitoba	9.95	individual	8.00
1992	Yukon	9.95	25-cents	8.00
1992	Alberta	9.95	651,812	8.00
1992	Prince Edward Island	9.95		8.00
1992	Ontario	9.95		8.00
1992	Nova Scotia	9.95		8.00
1992	Quebec	9.95		8.00
1992	Saskatchewan	9.95		8.00
1992	British Columbia	9.95		8.00
1992	13 Coin Set	129.45	84,397 sets	95.00

125TH ANNIVERSARY OF CANADA NICKEL UNCIRCULATED SET 1992. Released October 7th, 1992, this collection is mounted in a brilliantly coloured map of Canada, with each different twenty-five cent coin placed in the province or territory commemorated by its design. The Canada Day dollar is the central point of a compass. Each twenty-five cent coin is nickel and issued in "Brilliant uncirculated" condition.

Designers, modellers and specifications, please see page 123

Date	Description	Issue Price	Mintage	BU-65
1992	13 Coin Set with "Map" Holder	17.25	448,178	10.00

1867-1992, 125TH ANNIVERSARY MULE. An 1867-1992 obverse is muled with a 1993 Caribou reverse. Reportedly issued in a 1993 brilliant uncirculated set of 1993.

Designers, modellers and specifications, please see page 123

Date	Description	BU-65
1867-1992	Mule	Extremely rare

MILLENNIUM SILVER PROOF COMMEMORATIVE SET 1999.

Designers and Modellers: See page 125
Composition: .925 silver, .075 copper
Weight: 5.9 grams
Diameter: 23.9 mm
Thickness: 1.7 mm
Edge: Reeded
Die Axis: ↑↑

Case of Issue: (A) Royal blue flocked single coin case
(B) Royal blue flocked case, for twelve 25¢ coins

Date	Description	Issue Price	Mintage	BU-65
1999	January, A Country Unfolds	14.95	9,190	12.00
1999	February, Etched in Stone	14.95	8,691	12.00
1999	March, The Log Drive	14.95	8,765	12.00
1999	April, Our Northern Heritage	14.95	9,040	12.00
1999	May, The Voyageur	14.95	9,315	12.00
1999	June, From Coast to Coast	14.95	11,004	12.00
1999	July, A Nation of People	14.95	8,899	12.00
1999	August, The Pioneer Spirit	14.95	8,570	12.00
1999	September, Canada Through a Child's Eye	14.95	9,169	12.00
1999	October, A Tribute to First Nations	14.95	8,243	12.00
1999	November, The Airplane open the North	14.95	8,813	12.00
1999	December, This is Canada	14.95	11,715	12.00
1999	12 Coin Set	149.45	60,245	110.00

MILLENNIUM NICKEL SOUVENIR SET 1999. The twelve 25 cent nickel coins of 1999 were issued along with the Millennium medallion of 1999, inserted in a replica of a 1785 map of Canada. The medallion was only available in the millennium set. All coins are brilliant uncirculated.

It is in this set that the "No Denomination" coins of September and November are found. During the Fall of 1999, a Queen Elizabeth II Caribou obverse die became paired with the reverse dies of September and November millennium twenty-five cents coins creating two mules. The interesting result of this pairing is that for the first time Canada has a non-denomination legal tender coin.

The designers, modellers and specifications for the twenty-five cent coins are listed on page 124.

| Queen Elizabeth II / Caribou Twenty-five Cents Obverse | 1999 September Reverse | 1999 November Reverse |

1999 Medallion Obverse   1999 Medallion Reverse

Date	Description	Issue Price	Mintage	BU-63	BU-64	BU-65
1999	12 coins and 1999 medallion	24.95	1,499,973	15.	17.	20.
1999	September, no denomination	–	Incl. above	100.	125.	150.
1999	November, no denomination	–	incl. above	100.	125.	150.
1999	Medallion	–	Incl. above	10.	12.	15.

MILLENNIUM SILVER PROOF COMMEMORATIVE SET 2000.

Designers and Modellers: See page 125
Composition: .925 silver, .075 copper
Weight: 5.9 grams
Diameter: 23.9 mm
Thickness: 1.66 mm
Edge: Reeded
Die Axis: ↑↑

Case of Issue: (A) Royal blue flocked single coin case
(B) Royal blue flocked case, for twelve 25¢ coins

Date	Description	Issue Price	Mintage	PR-65
2000	January, Pride	14.95	N/A	12.
2000	February, Ingenuity	14.95	N/A	12.
2000	March, Achievement	14.95	N/A	12.
2000	April, Health	14.95	N/A	12.
2000	May, Natural Legacy	14.95	N/A	12.
2000	June, Harmony	14.95	N/A	12.
2000	July, Celebration	14.95	N/A	12.
2000	August, Family	14.95	N/A	12.
2000	September, Wisdom	14.95	N/A	12.
2000	October, Creativity	14.95	N/A	12.
2000	November, Freedom	14.95	N/A	12.
2000	December, Community	14.95	N/A	12.
2000	12 coin set	149.95	37,940	110.

MILLENNIUM NICKEL SOUVENIR SET 2000. The 2000 Souvenir Set features all twelve 25 cent nickel coins in brilliant uncirculated condition (MS65) plus the 2000 commemorative medallion which was only issued with the souvenir set. The coins are displayed on an easel featuring an aerial photograph of Canada. The designers, modellers and specifications for the twenty-five cent coins are listed on page 125.

"February" Twenty-five cent coin   2000 Millennium Medallion

2000 Mule, Coin Obverse with Medallion Obverse

Date	Description	Issue Price	Mintage	BU-63	BU-64	BU-65
2000	12 coins / 2000 medallion	$24.95	876,041	15.	20.	25.
2000	12 coins / 2000 medallion in plastic display case	$49.55	Incl. above	30.	40.	50.
2000	Medallion	—	Incl. above	5.	8.	12.
2000	Coin - Medallion mule	—	—	600.	1,200.	2,500.

COLOURIZED TWENTY-FIVE CENTS

MILLENNIUM 2000. Issued as part of the Millennium celebration set of coins, the twenty-five cent coins of January and July were highlighted in red.

Designers, modellers and specifications, same as for the July 2000 circulating 25-cent coins, see page 125.

Case of Issue: Blister packed on information card.

January 2000
Red: The two ribbons and
three maple leaves

Canada Day 2000
Red: The flag side panels
and the centre maple leaf

Date	Description	Issue Price	Mintage	BU-65
2000	January, Pride	8.95	49,719	20.00
2000	Canada Day, Celebration	8.95	26,106	75.00

THE SPIRIT OF CANADA, CANADA DAY 2001.

Designers:
  Obverse: Dora de Pédery-Hunt
  Reverse: Silke Ware
Modellers:
  Obverse: Dora de Pédery-Hunt
  Reverse: William Woodruff

Specifications are as for 2000.

Date	Description	Issue Price	Mintage	BU-65
2001	Canada Day	9.95	96,352	15.00

NATIONAL PRIDE, CELEBRATING CANADA'S 135th ANNIVERSARY, CANADA DAY 2002. The 2002 Canada Day twenty-five cents celebrates 135 years of National Pride. Presented to new Canadians at their citizenship ceremony during 'Celebrate Canada Day' week. This coin marks an important step for those who make Canada their home.

Designer:
    Obverse: Dora de Pédery-Hunt
    Reverse: Judith Chartier
Modeller:
    Obverse: Dora de Pédery-Hunt
    Reverse: N/A

Specifications are as for 2000

Date	Description	Issue Price	Mintage	BU-65
1952-2002P	Canada Day 2002	9.95	49,903	10.00

CANADA DAY 2003.

Photograph not
available
at press time

Designer:
    Obverse: Dora de Pédery-Hunt
    Reverse: N/A
Modeller:
    Obverse: Dora de Pédery-Hunt
    Reverse: N/A

Specifications are as for 2000

Date	Description	Issue Price	Mintage	BU-65
2003	Canada Day 2003	9.95	50,000	10.00

NUMISMATIC FIFTY CENTS

DISCOVERING NATURE SERIES
1995 - 2000

BIRDS OF CANADA; STERLING SILVER 50¢; 1995. The first set in the Discovering Nature Series was issued to commemorate birds that are native to Canada. This is the first of eight sets totalling 32 coins. They are the first sterling silver fifty cents issued since 1919.

Designers:
    Obverse: Dora de Pédery-Hunt
    Reverse: Jean Luc Grondin
Modellers:
    Obverse: Dora de Pédery-Hunt
    Reverse: Coin 1: Sheldon Beveridge
              Coin 2: Stan Witten
              Coin 3: Sheldon Beveridge
              Coin 4: Cosme Saffioti
Composition: .925 silver, .075 copper
Weight: 9.30 grams
Diameter: 27.13 mm
Thickness: 2.08 mm
Edge: Reeded
Die Axis: ↑↑

Case of Issue: Encapsulated coin in presentation box with illustrated booklet.

Coin No. 1
Atlantic Puffins

Coin No. 2
Whooping Crane

Coin No. 3
Gray Jays

Coin No. 4
White Tailed Ptarmigans

Date	Coin No.	Description	Issue Price	Mintage	PR-65
1995	1	Atlantic Puffin	–	Total	25.00
1995	2	Whooping Crane, 2 coin set	29.95	mintage	25.00
1995	3	Gray Jay	–	of all	25.00
1995	4	White-tailed Ptarmigans, 2 coin set	29.95	coins	25.00
1995		4 coin set	56.95	172,377	90.00

DISCOVERING NATURE SERIES
1995 - 2000

LITTLE WILD ONES; STERLING SILVER 50¢; 1996. The second set was issued to commemorate the young wildlife of Canada in their natural habitat.

Designers:
    Obverse: Dora de Pédery-Hunt
    Reverse: Dwayne Harty
Modellers:
    Obverse: Dora de Pédery-Hunt
    Reverse: Coin 5: Ago Aarand
               Coin 6: Sheldon Beveridge
               Coin 7: Stan Witten
               Coin 8: Sheldon Beveridge
Specifications:
    The physical and chemical properties
    are the same as the 1995 issue.

Case of Issue: (A) Two coin set; encapsulated coins
                  (B) Four coin set; encapsulated coins

Coin No. 5
Moose Calf

Coin No. 6
Wood Ducklings

Coin No. 7
Cougar Kittens

Coin number 8
Black Bear Cubs

Date	Coin No.	Description	Issue Price	Mintage	PR-65
1996	5	Moose Calf	—	Total	25.00
1996	6	Wood Duck, 2 coin set	29.95	mintage	25.00
1996	7	Cougar Kittens	—	of all	25.00
1996	8	Black Bear, 2 coin set	29.95	coins	25.00
1996		4 coin set	56.95	206,552	90.00

DISCOVERING NATURE SERIES
1995 - 2000

CANADA'S BEST FRIENDS; STERLING SILVER 50¢; 1997. The silver 50¢ set of 1997 honours the friendship and loyalty of four of Canada's favourite canine companions.

Designers:
Obverse: Dora de Pédery-Hunt
Reverse: Arnold A. Nagy
Modellers:
Obverse: Dora de Pédery-Hunt
Reverse: Coin 9: William Woodruff
Coin 10: Stan Witten
Coin 11: Sheldon Beveridge
Coin 12: Cosme Saffioti
Specifications:
The physical and chemical properties are the same as the 1995 issue.

Case of Issue: Encapsulated coin in presentation box, plus illustrated booklet.

Coin No. 9
Newfoundland

Coin No. 2
Nova Scotia Duck
Tolling Retriever

Coin No. 11
Labrador Retriever

Coin No. 4
Canadian Eskimo Dog

Date	Coin No.	Description	Issue Price	Mintage	PR-65
1997	9	Newfoundland	19.95	Total	20.00
1997	10	Nova Scotia Duck Tolling Retriever	19.95	mintage	20.50
1997	11	Labrador Retriever	19.95	of all	20.00
1997	12	Canadian Eskimo Dog	19.95	coins	20.00
1997		4 coin set	59.95	184,536	75.00

DISCOVERING NATURE SERIES
1995 - 2000

CANADA'S OCEAN GIANTS; STERLING SILVER 50¢; 1998. The silver 50¢ set of 1998 shows the grace and beauty of the whales that are seen off our coasts.

Designers:
    Obverse: Dora de Pédery-Hunt
    Reverse: Pierre Leduc
Modellers:
    Obverse: Dora de Pédery-Hunt
    Reverse: Pierre Leduc
            Coin 13: William Woodruff
            Coin 14: Sheldon Beveridge
            Coin 15: Cosme Saffioti
            Coin 16: Stan Witten
Specifications:
    The physical and chemical properties
    are the same as the 1995 issue

Case of Issue: Encapsulated coin in presentation box, plus illustrated booklet.

Coin No. 13
Killer Whale

Coin No. 14
Humpback Whale

Coin No. 15
Beluga Whale

Coin No. 16
Blue Whale

Date	Coin No.	Description	Issue Price	Mintage	PR-65
1998	13	Killer Whale	19.95	Total	20.00
1998	14	Humpback Whale	19.95	mintage	20.00
1998	15	Beluga Whale	19.95	of all	20.00
1998	16	Blue Whale	19.95	coins	20.00
1998		4 coin set	59.95	133,310	75.00

DISCOVERING NATURE SERIES
1995 - 2000

CATS OF CANADA; STERLING SILVER 50¢; 1999. Issued in 1999 to honour four species of domestic and wild felines found in Canada, a salute to our rich Canadian wildlife.

Designers:
    Obverse: Dora de Pédery-Hunt
    Reverse: John Crosby
Modellers:
    Obverse: Dora de Pédery-Hunt
    Reverse: Coin 17: Susan Taylor
                Coin 18: Susan Taylor
                Coin 19: Susan Taylor
                Coin 20: Susan Taylor
Specifications: The physical and chemical
    properties are the same as the 1995 issue

Case of Issue: Encapsulated coin in presentation box, plus illustrated booklet.

Coin No. 17
Tonkinese

Coin No. 18
Lynx

Coin No. 19
Cymric

Coin No. 20
Cougar

Date	Coin No.	Description	Issue Price	Mintage	PR-65
1999	17	Tonkinese	19.95	Total	25.00
1999	18	Lynx	19.95	mintage	25.00
1999	19	Cymric	19.95	of all	25.00
1999	20	Cougar	19.95	coins	25.00
1999		4 coin set	59.95	83,423	90.00

DISCOVERING NATURE SERIES
1995 - 2000

CANADIAN BIRDS OF PREY; STERLING SILVER 50¢, 2000. The sixth and last set of the series features the hunting birds indigenous to Canada.

Designers:
  Obverse: Dora de Pédery-Hunt
  Reverse: Coin 1 and 3, Jean-Luc Grondin
          Coin 2 and 4, Pierre Leduc
Modellers:
  Obverse: Dora de Pédery-Hunt
  Reverse: Coin 21: William Woodruff
          Coin 22: Susan Taylor
          Coin 23: Susan Taylor
          Coin 24: Stanley Witten
Specifications:
  The physical and chemical properties are the same as the 1995 issue

Case of Issue: Encapsulated coin in presentation box, plus illlustrated booklet.

Coin No. 21
Bald Eagle

Coin No. 22
Osprey

Coin No. 23
Great Horned Owl

Coin No. 24
Red-Tailed Hawk

Date	Coin No.	Description	Issue Price	Mintage	PR-65
2000	21	Bald Eagle	19.95	Total	22.50
2000	22	Osprey	19.95	mintage	22.50
2000	23	Great Horned Owl	19.95	of all	22.50
2000	24	Red-Tailed Hawk	19.95	coins	22.50
2000		4 Coin Set	59.95	123,628	80.00

CANADIAN SPORTS SERIES
1998 - 2000

CANADIAN SPORTS FIRSTS; STERLING SILVER 50¢; 1998. A new sport series of sterling silver 50¢ coins began in 1998 with the issue of the following four coins. The series will contain a total of twelve coins, four issued each of the years 1998, 1999 and 2000.

Designers:
    Obverse: Dora de Pédery-Hunt
    Reverse: Friedrich G. Peter
Modellers:
    Obverse: Dora de Pédery-Hunt
    Reverse: Coin 1: Sheldon Beveridge
              Coin 2: Ago Aarand
              Coin 3: Stan Witten
              Coin 4: Cosme Saffioti
Composition: .925 silver, .075 copper
Weight: 9.30 grams
Diameter: 27.13 mm
Thickness: 2.08 mm
Edge: Reeded
Die Axis: ↑↑

Case of Issue: Encapsulated coins in presentation box, plus illustrated booklet.

Coin No.1
First Official Amateur Figure Skating
Championships of 1888

Coin No. 2
First Canadian Ski Running and Ski
Jumping Championships of 1898

Coin No. 3
First Overseas Canadian Soccer
Tour of 1888

Coin No. 4
Gilles Villeneuve; Victory in the Grand
Prix of Canada for F1 Auto Racing 1978

Date	Coin No.	Description	Issue Price	Mintage	PR-65
1998	1	Skating	19.95	Total	20.00
1998	2	Skiing	19.95	mintage	20.00
1998	3	Soccer	19.95	of all	20.00
1998	4	Auto Racing	19.95	coins	20.00
1998		4 coin set	59.95	56,428	75.00

CANADIAN SPORTS SERIES
1998 - 2000

CANADIAN SPORTS FIRSTS; STERLING SILVER 50¢; 1999. The 1999 50¢ sterling silver coin set commemorates important dates in the history of Canadian sports. The designs reflect both the history of the sport and the growth and development into national pastimes.

Designers:
Obverse: Dora de Pédery-Hunt
Reverse: Donald H. Curley
Modellers:
Obverse: Dora de Pédery-Hunt
Reverse: Coin 5: William Woodruff
Coin 6: Stan Witten
Coin 7: Cosme Saffioti
Coin 8: Sheldon Beveridge
Specifications:
The physical and chemical properties are the same as the 1998 issue

Case of Issue: Singles: Encapsulated in a display folder and sleeve.
Set: Encapsulated coins in four hole presentation box, plus illlustrated booklets.

Coin No. 5
1904-1999 First Canadian Open
Golf Championship of 1904

Coin No. 6
1874-1999 First International Yacht Race
between Canada and U.S.A. in 1874

Coin No. 7
1909-1999 First Grey Cup in
Canadian Football

Coin No. 8
1891-1999 Invention of Basketball
by Canadian James Naismith

Date	Coin No.	Description	Issue Price	Mintage	PR-65
1999	5	Golf	19.95	Total	20.00
1999	6	Yachting	19.95	mintage	20.00
1999	7	Basketball	19.95	of all	20.00
1999	8	Football	19.95	coins	20.00
1999		4 coin set	59.95	52,115	60.00

CANADIAN SPORTS SERIES
1998 - 2000

CANADIAN SPORTS FIRSTS; STERLING SILVER 50¢; 2000. The 2000 50¢ Sterling Silver coin set celebrates the first competitions in Hockey, Curling, Steeplechase and Five Pin Bowling held in Canada. This is the last set in the twelve coin series.

Designers:
    Obverse: Dora de Pédery-Hunt
    Reverse: Brian Hughes
Modellers:
    Obverse: Dora de Pédery-Hunt
    Reverse: Coin 9: Stanley Witten
              Coin 10: Cosme Saffioti
              Coin 11: Susan Taylor
              Coin 12: William Woodruff
Specifications:
    The physical and chemical properties are the same as the 1998 issues.

Case: Singles: Encapsulated and housed in a lithographed metal box.
            Set: Twelve coin metal case.

Coin No. 9
1875-2000 First
Recorded Hockey Game

Coin No. 10
1760-2000 Introduction
of Curling to North America

Coin No. 11
1840-2000 First Steeplechase
Race in British North America

Coin No. 12
1910-2000 Birth of the
First 5-Pin Bowling League

Date	Coin No.	Description	Issue Price	Mintage	PR-65
2000	9	Hockey	19.95	Total	20.00
2000	10	Curling	19.95	mintage	20.00
2000	11	Steeplechase	19.95	of all	20.00
2000	12	Bowling	19.95	coins	20.00
2000		4 Coin Set	59.95	50,091	75.00

CANADIAN FESTIVALS SERIES
2001 - 2003

CANADIAN FESTIVALS, STERLING SILVER 50¢; 2001. The Royal Canadian Mint introduced a new series of sterling silver 50-cent coins in 2001 commemorating Canadian Festivals. Each coin represents a Canadian Province, Territory or Community, celebrating it's culture, history and traditions with colourful festivals. The 13-coin set will be issued over three years, starting in 2001 and ending 2003. and was available by subscription in 2001 for $249.95 with coins being shipped as they became available.

Designers:
    Obverse: Dora de Pédery-Hunt
    Reverse: See below
Modellers:
    Obverse: Dora de Pédery-Hunt
    Reverse: See below
Composition: .925 silver, .075 copper
Weight: 9.30 grams
Diameter: 27.13 mm
Thickness: 2.08 mm
Edge: Reeded
Die Axis: ↑↑

Case of Issue: A: Singles; Multicoloured printed card folder with encapsulated coin.
                 B: Thirteen coin set; Canadian Festivals subscription coffee table book.

Coin No. 1
Quebec Winter Carnival (Quebec)
Sylvie Daigneault, Stan Witten

Coin No. 2
Toonik Tyme (Nunavut)
John Mardon, José Osio

Coin No. 3 Newfoundland and Labrador
Folk Festival (Newfoundland)
David Craig, Cosme Saffioti

Coin No. 4 Festival of Fathers
(Prince Edward Island)
Brenda Whiteway, William Woodruff

Date	Coin No.	Description	Issue Price	Mintage	PR-65
2001	1	Quebec	21.95	Total	22.00
2001	2	Nunavut	21.95	mintage	22.00
2001	3	Newfoundland	21.95	all coins	22.00
2001	4	Prince Edward Island	21.95	58,123	22.00

CANADIAN FESTIVALS SERIES
2001-2003 (cont.)

CANADIAN FESTIVALS, STERLING SILVER 50¢; 2002. The second issue in the 13-coin set which commemorates festivals across Canada.

Designers:
> Obverse: Dora de Pédery-Hunt
> Reverse: See below

Modellers:
> Obverse: Dora de Pédery-Hunt
> Reverse: See below

Specifications:
> The physical and chemical properties are the same as the 2001 issue

Case of Issue: A: Singles; Multicoloured printed card folder with encapsulated coin.
B: Thirteen coin set; Canadian Festivals subscription coffee table book.

Coin No. 5
Annapolis Valley Blossom Festival
(Nova Scotia)
Bonnie Ross, José Osio

Coin No. 6
Stratford Festival of Canada
(Ontario)
Laurie McGaw, Susan Taylor

Coin No. 7
Folklorama
(Manitoba)
William Woodruff

Coin No. 8
Calgary Stampede
(Alberta)
Stan Witten

Coin No. 9
Squamish Days
Logger Sports
(British Columbia)
José Osio

Date	Coin No.	Description	Issue Price	Mintage	PR-65
2002	5	Nova Scotia	21.95	Total	22.00
2002	6	Ontario	21.95	mintage	22.00
2002	7	Manitoba	21.95	for all	22.00
2002	8	Alberta	21.95	coins	22.00
2002	9	British Columbia	21.95	58,998	22.00

CANADIAN FESTIVALS SERIES
2001-2003 (cont.)

CANADIAN FESTIVALS, STERLING SILVER 50¢; 2003. The third issue in the 13-coin set which commemorates festivals across Canada.

Designers:
    Obverse: Dora de Pédery-Hunt
    Reverse: See below
Modellers:
    Obverse: Dora de Pédery-Hunt
    Reverse: See below
Specifications:
    The physical and chemical properties
    are the same as the 2001 issue

Case of Issue: A: Singles; Multicoloured printed card folder with encapsulated coin.
                 B: Thirteen coin set; Canadian Festivals subscription coffee table book.

Photograph
not available
at press time

Coin No. 10
Yukon Festival
(Yukon)
Ken Anderson

Coin No. 11

Photograph
not available
at press time

Photograph
not available
at press time

Coin No. 12

Coin No. 13

Date	Coin No.	Description	Issue Price	Mintage	PR-65
2003	10	Yukon	21.95	N/A	22.00
2003	11	N/A	21.95	N/A	22.00
2003	12	N/A	21.95	N/A	22.00
2003	13	N/A	21.95	N/A	22.00
2001-03		Set Canadian Festivals (13 coins)	249.95	N/A	250.00

CANADIAN FOLKLORE AND LEGENDS SERIES
2001 - 2002

CANADA'S FOLKLORE AND LEGENDS; STERLING SILVER 50 CENTS; 2001. The first in a new series of 50-cent sterling silver coins celebrating Canadian Folklore and Legends. Official release date April 11, 2001.

Designer:
    Obverse: Dora de Pédery-Hunt
    Reverse: See below
Modeller:
    Obverse: Dora de Pédery-Hunt
    Reverse: See below
Composition: .925 silver .075 copper
Weight: 9.30 grams
Diameter: 27.13 mm
Thickness: 2.08 mm
Edge: Reeded
Die Axis: ↑↑

Case of Issue: Multicoloured printed card folder with encapsulated coin.

Coin No. 1
The Sled
Valentina Hotz-Entin
Susan Taylor

Coin No. 2
The Maiden's Cave
Peter Kiss
Susan Taylor

Coin No. 3
Les Petits Sauteux
Miyuki Tanobe
José Osio

Coin No. 4
The Pig That Wouldn't
Get Over the Stile
Laura Jolicoeur / José Osio

Coin No. 5
Shoemaker in Heaven
Francine Gravel
Cosme Saffioti

Coin No. 6
Le Vaisseau Fantome
Colette Boivin
William Woodruff

Date	Coin No.	Description	Issue Price	Mintage	PR-65
2001	1	The Sled	24.95	Total mintage	25.00
2001	2	The Maiden's Cave	24.95	of 2001 coins	25.00
2001	3	Les Petits Sauteux	24.95	28,979	25.00
2002	4	Pig That Wouldn't Get Over the Stile	24.95	Total mintage	25.00
2002	5	Shoemaker in Heaven	24.95	of 2002 coins	25.00
2002	6	Le Vaisseau Fantome	24.95	19,267	25.00

50 CENT STERLING SILVER COINS

50TH ANNIVERSARY OF THE CANADIAN TULIP FESTIVAL 2002. After World War II and the Dutch Royal Family's stay in Ottawa, Princess Juliana thanked Canadians for their hospitality with a personal gift of 20,000 tulip bulbs. The gift became the foundation for what was to become the annual Tulip Festival held in Ottawa.

Designer:
  Obverse: Dora de Pédery-Hunt
  Reverse: Anthony Testa
Modeller:
  Obverse: Dora de Pédery-Hunt
  Reverse: Stan Witten
Composition: .925 silver .075 copper,
  22-karat gold plate on design
Weight: 9.30 grams
Diameter: 27.13 mm
Thickness: 2.16 mm
Edge: Reeded
Die Axis: ↑↑

Case of Issue: Black leatherette, clam style; encapsulated coin; multicoloured sleeve; COA

Date	Description	Issue Price	Mintage	PR-65
2002	Golden Tulip	24.95	19,984	65.00

GOLDEN DAFFODIL, SYMBOL OF HOPE, 2003. The daffodil is the Canadian Cancer Society's symbol of hope. The Royal Canadian Mint donated $2.00 from the sale of each coin to the Cancer Society, with all funds going to support cancer research.

Designer:
  Obverse: Dora de Pédery-Hunt
  Reverse: Christie Paquet
Modeller:
  Obverse: Dora de Pédery-Hunt
  Reverse: Christie Paquet
Composition: .925 silver .075 copper,
  22-karat gold plate on design
Weight: 9.30 grams
Diameter: 27.13 mm
Thickness: 2.16 mm
Edge: Reeded
Die Axis: ↑↑

Case of Issue: Black leatherette, clam style; encapsulated coin; multicoloured sleeve; COA

Date	Description	Issue Price	Mintage	PR-65
2003	Golden Daffodil	34.95	55,000	35.00

COMMEMORATIVE DOLLARS 1968 TO DATE

The following pages list the silver, nickel and nickel bronze dollars issued by the numismatic department of the Royal Canadian Mint over the past years. The characteristics of these issues are itemized below.

COMMEMORATIVE DOLLAR SPECIFICATIONS

Specifications	Specimen Nickel Dollars 1968-1976 1982, 1984	Specimen/ Proof Silver Dollars 1971-1991	Proof Nickel/ Bronze Dollars 1987-date	Proof Silver Dollars 1992-2002	Proof Silver Dollars 2003
Composition:	1.00 Nickel	.500 Silver .500 Copper	Nickel Plated with Bronze	.925 Silver .075 Copper	99.99 Silver
Weight (grams):	15.62	23.30	7.00	25.175	25.175
Diameter (mm):	32.13	36.07	26.50	36.07	36.07
Thickness:			1.90	2.95	3.02
Edge:	Reeded	Reeded	11-Side Plain	Reeded	Reeded
Die axis:	↑↑	↑↑	↑↑	↑↑	↑↑

VOYAGEUR NICKEL DOLLAR 1968 AND 1969: A cased 1968 and 1969 nickel dollar was available from the numismatic department of the Mint during 1968-69. The department did not aggressively market this product until 1970. Thus the years 1968 and 1969 saw the development of the "cased dollar" line with the evolution of a "clam" style case.

Obverse: Designer: Arnold Machin   **Reverse:** Designer: Raymond Taylor
Modeller: Patrick Brindley   Modeller: Walter Ott
Case: Square, black leatherette with gold side trim. Gilt Royal Mint Building as crest. Blue inside with black insert and gilt Coat of Arms of Canada

Date	Description	Issue Price	Mintage	SP-65
1968	Voyageur, Nickel	N/A	N/A	3.00
1969	Voyageur, Nickel	N/A	N/A	3.00

MANITOBA CENTENNIAL NICKEL DOLLAR 1970. The year 1970 saw Canada's first commemorative nickel dollar, with a special reverse featuring a prairie crocus in recognition of the centenary of Manitoba's entry into Confederation.

Obverse: Designer: Arnold Machin   **Reverse:** Designer: Raymond Taylor
           Modeller: Patrick Brindley   Modeller: Walter Ott

Specifications: See page 259

Case: (A)   Square, black leatherette, gilt RCM crest, blue insert.
          (B)   Rectangular, maroon leatherette case, gold stamped crest of Canada,
                red inside with black insert.
          (C)   Rectangular, black leatherette case, gold stamped with the Japanese
                characters, Maple Leaf, Canada. Red interior with black insert. Card insert.
                (Sold at the Canada pavillion in Japan, during 1970.)

Date	Description	Issue Price	Mintage	SP-65
1970	Manitoba, Nickel, Case A	2.00	349,120	3.00
1970	Manitoba, Nickel, Case B	N/A	Incl. above	5.00
1970	Manitoba, Nickel, Case C	N/A	Incl. above	10.00

BRITISH COLUMBIA CENTENNIAL NICKEL DOLLAR 1971. The nickel dollar for 1971 commemorates the entry in 1871 of British Columbia into Confederation. Its design is based on the arms of the province, with a shield at the bottom and dogwood blossoms at the top. The design of the specimen nickel dollar is identical to the circulating issue. See page No. 156.

Obverse: Designer: Arnold Machin   **Reverse:** Designer: Thomas Shingles
          Modeller: Patrick Brindley   Modeller: Thomas Shingles
Specifications: See page 259
Case: Rectangular blue leatherette case, coat of arms of Canada stamped in silver, blue and black insert

Date	Description	Issue Price	Mintage	SP-65
1971	B.C. Centennial, Nickel	2.00	181,091	3.00

BRITISH COLUMBIA CENTENNIAL SILVER DOLLAR 1971. The first non-circulating silver dollar was issued to the public in 1971. It was a commemorative for the entry of British Columbia into Confederation in 1871. Its design is based upon the provincial arms. The obverse features a modification of the Machin portrait in which the portrait of the Queen was reduced slightly and her hair extensively redone.

Obverse: Designer: Arnold Machin   **Reverse:** Designer: Patrick Brindley
          Modeller: Patrick Brindley   Modeller: Patrick Brindley
Specifications: See page 259
Case: (A) Rectangular black leatherette, coat of arms, maroon and black insert
       (B) Rectangular black leatherette, coat of arms, white and black insert.

Date	Description	Issue Price	Mintage	SP-65
1971	B.C. Centennial, Silver	3.00	585,217	5.50

VOYAGEUR NICKEL DOLLAR 1972. The numismatic department of the Royal Canadian Mint issued a specimen nickel dollar of the same design as the circulating dollar.

Obverse:	Designer: Arnold Machin	Reverse:	Designer: E. Hahn
	Modeller: Patrick Brindley		Modeller: Terry Smith

Specifications: See page 259
Case: Rectangular blue leatherette case, blue and black insert.

Date	Description	Issue Price	Mintage	SP-65
1972	Voyageur, Nickel	2.00	143,392	3.00

VOYAGEUR SILVER DOLLAR 1972. The reverse of the 1972 silver dollar is the voyageur design somewhat modified from its last use on the 1966 silver dollar. One of the most noticeable differences is the substitution of beads for denticles at the rim.

Specifications: Designers and modellers are as for the nickel issue.
Case: Rectangular black leatherette case, maroon and black insert.

Date	Description	Issue Price	Mintage	SP-65
1972	Voyageur, Silver	3.00	341,581	5.50

PRINCE EDWARD ISLAND CENTENNIAL NICKEL DOLLAR 1973. The 100th anniversary of the entry of Prince Edward Island into Confederation was commemorated with the reverse design depicting the provincial legislature building in Charlottetown.

Obverse: Designer: Arnold Machin   **Reverse:** Designer: Terry Manning
         Modeller: Patrick Brindley   Modeller: Walter Ott
Specifications: See page 259
Case: Rectangular blue leatherette case, coat of arms, blue and black insert.

Date	Description	Issue Price	Mintage	SP-65
1973	P.E.I. Centennial, Nickel	2.00	466,881	3.00

ROYAL CANADIAN MOUNTED POLICE CENTENNIAL SILVER DOLLAR 1973. In 1973 the reverse of the silver dollar recognized the founding of the North West Mounted Police which later became the Royal Canadian Mounted Police.

Obverse: Designer: Arnold Machin   **Reverse:** Designer: Paul Cedarberg
         Modeller: Patrick Brindley   Modeller: Patrick Brindley
Specifications: See page 259
Case: (A)   Rectangular black leatherette case, coat of arms, maroon and black insert.
        (B)   Rectangular blue leatherette case, gilt RCMP crest, maroon and black insert.

Date	Description	Issue Price	Mintage	SP-65
1973	R.C.M.P., Silver, Case A	3.00	904,723	5.50
1973	R.C.M.P., Silver, Case B	3.00	Incl. above	15.00

WINNIPEG CENTENNIAL NICKEL DOLLAR 1974. The 1974 cased specimen nickel dollar carried the same design as the circulating dollar. See page 157.

Obverse:	Designer: Arnold Machin	Reverse:	Designer: Paul Pederson
	Modeller: Patrick Brindley		Modeller: Patrick Brindley

Specifications: See page 259

Case: Rectangular blue leatherette case, coat of arms, blue and black plastic insert.

Date	Description	Issue Price	Mintage	SP-65
1974	Winnipeg Centennial, Nickel	2.00	363,786	3.00
1974	Winnipeg Centennial, Nickel, Double Yoke (Die)	2.00	Incl. above	275.00

Note: See page 344 for illustration of 1974 Specimen double die variety.

WINNIPEG CENTENNIAL SILVER DOLLAR 1974. The 100th anniversary of the establishment of Winnipeg, Manitoba, as a city was marked by the reverse of the 1974 silver dollar. The design is identical to that of the nickel dollar.

Obverse:	Designer: Arnold Machin	Reverse:	Designer: Paul Pederson
	Modeller: Patrick Brindley		Modeller: Patrick Brindley

Specifications: See page 259

Case: Rectangular black leatherette case, coat of arms, maroon and black plastic insert.

Date	Description	Issue Price	Mintage	SP-65
1974	Winnipeg Centennial, Silver	3.50	628,183	5.00

VOYAGEUR NICKEL DOLLAR 1975. Issued by the numismatic department of the Royal Canadian Mint as a specimen quality example of the circulating nickel dollar.

Obverse:	Designer: Arnold Machin	Reverse:	Designer: E. Hahn
	Modeller: Patrick Brindley		Modeller: Terry Smith

Specifications: See page 259
Case: Rectangular blue leatherette case, coat of arms, blue and black insert.

Date	Description	Issue Price	Mintage	SP-65
1975	Voyageur, Nickel	2.50	88,102	3.00

CALGARY CENTENNIAL SILVER DOLLAR 1975. For the centenary of the founding of Calgary, Alberta, the silver dollar of 1975 bore a special reverse showing a cowboy atop a bucking bronco. Oil wells and the modern city skyline appear in the background.

Obverse:	Designer: Arnold Machin	Reverse:	Designer: D. D. Paterson
	Modeller: Patrick Brindley		Modeller: Patrick Brindley

Specifications: See page 259
Case: Rectangular black leatherette case, coat of arms, maroon and black insert.

Date	Description	Issue Price	Mintage	SP-65
1975	Calgary Centennial, Silver	3.50	833,095	5.50

VOYAGEUR NICKEL DOLLAR 1976. Issued by the numismatic department of the Royal Canadian Mint in specimen quality. This was the last year of issue for a single voyageur nickel dollar.

| Obverse: | Designer: Arnold Machin | Reverse: | Designer: E. Hahn |
| | Modeller: Patrick Brindley | | Modeller: Terry Smith |

Specifications: See page 259
Case: Rectangular blue leatherette case, coat of arms, blue and black insert.

Date	Description	Issue Price	Mintage	SP-65
1976	Voyageur, Nickel	2.50	74,209	3.00

LIBRARY OF PARLIAMENT CENTENNIAL SILVER DOLLAR 1976. The reverse of the 1976 silver dollar was employed to commemorate the 100th anniversary of the completion of the Library of Parliament. This attractive building was the only part of the original centre block of the Parliament Buildings that was saved during the disastrous fire of 1916. It is still in use and is a popular tourist attraction in Ottawa.

Obverse:	Designer: Arnold Machin	Reverse:	Designers: Walter Ott,
	Modeller: Patrick Brindley		Patrick Brindley
			Modeller: Walter Ott

Specifications: See page 259
Case: (A) Rectangular black leatherette case, coat of arms, maroon and black insert.
(B) Rectangular blue leatherette case, coat of arms, light blue insert with purple satin cloth printed "Library of Parliament - Bibliotheque du Parlement 1876-1976."

Date	Description	Issue Price	Mintage	SP-65
1976	Library of Parliament, Silver Case A	4.00	483,722	6.00
1976	Library of Parliament, Silver Case B	4.00	Incl above	10.00

QUEEN ELIZABETH II SILVER JUBILEE SILVER DOLLAR 1977. During 1977 the Queen celebrated the 25th anniversary of her accession to the throne. Many countries, including Canada, recognized the event with a special commemorative coin. The design on the reverse depicts the throne of the Senate of Canada, which is used by the Queen or the Governor General for ceremonial occasions. The obverse was specifically designed for this coin and bears a special legend and the dates 1952-1977.

Obverse:	Designer: Arnold Machin	Reverse:	Designer: Raymond Lee
	Modeller: Royal Mint Staff		Modeller: Ago Aarand

Specifications: See page 259

Case:
    (A) Rectangular black leatherette case, coat of arms, maroon and black plastic insert.
    (B) Rectangular maroon leatherette case, coat of arms, maroon and black plastic insert.
    (C) Rectangular maroon velveteen case, coat of arms, maroon velveteen insert.

Date	Description	Issue Price	Mintage	SP-65
1977	Jubilee, Silver, Case A	4.25	744,848	5.50
1977	Jubilee, Silver, Case B	4.25	Incl. above	15.00
1977	Jubilee, Silver, Case C	4.25	Incl. above	15.00

COMMONWEALTH GAMES SILVER DOLLAR 1978. The 1978 silver dollar commemorated the 11th Commonwealth Games, held in Edmonton, Alberta, August 3-12 of that year. The reverse design features the symbol of the Games in the centre, and the official symbols of the ten sports which comprise the Games along the perimeter. The obverse was made specifically for this issue.

Obverse: Designer: Arnold Machin   Reverse: Designer: Raymond Taylor
          Modeller: Royal Mint Staff   Modeller: Victor Coté
Specifications: See page 259
Case: Rectangular black leatherette case, coat of arms, maroon and black plastic
                 insert.

Date	Description	Issue Price	Mintage	SP-65
1978	Commonwealth Games	4.50	640,000	5.50

GRIFFON TRICENTENNIAL SILVER DOLLAR 1979. The 300th anniversary of the first voyage by a commercial ship on the Great Lakes was commemorated on the reverse of the 1979 silver dollar.

Obverse: Designer: Arnold Machin   Reverse: Designer: Walter Schluep
          Modeller: Patrick Brindley   Modeller: Terry Smith
Specifications: See page 259
Case: Square black leatherette, maroon insert, capsule.

Date	Description	Issue Price	Mintage	SP-65
1979	Griffon	5.50	688,671	10.00

ARCTIC TERRITORIES CENTENNIAL SILVER DOLLAR 1980. The 1980 commemorative silver dollar marked the centenary of the transfer of the Arctic islands from the British Government to the government of the Dominion of Canada.

Obverse: Designer: Arnold Machin   **Reverse:** Designer: D. D. Paterson
        Modeller: Patrick Brindley   Modeller: Walter Ott
Specifications: See page 259
Case: Square black leatherette, maroon insert, capsule.

Date	Description	Issue Price	Mintage	SP-65
1980	Arctic	22.00	389,564	20.00

TRANS-CANADA RAILWAY CENTENNIAL SILVER DOLLAR 1981. The 1981 silver dollar commemorates the 100th anniversary of the approval by the Canadian government to build the Trans-Canada Railway. This is the first year of issue by the Mint of two different qualities of silver dollars.

Obverse: Designer: Arnold Machin   **Reverse:** Designer: Christopher Gorey
        Modeller: Patrick Brindley   Modeller: Walter Ott
Specifications: See page 259
Case: Proof – Square black leatherette, maroon insert, capsule
.   Uncirculated – Clear plastic, black insert.

Date	Description	Issue Price	Mintage	Price
1981	Railway, PR-65	18.00	353,742	15.00
1981	Railway, BU-65	14.00	148,647	8.00

CONSTITUTION NICKEL DOLLAR 1982. The reverse features a faithful reproduction of the celebrated painting of the Fathers of Confederation. This nickel dollar commemorates the Constitution with the inscription "1867 CONFEDERATION" above the painting and "CONSTITUTION 1982" beneath it. The condition of this dollar is "select uncirculated" as offered by the Mint.

Obverse:	Designer: Arnold Machin	Reverse:	Designer: Ago Aarand
	Modeller: Royal Mint Staff		Modeller: RCM Staff

Specifications: See page 259
Case: Maroon case with maple leaf logo, maroon insert, capsule.

Date	Description	Issue Price	Mintage	PR-65
1982	Consitution	9.75	107,353	9.00

REGINA CENTENNIAL SILVER DOLLAR 1982. Issued to commemorate the centennial of the founding of Regina in 1882.

Obverse:	Designer: Arnold Machin	Reverse:	Designer: Huntley Brown
	Modeller: Patrick Brindley		Modeller: Walter Ott

Specifications: See page 259
Case: Proof – Square black leatherette case, maroon insert, capsule.
Uncirculated – Clear plastic case, black insert.

Date	Description	Issue Price	Mintage	Price
1982	Regina Centennial, PR-65	15.25	577,959	6.50
1982	Regina Centennial, BU-65	10.95	144,989	10.00

WORLD UNIVERSITY GAMES SILVER DOLLAR 1983. Issued to commemorate the World University Games held in Edmonton, Alberta, during July of that year.

Obverse: Designer: Arnold Machin   **Reverse:** Designer: Carola Tietz
           Modeller: Patrick Brindley   Modeller: Walter Ott
Specifications: See page 259
Case: Proof – Square black leatherette case, maroon insert, capsule.
                 Uncirculated – Clear plastic case, black insert.

Date	Description	Issue Price	Mintage	Price
1983	World Games, PR-65	16.15	340,068	7.00
1983	World Games, BU-65	10.95	159,450	6.00

JACQUES CARTIER NICKEL DOLLAR 1984. The 450th year of Jacques Cartier's landing at Gaspe, Quebec, was honoured on July 24, 1984, by the issuing of a commemorative nickel dollar.

Obverse: Designer: Arnold Machin   **Reverse:** Designer: Hector Greville
           Modeller: Royal Mint Staff   Modeller: Victor Coté
Specifications: See page 259
Case: Rectangular green velvet case, green insert, capsule.

Date	Description	Issue Price	Mintage	PR-65
1984	Jacques Cartier, Nickel	9.75	87,776	6.00

TORONTO SESQUICENTENNIAL SILVER DOLLAR 1984. Issued to commemorate the 150th anniversary of the incorporation of the City of Toronto in 1834.

Obverse: Designer: Arnold Machin   **Reverse:** Designer: D. J. Craig
Modeller: Patrick Brindley   Modeller: Walter Ott
Specifications: See page 259
Case: Proof – Square black leatherette case, maroon insert, capsule.
Uncirculated – Clear plastic case, black insert.

Date	Description	Issue Price	Mintage	Price
1984	Toronto Sesquicentennial, PR-65	17.50	571,079	7.50
1984	Toronto Sesquicentennial, BU-65	11.40	133,563	7.00

NATIONAL PARKS CENTENNIAL SILVER DOLLAR 1985. The 1985 silver dollar commemorates the 100th anniversary of an important part of Canada's heritages, the National Parks.

Obverse: Designer: Arnold Machin   **Reverse:** Designer: Karel Rohlicek
Modeller: Patrick Brindley   Modeller: Walter Ott
Specifications: See page 259
Case: Proof – Square black leatherette case, maroon insert, capsule.
Uncirculated – Clear plastic case, black insert.

Date	Description	Issue Price	Mintage	Price
1985	National Parks, PR-65	17.50	537,297	12.00
1985	National Parks, BU-65	12.00	162,873	7.00

VANCOUVER CENTENNIAL SILVER DOLLAR 1986. Issued to commemorate the 100th anniversary of the founding of Vancouver and the arrival of the first trans-Canada train in Vancouver. Canadian Pacific Engine No. 371 was the first to arrive in 1886.

Obverse: Designer: Arnold Machin
        Modeller: Patrick Brindley

Reverse: Designer: Elliott John Morrison
        Modeller: Ago Aarand,
                  Victor Coté

Specifications: See page 259
Case: Proof: Square black leatherette case, maroon insert, capsule.
        Uncirculated: Clear plastic case, black insert.

Date	Description	Issue Price	Mintage	Price
1986	Vancouver Centennial, PR-65	18.00	496,418	8.00
1986	Vancouver Centennial, BU-65	12.25	124,574	7.00

THE LOON NICKEL/BRONZE DOLLAR 1987. A proof striking of the loon dollar was issued by the numismatic department of the Royal Canadian Mint in 1987.

Obverse: Designer: Arnold Machin
        Modeller: Patrick Brindley

Reverse: Designer: R. R. Carmichael
        Modeller: Terry Smith

Specifications: See page 259
Case: Blue velvet case, blue velvet insert, capsule.

Date	Description	Issue Price	Mintage	PR-65
1987	Loon, Nickel/Bronze	13.50	178,120	10.00

JOHN DAVIS SILVER DOLLAR 1987. The 400th anniversary of John Davis' historic expedition in search of the North West Passage is commemorated on the 1987 silver dollar.

Obverse: Designer: Arnold Machin
Modeller: Patrick Brindley

Reverse: Designer: Christopher Gorey
Modeller: Ago Aarand,
Victor Coté

Specifications: See page 259
Case: Proof: Square black leatherette case, maroon insert, capsule.
Uncirculated: Clear plastic black insert.

Date	Description	Issue Price	Mintage	Price
1987	John Davis, PR-65	19.00	405,688	12.00
1987	John Davis, BU-65	14.00	118,722	8.00

SAINT-MAURICE IRONWORKS SILVER DOLLAR 1988. The 250th anniversary of the Saint-Maurice Ironworks, Canada's first heavy industry, is commemorated on the 1988 silver dollar.

Obverse: Designer: Arnold Machin
Modeller: Patrick Brindley

Reverse: Designer: R. R. Carmichael
Modeller: Sheldon Beveridge

Specifications: See page 259
Case: Proof: Square, black leatherette case, maroon insert, capsule.
Uncirculated: Clear plastic case, black insert.

Date	Description	Issue Price	Mintage	Price
1988	Saint-Maurice Ironworks, PR-65	20.00	259,230	20.00
1988	Saint-Maurice Ironworks, BU-65	15.00	106,702	9.00

MACKENZIE RIVER BICENTENNIAL SILVER DOLLAR 1989. The bicentennial of the first full length voyage of the Mackenzie River by Alexander Mackenzie and his European crew, all the way to the Arctic Ocean, is commemorated on the 1989 silver dollar.

Obverse: Designer: Arnold Machin   **Reverse:** Designer: John Mardon
      Modeller: Patrick Brindley   Modeller: Sheldon Beveridge
Specifications: See page 259
Case: Proof: Square black leatherette case, maroon insert, capsule.
              Uncirculated: Clear plastic black insert.

Date	Description	Issue Price	Mintage	Price
1989	Mackenzie River Bicentennial, PR-65	21.75	272,319	20.00
1989	Mackenzie River Bicentennial, BU-65	16.25	110,650	9.00

HENRY KELSEY TRICENTENNIAL SILVER DOLLAR 1990. The 300th anniversary of Henry Kelsey's ventures into the Canadian West is commemorated on the 1990 silver dollar.

Obverse: Designer: Dora de Pédery-Hunt   **Reverse:** Designer: D. J. Craig
      Modeller: Dora de Pédery-Hunt   Modeller: Ago Aarand
Specifications: See page 259
Case: Proof: Square black leatherette case, maroon insert, capsule.
              Uncirculated: Clear plastic case, black insert.

Date	Description	Issue Price	Mintage	Price
1990	Henry Kelsey, PR-65	22.95	222,983	20.00
1990	Henry Kelsey, BU-65	16.75	85,763	9.00

FRONTENAC SILVER DOLLAR 1991. Commemorates the 175th anniversary of the first steamship to sail on the Great Lakes. Built by a partnership of Kingston merchants in 1815, the Frontenac established a regular passenger and freight route between Prescott and Burlington by 1817, thus becoming the first Canadian built steamship to operate on Lake Ontario.

Obverse:	Designer: Dora de Pédery-Hunt	**Reverse:**	Designer: D. J. Craig
	Modeller: Dora de Pédery-Hunt		Modeller: Sheldon Beveridge

Specifications: See page 259
Case: Proof: Square black leatherette case, maroon insert, capsule.
Uncirculated: Clear plastic case, black insert.

Date	Description	Issue Price	Mintage	Price
1991	Frontenac, PR-65	22.95	222,892	42.50
1991	Frontenac, BU-65	16.75	82,642	9.00

125TH ANNIVERSARY OF CANADA NICKEL/BRONZE DOLLAR 1992. Issued as part of the "125" coin program by the numismatic department of the Mint. This proof coin is the companion piece to the circulating issue of the same design. For more information on this coin see page 165.

Obverse:	Designer: Dora de Pédery-Hunt	**Reverse:**	Designer: Rita Swanson
	Modeller: Dora de Pédery-Hunt		Modeller: Ago Aarand

Specifications: See page 259
Case: Royal blue flocked case, blue insert, capsule.

Date	Description	Issue Price	Mintage	PR-65
1992	125th Anniversary of Canada	19.95	24,227	12.00

KINGSTON TO YORK STAGECOACH SILVER DOLLAR 1992. Commemorating the 175th anniversary of the first stage coach service between Kingston and York in January 1817. Samuel Purdy was only able to maintain regular service during the winter months, hence the sleigh with runners. This is the first issue of a dollar coin in sterling silver since the pattern dollar was struck in London by the Royal Mint in 1911.

Obverse:	Designer: Dora de Pédery-Hunt	Reverse:	Designer: Karsten Smith
	Modeller: Dora de Pédery-Hunt		Modeller: Susan Taylor

Specifications: See page 259
Case: Proof: Square black leatherette case, maroon insert, capsule.
Uncirculated: Clear plastic case, black insert.

Date	Description	Issue Price	Mintage	Price
1992	Stagecoach, PR-65	23.95	187,612	15.00
1992	Stagecoach, BU-65	17.50	78,160	9.00

STANLEY CUP SILVER DOLLAR 1893-1993. Commemorating the 100th anniversary of the Stanley Cup, first presented during the 1892 - 1893 season to the Montreal Amateur Athletic Association team by Lord Stanley.

Obverse:	Designer: Dora de Pédery-Hunt	Reverse:	Designer: Stewart Sherwood
	Modeller: Dora de Pédery-Hunt		Modeller: Sheldon Beveridge

Specifications: See page 259
Case: Proof: Square black leatherette case, maroon insert, capsule.
Uncirculated: Clear plastic case, black insert.

Date	Description	Issue Price	Mintage	Price
1993	Stanley Cup, PR-65	23.95	294,314	15.00
1993	Stanley Cup, BU-65	17.50	88,150	9.00

RCMP NORTHERN DOG TEAM PATROL SILVER DOLLAR 1994. Issued to commemorate the 25th anniversary of the last RCMP Northern Dog Team Patrol.

Obverse: Designer: Dora de Pédery-Hunt Reverse: Designer: Ian D. Sparkes
       Modeller: Dora de Pédery-Hunt   Modeller: Ago Aarand
Specifications: See page 259
Case: Proof: Silver sleeve; square black leatherette case, maroon insert, encapsulated coin.
             Uncirculated: Clear plastic case, black insert.

Date	Description	Issue Price	Mintage	Price
1994	RCMP Dog Team Patrol, PR-65	24.50	178,485	37.50
1994	RCMP Dog Team Patrol, BU-65	17.95	65,295	10.00

REMEMBRANCE NICKEL/BRONZE DOLLAR 1994. The war memorial was first built to commemorate the participation of all Canadians in the First World War. The memorial was rededicated in 1982 to include veterans of the Second World War and the Korean War. For circulating issue please see page 166.

Obverse: Designer: Dora de Pédery-Hunt Reverse: Designer: R.C.M. Staff
       Modeller: Dora de Pédery-Hunt   Modeller: T. Smith, Ago Aarand
Specifications: See page 259
Case: Royal blue flocked case, blue insert, capsule.

Date	Description	Issue Price	Mintage	PR-65
1994	Remembrance	16.95	54,524	12.00

325TH ANNIVERSARY OF THE FOUNDING OF THE HUDSON'S BAY COMPANY SILVER DOLLAR 1995. From 1670 to the current day the history of the Hudson's Bay Company has been intertwined with that of Canada.

Obverse: Designer: Dora de Pédery-Hunt **Reverse:** Designer: Vincent McIndoe
    Modeller: Dora de Pédery-Hunt   Modeller: Susan Taylor
Specifications: See page 259
Case: Proof: Silver sleeve, square black leatherette case, maroon insert, encapsulated coin.
    Uncirculated: Clear plastic case, black insert.

Date	Description	Issue Price	Mintage	Price
1995	325th Anniv. Hudson's Bay Co., PR-65	24.50	166,259	22.50
1995	325th Anniv. Hudson's Bay Co., BU-65	17.95	61,819	10.00

PEACEKEEPING IN CONJUNCTION WITH THE 50TH ANNIVERSARY OF THE UNITED NATIONS NICKEL/BRONZE DOLLAR 1995. Issued to commemorate Canada's role in the United Nations peacekeeping forces. For circulating issue see page 166.

Obverse: Designer: Dora de Pédery-Hunt **Reverse:** Designers: J. K. Harman,
    Modeller: Dora de Pédery-Hunt   R. G. Henriguez,
                                                C. H. Oberlander
                              Modellers: Susan Taylor
                                               Ago Aarand

Specifications: See page 259
Case: Royal blue flocked display case, blue insert, capsule

Date	Description	Issue Price	Mintage	PR-65
1995	Peacekeeping	17.95	43,293	10.00

200TH ANNIVERSARY OF JOHN McINTOSH, SILVER DOLLAR 1996. John McIntosh arrived in Canada in 1796 and settled in Ontario. Issued to pay tribute to the originator of Canada's most important commercial apple.

Obverse: Designer: Dora de Pédery-Hunt   **Reverse**: Designer: Roger Hill
             Modeller: Dora de Pédery-Hunt   Modeller: Sheldon Beveridge
Specifications: See page 259
Case: Proof: Silver sleeve multicoloured sleeve, black leatherette case,
                 maroon flock insert, encapsulated coin, COA.
                 Uncirculated: Plastic capsule with silver sleeve.

Date	Description	Issue Price	Mintage	Price
1996	Silver, PR-65	29.95	133,779	42.50
1996	Silver, BU-65	19.95	58,834	10.00

25TH ANNIVERSARY OF THE 1972 CANADA/RUSSIA HOCKEY SERIES, SILVER DOLLAR 1997. Paul Henderson's winning goal won the 1972 series for Canada. In 1997 two gift packages were offered. (1) A sterling silver Pin / uncirculated dollar. (2) A numbered colour reproduction print / uncirculated dollar.

Obverse: Designer: Dora de Pédery-Hunt   **Reverse**: Designer: Walter Burden
             Modeller: Dora de Pédery-Hunt   Modeller: Stan Witten
Specifications: See page 259
Case: Proof: Multicoloured sleeve, black leatherette case, maroon flock insert,
                 encapsulated coin, COA
                 Uncirculated: Plastic capsule with silver sleeve

Date	Description	Issue Price	Mintage	Price
1997	Silver, PR-65	29.95	184,965	42.50
1997	Silver, BU-65	19.95	155,252	12.00
1997	Silver, BU-65, with pin	29.95	N/A	16.00
1997	Silver, BU-65, with print	24.95	N/A	16.00
1997	Silver, BU-65, with phone card and stamp set	N/A	N/A	16.00

10TH ANNIVERSARY OF THE ONE DOLLAR LOON 1997. The Flying Loon (nickel-bronze) one dollar coin was issued only in "O'Canada" (SP-65) specimen sets. The sterling silver Flying Loon was issued singly. All were sold by the Numismatic Department of the Royal Canadian Mint as a limited edition during 1997.

Obverse:	Designer: Dora de Pédery-Hunt	Reverse:	Designer: Jean-Luc Grondin
	Modeller: Dora de Pédery-Hunt		Modeller: Sheldon Beveridge

	Nickel-bronze	Sterling Silver
Composition:	Nickel electro-plated with bronze	92.5% silver, 7.5% copper
Weight:	7.0 grams	25.175 gms
Diameter:	26.5 mm, 11 sided	26.07 mm, 11 sided
Thickness:	1.95 mm	3.04 mm
Edge:	Plain	Plain
Die Axis:	↑↑	↑↑
Case of Issue:	In sets	Black case with silver coloured strap

Date	Description	Issue Price	Mintage	Price
1997	Nickel-bronze, SP-65	–	–	25.00
1997	Silver proof, PR-65	49.95	24,995	100.00

Note: No issue price or mintage is given for the 10th anniversary nickel-bronze dollar as an individual coin, it was only issued in the specimen sets of 1997. (see page 357).

125TH ANNIVERSARY OF THE ROYAL CANADIAN MOUNTED POLICE, SILVER DOLLAR, 1998.

The design by Adeline Halvorson features a mounted police officer in a 1900s uniform.

Obverse: Designer: Dora de Pédery-Hunt **Reverse:** Designer: Adeline Halvorson
Modeller: Dora de Pédery-Hunt Modeller: Sheldon Beveridge
Specifications: See page 259
Case: Proof: Multicoloured sleeve, dark green clam display case, green insert, encapsulated coin, COA.
Uncirculated: plastic capsule and container.

Date	Description	Issue Price	Mintage	Price
1998	125th Anniv. RCMP, PR-65	29.95	130,795	27.50
1998	125th Anniv. RCMP, BU-65	19.95	81,376	12.00
1998	125th Anniv. RCMP, BU-65, with pin	29.95	N/A	16.00

225th ANNIVERSARY OF THE VOYAGE OF JUAN PEREZ AND THE SIGHTING OF THE QUEEN CHARLOTTE ISLANDS, SILVER DOLLAR 1999.

In 1774 Juan Perez led an expedition which made the first documented sighting of the Queen Charlotte Islands. The reverse of this coin illustrates the 225 ton frigate 'The Santiago,' one of the Queen Charlotte Islands and the Haida canoes approaching the ship.

Obverse: Designer: Dora de Pédery-Hunt **Reverse:** Designer: D. J. Craig
Modeller: Dora de Pédery-Hunt Modeller: Stanley Witten
Specifications: See page 259
Case: Proof: Multicoloured sleeve, dark green clam display case, green insert, encapsulated coin, COA.
Uncirculated: Plastic capsule and container.

Date	Description	Issue Price	Mintage	Price
1999	25th Anniv. Voyage Perez, PR-65	29.95	126,435	25.00
1999	25th Anniv. Voyage Perez, BU-65	19.95	67,655	13.00
1999	25th Anniv, Voyage Perez, BU-65 Journal Gift Set	N/A	N/A	18.00

INTERNATIONAL YEAR OF OLDER PERSONS 1999. The United Nations, in October 1999, declared 1999 as the International Year of Older Persons. This coin was struck to support Canada's concept of "A Society for All Ages."

Obverse: Designer: Dora de Pédery-Hunt **Reverse:** Designer: S. Armstrong-Hodgson
 Modeller: Dora de Pédery-Hunt Modeller: William Woodruff
Specifications: See page 259
Case: Multicoloured case, black insert, encapsulated coin, COA.

Date	Description	Issue Price	Mintage	PR-65
1999	International Year of Older Persons	49.95	24,976	40.00

VOYAGE OF DISCOVERY 2000. Poised on the launch pad to the next millennium, Canada's voyage of discovery promises to be one of energy, ability and achievement.

Obverse: Designer: Dora de Pédery-Hunt **Reverse:** Designer: D. F. Warkentine
 Modeller: Dora de Pédery-Hunt Engraver: Cosme Saffioti
Specifications: See page 259
Case: Proof: Dark green clam display case with green insert encapsulated coin, COA.
 Uncirculated: Multicoloured slide case with encapsulated coin.

Date	Description	Issue Price	Mintage	Price
2000	Voyage of Discovery, PR-65	29.95	121,575	30.00
2000	Voyage of Discovery, BU-65	19.95	62,975	15.00

50TH ANNIVERSARY OF THE NATIONAL BALLET OF CANADA 2001. The National Ballet of Canada, a company with more than 50 dancers and its own full symphony orchestra, is Canada's premier dance company which ranks as one of the world's top international companies. Founded in 1951 by English dancer Celia Franca, the classical company is the only Canadian company to present a full range of traditional full evening ballet classics.

Obverse: Designer: Dora de Pédery-Hunt   Reverse: Designer: Scott McKowen
         Modeller: Dora de Pédery-Hunt   Engraver: Susan Taylor
Specifications: See page 259
Case: Proof: Multicoloured sleeve, dark green clam display case, green insert,
                encapsulated coin, COA
         Uncirculated: Multicoloured sleeve, black plastic holder, encapsulated coin.

Date	Description	Issue Price	Mintage	Price
2001	50th Anniv. National Ballet, PR-65	30.95	89,390	30.00
2001	50th Anniv. National Ballet, BU-65	20.95	53,668	20.00

90TH ANNIVERSARY OF THE STRIKING OF CANADA'S 1911 SILVER DOLLAR 2001. The 1911 Canadian silver dollar is the most valuable Canadian coin known. Only three examples exist, two sterling silver trial strikes and one lead strike.

Obverse: Designer: Dora de Pédery-Hunt   Reverse: Designer: RCM Engravers
         Modeller: Dora de Pédery-Hunt   Engraver: Cosme Saffioti
Specifications: See page 259
Case: Unknown

Date	Description	Issue Price	Mintage	PR-65
2001	90th Anniversary	49.95	24,996	65.00

50TH ANNIVERSARY OF HER MAJESTY QUEEN ELIZABETH II'S ACCESSION TO THE THRONE 2002. For the first time a silver dollar carries a double date (1952-2002) on the obverse.

Obverse: Designer: Dora de Pédery-Hunt **Reverse:** Designer: RCM Engravers
Modeller: Dora de Pédery-Hunt   Engraver: Susan Taylor
Specifications: See page 259
Case: Proof: Multicoloured sleeve, dark green clam display case, green insert, encapsulated coin, COA
Uncirculated: Multicoloured sleeve, black plastic holder, encapsulated coin

Date	Description	Issue Price	Mintage	Price
2002	50th Anniv. Queen Elizabeth, PR-65	30.95	119,233	32.50
2002	50th Anniv. Queen Elizabeth, BU-65	20.95	65,582	21.00

Note: A 24 karat gold plated variety was issued in a special edition proof set, set page 363.

15TH ANNIVERSARY OF THE ONE DOLLAR LOON, 2002. First struck in 1987, the one dollar coin with the image of a solitary Common Loon soon became Canada's most popular coin, affectionately called the "Loonie." This commemorative dollar, depicting a loon family, was issued only in special edition specimen sets for 2002. (See page 358).

Obverse: Designer: Dora de Pédery-Hunt **Reverse:** Designer: Dora de Pédery-Hunt
Modeller: Dora de Pédery-Hunt   Engraver: Cosme Saffioti
Specifications: See page 259

Date	Description	Issue Price	Mintage	SP-65
2002	Family of Loons			See specimen set, page 358

CENTRE ICE 2002. A "Centre Ice" 22-karat gold-plated loon dollar coin was issued as part of a souvenir album, entitled "Going For Gold," jointly offered by the Mint, Post Office and MacLean's Magazine to commemorate the Olympic gold medals for hockey won by Canadian teams in 2002.

Obverse: Designer: Dora de Pédery-Hunt   **Reverse:** Designer: Dora de Pédery-Hunt
            Modeller: Dora de Pédery-Hunt   Engraver: Cosme Saffioti
Specifications: As shown on page 259, but 22 karat gold plated, with privy mark.

Date	Description	Issue Price	Mintage	PR-65
2002	Centre Ice	54.95	25,000	55.00

QUEEN ELIZABETH THE QUEEN MOTHER 2002. Available only in proof condition this silver dollar honoured the life of Queen Elizabeth the Queen Mother.

Obverse: Designer: Dora de Pédery-Hunt   **Reverse:** Designer:
            Modeller: Dora de Pédery-Hunt   Engraver:
Specifications: See page 259
Case: N/A

Date	Description	Issue Price	Mintage	PR-65
2002	Queen Mother	49.95	9,984	175.00

100TH ANNIVERSARY OF THE COBALT SILVER DISCOVERY 2003. It is 100 years since Fred LaRose, a blacksmith, threw his hammer at a fox, of course missing the fox, but striking a rock revealing a gleaming view of silver. This is the first issue of a pure silver (.9999 fine) dollar by the Royal Canadian Mint.

Obverse: Designer: Dora de Pédery-Hunt **Reverse:** Designer: Dora de Pédery-Hunt
Modeller: John Mardon Engraver: N/A
Specifications: See page 259
Case: Proof – Black leatherette exterior; black velour interior;
multicoloured sleeve; encapsulated coin; COA
Brilliant – Plastic

Date	Description	Issue Price	Mintage	Price
2003	Cobalt, PR-65	33.95	125,000	35.00
2003	Cobalt, BU-65	24.95	75,000	25.00

NUMISMATIC TWO DOLLARS

SPECIFICATIONS OF THE TWO DOLLAR NUMISMATIC ISSUES

A. BI-METALLIC, NICKEL–ALUMINUM BRONZE TWO DOLLAR COIN. Issued in proof and uncirculated condition, this coin is the numismatic counterpart of the circulating issue listed on page 164.

Composition:
    Outer Ring: .990 Ni
    Inner Core: .092 Cu, .060 Au, .020 Ni
Weight: 7.3 gms
Edge: Interrupted Serration

Diameter:
    Outer Ring: 28 mm
    Inner Core: 16.8 mm
Thickness: 1.80 mm
Die Axis: ↑↑

B. BI-METALLIC, STERLING SILVER–GOLD-PLATED TWO DOLLAR COIN. Two thicknesses were issued in proof condition, standard and Piedfort.

Composition:
    Outer Ring: 92.5 Ag, 7.5 Cu
    Inner Core: 7.5 Cu, 92.5 Ag, 24kt Au-pltd
Weight:
    Standard: 8.83 gms
    Ring: 5.86 gms
    Core: 2.97 gms
    Piedfort: 17.66 gms
    Ring: 11.72 grams
    Core: 5.94 grams

Edge: Interrupted Serration
Diameter:
    Outer Ring: 28.07 mm
    Inner Core: 16.8 mm
Thickness:
    Standard: 1.9 mm
    Piedfort: 3.6 mm
Die Axis: ↑↑

C. BI-METALLIC, GOLD–GOLD TWO DOLLAR COIN. The two dollar coin was issued only in proof condition.

Composition:
    Outer Ring: .052 Cu, .770 Ag,
        .172 Au (14 kt white gold)
    Inner Core: .042 Cu, .041 Ag,
        .917 Au (22kt)
Weight: 11.4 gms
    Ring: 6.314 grams
    Core: 5.09 grams

Diameter:
    Outer Ring: 28.0 mm
    Inner Core: 16.80 mm
Edge: Interrupted Serration
Thickness: 1.80 mm
Die Axis: ↑↑

POLAR BEAR TWO DOLLAR COIN, 1996. Issued in 1996 by the Numismatic Department of the Royal Canadian Mint to commemorate the introduction of the two dolllar coin replacing the two dollar bank note. Three different compositions were used to produce the numismatic two dollar coins of 1996. 1996 two dollar Piedfort was not issued singly; it was issued as part of a set. See page 342.

Obverse: Designer: Dora de Pédery-Hunt   **Reverse:** Designer: Brent Townsend
         Modeller: Dora de Pédery-Hunt   Modeller: Ago Aarand

Issued: 1. Brilliant Uncirculated: Bi-metallic, nickel/aluminim, specification A.
2. Proof: Bi-metallic, nickel/aluminum, specification A.
3. Piedfort: Bi-metallic, sterling silver/gold-plated sterling silver, specification B.
4. Proof: Bi-metallic, gold/gold, specification C.

Case: A. Brilliant Uncirculated: Presentation folder with Polar Bear.
Proof: Black suede, blue flock inside, encapsulated coin.
B. Piedfort: Blue leatherette display case, blue flock inside, encapsulated coin.
C. Blue ultrasuede, blue inside, encapsulated coin.

Date	Description	Issue Price	Mintage	Condition	Price
1996	BU-65	10.95	74,669	MS-65	9.00
1996	PR-65	24.95	66,843	PR-65	25.00
1996	Piedfort, PR-65	N/A	N/A	PR-65	100.00
1996	Gold, PR-65	299.95	5,000	PR-65	300.00

NUNAVUT TWO DOLLAR PROOF COMMEMORATIVE, 1999. Issued to commemorate the formation of Nunavut, Canada's third territory, in 1999.

Obverse: Designer: Dora de Pédery-Hunt **Reverse:** Designer: G. Arnaktauyok
Modeller: Dora de Pédery-Hunt Modeller: Ago Aarand, José Osio

Issued: 1. Proof: Bi-metallic, sterling silver/gold-plated sterling silver, specification B.
2. Proof: Bi-metallic, gold/gold, specification C.

Case: Antique oval clam style case lined with black suede.

Date	Description	Issue Price	Mintage	PR-65
1999	Silver	24.95	39,873	25.00
1999	Gold	299.95	4,298	250.00

Varieties $2.00 1999 Nunavut. The ring varieties of the Nunavut reverse design appears to be a function of the alloy and its flow characteristics for interlocking the core and outer ring together.

Narrow Ring
Business Strike and
Brilliant Uncirculated

Wide Ring
Specimen Sets

No Ring
Proof Single

Note: A $2.00 Nunavut mule was issued when the brilliant uncirculated $2.00 obverse die was married with the proof $2.00 reverse die.

POLAR BEARS TWO DOLLAR COMMEMORATIVE 2000. Commemorating the Path of Knowledge reflected in experience, wisdom and knowledge that is passed down from generation to generation.

Obverse: Designer: Dora de Pédery-Hunt   **Reverse:** Designer: Tony Bianco
         Modeller: Dora de Pédery-Hunt   Modeller: Cosme Saffioti

Issued: 1.   Proof: Bi-metallic, sterling silver/gold-plated sterling silver, specification B.
         2.   Proof: Bi-metallic, gold/gold, specification C.
Case: N/A

Date	Description	Issue Price	Mintage	PR-65
2000	Silver	24.95	39,768	25.00
2000	Gold	299.95	5,881	250.00

NUMISMATIC FIVE DOLLARS

NORMAN BETHUNE FIVE DOLLAR COIN 1998. In 1998 the Royal Canadian Mint produced a $5 silver coin to commemorate the 60th anniversary of Dr. Norman Bethune's arrival in China. The coin was issued as part of a two coin set, in conjunction with China Gold Coin Incorporation (CGCI).

Obverse: Designer: Dora de Pédery-Hunt **Reverse:** Designer: Harvey Chan
Modeller: Dora de Pédery-Hunt Modellers: Ago Aarand,
Stan Witten

Case: Brown leatherette two-coin display with outer box covered in Chinese brocade, COA.

Mint	Composition	Weight (g)	Diameter	Edge	Thickness
CGCI	.9999 silver	31.10	40.0	Reeded	N/A
RCM	.9999 silver	31.39	38.0	Reeded	3.3 mm

Date	Description	Issue Price	Mintage	PR-65
1998	Bethune - CGCI	–	–	20.00
1998	Bethune - RCM	–	–	20.00
1998	2 coin set	98.00	65,831	35.00

THE VIKING SETTLEMENT FIVE DOLLAR COIN 1999. Issued to commemorate The Vikings landing at L'Anse-aux-Meadows, Newfoundland, circa 1000 A.D. Norway issued a 20 Kroner coin in 1999 also commemorating the same Viking Landing. These two coins were offered as a set.

Obverse: Designer: Dora de Pédery-Hunt **Reverse:** Designer: Donald Curley
Modeller: Dora de Pédery Hunt Modeller: Stan Witten

Composition:
.810 Copper **Thickness:** 2.5 mm
.090 Nickel **Weight:** 9.9 grams
.100 Zinc **Diameter:** 27.0 mm
Edge: Plain

Case: Oval, immitation resin stone; printed outer cardboard sleeve; two hole box, brown insert, encapsulated coins

Date	Description	Issue Price	Mintage	PR-65
1999	Canada $5, Norway 20KR, 2 coins	N/A	28,540	35.00

100TH ANNIVERSARY OF THE FIRST WIRELESS TRANSMISSION 1901-2001. On December 12th, 1901, Guglieimo Marconi (1874-1937) successfully transmitted the first wireless message across the Atlantic from Poldhu in Cornwall, England, to Signal Hill in St. John's, Newfoundland. Issued to commemorate this anniversary the Royal Canadian Mint, in conjunction with the Royal Mint, issued this two-coin set.

	CANADA $5 PROOF	**BRITISH £2 REVERSE PROOF**
Designers:		
Obverse:	Dora de Pédery-Hunt	Ian Rank-Bradley
Reverse:	Cosme Saffioti	Robert Evans
Engravers:		
Obverse:	Dora de Pédery-Hunt	Royal Mint Staff
Reverse:	Cosme Saffioti	Robert Evans
Composition:		
	Coin: .925 silver, .075 copper	Coin: .925 silver, .075 copper
	Cameo: 24-karat gold plate	Outer circle: Plated 22kt gold
		Inner disc: .925 silver, .075 copper
Weight:	16.96 gms	24.0 gms
Diameter:	28.40 mm	28.40 mm
Thickness:	N/A	N/A
Edge:	Serrated	Lettering
Die Axis:	↑↑	↑↓
Case:	Two-coin clam-style case	

Date	Description	Issue Price	Mintage	PR-65
2001	2 coins, Canada $5, British £2	99.95	15,011	75.00

FIVE AND TEN DOLLARS

MONTREAL SUMMER OLYMPICS, 1973-1976. In 1976, Montreal, Quebec, hosted the XXI Olympiad. To commemorate and help finance Canada's first Olympics, the federal government agreed to produce a series of twenty-eight silver and two gold coins (see section following for the $100 gold coins). There are seven series of silver coins. Each series has two $5 and two $10 coins, making a total of fourteen coins of each denomination. Each series depicts different Olympic themes on the reverse and has a common design (except for the date) on the obverse. The date on the coins is usually the year of minting. Orders for the Olympic coins were accepted up to the end of December 1976, so a small unit continued to function into 1977 on the Olympic Coin Program. Mintage by series was never recorded, but the annual reports of the Royal Canadian Mint give the following figures by year: 1973 - 537,898 $10, 543,098 $5; 1974 - 3,949,878 $10, 3,981,140 $5; 1975 - 4,952,433 $10, 3,970,000 $5; 1976 - 3,970,514 $10, 3,775,259 $5. These figures do not necessarily coincide with the actual post office sales figures for the coins.

The Olympic coins were offered to the collector in two qualities, uncirculated and proof. The uncirculated issues were packaged and offered for sale in four different formats: (1) encapsulated (single coins only in styrene crystal capsules); (2) one-coin "standard" case (single coins in black case with red interior); (3) four-coin "custom" set (two $5 and two $10 coins by series in black case with gold trim and red insert); and (4) four-coin "prestige" set (two $5 and two $10 coins by series in matte black leatherette case with blue insert).

The proof coins were only offered in sets, and the "deluxe" case of issue was made of Canadian white birch with a specially tanned steer hide cover and black insert.

Because of the fluctuating price of silver during the years of the program (1973 to 1976), the original issue prices varied somewhat from series to series.

Original Issue Prices

Package Type	Series I	Series II	Series III-VII
$5 Encapsulated	6.00	7.50	8.00
$10 Encapsulated	12.00	15.00	15.75
Set of 4 Encapsulated	36.00	45.00	47.50
$5 in Standard Case	7.50	9.00	9.00
$10 in Standard Case	14.00	17.00	17.00
Set of 4 in Standard Case	43.00	52.00	52.00
Custom Set	45.00	55.00	55.00
Prestige Set	50.00	60.00	60.00
Deluxe Proof Set	72.50	82.50	82.50

$5 COIN
Composition: .925 silver, .075 copper
Weight: 24.30 grams **Edge:** Reeded
Diameter: 38.00 mm **Die Axis:** ↑↑

$10 COIN
Composition: .925 silver, .075 copper
Weight: 48.60 grams **Edge:** Reeded
Diameter: 45.00 mm **Die Axis:** ↑↑

SERIES I

Coin No. 1
World Map

Coin No. 2
Map of North America

Coin No. 3
Montreal Skyline

Coin No. 4
Kingston and Sailboats

Theme: Geographic
Official Release Date:

December 13, 1973. (The Series I issuing period began in late 1973 and was carried over into 1974. During the last half of the period a 1974 dated obverse die - possibly made in advance for the Series II coins - was mated inadvertently with a Series I reverse die of the Map of the World resulting in the production and release of a Series I mule dated 1974.)

Designer of Reverse:

Georges Huel, worked by invitation.

Modellers:

1 ($10 Map of the World): design was photochemically etched
2 ($5 Map of North America): design was photochemically etched
3 ($10 Montreal Skyline): Ago Aarand
4 ($5 Kingston and Sailboats): Terrence Smith

Date	$5 Coin	$10 Coin	Custom Set	Prestige Set	Proof Set
1973	6.00	12.00	32.50	32.50	35.00
1974 Mule	—	300.00	—	—	—

SERIES II

Coin No. 5
Head of Zeus

Coin No. 6
Athlete with Torch

Coin No. 7
Temple of Zeus

Coin No. 8
Olympic Rings and Wreath

Theme: Olympic Motifs
Official Release Date: September 16, 1974
Designer of Reverse: Anthony Mann, winner of an invitational competition.
Modellers:

        5 ($10 Head of Zeus): Patrick Brindley
        6 ($5 Athlete with Torch): Patrick Brindley
        7 ($10 Temple of Zeus): Walter Ott
        8 ($5 Olympic Rings and Wreath): Walter Ott

Date	$5 Coin	$10 Coin	Custom Set	Prestige Set	Proof Set
1974	6.00	12.00	32.50	32.50	35.00

SERIES III

Coin No. 9
Lacrosse

Coin No. 10
Canoeing

Coin No. 11
Cycling

Coin No. 12
Rowing

Theme: Early Canadian Sports
Official Release Date: April 16, 1975
Designer of Reverse: Ken Danby, winner of an invitational competition.
Modellers:

9 ($10 Lacrosse): Walter Ott
10 ($5 Canoeing): Patrick Brindley
11 ($10 Cycling): Ago Aarand
12 ($5 Rowing): Terrence Smith

Date	$5 Coin	$10 Coin	Custom Set	Prestige Set	Proof Set
1974	6.00	12.00	32.50	32.50	35.00

SERIES IV

Coin No. 13
Men's Hurdles

Coin No. 14
Marathon

Coin No. 15
Women's Shot Put

Coin No. 16
Women's Javelin

Theme: Olympic Track and Field Sports
Official Release Date: August 12, 1975
Designer of Reverse: Leo Yerxa, winner of an invitational competition.
Modellers:

        13 ($10 Men's Hurdles): Patrick Brindley
        14 ($5 Marathon): Walter Ott
        15 ($10 Women's Shot Put): Patrick Brindley
        16 ($5 Women's Javelin): Walter Ott

Date	$5 Coin	$10 Coin	Custom Set	Prestige Set	Proof Set
1975	6.00	12.00	32.50	32.50	35.00

SERIES V

Coin No. 17
Paddling

Coin No. 18
Diving

Coin No. 19
Sailing

Coin No. 20
Swimming

Theme: Olympic Summer Sports
Official Release Date: December 1, 1975
Designer of Reverse: Lynda Cooper, winner of an open national competition.
Modellers:

17 ($10 Paddling): design was photochemically etched
18 ($5 Diving): design was photochemically etched
19 ($10 Sailing): design was photochemically etched
20 ($5 Swimming): design was photochemically etched

Date	$5 Coin	$10 Coin	Custom Set	Prestige Set	Proof Set
1975	6.00	12.00	32.50	32.50	35.00

SERIES VI

Coin No. 21
Field Hockey

Coin No. 22
Fencing

Coin No. 23
Soccer

Coin No. 24
Boxing

Theme: Olympic Team and Body Contact Sports
Official Release Date: March 1, 1976
Designer of Reverse: Shigeo Fukada, winner of an open international competition.
Modellers:

> 21 ($10 Field Hockey): design was photochemically etched
> 22 ($5 Fencing): design was photochemically etched
> 23 ($10 Soccer): design was photochemically etched
> 24 ($5 Boxing): design was photochemically etched

Date	$5 Coin	$10 Coin	Custom Set	Prestige Set	Proof Set
1976	6.00	12.00	32.50	32.50	35.00

SERIES VII

Coin No. 25
Olympic Stadium

Coin No. 26
Olympic Village

Coin No. 27
Olympic Velodrome

Coin No. 28
Olympic Flame

Theme: Olympic Games Souvenir Designs
Official Release Date: June 1, 1976
Designer of Reverse: Elliott John Morrison, winner of an invitational competition.
Modellers:

25 ($10 Olympic Stadium): Ago Aarand
26 ($5 Olympic Village): Sheldon Beveridge
27 ($10 Olympic Velodrome): Terrence Smith
28 ($5 Olympic Flame): Walter Ott

Date	$5 Coin	$10 Coin	Custom Set	Prestige Set	Proof Set
1976	6.00	12.00	32.50	32.50	35.00

FIFTEEN DOLLAR COINS

100TH ANNIVERSARY OF THE OLYMPIC MOVEMENT, 1996. The International Olympic Committee initiated a commemorative coin programme to mark the centennial of the modern Olympic movement in 1996. Five mints, Canada, Australia, France, Austria and Greece participated by issuing one gold and two silver coins over a five year period. The total collection comprises five gold and ten silver coins.

The Royal Canadian Mint issued the first three coins in 1992. The silver fifteen dollar coins are listed here, the gold on page 322.

The standard catalogue lists only the coins issued by RCM.

Designers:
Obverse: Dora de Pédery-Hunt
Reverse: Coin 1: David Craig
          Coin 2: Stewart Sherwood
Modellers:
Obverse: Coin 1: Dora de Pédery-Hunt
Reverse: Coin 1: Sheldon Beveridge
          Coin 2: Terry Smith
Composition: .925 silver, .075 copper
Thickness: 3.1 mm
Weight: 33.63 grams
Edge: Lettering: Citius, Altius, Fortius
Diameter: 40.0 mm
Die Axis: ↑↑

Coin No. 1
Speed Skater, Pole Vaulter, Gymnast

Coin No. 2
The Spirit Of The Generations

Case of Issue:
Single Coin: Burgundy leatherette case
Set: Wooden display case

Date	Description	Issue Price	Mintage	PR-65
1992	Skater	$46.95	105,645	30.00
1992	Spirit	$46.95	Incl. above	30.00

CHINESE LUNAR CALENDAR STERLING SILVER COIN SERIES 1998-2009. Starting in 1998 with the year of the Tiger, the mint embarked on issuing a twelve year series of Chinese Lunar calendar coins. The twelve sterling silver coins were issued one per year to commemorate the start of each new year of the twelve year cycle. The coins are available singly or by subscription. The subscription was for a five year period beginning in 1999 and ending in 2003. The five coins, shipped one per year, were offered at a fixed price of $428.28 including a sterling silver medallion housed in a 13-hole presentation box made of embossed red velvet and gold moiré. The single presentation box is a smaller version of the larger one, red and gold moiré.

YEAR OF THE TIGER 1998

YEAR OF THE RABBIT 1999

Designers:		Modellers:	
Obverse:	Dora de Pédery-Hunt	Obverse:	Dora de Pédery-Hunt
Reverse:	Harvey Chain	Reverse:	1998: Stan Witten
Composition:	.925 silver, .075 copper		1999: José Osio
	24-karat gold plated cameo	**Thickness:** 3.35 mm	
Weight:	34.00 grams	**Edge:** Reeded	
Diameter:	40.0 mm	**Die Axis:** ↑↑	
Case:	Embossed red velvet boxes with gold moiré sides containing either a single or		
	thirteen coin insert.		

Date	Description	Issue Price	Mintage Single	PR-65
1998	Year of the Tiger	68.88	68,888	450.00
1999	Year of the Rabbit	72.88	77,791	50.00

YEAR OF THE DRAGON 2000

YEAR OF THE SNAKE 2001

Designers:
Obverse: Dora de Pédery-Hunt
Reverse: Harvey Chain
Composition: .925 silver, .075 copper
24-karat gold plated cameo
Weight: 34.00 grams
Diameter: 40.0 mm
Case: Embossed red velvet boxes with gold moiré sides containing either a single or thirteen coin insert.

Modellers:
Obverse: Dora de Pédery-Hunt
Reverse: 2000: José Osio
2001: José Osio
Thickness: 3.35 mm
Edge: Reeded
Die Axis: ↑↑

Date	Description	Issue Price	Mintage Single	Market Price
2000	Year of the Dragon	72.88	88,634	75.00
2001	Year of the Snake	78.88	60,754	70.00

YEAR OF THE HORSE 2002

YEAR OF THE SHEEP 2003

Photograph not
available
at press time

Designers:

    Obverse: Dora de Pédery-Hunt
    Reverse: Harvey Chain

Composition: .925 silver, .075 copper
          24-karat gold plated cameo

Weight: 34.00 grams

Diameter: 40.0 mm

Case: Embossed red velvet boxes with gold moiré sides containing either a single or thirteen coin insert.

Modellers:

    Obverse: Dora de Pédery-Hunt
    Reverse: 2002: José Osio
              2003: N/A

Thickness: 3.35 mm

Edge: Reeded

Die Axis: ↑↑

Date	Description	Issue Price	Mintage Set	Mintage Single	PR-65
2002	Year of the Horse	78.88	–	59,395	80.00
2003	Year of the Sheep	78.88	–	N/A	80.00
1998-2003	Set One, 6 coins	428.28	6868	6877	750.00

TWENTY DOLLAR COINS

CALGARY WINTER OLYMPICS, 1985 - 1988. In 1988, Calgary, Alberta, hosted the XV Olympic Winter Games. To commemorate and assist in the financing, the Federal Government, through the Royal Canadian Mint, agreed to produce a series of ten sterling silver coins and one gold coin. The silver coins were issued in sets of two $20.00 coins over the period September 1985 through September 1987. Unlike the 1976 Olympic coins, the Calgary Winter Olympic coins were issued in proof quality only.

The date on the coins (obverse) is the year of minting while the reverse carries the date 1988, the year of the games. Mintage is limited to a total of 5,000,000 coins, resulting if minted in equal numbers, in 500,000 complete sets of the ten coins series.

The first offering of the coins for sale by the Royal Canadian Mint was based on 350,000 complete sets at $370.00 per set. By the fifth series the complete set was being offered at $420.00.

Edge lettering was used for the first time on Canadian silver coins. "XV OLYMPIC WINTER GAMES - JEUX OLYMPIQUES D'HIVER" appeared on all ten silver coins. There are existing varieties that have missed the edge lettering process.

Designer: Arnold Machin
Composition: .925 silver, .075 copper
Weight: 34.07 grams
Diameter: 40 mm
Edge: Lettered
Die Axis: ↑↑

FIRST SERIES

Coin No. 1
Downhill Skiing

Coin No. 2
Speed Skating

Official Release Date: September 16, 1985
Official Issue Price: $37.00 per coin, $74.00 per series
Reverse Designers: 1: Ian Stewart, 2: Friedrich Peter
Sculpture Engravers: 1: Terrence Smith, 2: Ago Aarand
Case: Green Velvet, Olympic Logo, one or two coin display.

Date	Description	Quantity Minted	PR-65 Single	PR-65 Set
1985	Downhill Skiing	406,360	25.00	—
1985	Speed Skating	354,222	25.00	48.00
1985	Speed Skating, no edge lettering	Incl. above	200.00	—

SECOND SERIES

Coin No. 3
Hockey

Coin No. 4
Biathlon

Official Release Date: February 25, 1986
Official Issue Price: $37.00 per coin, $74.00 per series
Reverse Designers: 3: Ian Stewart, 4: John Mardon
Sculpture Engravers: 3: Victor Coté, 4: Sheldon Beveridge
Case: Green Velvet, Olympic Logo, one or two coin display.

Date	Description	Quantity Minted	PR-65 Single	PR-65 Set
1986	Hockey	396,602	25.00	–
1986	Hockey, no edge lettering	Incl. above	150.00	–
1986	Biathlon	308,086	25.00	48.00
1986	Biathlon, no edge lettering	Incl. above	150.00	–

THIRD SERIES

Coin No. 5
Cross-Country Skiing

Coin No. 6
Free-Style Skiing

Official Release Date: August 18, 1986
Official Issue Price: $39.50 per coin, $79.00 per series
Reverse Designers: 5: Ian Stewart, 6: Walter Ott
Sculpture Engravers: 5: Terrence Smith, 6: Walter Ott
Case: Green Velvet, Olympic Logo, one or two coin display.

Date	Description	Quantity Minted	PR-65 Single	PR-65 Set
1986	Cross-Country Skiing	303,199	25.00	–
1986	Free-Style Skiing	294,322	25.00	48.00
1986	Free-Style Skiing, no edge lettering	Incl. above	200.00	–

FOURTH SERIES

Coin No. 7
Figure Skating

Coin No. 4
Curling

Official Release Date: March 14, 1987
Official Issue Price: $39.50 per coin, $79.00 per series
Reverse Designers: 7: Raymond Taylor, 8: Ian Stewart
Sculpture Engravers: 7: Walter Ott, 8: Sheldon Beveridge
Case: Green Velvet, Olympic Logo, one or two coin display.

Date	Description	Quantity Minted	PR-65 Single	PR-65 Set
1987	Figure Skating	334,875	25.00	—
1987	Curling	286,457	25.00	48.00

FIFTH SERIES

Coin No. 9
Ski-Jumping

Coin No. 10
Bobsleigh

Official Release Date: August 11, 1987
Official Issue Price: $42.00 per coin, $84.00 per series
Reverse Designers: 9: Raymond Taylor, 10: John Mardon
Sculpture Engravers: 9: David Kierans, 10: Victor Coté
Case: Green Velvet, Olympic Logo, one or two coin display.

Date	Description	Quantity Minted	PR-65 Single	PR-65 Set
1987	Ski-Jumping	290,954	25.00	—
1987	Bobsleigh	274,326	25.00	48.00

AVIATION COMMEMORATIVES, 1990 - 1999. Canada's aviation heroes and achievements are commemorated on this series of twenty dollar sterling silver coins. The series consists of ten coins issued two per year over five years. For the first time each coin design contains a 24 karat gold covered oval cameo portrait of the aviation hero commemorated. All coins were issued in proof quality and a maximum of 50,000 of each coin was offered for sale during the program.

Specifications common to the series are:

Obverse:

Designer: Dora de Pédery-Hunt
Modeller: Dora de Pédery-Hunt

Composition: .925 silver, .075 copper
with 24 karat gold cameo

Weight: 31.103 grams
Diameter: 38 mm
Edge: Interrupted serration
Thickness: 3.5 mm
Die Axis: ↑↑

Case of Issue: Aluminum case in the shape of a wing. Two and ten coin display cases. The issue price of the ten coin case was $37.00

FIRST SERIES

Coin No. 1
Avro Anson and the
North American Harvard
Robert Leckie

Coin No. 2
Avro Lancaster
J. E. Fauquier

Official Release Date: September 15, 1990
Reverse Designers: 1: Geoff Bennett
2: R.R. Carmichael
Portrait Engravers: 1: Terrence Smith
2: Sheldon Beveridge

Engravers: 1: Sheldon Beveridge
2: Ago Aarand

Date	Coin No.	Description	Issue Price	Mintage	PR-65
1990	1	Anson and Harvard, Leckie	55.50	41,844	50.00
1990	2	Lancaster, Fauquier	55.50	43,596	125.00

FIRST SERIES (cont.)

Coin No. 3
A.E.A. Silver Dart
F.W. Baldwin and
John A.D. McCurdy

Coin No. 4
de Havilland Beaver
Phillip C. Garratt

Official Release Date: May 16, 1991

Reverse Designers: 3: George Velinger
4: Peter Mossman

Portrait Engravers: 3: Terrence Smith
4: William Woodruff

Engravers: 3: Sheldon Beveridge
4: Ago Aarand

Date	Coin No.	Description	Issue Price	Mintage	PR-65
1991	3	Silver Dart, Baldwin, McCurdy	55.50	35,202	40.00
1991	4	Beaver, Garratt	55.50	36,197	40.00

Coin No. 5
Curtiss JN-4 (Canuck)
Sir Frank Wilton Baillie

Coin No. 6
de Havilland Gipsy Moth
Murton A. Seymour

Official Release Date: August 13, 1992

Reverse Designers: 5: George Velinger
6: John Mardon

Portrait Engravers: 5: Terry Smith
6: Susan Taylor

Engravers: 5: Sheldon Beveridge
6: Ago Aarand

Date	Coin No.	Description	Issue Price	Mintage	PR-65
1992	5	Curtiss, Baillie	55.50	33,105	40.00
1992	6	Gipsy Moth, Seymou	55.50	32,537	40.00

FIRST SERIES (cont.)

Coin No. 7
Fairchild 71c
James A Richardson

Coin No. 8
Lockheed 14 Super Electra
Zebulon Lewis Leigh

Official Release Date: May 3, 1993

Reverse Designers: 7: R. R. Carmichael
8: R. R. Carmichael

Engravers: 7: Susan Taylor
8: Sheldon Beveridge

Portrait Engravers: 7: Susan Taylor
8: Sheldon Beveridge

Date	Coin No.	Description	Issue Price	Mintage	PR-65
1993	7	Fairchild, Richardson	55.50	32,199	40.00
1993	8	Lockheed, Leigh	55.50	32,550	40.00

Coin No. 9
Curtiss HS-2L
Stuart Graham

Coin No. 10
Canadian Vickers Vedette
Wilfred T. Reid

Official Release Date: March 24, 1994

Reverse Designers: 9: John Mardon
10: R. R. Carmichael

Engravers: 9: Sheldon Beveridge
10: Sheldon Beveridge

Portrait Engravers: 9: Susan Taylor
10: Sheldon Beveridge

Date	Coin No.	Description	Issue Price	Mintage	PR-65
1994	9	Curtiss, Graham	55.50	31,242	40.00
1994	10	Vedette, Reid	55.50	30,880	40.00
1990-1994		Series One, 10 coin set			475.00

SECOND SERIES

This is the second series of the aviation cameo coins of Canada. The theme of this series is "Powered Flight in Canada – Beyond World War II." The obverse physical and chemical specifications are the same as the first series.

Coin No. 1
Fleet 80 Canuck
J.Omer (Bob) Noury

Coin No. 2
DHC-1 Chipmunk
W/C Russell Bannock

Official Release Date: September 16, 1995
Reverse Designers: 1: Robert Bradford
2: Robert Bradford
Portrait Engravers: 1: Cosme Saffioti
2: Ago Aarand

Engravers: 1: Cosme Saffioti
2: William Woodruff

Coin No. 3
Avro Canada CF-100 Canuck
Janus Zurakowski

Coin No. 4
Avro Canada CF-105 Arrow
James A. Chamberlin

Official Release Date: July 25, 1996
Reverse Designers: 3: Jim Bruce
4: Jim Bruce
Portrait Engravers: 3: Cosme Saffioti
4: Sheldon Beveridge

Engravers: 3: Stan Witten
4: William Woodruff

Date	Coin No.	Description	Issue Price	Mintage	PR-65
1995	1	The Fleet 80 Canuck	57.95	17,438	40.00
1995	2	DHC-1 Chipmunk	57.95	17,722	40.00
1996	3	CF- 100 Canuck	57.95	18,508	100.00
1996	4	CF-105 Arrow	57.95	27,163	40.00

SECOND SERIES (cont.)

Coin No. 5	Coin No. 6
Canadair F-86 Sabre	Canadair CT-114 Tutor
Fern Villeneuve	Edward Higgins

Official Release Date: August 15, 1997

Reverse Designers: 5: Ross Buckland
6: Ross Buckland

Engravers: 5: William Woodruff
6: Stan Witten

Portrait Engravers: 5: Cosme Saffioti
6: Ago Aarand

Coin No. 7	Coin No. 8
Canadair CP-107 Argus	Canadair CL-215 Waterbomber
William S. Longhurst	Paul Gagnon

Official Release Date: June 5, 1998

Reverse Designers: 7: Peter Mossman
8: Peter Mossman

Engravers: 7: Sheldon Beveridge
8: Stan Witten

Portrait Engravers: 7: Cosme Saffioti
8: William Woodruff

Date	Coin No.	Description	Issue Price	Mintage	PR-65
1997	5	F86 Sabre	57.95	16,440	40.00
1997	6	Tutor Jet	57.95	18,414	40.00
1998	7	Argus	57.95	14,711	40.00
1998	8	Waterbomber	57.95	15,237	40.00
1998	7, 8	2 coin set	N/A	N/A	100.00

Note: In 1998 a special issue of a two-coin set (coin 7 and 8) boxed with cardboard model was offered.

SECOND SERIES (cont.)

Coin No. 9
de Havilland DHC-6 Twin Otter
George A. Neal

Coin No. 10
de Havilland DHC-8 Dash 8
Robert H. (Bob) Fowler

Official Release Date: April 15, 1999
Reverse Designers: 9: Neil Aird
10: Neil Aird
Portrait Engravers: 9: Cosme Saffioti
10: Cosme Saffioti

Engravers: 9: Cosme Saffioti
10: William Woodruff

Date	Coin No.	Description	Issue Price	Mintage	PR-65
1999	9	Twin Otter	57.95	14,173	40.00
1999	10	Dash 8	57.95	14,138	40.00
1995-1999 set		Series Two, 10 coin set	N/A	N/A	400.00

TRANSPORTATION ON LAND, SEA AND RAIL, 2000 to 2003. Canada's first sterling silver hologram cameo twenty dollar coins were issued in 2000. This new series of nine coins commemorates Canadian achievements in transportation. Each coin bears a 24-karat goldplated holographic cameo of famous Canadian methods of transportation.

LAND, SEA AND RAIL 2000

Obverse

Coin No. 1
H.S. Taylor Steam Buggy
John Mardon / Cosme Saffioti

Coin No. 2
The Bluenose
J. Franklin Wright / Stanley Witten

Coin No. 3
The Toronto
J. Mardon / S. Witten / C. Saffioti

Obverse:
    Designer: Dora de Pédery-Hunt
    Modeller: Dora de Pédery-Hunt
Composition: .925 silver, .075 copper
Diameter: 38.0 mm
Edge: Interrupted serration

Reverse: See above
Specifications: The following are common to the transportation commemorative series
Weight: 31.103 grams
Thickness: 3.5 mm
Die Axis: ↑↑

Case of Issue: Charcoal coloured anodized aluminum case with RCM logo, black flocked insert, COA.

Official Release Date: April 18, 2000

Date	Coin No.	Description	Issue Price	Mintage	PR-65
2000	1	H.S. Taylor Steam Buggy	59.95	Total	65.00
2000	2	The Bluenose	59.95	mintage	200.00
2000	3	The Toronto	59.95	all coins	75.00
2000	–	3 coin set	179.85	44,367	325.00

LAND, SEA AND RAIL 2001

Obverse

Coin No. 4
The Russell 'Light Four
Model L Touring Car
John Mardon / José Osio

Coin No. 5
The Marco Polo
J. Franklin Wright / Stan Witten

Coin No. 6
The Scotia
Don Curely/ William Woodruff

Official Release Date: April 17, 2001

Date	Coin No.	Description	Issue Price	Mintage	PR-65
2001	4	Russell	59.95	Total	60.00
2001	5	The Marco Polo	59.95	mintage	75.00
2001	6	The Scotia	59.95	all coins	60.00
2001	–	3 coin set	179.85	41,828	195.00

LAND, SEA AND RAIL 2002

Obverse

Coin No. 7
The Gray-Dort
John Mardon / Cosme Saffioti

Coin No. 8
The William Lawrence
Bonnie Ross / William Woodruff

Coin No. 9
D-10 Locomotive
Dan Fell / William Woodruff

Official Release Date: April, 2002

Date	Coin No.	Description	Issue Price	Mintage	PR-65
2002	7	The Gray-Dort	59.95	Total mintage	60.00
2002	8	The William Lawrence	59.95	all coins	60.00
2002	9	The D-10 Locomotive	59.95	33,244	60.00
2002	–	3 coin set	195.00	2,500	180.00

Note: The 2002 Land, Sea and Rail collection was offered with matching COA in a limited edition of 2,500.

LAND, SEA AND RAIL 2003

Photograph not
available
at press time

Obverse

Coin No. 1
HMCS Bras d'Or
Hydrofoil designed by
DeHavilland in 1967
Donald Curley

Coin No. 2
C.N.R. FA-1 Diesel Electric
Locomotive - No. 9400
John Mardon

Coin No. 3
Bricklin SV-1 (Land)
designed by Malcolm in 1974
Brian Hughes

Official Release Date: N/A

Date	Coin No.	Description	Issue Price	Mintage	PR-65
2003	1	HMCS Bras d'or	59.95	15,000	60.00
2003	2	C.N.R. FA-1 Diesel Electric Locomotive	59.95	15,000	60.00
2003	3	Bricklin SV-1	59.95	15,000	60.00
2003	—	3 coin set	N/A	N/A	N/A

GOLD 20 DOLLAR COIN

CENTENNIAL OF CONFEDERATION COMMEMORATIVE 1967. The highlight of the coins issued in 1967 to mark the centenary of Canadian Confederaton was a $20 gold coin. It was issued only as part of a $40.00 specimen set (see page 342 for the set listing), but many were later removed from the sets for separate trading. The reverse design is an adaption of the Canadian coat of arms, as on the 50-cent piece of 1960-1966. It is the only coin in the Centennial set that bears the single date 1967 instead of 1867-1967.

Designer: Portrait: Arnold Machin
Reverse: RCM staff
Modeller: Obverse: Myron Cook, using
the Machin portrait model
Reverse: Myron Cook, using
the Thomas Shingles model of
the Canadian coat-of-arms
Composition: .900 gold, .100 copper
Weight: 18.27 grams
Diameter: 27.05 mm
Edge: Reeded
Die Axis: ↑↑
Case of Issue: Black or brown leather
with black flock insert

Date	Description	Issue Price	Mintage	SP-65
1967	Confederation Commemorative	Not issued singly	334,288	300.00

GOLD 100 DOLLAR COINS (14kt)

OLYMPIC COMMEMORATIVES 1976. As part of the series of collectors coins struck to commemorate and help finance the XXI Olympiad, two separate $100 gold coins were issued in 1976. The reverse design for each shows an ancient Grecian athlete being crowned with laurel by the goddess Pallas Athena. The uncirculated edition (uniformly shiny surface) is 14k gold and has rim denticles. The proof edition (mirror fields and matte devices and legends) is 22k gold, slightly smaller, and lacks rim denticles.

Designer: Portrait: Arnold Machin
Reverse: Dora de Pédery-Hunt
Modeller: Obverse: Walter Ott, using
the Machin portrait model
Reverse: Dora de Pédery-Hunt
and Walter Ott
Composition: .583 gold,
.417 copper alloy
Weight: 13.338 grams
Diameter: 27.00 mm
Edge: Reeded
Die Axis: ↑↑
Case of Issue: Plastic flip in a brown sleeve

Date	Description	Issue Price	Mintage	MS-65
1976	Olympic Commemorative	105.00	650,000	150.00

Note: Canadian gold coins trade at a small premium over gold value. Please refer to the bullion value for pricing if there is a major change in the price of gold.

GOLD 100 DOLLAR COINS (22kt) 1976-1986

Designer & Modeller: As previous
Composition: .917 gold, .083 copper alloy
Weight: 16.966 grams
Diameter: 25.00 mm
Edge: Reeded
Die Axis: ↑↑
Case of Issue: Cowhide and wood with
    black suede insert, COA

Date	Description	Issue Price	Mintage	PR-65
1976	Olympic Commemorative	150.00	350,000	300.00

ELIZABETH II SILVER JUBILEE COMMEMORATIVE 1977. Following the sales success of the Olympic $100 coins, the government decided to embark upon a program to issue a $100 coin every year. The 1977 coin formed part of a two-coin set - the other coin was the silver dollar, issued in recognition of the Queen's Silver Jubilee. The special reverse shows a bouquet of flowers made up of the official flowers of the provinces and territories. All of the issue was of proof quality, with mirror fields and matte devices and legends.

Designer: Obverse: Arnold Machin
    Reverse: Raymond Lee
Modeller: Reverse - Walter Ott
Composition: .917 gold, .083 silver
Weight: 16.965 grams
Diameter: 27.00 mm
Edge: Reeded
Die Axis: ↑↑
Case of Issue: Black leatherette case
    with maroon insert and plastic
    coin holder, COA

Date	Description	Issue Price	Mintage	PR-65
1977	Silver Jubilee Commemorative	140.00	180,396	300.00

CANADIAN UNITY COIN 1978. The reverse of the proof $100 gold coin for 1978 depicts twelve Canada geese flying in formation. The image represents the ten provinces and two territories, and so promotes Canadian unity.

Designer: Obverse: Arnold Machin
    Reverse: Roger Savage
Modeller: Obverse: Royal Canadian Mint
    staff, using the Machin model
    Reverse: Ago Aarand
Specifications: Same as 1977
Case of Issue: Black leatherette case with
    blue insert and plastic coin holder,
    COA

Date	Description	Issue Price	Mintage	PR-65
1978	Canadian Unity	150.00	200,000	300.00

INTERNATIONAL YEAR OF THE CHILD COMMEMORATIVE 1979. Children playing hand in hand beside a globe adorn the reverse of the 1979 $100 gold coin struck in honour of the International Year of the Child.

Designer: Obverse: Arnold Machin
Reverse: Carola Tietz
Modeller: Obverse: RCM staff using the Machin model
Reverse: Victor Coté
Specifications: Same as 1977
Case of Issue: Brown leatherette with brown flocked insert. Brown plastic coin holder, COA

Date	Description	Issue Price	Mintage	PR-65
1979	International Year of the Child	185.00	250,000	300.00

ARCTIC TERRITORIES COMMEMORATIVE 1980. The gold $100 coin for 1980 is a commemorative marking the 100th anniversary of the transfer of the Arctic Islands from the British government to the government of the Dominion of Canada. Its reverse shows an Inuk paddling a kayak near a small iceberg and has no lettering or date. The obverse features the Machin bust of Queen Elizabeth, with the legend and date.

Designer: Obverse: Arnold Machin
Reverse: Arnaldo Marchetti
Modeller: Obverse: RCM staff using the Machin model
Reverse: Sheldon Beveridge
Specifications: Same as 1977
Case of Issue: Brown leatherette with brown flocked insert., encapsulated coin encapsulated, COA

Date	Description	Issue Price	Mintage	PR-65
1980	Arctic Territories Commemorative	430.00	130,000	300.00

"O CANADA" COMMEMORATIVE 1981. The $100 gold coin for 1981 marks the decision of the Canadian Parliament, on July 1, 1980, to adopt the song "O Canada" as our national anthem.

Designer: Obverse: Arnold Machin
Reverse: Roger Savage
Modeller: Obverse: RCM staff using the Machin model
Reverse: Walter Ott
Specifications: Same as 1977
Case of Issue: Same as 1980

Date	Description	Issue Price	Mintage	PR-65
1981	National Anthem	300.00	100,950	300.00

PATRIATION OF THE CANADIAN CONSTITUTION 1982. The $100 gold coin for 1982 commemorates the patriation of the Constitution of Canada. The reverse of the coin portrays this historical event by a page turning in an open book bearing the coat of arms of Canada and a maple leaf. The obverse of this coin, the seventh in the 22 karat $100 series, depicts Arnold Machin's effigy of Her Majesty Elizabeth II and the legend "100 Dollars" and "Elizabeth II."

Designer: Obverse: Arnold Machin
Reverse: Friedrich Peter
Modeller: Obverse: RCM staff using the
Machin model
Reverse: Walter Ott
Specifications: Same as 1977
Case of Issue: Same as 1980

Date	Description	Issue Price	Mintage	PR-65
1982	Canadian Constitution	290.00	121,706	300.00

SIR HUMPHREY GILBERT'S LANDING IN NEWFOUNDLAND 1983. The $100 gold coin for 1983 commemorates Gilbert's landing in Newfoundland to proclaim it as Britain's first overseas colony. The word "CANADA" appears on the edge for the first time in Canadian coinage.

Designer: Obverse: Arnold Machin
Reverse: John Jaciw
Modeller: Obverse: RCM staff using
Machin model
Reverse: Walter Ott
Edge: Lettered, Reeded
Specifications: Same as 1977
Case of Issue: Same as 1980

Date	Description	Issue Price	Mintage	PR-65
1983	Sir Humphrey Gilbert's Landing	310.00	83,128	300.00

JACQUES CARTIER'S VOYAGE OF DISCOVERY 1984. The $100 gold coin for 1984 commemorates Cartier's landing at Gaspé, Bonaventure in 1534. The reverse portrays a profile of Jacques Cartier and a ship of his era. Arnold Machin's effigy of Her Majesty Queen Elizabeth II is continued. The edge security lettering of 1983 was not continued in 1984.

Designer: Obverse: Arnold Machin
Reverse: Carola Tietz
Modeller: Obverse: RCM staff using
Machin model
Reverse: Walter Ott
Specifications: Same as 1977
Case of Issue: Same as 1981

Date	Description	Issue Price	Mintage	PR-65
1984	Jacques Cartier Voyage	325.00	67,662	300.00

NATIONAL PARKS CENTENARY 1985. The $100 gold coin of 1985 commemorates the centennial of an important part of Canada's heritage, the National Parks. The reverse of the coin portrays a bighorn sheep poised on a cliff in the Canadian Rockies.

Designer: Obverse: Arnold Machin
Reverse: Hector Greville
Modeller: Reverse: Walter Ott
Specifications: Same as 1977
Case of Issue: Brown leatherette book type case, with maple leaf emblem. Inside: Beige satin, encapsulated coin. All enclosed in a brown plastic box, COA

Date	Description	Issue Price	Mintage	PR-65
1985	National Parks Centenary	325.00	58,520	300.00

INTERNATIONAL YEAR OF PEACE 1986. The $100 gold coin for 1986 signifies Canada's support for world peace. The reverse depicts a branch of maple leaves intertwined with a branch of olive leaves, symbols of Canada and Peace coming together. The words "Peace-Paix" forming a circle are superimposed on the design.

Designer: Obverse: Arnold Machin
Reverse: Dora de Pédery-Hunt
Modeller: Obverse: RCM staff
Reverse: Dora de Pédery-Hunt
Specifications: Same as 1977
Case of Issue: Same as 1985

Date	Description	Issue Price	Mintage	PR-65
1986	International Year of Peace	325.00	76,255	300.00

GOLD 100 DOLLAR COINS (14kt) 1987 TO DATE

XV OLYMPIC WINTER GAMES 1987. The $100 gold coin for 1987 commemorates the XV Olympic Winter Games held in Calgary in 1988. The reverse portrays a hand holding the Olympic Torch with a stylized flame forming an image of the Canadian Rocky Mountains. This is the second $100 gold coin to have a lettered edge. The inscription reads "XV Olympic Winter Games - XVes Jeux Olympiques D'Hiver."

Designer: Obverse: Arnold Machin
Reverse: Friedrich Peter
Modeller: Reverse: Ago Aarand
Composition: .583 gold, .417 silver
Weight: 13.338 grams
Diameter: 27 mm
Edge: Lettered
Die Axis: ↑↑
Case of Issue: Same as 1985

Date	Description	Issue Price	Mintage	PR-65
1987	XV Olympic Winter Games	255.00	145,175	160.00

THE BOWHEAD WHALE (BALAENA MYSTICETUS) 1988. The $100 gold coin for 1988 celebrates a precious national treasure. The reverse portrays a bowhead whale and her calf surrounded by a circle.

Designer: Obverse: Arnold Machin
Reverse: Robert R. Carmichael
Modeller: Ago Aarand
Composition: 0.583 gold, .4167 silver
Weight: 13.338 grams
Diameter: 27.00 mm
Thickness: 2.15 mm
Edge: Reeded
Die Axis: ↑↑
Case of Issue: Same as 1987

Date	Description	Issue Price	Mintage	PR-65
1988	Bowhead Whale	255.00	52,239	160.00

SAINTE-MARIE 1639-1989. In 1639 the French Jesuits founded a fortified mission village near Midland, Ontario, which they named Sainte-Marie among the Hurons. 1989 was the 350th anniversary of this first self-sufficient settlement in Ontario, where one-fifth of the European population of Canada lived.

Designer: Obverse: Arnold Machin
Reverse: David J. Craig
Modeller: Obverse: Patrick Brindley
Reverse: Ago Aarand
Specifications: Same as 1988
Case of Issue: Same as 1985

Date	Description	Issue Price	Mintage	PR-65
1989	Sainte-Marie	245.00	63,881	160.00

INTERNATIONAL LITERACY YEAR 1990. The General Assembly of the United Nations declared 1990 as the International Year of Literacy, setting the stage for the eradicatioan of illiteracy around the world by the year 2000.

Designer: Obverse: Dora de Pédery-Hunt
Reverse: John Mardon
Modeller: Obverse: Dora de Pédery-Hunt
Reverse: Ago Aarand
Susan Taylor
Specifications: Same as 1988
Case of Issue: Same as 1985

Date	Description	Issue Price	Mintage	PR-65
1990	International Literacy	245.00	49,940	160.00

EMPRESS OF INDIA 1991. Commemorating the 100th anniversary of the Empress of India's first arrival in Vancouver from Yokohama, Japan. The Canadian Pacific's trans-Pacific Empress ships were among the world's first cruise ships.

Designer: Obverse: Dora de Pédery-Hunt
Reverse: Karsten Smith
Modeller: Obverse: Dora de Pédery-Hunt
Reverse: Sheldon Beveridge
Specifications: Same as 1988
Case of Issue: Same as 1985

Date	Description	Issue Price	Mintage	PR-65
1991	Empress of India	245.00	33,966	160.00

CITY OF MONTREAL, 350TH ANNIVERSARY 1642-1992. On May 17, 1642, three vessels arrived from France landing Maisonneuve and his men on an island in the St. Lawrence River. They called the island Ville-Marie which was renamed Montreal in the early 1700's.

Designer: Obverse: Dora de Pédery-Hunt
Reverse: Stewart Sherwood
Modeller: Obverse: Dora de Pédery-Hunt
Reverse: Ago Aarand,
Cosme Saffioti
Specifications: Same as 1988
Case of Issue: Same as 1985

Date	Description	Issue Price	Mintage	PR-65
1992	Montreal	239.85	28,190	160.00

1893 THE ERA OF THE HORSELESS CARRIAGE 1993. The five vehicles pictured on the reverse of the 1993 gold coin are, clockwise from the left, the French Panhard-Levassor's Daimler, the American Duryea, the German Benz Victoria, the Simmonds Steam Carriage and, in the centre, the first Canadian built electric car, the Featherstonhaugh

Designer: Obverse: Dora de Pédery-Hunt
Reverse: John Mardon
Modeller: Obverse: Dora de Pédery-Hunt
Reverse: Ago Aarand,
William Woodruff
Specifications: Same as 1988
Case of Issue: Same as 1985

Date	Description	Issue Price	Mintage	PR-65
1993	Horseless Carriage	239.85	25,971	160.00

THE HOME FRONT 1994. This coin is part of the Remembrance & Peace Issue. The design was taken from a 1945 painting by P. Clark, entitled "Maintenance Jobs in the Hangar."

Designer: Obverse: Dora de Pédery-Hunt
Reverse: Paraskeva Clark
Modeller: Obverse: Dora de Pédery-Hunt
Reverse: Susan Taylor,
Ago Aarand
Specifications: Same as 1988
Case of Issue: Same as 1985

Date	Description	Issue Price	Mintage	PR-65
1994	Home Front	249.95	17,603	185.00

275TH ANNIVERSARY OF THE FOUNDING OF LOUISBOURG 1995. Louisbourg, built in 1720 as a strategic centre for the French military in North America, is commemorated on the $100.00 gold coin of 1995.

Designer: Obverse: Dora de Pédery-Hunt
Reverse: Lewis Parker
Modeller: Obverse: Dora de Pédery-Hunt
Reverse: Sheldon Beveridge
Specifications: Same as 1988
Case of Issue: Same as 1985

Date	Description	Issue Price	Mintage	PR-65
1995	Louisbourg	249.95	16,916	185.00

100TH ANNIVERSARY OF THE FIRST MAJOR GOLD DISCOVERY IN THE KLONDIKE 1996. In 1896 the Gold Rush began when George and Kate Carmack, Skookum Jim and Dawson Charlie made the Klondike's first major gold find. 1996 was the last $100.00 gold coin to be packaged in the book type cases.

Designer: Obverse: Dora de Pédery-Hunt
Reverse: John Mantha
Modeller: Obverse: Dora de Pédery-Hunt
Reverse: Cosme Saffioti
Specifications: Same as 1988
Case of Issue: Same as 1985

Date	Description	Issue Price	Mintage	PR-65
1996	Klondike Gold Rush	259.95	17,973	225.00

150TH ANNIVERSARY OF ALEXANDER GRAHAM BELL'S BIRTH 1997. The $100 gold coin of 1997 honours the creative genius of Alexander Graham Bell. He was born in Scotland in 1847. In 1874 while in Ontario, he carried out the experiments that led to the invention of the telephone. The $100 gold coin was offered for the first time with or without a case

Designer: Obverse: Dora de Pédery-Hunt
Reverse: Donald H. Curley
Modeller: Obverse: Dora de Pédery-Hunt
Reverse: Sheldon Beveridge
Edge: Reeded
Specifications: Same as 1988
Original Issue Price: With case: $259.95
Without case: $254.95
Case of Issue: Black suede clam type case, black suede inside, encapsulated coin

Date	Description	Issue Price	Mintage	PR-65
1997	Alexander Graham Bell	See above	14,030	225.00

75TH ANNIVERSARY OF THE NOBEL PRIZE FOR THE DISCOVERY OF INSULIN 1998. The discovery of insulin by Frederick Banting and John MacLeod earned them the Nobel Prize for Physiology and Medicine in 1923.

Designer: Obverse: Dora de Pédery-Hunt
Reverse: Robert R. Carmichael
Modeller: Obverse: Dora de Pédery-Hunt
Reverse: Stan Witten
Specifications: Same as 1988
Original Issue Price: With case: $259.95
Without case: $254.95
Case of Issue: Same as 1997

Date	Description	Issue Price	Mintage	PR-65
1998	Nobel Prize	See above	11,220	225.00

50TH ANNIVERSARY OF NEWFOUNDLAND'S CONFEDERATION WITH CANADA IN 1949, 1999. Issued to celebrate the 50th anniversary of Newfoundland's union with Canada on March 31, 1949.

Designer: Obverse: Dora de Pédery-Hunt
Reverse: J. Gale-Vaillancourt
Modeller: Obverse: Dora de Pédery-Hunt
Reverse: William Woodruff
Specifications: Same as 1988
Original Issue Price: With case: $259.95
Without case: $254.95
Case of Issue: Black suede clam type case, black suede inside, encapsulated coin

Date	Description	Issue Price	Mintage	PR-65
1999	Newfoundland	See above	10,242	275.00

150TH ANNIVERSARY OF THE SEARCH FOR THE NORTHWEST PASSAGE IN1850, 2000. The Franklin Expedition, which was lost on its voyage to discover a Northwest passage to the far east, is commemorated on the 100 dollar gold coin for 2000.

Designer: Obverse: Dora de Pédery-Hunt
Reverse: John Mardon
Modeller: Obverse: Dora de Pédery-Hunt
Reverse: Stan Witten
Specifications: Same as 1988
Original Issue Price: With case: $269.95
Without case: $254.95
Case of Issue: Metal presentation case
with wood insert, COA

Date	Description	Issue Price	Mintage	PR-65
2000	Northwest Passage	See above	10,547	260.00

125TH ANNIVERSARY OF THE LIBRARY OF PARLIAMENT 2001. The Library of parliament is one of the most famous symbols of the Canadian Confederation. "This beautiful building is an architectural marvel, and a treasure for all Canadians to cherish."

Designer: Obverse: Dora de Pédery-Hunt
Reverse: Robert R. Carmichael
Engraver: Obverse: Dora de Pédery-Hunt
Reverse: Susan Taylor
William Woodruff
Specifications: Same as 1988
Original Issue Price: With case $274.95
Without case $260.95
Case of Issue: Same as 2000

Date	Description	Issue Price	Mintage	PR-65
2001	Library of Parliament	See above	8,080	260.00

COMMEMORATING CANADA'S OIL INDUSTRY 2002. Struck to commemorate the major economic importance of oil to the Canadian economy and Canada's place as one of the major oil producers of the world. The sea of 'black gold' at the foot of the oil rig commemorates the major discovery of the Leduc oil field on February 13, 1947.

Designer: Obverse: Dora de Pédery-Hunt
Reverse: John Mardon
Engraver: Obverse: Dora de Pédery-Hunt
Reverse: Stan Witten
Specifications: Same as 1988
Original Issue Price: With case $274.95
Without case $260.95
Case of Issue: Same as 2000

Date	Description	Issue Price	Mintage	PR-65
2002	Oil Rig	See above	9,992	400.00

100TH ANNIVERSARY OF THE DISCOVERY OF MARQUIS WHEAT 2003. After 10 years of experiments, Dr. William Saunders and his sons Percy and Charles, discovered the marquis wheat variety, making Canada forever known as the world's bread basket.

Designer: Obverse: Dora de Pédery-Hunt
Reverse: Thom Nelson
Engraver: Obverse: Dora de Pédery-Hunt
Reverse: Stan Witten
Specifications: Same as 1988
Original Issue Price: With case $289.95
Without case $277.95
Case of Issue: Same as 2000

Date	Description	Issue Price	Mintage	PR-65
2003	Marquis Wheat	See above	10,000	290.00

Note: All proof coins are a frosted relief on a brilliant background.

GOLD HOLOGRAM 150 DOLLAR COINS

YEAR OF THE DRAGON 2000. This coin commemorates the coincidence of the year of the Dragon and the Dawn of a New Millennium, an occurrence that happens once every three thousand years. This is the second hologram coin issued and the first of the Chinese Lunar series of coins.

Designer:
   Obverse: Dora de Pédery-Hunt
   Reverse: Harvey Chan
   Obverse: Dora de Pédery-Hunt
Modellers:
   Reverse: Harvey Chan
   Reverse: RCM Engineering Staff

Composition: .750 gold, .250 silver
Weight: 13.61 grams
Diameter: 28.0 mm
Thickness: 1.81 mm
Edge: Serrated
Die Axis: ↑↑
Case of Issue: Gold satin clam style case with gold foil outer box.

Date	Description	Issue Price	Mintage	PR-65
2000	Year of the Dragon	388.88	8,874	600.00

YEAR OF THE SNAKE 2001. To celebrate the arrival of the year of the Snake in the Chinese Lunar Calendar, the Royal Canadian Mint introduced the second in the series of $150 Hologram gold coins.

Designers, modellers and specifications same as for the 2000 coin.

Date	Description	Issue Price	Mintage	PR-65
2001	Year of the Snake	388.88	6,571	400.00

YEAR OF THE HORSE 2002. The seventh sign of the Chinese lunar calendar is the horse. This is the third hologram coin of the series.

Designers, modellers and specifications same as for the 2000 coin.

Date	Description	Issue Price	Mintage	PR-65
2002	Year of the Horse	388.88	6,596	400.00

YEAR OF THE SHEEP 2003. The eighth sign of the Chinese lunar calendar is the Sheep. This is the fourth hologram coin of the series.

Designers, modellers and specifications same as for the 2000 coin.

Case: Multicoloured outer container, clam-style

Date	Description	Issue Price	Mintage	PR-65
2003	Year of the Sheep	398.88	6,888	400.00

GOLD 175 DOLLAR COIN

100TH ANNIVERSARY OF THE OLYMPIC MOVEMENT 1992-1996. Commemorating the 100th anniversary of the Olympic movement in 1996, Canada and four other countries, Australia, France, Austria and Greece, issued a three coin set, one gold and two silver coins. They were issued each year beginning with Canada in 1992. See page No. 296 for the Royal Canadian Mint silver issues. Only the Royal Canadian Mint issued coins are listed in the Standard Catalogue.

Designers:
    Obverse: Dora de Pédery-Hunt
    Reverse: Stewart Sherwood
Composition: .916 Gold, .084 Copper
Diameter: 28.00 mm
Edge: Lettering: Citius, altius, fortius

Modellers:
    Obverse: Dora de Pédery-Hunt
    Reverse: Ago Aarand
Weight: 16.97g
Thickness: 2.00 mm
Die Axis: ↑↑

Date	Description	Issue Price	Mintage	PR-65
1992	Flame	429.75	22,092	375.00

GOLD 200 DOLLAR COINS

CANADA FLAG SILVER JUBILEE 1990. Issued to commemorate the 25th anniversary of the proclamation approving Canada's flag.

Designer:
    Obverse: Dora de Pédery-Hunt
    Reverse: Stewart Sherwood
Modellers:
    Obverse: Dora de Pédery-Hunt
    Reverse: Ago Aarand
Composition: .916 gold, .083 silver
Weight: 17.13 grams
Diameter: 29.0 mm
Thickness: 2.0 mm
Edge: Reeded
Die Axis: ↑↑
Case of Issue: Same as 1991

Date	Description	Issue Price	Mintage	PR-65
1990	Canada Flag	395.00	20,980	300.00

A NATIONAL PASSION 1991. The 1991 two hundred dollar proof gold coin was issued as a tribute to the spirit and vitality of Canadian youth and the national game of hockey.

Designer:
    Obverse: Dora de Pédery-Hunt
    Reverse: Stewart Sherwood
Modeller:
    Obverse: Dora de Pédery-Hunt
    Reverse: Susan Taylor
Specifications: Same as 1990
Case of Issue: Woven Jacquard case, certificate, encapsulated coin

Date	Description	Issue Price	Mintage	PR-65
1991	A National Passion	425.00	10,215	300.00

NIAGARA FALLS 1992. The 1992 two hundred dollar gold coin was issued as a tribute to the beauty and majesty of Niagara Falls. The coin features two children playing near the falls.

Designer:
    Obverse: Dora de Pédery-Hunt
    Reverse: John Mardon
Modeller:
    Obverse: D. De Pédery-Hunt
    Reverse: Susan Taylor
Specifications: Same as 1990
Case of Issue: Same as 1991

Date	Description	Issue Price	Mintage	PR-65
1992	Niagara Falls	389.65	9,465	300.00

ROYAL CANADIAN MOUNTED POLICE 1993. The 1993 issue of the two hundred dollar gold coin pays tribute to the unique contribution of the R.C.M.P. to Canadian history.

Designer:
    Obverse: Dora de Pédery-Hunt
    Reverse: Stewart Sherwood
Modeller:
    Obverse: Dora de Pédery-Hunt
    Reverse: Susan Taylor
Specifications: Same as 1990
Case of Issue:Same as 1991

Date	Description	Issue Price	Mintage	PR-65
1993	R.C.M.P.	389.65	10,807	300.00

ANNE OF GREEN GABLES 1994: Issued as a tribute to the famous character in the novel by Canadian writer Lucy Maud Montgomery, this is the last coin in the youth and heritage series.

Designer:
    Obverse: Dora de Pédery-Hunt
    Reverse: Pheobe Gilman
Modeller:
    Obverse: Dora de Pédery-Hunt
    Reverse: Susan Taylor
Specifications: Same as 1990
Case of Issue:Same as 1991

Date	Description	Issue Price	Mintage	PR-65
1994	Anne of Green Gables	399.95	10,655	300.00

THE SUGAR BUSH 1995. Commemorating the time honoured rite of spring known in Canada as "sugaring off."

Designer:
    Obverse: Dora de Pédery-Hunt
    Reverse: J.D. Mantha
Modeller:
    Obverse: Dora de Pédery-Hunt
    Reverse: Sheldon Beveridge
Specifications: Same as 1990
Case of Issue:Same as 1991

Date	Description	Issue Price	Mintage	PR-65
1995	Sugar Bush	399.95	9,579	300.00

TRANSCONTINENTAL LANDSCAPE 1996. Issued to commemorate the railway, a central symbol of national life.

Designer:
  Obverse: Dora de Pédery-Hunt
  Reverse: Suzanne Duranceau
Modeller:
  Obverse: Dora de Pédery-Hunt
  Reverse: Cosme Saffioti
Specifications: Same as 1990
Case of Issue: Same as 1991

Date	Description	Issue Price	Mintage	PR-65
1996	Transcontinental Landscape	414.95	8,047	350.00

HAIDA "RAVEN BRINGING LIGHT TO THE WORLD" 1997. The first issue of a four year program, celebrating Canadian Native cultures and traditions. The $200 gold coin in 1997 was available with or without a case because the mint offered a four-coin case to house the set.

Designer:
  Obverse: Dora de Pédery-Hunt
  Reverse: Robert Davidson
Modeller:
  Obverse: Dora de Pédery-Hunt
  Reverse: C. Saffioti, A. Aarand
Specifications: Same as 1990
Original Issue Price:
  With case: $414.95
  Without case: $409.95
Case of Issue: Same as 1998

Date	Description	Issue Price	Mintage	PR-65
1997	Haida	See above	11,610	625.00

THE LEGEND OF THE WHITE BUFFALO 1998. The second issue of the four year program, celebrating Canadian Native cultures and traditions. The $200 gold coin was available with or without a case.

Designer:
  Obverse: Dora de Pédery-Hunt
  Reverse: Alex Janvier
Modeller:
  Obverse: Dora de Pédery-Hunt
  Reverse: Cosme Saffioti
Specifications: Same as 1990
Original Issue Price:
  With case: $414.95
  Without case: $409.95
Case of Issue: Encapsulated coin in
  metal trimmed presentation case.

Date	Description	Issue Price	Mintage	PR-65
1998	Buffalo	See above	7,149	350.00

MIKMAQ BUTTERFLY 1999. The third in the four coin series celebrating Canadian native cultures and traditions. The coin depicts a butterfly in the traditional Mikmaq double curve symbol of the balance between the physical and spiritual worlds.

Designer:
 Obverse: Dora de Pédery-Hunt
 Reverse: Alan Syliboy
Modeller:
 Obverse: Dora de Pédery-Hunt
 Reverse: Cosme Saffioti
Specifications: Same as 1990
Original Issue Price:
 With case: $414.95
 Without case: $409.95
Case of Issue: Encapsulated coin in
  metal trimmed presentation case.

Date	Description	Issue Price	Mintage	PR-65
1999	Mikmaq Butterfly	See above	6,510	350.00

MOTHER AND CHILD 2000. This is the fourth and last coin in the four coin Native Cultures and Traditions series.

Designer:
 Obverse; Dora de Pédery-Hunt
 Reverse: Germaine Arnaktauyok
Modeller:
 Obverse: Dora de Pédery-Hunt
 Reverse: Susan Taylor
Specifications: Same as 1990
Original Issue Price:
 With Case: $414.95
 Without case: $409.95
Case of Issue: Encapsulated coin in
  metal trimmed presentation case.

Date	Description	Issue Price	Mintage	PR-65
2000	Mother and Child	See above	7,410	350.00

Note: A special collector case designed by Maryanne Barkhouse for the "Canadian Native Cultures and Traditions" series was issued in 1998. The box was made of imitation stone resin, with the Arctic Fox as the central panel, and on each side an animal on which the native aboriginal depended. The four-coin case was available directly from the Mint, priced at $79.95. The complete four-coin set in case, $1,600.00.

CORNELIUS KRIEGHOFF 2001. The 2001 $200 gold coin is the first in a four coin series featuring Canadian art and artists. Cornelius Krieghoff's famous painting "The Habitant Farm" is featured on the reverse.

Designer:
  Obverse: Dora de Pédery-Hunt
  Reverse: Cornelius Krieghoff
Engraver:
  Obverse: Dora de Pédery-Hunt
  Reverse: Susan Taylor
Specifications: Same as 1990
Original Issue Price:
  With case: $424.95
  Without case: $412.95
Case of Issue: Encapsulated coin in metal trimmed presentation case

Date	Description	Issue Price	Mintage	PR-65
2001	Cornelius Krieghoff	See above	5,406	350.00

TOM THOMPSON 2002. The second coin of the four-coin series honouring Canada's famous painters. Thompson's (1877-1917) 'The Jack Pine" painted in 1916 in Algonquin Park, is one of Canada's most familiar images.

Designer:
  Obverse: Dora de Pédery-Hunt
  Reverse: Tom Thompson
Engraver:
  Obverse: Dora de Pédery-Hunt
  Reverse: Susan Taylor
Specifications: Same as 1990
Original Issue Price:
  With case: $424.95
  Without case: $412.95
Case of Issue: Encapsulated coin in metal trimmed presentation case

Date	Description	Issue Price	Mintage	PR-65
2002	Tom Thompson	See above	5,264	425.00

LIONEL LEMOINE FITZGERALD 2003. The third gold coin in the Canadian Art series features Fitzgerald's 'Houses,' painted 1929. The rural life of the small prairie towns is the theme of this magnificent painting.

Designer:
   Obverse: Dora de Pédery-Hunt
   Reverse: L. LeMoine Fitzgerald
Engraver:
   Obverse: Dora de Pédery-Hunt
   Reverse: Cosme Saffioti
Specifications: Same as 1990
Original Issue Price:
   With case: $424.95
   Without case: $412.95
Case of Issue: Encapsulated coin in
   metal trimmed presentation case

Date	Description	Issue Price	Mintage	PR-65
2002	Fitzgerald's 'Houses'	See above	10,000	425.00

GOLD 300 DOLLAR COINS

TRIPLE CAMEO PORTRAITS OF QUEEN ELIZABETH II, 2002. This silver (.9999) coin bears triple cameo, 14kt gold portraits of Queen Elizabeth II: 1953-1964 portrait by Mary Gillick; 1965-1989 portrait by Arnold Machin; 1990 to date portrait by Dora de Pédery-Hunt.

Designer: Obverse: Dora de Pédery-Hunt	**Modeller:** Obverse: Dora de Pédery-Hunt
Reverse:	Reverse:
Composition: .999 gold, 38.67 grams	**Weight:** 60.0 grams
.9999 silver, 26.33 grams	
Diameter: 50.0 mm	**Thickness:** N/A
Edge: N/A	**Die Axis:** ↑↑

Case of Issue: Anodized gold-coloured aluminum box with cherry wood stained siding.

Date	Description	Issue Price	Mintage	PR-65
2002	Triple Cameo Portraits	$1,095.95	993	1,100.

GOLD 350 DOLLAR COINS

90TH ANNIVERSARY OF THE ROYAL CANADIAN MINT 1998. To mark their 90th anniversary, the Mint issued a 99.999 per cent pure gold coin.

Designer: Obverse: Dora de Pédery-Hunt
     Reverse: Pierre Leduc
Composition: .99999 gold
Diameter: 34.0 mm
Edge: Reeded

Modeller: Obverse: Dora de Pédery-Hunt
     Reverse: Ago Aarand
Weight: 38.05 grams
Thickness: 2.7 mm
Die Axis: ↑↑

Case of Issue: Anodized gold-coloured aluminum box with cherry wood stained siding.

Date	Description	Issue Price	Mintage	PR-65
1998	Floral	$999.99	1999	1,150.

A GOLDEN SLIPPER, PRINCE EDWARD ISLAND'S PROVINCIAL FLOWER 1999.

Designer: Obverse: Dora de Pédery-Hunt
     Reverse: Henry Purdy
Specifications: Same as 1998

Modeller: Obverse: Dora de Pédery-Hunt
     Reverse: José Osio
Case of Issue: Same as 1998

Date	Description	Issue Price	Mintage	PR-65
1999	Golden Slipper	$999.99	1,990	1,150.

THE PACIFIC DOGWOOD, BRITISH COLUMBIA'S PROVINCIAL FLOWER 2000.

Designer: Obverse: Dora de Pédery Hunt   **Modeller:** Obverse: Dora de Pédery Hunt
            Reverse: Caren Heine   Reverse: José Osio
Specifications: Same as 1998   **Case of Issue:** As 1998

Date	Description	Issue Price	Mintage	PR-65
2000	Pacific Dogwood	$999.99	1,971	1,100.

THE MAYFLOWER, NOVA SCOTIA'S PROVINCIAL FLOWER 2001.

Designer: Obverse: Dora de Pédery Hunt   **Modeller:** Obverse: Dora de Pédery Hunt
            Reverse: Bonnie Ross   Reverse: Susan Taylor
Specifications: Same as 1998   **Case of Issue:** As 1998

Date	Description	Issue Price	Mintage	PR-65
2001	The Mayflower	$999.99	1,988	1,100.

THE WILD ROSE, ALBERTA'S PROVINCIAL FLOWER 2002. Rosa Acicularis (The Wild Rose) is the official floral emblem of Alberta. First adopted as the provincial flower in 1930, the wild rose is the fifth in the floral gold coin signature series.

Designer: Obverse: Dora de Pédery Hunt   **Modeller:** Obverse: Dora de Pédery Hunt
             Reverse: Dr. Andreas Kare Hellum   Reverse: William Woodruff
Specifications: Same as 1998   **Case of Issue:** As 1998

Date	Description	Issue Price	Mintage	PR-65
2002	The Wild Rose	$1,099.99	1,803	1,100.

THE WHITE TRILLIUM, ONTARIO'S PROVINCIAL FLOWER 2003.

Photograph not
available
at press time

Designer: Obverse: Dora de Pédery Hunt   **Modeller:** Obverse: Dora de Pédery Hunt
             Reverse: N/A   Reverse: N/A
Specifications: Same as 1998   **Case of Issue:** As 1998

Date	Description	Issue Price	Mintage	PR-65
2002	The White Trillium	$1,099.99	N/A	1,100.

COLLECTOR SETS

Although some silver dollars of proof-like quality were issued prior to 1954, it has not been confirmed that any entire sets were issued. Certainly some minor coins in the sets of 1950-1952 are proof-like, but either the few proof-likes made were mixed up with circulation strikes in making up the sets, or certain denominations were not made as proof-likes to begin with. In any event, the majority of the coins in the sets sold to the public by the Mint in 1950-1953 were no more than circulation strikes that had not gone through mint bags. Beginning in 1954 and continuing through 1969, all mint sets that the Royal Canadian Mint sold to the public were Proof-like. The quality was somewhat inferior in 1965 as a result of greatly increased production, and in 1968-1969 because of the inexperience of the Mint in producing larger proof-like coins in nickel.

During the period 1953 to 1970, specimen sets were also produced in some years. This generally does not pose a difficulty because the specimen coins were either issued in special packaging or were markedly better quality than the corresponding proof-like coins.

PROOF-LIKE AND BRILLIANT UNCIRCULATED SETS
1954-2003

SIX COIN SILVER PROOF-LIKE SETS 1954-1960

Proof-like sets issued from 1953 to 1960 came in flat white cardboard holders housed in cellophane envelopes. The black stamp, "ROYAL CANADIAN MINT / OTTAWA, CANADA," appears on some 1960 holders.

Proof-like Sets as Issued 1954-1960

Date	No. of Coins	Issue Price	Mintage	PL-65
1954 Shoulder Fold	6	2.50	3,000	400.00
1954 No Shoulder Fold	6	2.50	Incl. above	1,000.00
1955 Normal Water Lines Dollar	6	2.50	6,300	275.00
1955 Arnprior Dollar	6	2.50	Incl. above	375.00
1956	6	2.50	6,500	150.00
1957	6	2.50	11,862	125.00
1958	6	2.50	18,259	85.00
1959	6	3.00	31,577	45.00
1960	6	3.00	64,097	35.00

SIX COIN SILVER PROOF-LIKE SETS 1961-1967

This was a continuation of the set offered previously. It contained one of each denomination (for a total of six coins) packaged in a flat pliofilm pouch.

The 1961 set, which of course was the first set packaged under the system, did not come wtihout problems. The one cent coin was prone to discolouring, making a brilliant, red PL-65 cent a scarcity.

Date	No. of Coins	Issue Price	Mintage	PL-65
1961	6	3.00	98,373	30.00
1962	6	3.00	200,950	20.00
1963	6	3.00	673,006	11.00
1964	6	3.00	1,653,162	11.00
1965 Variety 1 Dollar	6	4.00	2,904,352	10.00
1965 Variety 2 Dollar	6	4.00	Incl. above	10.00
1966 Large Beads Dollar	6	4.00	672,514	10.00
1967	6	4.00	963,714	15.00

Note: The third, fourth and fifth varieties of the 1965 silver dollar were not packaged in the proof-like sets issued by the mint.

SIX COIN NICKEL PROOF-LIKE SETS 1968-1976

This was a continuation of the sets previously offered, only now the four coins 10 cents to the one dollar were nickel in composition. Naturally the one cent and five cent remained the same and the Pliofilm packaging was continued. The coin finish was Proof-like until 1976, and from 1977 to 1980 the finish was brilliant relief – brilliant background.

1968 Double Waterlines
Double Die

1974 Double Yoke
Double Die

Date	No. of Coins	Issue Price	Mintage	PL-65
1968	6	4.00	521,641	3.25
1968 Small Island $1	6	4.00	Incl. above	17.00
1968 No Island $1	6	4.00	Incl. above	15.00
1968 Double Waterlines	6	4.00	Incl. above	85.00
1969	6	4.00	326,203	3.50
1970	6	4.00	349,120	4.50
1971	6	4.00	253,311	4.50
1972	6	4.00	224,275	6.00
1973 Large Bust 25¢	6	4.00	243,695	225.00
1973 Small Bust 25¢	6	4.00	Incl. above	4.50
1974	6	5.00	213,589	4.00
1974 Double Yoke	6	5.00	Incl. above	300.00
1975	6	5.00	197,372	4.25
1976	6	5.15	171,737	4.75

SIX COIN NICKEL PROOF-LIKE SETS 1977-1980

In 1977 the quality of the pliofilm sets began to improve. Probably as a result of the numismatic presses purchased in 1972 to produce Canada's first officially recognized proof coins for the Montreal Olympic proof sets. The finish on the coins within the sets is brilliant relief − brilliant background.

Date	No. of Coins	Issue Price	Mintage	PL-65
1977	6	5.15	225,307	5.25
1977 Short Water Lines	6	5.15	Incl. above	9.50
1978 Square Jewels	6	5.25	260,000	4.50
1978 Round Jewels	6	5.25	Incl. above	15.00
1979	6	6.25	187,624	4.50
1979 Pointed	6	6.25	Incl. above	6.50
1980	6	8.00	169,390	5.25

SIX COIN NICKEL BRILLIANT UNCIRCULATED SETS 1981-1996

In 1980 the Mint's marketing department began a restructuring of the mix of coins offered to collectors. The old issue of Proof-like sets (not a term recognized by the R.C.M.) was officially named "The Brilliant Uncirculated Set."

The quality improvement which began in 1977 continued with the 1981 introduction of a confirmed finish on the pliofilm set – brilliant relief on brilliant background.

In 1996 the finish was changed on the coins to brilliant relief – parallel finish background. The Pliofilm package continued.

Date and Mint Mark	One Dollar Coins	No. of Coins	Issue Price	Mintage	MS-65
1981	Voyager	6	5.00	186,250	5.25
1982	Voyager	6	5.00	203,287	4.75
1983	Voyager	6	5.00	190,838	9.00
1984	Voyager	6	5.00	181,415	7.75
1985	Voyager, Plioflim	6	6.95	173,924	9.25
1985	Voyager, Hard Plastic	6	N/A	Incl. above	30.00
1986	Voyager	6	6.95	167,338	9.25
1987	Voyager	6	6.95	212,136	7.00
1988	Loon	6	6.95	182,048	7.00
1989	Loon	6	7.70	158,636	12.50
1990	Loon	6	7.70	170,791	12.50
1991	Loon	6	8.50	147,814	45.00
1992	Loon	6	9.50	217,597	17.00
1993	Loon	6	9.50	171,680	6.25
1993 CNA	Loon	6	9.50	Incl. above	12.00
1994	Loon	6	9.75	141,676	8.25
1995	Loon	6	9.75	143,892	10.50
1996	Loon	6	11.95	120,217	30.00
1996 5¢ NR 6	Loon	6	11.95	Incl. above	30.00

Note: The 1996 Brilliant Uncirculated set contains the 5¢ NR 6 variety.

SEVEN COIN NICKEL BRILLIANT UNCIRCULATED SETS 1997-2000

In 1997 the two dollar Polar Bear coin was added to the set. In mid-1997 the RCM transferred production of the uncirculated sets to Winnipeg. The Ottawa and Winnipeg issues of 1997 can be distinguished by the method of packaging, not by the finish of the coins. They are indicated by (O) for Ottawa and (W) for Winnipeg in the listings. No mint marks appear on 1997-dated coins. The finish on both sets (1997) is technically equal, which is Brilliant Relief - Parallel Finish on background.

In 1998 the finish on the coins returned to a brilliant relief with a brilliant background, and this was continued until 2000. To distinguish the coins produced at the Winnipeg mint in 1998, a "W" was added to all coins from one cent through two dollars. This is the first time the Canadian mint placed a mint mark on Canadian coins. When the set production was moved back to Ottawa, in mid-1998, the coins were struck without a mint mark. In 2000, the mint mark appeared again as set production was moved back to the Winnipeg mint. The packaging of the sets in transparent plastic film was continued, and 2000 was the last year of issue for sets containing pure nickel coinage. The Winnipeg mint mark 'W' is found on the obverse, to the lower right of the portrait.

1997 Ottawa Uncirculated Set – The $1.00 Loon coin is at top right.

1997 Winnipeg Uncirculated Set – The $1.00 Loon coin is top left.

SEVEN COIN NICKEL BRILLIANT UNCIRCULATED SETS, 1997-2000 cont'd

"W" Mint Mark

Date and Mint Mark	One/Two Dollar Coins	No. of Coins	Issue Price	Mintage	MS-65
1997 (O)	Loon/Polar Bear	7	13.95	174,692	27.50
1997 (W)	Loon/Polar Bear	7	13.95	Incl. above	11.50
1998 (O)	Loon/Polar Bear	7	13.95	145,439	19.00
1998 (W)	Loon/Polar Bear	7	13.95	Incl. above	27.50
1999	Loon/Polar Bear	7	13.95	117,318	12.75
1999	Loon/Nunavut	7	13.95	74,821	12.75
1999	Loon/Nunavut Mule	7	13.95	Incl. above	350.00
2000	Loon/Polar Bear	7	15.95	186,985	12.75
2000	Loon/Polar Bears	7	15.95	Incl. above	12.75

Note: See page 355, Brilliant Uncirculated Singles for the images of the 1999 Nunavut Mule.

FIVE COIN MULTI-PLY PLATED STEEL BRILLIANT UNCIRCULATED SET 1999

Multi-Ply Plated coinage was issued to the vending industry for test purposes in 1999. The industry's request was for "actual coins" that would be used in circulation, not "test" coinage that may or may not be issued. Five denominations, one cent through to the fifty cents, were issued to the industry on a deposit basis. Naturally not all were returned, for some found their way into the numismatic market. Finding superior demand for the legal tender "test coinage," the mint issued a six-piece set containing five multi-ply plated steel coins and a medallion for sale to the numismatic market. The finish on the coins is brilliant relief, brilliant background.

Date and Mint Mark	One/Two Dollar Coins	No. of Coins	Issue Price	Mintage	MS-65
1999P	Medallion	5	99.95	20,000	45.00

SEVEN COIN MULTI-PLY PLATED STEEL UNCIRCULATED SETS 2001 TO DATE

No multi-ply plated steel sets were issued in 2000. The finish on the multi-ply plated steel coins is brilliant relief – brilliant background, continuing from the 2000 nickel sets.

In 2002, to commemorate the Golden Jubilee of Queen Elizabeth II, the Mint issued double dated (1952-2002) plated steel coinage. These coins were used in the collectors sets, and are identical to those of the previous year except for the double dates. Special Edition Jubilee Sets are found on page 363.

Date and Mint Mark	One/Two Dollar Coins	No. of Coins	Issue Price	Mintage	MS-65
2001P	Loon/Bear	7	15.95	115,897	16.00
1952-2002P	Loon/Bear	7	15.95	97,279	16.00
2003P	Loon/Bear	7	15.95	N/A	16.00
2004P	Loon/Bear	7	15.95	N/A	16/00

CUSTOM PROOF-LIKE SETS 1971 - 1976

The custom set contained one of each denomination, with an extra cent to show the obverse. The quality of the coins is brilliant releif – brilliant background. Marketing of these sets ceased in 1976.

Cases: **1971:** Coins in black vinyl-covered case with Canada's coat of arms and the word "CANADA" stamped in gold on the top.

1972-1973: as 1971, except the vinyl is red.

1974 - 1976: as 1971, except the vinyl is maroon.

Date	One Dollar Coins	No. of Coins	Price	Mintage	BU-65
1971	B.C.	7	6.50	33,517	7.50
1972	Voyageur	7	6.50	38,198	7.50
1973LB 25¢	P.E.I.	7	6.50	49,376	200.00
1973SB 25¢	P.E.I.	7	6.50	Incl. above	7.50
1974	Voyageur	7	8.00	44,296	7.50
1975	Voyageur	7	8.00	36,581	7.50

"OH! CANADA" NICKEL BRILLIANT
UNCIRCULATED SETS, 1994 - 2000

First issued in 1994, this set included the nickel-bronze dollar current to that year. In 1997 this set was expanded to include the two dollar polar bear coin. In 1998 the packaging of the "Oh! Canada" sets changed from card displays to clear plastic display units.

Date and Mint Mark	One/Two Dollar Coins	No. of Coins	Issue Price	Mintage	MS-65
1994	Loon/None	6	16.95	18,794	15.00
1995	Peacekeeping/None	6	16.95	50,927	12.00
1996	Loon/None	6	16.95	31,083	18.00
1997	Flying Loon/Polar Bear	7	21.95	84,124	35.00
1998	Loon/Polar Bear	7	21.95	42,710	22.00
1998W	Loon/Polar Bear	7	21.95	24,792	22.00
1999	Loon/Polar Bear	7	21.95	82,754	20.00
2000	Loon/Polar Bear	7	21.95	107,884	12.00
2000W	Loon/Polar Bear	7	21.95	Inc. above	20.00

"OH CANADA" MULTI-PLY PLATED STEEL
BRILLIANT UNCIRCULATED SETS, 2001 TO DATE

In 2001 the five subsidiary coins of the "Oh! Canada" set were replaced by the five Multi-Ply Plated Steel coins. In the 2002 set all coins bear the double date '1952-2002' to commemorate the Golden Jubilee of Her Majesty Queen Elizabeth II.

Date and Mint Mark	One/Two Dollar Coins	No. of Coins	Issue Price	Mintage	MS-65
2001P	Loon/Polar Bear	7	22.95	66,726	12.00
1952-2002P	Loon/Polar Bear	7	22.95	60,484	20.00
2003P	Loon/Polar Bear	7	22.95	N/A	23.00

SPECIAL ISSUES "OH CANADA"
BRILLIANT UNCIRCULATED SETS

The "Oh! Canada" sets are found with a variety of packaging designed for different markets. The known designs are listed here:

1998	CIBC, Smart Start	$22.00
2001P	Calgary	$11.00
	St. John's	$13.00
	Niagara Falls	$11.00
	Vancouver	$12.00
	Whistler	$10.00
	R.C.M.	$10.00
	Montreal, regular	$10.00
	Halifax	$13.00
	Quebec City	$10.00
	Banff	$11.00

"BUNDLE OF JOY/TINY TREASURES"
NICKEL BRILLIANT UNCIRCULATED SETS, 1995 - 2000

First issued in 1995, this uncirculated set was specially packaged for the gift market using the six uncirculated denominations of the time. In 1997 this set was expanded to include the two dollar polar bear coin. In 1998 the name changed from "Bundle of Joy" to "Tiny Treasures" uncirculated sets. Also in the same year the packaging of the sets of "Tiny Treasures" changed from card displays to clear plastic display units.The movement of set production to Winnipeg and back to Ottawa that occurred in 1998 with the uncirculated sets also took place with the "Oh! Canada" and "Tiny Treasures" sets. In 2000 the production of the sets occurred in both the Ottawa and Winnipeg mints.

Date and Mint Mark	One/Two Dollar Coins	No. of Coins	Issue Price	Mintage	MS-65
1995	Loon	6	19.95	36,443	18.00
1996	Loon	6	19.95	56,618	18.00
1997(O)	Loon/Polar Bear	7	21.95	55,199	20.00
1998	Loon/Polar Bear	7	21.95	46,139	20.00
1998W	Loon/Polar Bear	7	21.95	12,625	28.00
1999	Loon/Polar Bear	7	21.95	67,694	20.00
2000	Loon/Polar Bear	7	21.95	82,964	20.00
2000W	Loon/Polar Bear	7	21.95	Inc. above	20.00
2000	Loon/Polar Bears	7	21.95	Inc. above	12.00

"TINY TREASURES" MULTI-PLY PLATED STEEL
BRILLIANT UNCIRCULATED SETS, 2001 TO DATE

As with the uncirculated sets of 2001 the nickel coinage of the previous year was replaced with the new patented Multi-Ply Plated Steel coins. In the 2002 set all coins bear the double date '1952-2002' to commemorate the Golden Jubilee of Her Majesty Queen Elizabeth II.

Date and Mint Mark	One/Two Dollar Coins	No/ of Coins	Issue Price	Mintage	MS-65
2001P	Loon/Polar Bear	7	22.95	52,085	12.00
1952-2002P	Loon/Polar Bear	7	22.95	49,963	20.00
2003P	Loon/Polar Bear	7	22.95	N/A	23.00

PROOF-LIKE AND BRILLIANT UNCIRCULATED SINGLE COINS

During the last fifty years, for one reason or another, collectors of Canadian coins reverted to stripping individual coins from sets issued by the Numismatic Department of the Mint. Besides condition at times being the driving force, there developed in the 1990s another need. Business strikes were just not available if the series was to be maintained. For example the 1992 Caribou twenty-five cents was not issued as a business strike, therefore collectors who wished to maintain that series had to extract the brilliant uncirculated coins from the sets.

PROOF-LIKE SINGLES 1950-1953

All proof-like singles, 1¢ – $1.00, originated from sets, either sold by the Mint on request or given by the Mint Master to persons visiting his office. Of course, on special government occasions coins were struck as presentation gifts to visiting dignitaries. These sets came in either a brown kraft envelope, with the coins enclosed in a cellophane packet, approximately 2" x 3", or in a small white cardboard box of the same dimensions.

Early singles prior 1953 exist but not in sufficient quantities to merit listing. The sets were surprise packages because there was no condition consistency in their contents. More often than not the quality of the six coins was mixed from brilliant uncirculated to specimen. We must remember these sets were considered gifts and thus there was no need for a uniform quality to be adhered to.

The coins listed below all originated from the Mint via this gateway. The quality of the coins listed is proof-like (PL-65). Set prices are not listed simply because they were seldom found, and if available they were more than likely assembled after the fact.

Date and Mint Mark	1¢	5¢	10¢	25¢	50¢	$1
1950	—	—	—	—	—	375.
1950 Arn.	—	—	—	—	—	2,500.
1950 SWL	—	—	—	—	—	1,500.
1951	2,500.	—	—	150.	350.	325.
1951 Arp.	—	—	—	—	—	2,000.
1952 WL	—	—	—	500.	350.	600.
1952 NWL	—	—	—	—	—	350.
1952 SWL	—	—	—	—	—	2,000.
1953 NSF	125.	125.	125.	200.	700.	1,200.
1953 SF	50.	50.	75.	150.	350.	850.

NUMISMATIC ONE DOLLAR

PROOF-LIKE SILVER DOLLARS 1954-1964

In 1954 the Royal Canadian Mint began a program of selling specially struck dollar coins to collectors. These proof-like dollars were packaged in cellophane envelopes between the years 1954 and 1961, and from 1962 to 1964 in pliofilm pouches. Listed below are the issue price and mintage of each year.

Date	Issue Price	Mintage	Date	Issue Price	Mintage
1954	1.25	5,300	1959	1.25	13,583
1955	1.25	7,950	1960	1.25	18,631
1955 Arn	1.25	Incl. above	1961	1.25	22,555
1956	1.25	10,212	1962	1.25	47,591
1957	1.25	16,241	1963	1.25	290,529
1958	1.25	33,237	1964	1.25	1,209,279

PROOF-LIKE NICKEL DOLLARS

Proof-like nickel dollars were issued for collectors in 1968 and 1969. They were packaged by the Royal Canadian Mint in pliofilm strips of five coins per strip. This method of packaging was discontinued in 1969.

Date and Description	Issue Price	Mintage
1968	1.25	885,124
1969	1.25	211,112

PROOF-LIKE SINGLES (PL-65) 1954-1967

As in the previous listing all single proof-like coins are from sets. However, beginning in 1954 the sets were on sale to the public, and quality became consistant throughout the set, meaning all coins were proof-like, a term the Mint never recognized nor attempted for they were sold under the term brilliant uncirculated "business strikes." In order to avoid complaints regarding quality the premium over face value was minimal — .59 cents, leaving no room to engage in a discussion over quality.

It is in this series that cameo coins are found. Struck from a silver-copper alloy they were easier to strike than the late pure nickel coinage. The ease of striking, coupled with new dies produced cameo coins. The newer the die the better the potential cameo reproduction.

Date and Mint Mark	1¢	5¢	10¢	25¢	50¢	$1
1954 NSF	450.00	–	–	–	–	–
1954	75.00	40.00	40.00	135.00	200.00	300.00
1954 NSF	500.00	–	–	–	–	–
1955	60.00	30.00	30.00	105.00	130.00	200.00
1956	40.00	15.00	15.00	55.00	665.00	110.00
1957	35.00	12.50	12.50	50.00	60.00	100.00
1958	22.00	6.00	6.00	25.00	30.00	55.00
1959	17.50	5.00	5.00	12.00	15.00	25.00
1960	15.00	4.00	4.00	10.00	12.00	20.00
1961	15.00	3.00	3.00	8.00	11.00	18.00
1962	2.00	2.00	2.00	6.00	7.00	12.00
1963	1.00	1.00	1.00	3.75	4.75	7.50
1964	1.00	1.00	1.00	3.50	4.50	7.00
1965	1.00	1.00	1.00	3.50	4.50	7.00
1966	1.00	1.00	1.00	3.50	4.50	7.00
1967	2.00	2.00	2.00	5.00	6.50	10.00

PROOF-LIKE SINGLES 1968-1976

With the withdrawal of silver from circulating coinage and its replacement by nickel, two factors emerged in the production of coinage for sets: (1) coinage became a little more difficult to produce due to the hardness of nickel; (2) the high pressure needed to bring design to the coins. Cameo coinage for all intents and purposes no longer existed. It is not that it was gone forever, but that it is very seldom found in this series. Frosted relief on a mirror field appeared in 1973 on the Montreal Olympic silver $5 and $10 coins.

Date and Mint Mark	1¢	5¢	10¢	25¢	50¢	$1
1968	1.00	1.00	1.00	2.00	2.50	3.50
1968 Small Island	–	–	–	–	–	14.00
1968 No Island	–	–	–	–	–	12.00
1968 XWL, Double Die	–	–	–	–	–	100.00
1969	1.00	1.00	1.00	2.25	2.50	3.50
1970	1.00	1.00	1.00	2.75	2.75	4.00
1971	1.00	1.00	1.00	2.25	2.75	4.00
1972	1.00	1.00	1.00	2.25	2.75	4.00
1973	1.00	1.00	1.00	2.50	3.00	4.50
1973	–	–	–	185.00	–	–
1974	1.00	1.00	1.00	2.00	2.75	4.00
1975	1.00	1.00	1.00	2.00	2.75	4.25
1976	1.00	1.00	1.00	2.00	2.75	4.50

Note: For 1968 XWL, Double Die image, please refer to page 344.

BRILLIANT UNCIRCULATED SINGLES 1977-1980

1976 was the last year for proof-like coinage, and 1977 was the beginning of the brilliant uncirculated sets offered by the Royal Canadian Mint, a term recognized and supported in their marketing plans. The finish was brilliant relief – brilliant background.

Date and Mint Mark	1¢	5¢	10¢	25¢	50¢	$1
1977	1.00	1.00	1.00	2.00	2.75	4.25
1977 SWL	–	–	–	–	–	8.50
1978	1.00	1.00	1.00	2.00	2.75	4.25
1978 Round Jewel	–	–	–	–	12.50	–
1979	1.00	1.00	1.00	2.00	2.50	4.25
1979 Ptd Bust	–	–	–	–	5.00	–
1980	1.00	1.00	1.00	2.00	2.75	4.25

BRILLIANT UNCIRCULATED SINGLES 1981–1995

In 1981 the Royal Canadian Mint continued the revamping process of collector sets. The brilliant uncirculated set is continued, the specimen set is now recognized as containing specimen coinage, a condition above brilliant uncirculated, and the proof set, known in the 1970s as the double dollar set, is now recognized as proof quality for the first time by the Royal Canadian Mint.

Date and Mint Mark	1¢	5¢	10¢	25¢	50¢	$1
1981	1.00	1.00	1.00	2.00	2.75	4.25
1982	1.00	1.00	1.00	2.00	2.575	4.00
1983	1.50	1.50	2.00	2.50	3.75	7.25
1984	1.50	1.50	2.00	2.50	4.00	6.50
1985	1.50	1.50	2.00	2.50	4.00	7.50
1986	1.50	1.50	2.00	2.50	4.00	7.50
1987	1.50	1.50	1.75	2.25	3.50	5.50
1988	1.50	1.50	1.75	2.25	3.50	5.50
1989	2.00	2.00	2.50	4.50	6.00	9.00
1990	2.00	2.00	2.50	4.50	6.00	9.00
1991	3.50	8.00	3.50	22.00	15.00	15.00
1992	2.50	2.50	3.00	10.00	6.00	10.00
1993	1.00	1.00	1.00	2.25	3.00	4.50
1994	1.50	1.50	2.00	2.50	4.00	6.50
1995	1.75	1.75	2.25	4.00	5.00	8.00

SPECIMEN AND BRILLIANT UNCIRCULATED SINGLES 1996–1997

In 1996, for whatever reason, the Royal Canadian Mint chose to package specimen quality coinage instead of the normal brilliant uncirculated quality in pliofilm packets, the same that had been historically used for the past 35 years. Specimen quality is brilliant relief – parallel finish background. Specimen dies, after striking approximately 1,000 coins lose the parallel finish background and are turned over to the production of brilliant uncirculated coinage. This may explain the variation in quality that is found in these sets. The quality reverted to brilliant uncirculated, brilliant relief – brilliant background, in 1998.

Date and Mint Mark	1¢	5¢	10¢	25¢	50¢	$1	$2
1996	3.00	3.00	4.00	10.00	15.00	20.00	–
1997	1.75	1.75	2.00	6.00	4.00	8.00	6.00

BRILLIANT UNCIRCULATED SINGLES 1999-2003

In this series two Canadian first are recognized: (1) mint marks denoting the production of coins at either of the Ottawa or Winnipeg mints; (2) the innovation of the "P" mark to distinguinsh the plated steel variety of coinage introduced in 1999.

Again, the finish is brilliant relief – brilliant background.

1999 $2.00 Nunavut nickel/copper
brilliant uncirculated

Narrow ring
obverse and reverse

$2.00 brilliant uncirculated
nickel/copper mule

Narrow ring obverse
No ring reverse

1999 $2.00 Nunavut
silver proof

Narrow ring obverse
No ring reverse

The brilliant uncirculated nickel/copper mule is found only in brilliant uncirculated sets.

Date and Mint Mark	1¢	5¢	10¢	25¢	50¢	$1	$2
1998O	2.25	2.25	2.50	9.00	4.00	8.00	6.00
1998W	2.00	2.00	3.00	7.00	4.00	8.00	6.00
1999 Bear	2.00	2.00	2.50	7.00	4.00	8.00	6.00
1999 Nunavut	–	–	–	–	–	–	8.00
1999 Nunavut Mule	–	–	–	–	–	–	250.00
1999P	10.00	10.00	10.00	20.00	25.00	–	–
2000	2.00	2.00	2.50	7.00	4.00	8.00	6.00
2000W	2.00	2.00	2.50	7.00	4.00	8.00	6.00
2001P	2.25	2.25	2.50	3.50	5.00	7.00	10.00
1952-2002P	2.25	2.25	2.50	3.50	5.00	7.00	10.00
2003P	2.25	2.25	2.50	3.50	5.00	7.00	10.00

CUSTOM SETS 1971-1980

PROOF-LIKE CUSTOM SETS 1971-1976

The custom set contained one of each denomination with an extra cent to show the obverse. The quality of the coins is brilliant relief – brilliant background. Marketing of these sets ceased in 1976.

Cases: **1971:** Coins in black vinyl-cover case with Canada's coat of arms and the word "CANADA" stamped in gold on the top.

1972-1973: As 1971, except the vinyl is red.

1974-1976: As 1971, except the vinyl is maroon.

Date	One Dollar Coins	No. of Coins	Issue Price	Mintage	SP-65
1971	B.C.	7	6.50	33,517	7.50
1972	Voyageur	7	6.50	38,198	7.50
1973 LB 25¢	P.E.I.	7	6.50	49,376	200.00
1973 SM 25¢	P.E.I.	7	6.50	Incl. above	7.50
1974	Voyageur	7	8.00	44,296	7.50
1975	Voyageur	7	8.00	36,851	7.50
1976	Voyageur	7	8.15	28,162	8.50

CUSTOM SPECIMEN SETS 1977-1980

With the end of the 1976 Montreal Olympic Coin program, and with a new numismatic production facility now in place, the Mint turned their sights to improving the quality of their numismatic product line. The quality of the custom sets was upgraded to specimen. The packaging remained constant except for the modifications listed below.

Cases: **1977 to 1978:** Coins in maroon vinyl-covered case with Canada's coat of arms and the word "CANADA" stamped in gold on the top.

1979-1980: As 1977, except a gold maple leaf replaces the coat of arms and "CANADA"

Date	One Dollar Coins	No. of Coins	Issue Price	Mintage	SP-65
1977	Voyageur	7	8.15	44,198	8.50
1978	Voyageur	7	8.75	41,000	8.60
1979	Voyageur	7	10.75	31,174	8.50
1980	Voyageur	7	12.50	41,447	9.50

SPECIMEN SETS

SIX COIN NICKEL SPECIMEN SETS 1981-1996

1981 saw the first official issue of specimen coinage. The package was redesigned, and the coins were marketed as being of specimen quality, and the contents of the set reduced to six coins. The finish on the coins from 1981 to 1995 was brilliant relief – brilliant background, and in 1996 was changed to brilliant relief – parallel background.

Cases: **1981-1987:** Blue leatherette, booklet type (103 mm x 141 mm), inside a hinged blue plastic frame housing, six encapsulated coins. All enclosed in a silver box.

1988-1996: Blue leatherette, wallet type, (96 mm x 153 mm) silver stamped mint crest, inside clear plastic frame with blue plastic insert. All enclosed in a silver sleeve.

Date	One Dollar Coins	No. of Coins	Issue Price	Mintage	SP-65
1981	Voyageur	6	10.00	71,300	8.50
1982	Voyageur	6	11.50	62,298	8.50
1983	Voyageur	6	12.75	60,329	8.50
1984	Voyageur	6	12.95	60,030	8.50
1985	Voyageur	6	12.95	61,533	9.50
1986	Voyageur	6	12.95	67,152	9.50
1987	Voyageur	6	14.00	74,441	11.00
1988	Loon	6	14.00	70,205	16.00
1989	Loon	6	16.95	66,855	21.00
1990	Loon	6	17.95	76,611	21.00
1991	Loon	6	17.95	68,552	50.00
1992	Loon	6	18.95	78,328	29.00
1993	Loon	6	18.95	77,351	23.00
1994	Loon	6	19.25	75,973	24.00
1995	Loon	6	19.25	77,326	22.00
1996	Loon	6	19.25	62,125	32.50

SEVEN COIN NICKEL SPECIMEN SETS 1997-2000

In 1997 the two dollar coin was added to the set, raising the the number of coins back to seven. The set continued as specimen quality with the packaging being revised in 1998. The finish on the coins was continued as brilliant relief – brilliant parallel background.

Case of Issue: **1997: as 1996** and previous
1998 to Date: Green leatherette outer cover with RCM logo. All enclosed in a multicoloured box.

Date	One/Two Dollar Coins	No. of Coins	Issue Price	Mintage	SP-65
1997	Flying Loon/Polar Bear	7	26.95	97,595	47.50
1998	Loon/Polar Bear	7	26.95	67,697	32.50
1999	Loon/Polar Bear	7	26.95	46,786	37.50
1999	Loon/Nunavut	7	26.95	45,104	40.00
2000	Loon/Polar Bear	7	34.95	87,965	35.00
2000	Loon/Polar Bears	7	34.95	Inc. above	35.00

SEVEN COIN MULTI-PLY PLATED STEEL SPECIMEN SETS, 2001 TO DATE

The 2002 specimen set is a double anniversary set issued to commemorate the Golden Jubilee of Queen Elizabeth II, and the 15th anniversary of the Loon dollar coin which was introduced in 1987. This is the only set which contains the "Family of Loons." The finish on the coins is the same as that of 1997-2000.

Date	One/Two Dollar Coins	No. of Coins	Issue Price	Mintage	SP-65
2001P	Loon/Polar Bear	7	39.95	54,613	35.00
1952-2002P	Loon Family/Polar Bear	7	39.95	66,268	40.00
2003P	Loon/Polar Bear	7	39.95	N/A	40.00

PRESTIGE SETS 1971-1980

When it was first introduced in 1971, the prestige set (double dollar set) had two nickel dollars, with the second nickel dollar being used to display the obverse. This was also true for the 1972 set, however from 1973 on the second nickel dollar was replaced with a silver dollar. The quality of the coins in the prestige set are specimen until 1980 and proof thereafter.

Cases: **1971-1973:** Crest of Canada; black leather, book type with clasp. Red satin inside red flocked 7-hole stationary display - coloured flocked jackets.

1974-1978: Crest of Canada; black leather, book type with clasp. Red satin inside, hinged black plastic 7-hole display - coloured flocked jackets.

1979-1980: Maple Leaf; black cardboard box, book type with clasp. Red satin inside, hinged black plastic 7-hole display - coloured flocked jackets.

SPECIMEN SETS 1971-1980

Date	One Dollar Coins	No. of Coins	Issue Price	Mintage	SP-65
1971	B.C./B.C.	7	12.00	66,860	18.00
1972	Voyageur/Voyageur	7	12.00	36,349	29.00
1973 LB 25¢	P.E.I./R.C.M.P.	7	12.00	119,891	180.00
1973 SB 25¢	P.E.I./R.C.M.P.	7	12.00	Incl. above	21.00
1974	Winnipeg/Winnipeg	7	15.00	85,230	14.00
1975	Voyaguer/Calgary	7	15.00	97,263	14.00
1976	Voyaguer/Parliament	7	16.00	87,744	14.00
1977	Voyageur/Jubilee	7	16.00	142,577	14.00
1977 SWL	Voyageur/Jubilee	7	16.00	Incl. above	18.00
1978	Voyageur/Edmonton	7	16.50	147,000	14.00
1978 RB	Voyaguer/Edmonton	7	16.50	Incl. above	28.00
1979	Voyageur/Griffon	7	18.50	155,698	16.00
1980	Voyageur/Polar Bear	7	36.00	162,875	26.00

PROOF SETS 1981 TO DATE

In the product mix reorganization of 1981 the prestige set of previous years was now upgraded to proof status, frosted relief – brilliant (mirror) background.

Cases: **1981-1985:** Maple Leaf; black cardboard box, book type with clasp. Red satin inside, hinged black plastic 7-hole display - coloured flocked jackets.

1986-1997: Maple leaf; black plastic box, wallet type. Red satin inside, hinged black plastic 7-hole display - coloured flocked jacket.

1998 to date: Mint logo; dark green leather case with black plastic 8-hole insert, green interior with outer box

SEVEN COIN NICKEL PROOF SETS 1981-1995

Date	One Dollar Coins	No. of Coins	Issue Price	Mintage	PR-65
1981	Voyageur/Train	7	36.00	199,000	22.00
1982	Voyageur/Skull	7	36.00	180,908	15.00
1983	Voyageur/Games	7	36.00	166,779	16.00
1984	Voyageur/Toronto	7	40.00	161,602	22.50
1985	Voyageur/Parks	7	40.00	153,950	25.00
1986	Voyageur/Vancouver	7	40.00	176,224	22.50
1987	Voyageur/Davis Strait	7	43.00	175,686	22.50
1988	Loon/Ironworks	7	43.00	175,259	27.50
1989	Loon/MacKenzie	7	46.95	154,693	27.50
1990	Loon/Kelsey	7	48.00	158,068	27.50
1991	Loon/Empress	7	48.00	131,888	87.50
1992	Loon/Stagecoach	7	49.75	147,061	40.00
1993	Loon/Hockey	7	49.75	143,065	30.00
1994	Loon/Dogsled Team	7	50.75	104,485	47.50
1995	Loon/Hudson's Bay	7	50.75	101,560	32.50

SEVEN COIN SILVER PROOF SETS 1996

Beginning in 1996 the five cent, ten cent, twenty-five cent and fifty cent coins were struck in sterling silver (92.5% Ag and 7.5% Cu). All other specifications remained the same. The sterling silver and loon dollars, along with the one cent coin remained unchanged.

Date	One Dollar Coins	No. of Coins	Issue Price	Mintage	PR-65
1996	Loon/McIntosh	7	66.25	112,835	60.00

EIGHT COIN SILVER PROOF SETS 1997 TO DATE

In 1997 the two dollar coin was added to the set, raising the total to eight coins. The two dollar coin, following the practice established in 1996, was made of sterling silver with a gold plated centre. The one cent coin up to and including 2003, is not the multi-ply plated steel variety, but of bronze composition.

Date	One/Two Dollar Coins	No. of Coins	Issue Price	Mintage	PR-65
1997	Loon/Hockey/Bear	8	79.95	113,647	67.50
1998	Loon/R.C.M.P./Bear	8	79.95	93,632	77.50
1999	Loon/ Queen Charlotte/Bear	8	79.95	95,113	135.00
2000	Loon/Discovery/Bear	8	79.95	90,921	95.00
2001	Loon/Ballet/Bear	8	81.95	74,194	85.00
1952-2002	Loon/Queen Elizabeth II / Bear	8	81.95	65,461	100.00
1952-2002	ANA Edition as above	8	59.99	500	125.00
2003	Loon/Cobalt/Bear	8	81.95	N/A	85.00

Note: ANA 2002 Building Fund Sets contain a numbered ANA certificate of authenticity.

PROOF SINGLES 1981 TO DATE

The finish on all coins is proof, frosted relief − brilliant (mirror) background

Date and Mint Mark	PROOF-65						
	1¢	5¢	10¢	25¢	50¢	$1	$2
1981	5.00	5.00	5.00	6.00	6.00	7.00	−
1982	5.00	5.00	5.00	6.00	6.00	7.00	−
1983	5.00	5.00	5.00	6.00	6.00	7.00	−
1984	5.00	5.00	5.00	6.00	6.00	7.00	−
1985	5.00	5.00	5.00	6.00	6.00	7.00	−
1986	5.00	5.00	5.00	6.00	6.00	7.00	−
1987	5.00	5.00	5.00	6.00	6.00	7.00	−
1988	5.00	5.00	5.00	6.00	6.00	7.00	−
1989	5.00	5.00	5.00	6.00	6.00	7.00	−
1990	5.00	5.00	5.00	6.00	6.00	7.00	−
1991	10.00	10.00	10.00	15.00	20.00	30.00	−
1992	7.50	7.50	7.50	10.00	10.00	18.00	−
1993	5.00	5.00	5.00	6.00	6.00	7.00	−
1994	5.00	5.00	5.00	6.00	6.00	7.00	−
1995	5.00	5.00	5.00	6.00	6.00	7.00	−
1996	4.00	4.00	4.00	6.00	6.00	6.00	12.00
1997	4.00	4.00	4.00	6.00	6.00	9.00	18.00
1998	4.00	4.00	4.00	6.00	6.00	18.00	35.00
1999	4.00	4.00	4.00	12.00	12.00	35.00	75.00
2000	4.00	4.00	4.00	8.00	8.00	22.00	45.00
2001	4.00	4.00	4.00	6.00	6.00	22.00	45.00
1952-2002	4.00	4.00	4.00	8.00	8.00	25.00	50.00
2003	4.00	4.00	4.00	5.00	6.00	18.00	35.00

SPECIAL ISSUES

100TH ANNIVERSARY OF CONFEDERATION 1867-1967

In 1967 the Royal Canadian Mint produced two special cased coins sets to mark the 100th anniversary of Confederation. The silver medallion set in the red leather-covered case contained one each of the 1¢ to $1 (proof-like quality) and a sterling silver medallion designed and modelled by Thomas Shingles. The gold presentation set contained a $20 gold coin and one each of the 1¢ to $1, all of specimen quality. The coins were housed in a black leather-covered case.

Date	Description	No of Coins	Issue Price	Mintage	PR-65
1967	Silver Medallion	6 + med.	12.00	72,463	25.00
1967	20 Dollar Gold	7	40.00	337,687	350.00

SPECIAL LIMITED EDITION PROOF SETS

First issued in 1994 these proof sets were limited to 50,000. They contained the silver dollar commemorative, along with the bronze/nickel commemorative of the year. The other five coins are the same as contained in the prestige set of that year. Limited edition proof sets were not issued after 1995

Case: Burgundy display case, wallet type, dated on spine with year of issue.
Interior: White satin with brown plastic display frame - burgundy plastic box.

Date	Dollar Coins	No. of Coins	Issue Price	Mintage	PR-65
1994	Remembrance/ Dog Team Patrol	7	59.50	49,222	40.00
1995	Peacekeeping/ Hudson's Bay	7	66.95	49,802	40.00

COMMEMORATING THE INTRODUCTION OF THE TWO DOLLAR COIN 1996

To inaugurate the launch of Canada's new two dollar coin the Royal Canadian Mint issued three variations, each packaged with a two dollar bank note. The proof coin is accompanied by an uncirculated replacement (BRX) note and the uncirculated coin is accompanied by one of the last $2 bank notes printed. Also a special two dollar set with a Piedfort coin struck in sterling silver with a gold plated inner core, (see page 288) and two uncut uncirculated replacement (BRX) two dollar bank notes was issued.

Cases: Unc: Blue presentation box
Proof : Presentation folder illustrated with polar bears
Piedfort: Blue leatherette display case with flocked interior

Date	Description	Mintage	Issue Price	Market Price
1996	$2 Unc, $2 Note	91,427	29.95	10.00
1996	$2 Proof, $2 BRX Note	27,103	79.95	25.00
1996	$2 Piedfort, uncut pair, $2 BRX Notes	11,526	179.95	90.00

90th ANNIVERSARY OF THE ROYAL CANADIAN MINT 1908-1998

Issued to commemorate the 90th Anniversary of the Royal Canadian Mint, this five coin set features the same reverse designs as the original 1908 coins, except for the double date 1908-1998. The set was issued in two finishes, matte and mirror proof. The matte set cent does not carry the country of origin, "Canada." This error was corrected on the mirror proof set.

Designer:
   Obverse: Dora de Pédery-Hunt
   Reverse: 1¢ – G. W. DeSaulles
         5¢, 10¢, 25¢, 50¢ –
         W. H. J. Blakemore

Modeller:
   Obverse: Dora de Pédery-Hunt
   Reverse: Ago Aarand

Case of Issue: Burgundy leather clam type case, gold Mint logo

Specifications

Coin	Composition	Weight	Diameter	Edge	Die Axis
1¢	Copper plated on .925 silver, .075 copper	5.67	25.4	Plain	↑↑
5¢	.925 silver, .075 copper	1.17	15.494	Reeded	↑↑
10¢	.925 silver, .075 copper	2.23	18.034	Reeded	↑↑
25¢	.925 silver, .075 copper	5.81	23.62	Reeded	↑↑
50¢	.925 silver, .075 copper	11.62	29.72	Reeded	↑↑

Pricing

Date	Description	Mintage	Issue Price	Market Price
1998	Antique, 5 Coin Set	24,893	99.00	50.00
1998	Proof, 5 Coin Set	18,376	99.00	50.00

GOLDEN JUBILEE SETS OF QUEEN ELIZABETH II 1952-2002

The Golden Jubilee 50-cent proof coin is included in four different collectors' sets, where it replaces the regular issue. The proof coin is sterling silver in keeping with the previous sets.

The Special Edition Uncirculated Set contains the Golden Jubilee 50-cent piece, and the 1952-2002 Canada Day 25-cent coin; the balance of the coins being the regular double-dated Jubilee 2002P issue.

The Special Edition Proof Set contains a commemorative silver dollar and 50-cent coin, both gold plated; the balance of the coins being the regular proof set issues of 2002.

Date	Description	No. of Coins	Mintage	Issue Price	Market Price
1952-2002	Keepsake Booklet	5 x 50¢	200,170	4.95	6.00
1952-2002	Keepsake Booklet	10 x 50¢	116,034	9.95	11.00
1952-2002	Special Edition Uncirculated Set	7	49,860	15.95	16.00
1952-2002	Special Edition Proof Set	8	32,642	99.95	100.00

FIVE AND TEN DOLLAR GOLD COMMEMORATIVES 1912 - 2002

Issued to mark the 90th anniversary of Canada's first five and ten dollar gold coins in 1912, the double-dated 1912-2002 coins carry on a commemorative series which began in 1998, with the issue recalling the first set of coins struck at the Ottawa Mint. Basing the overall design on the 1912 specimen coins from the Bank of Canada collection, the 1912-2002 gold coins differ only in the date and, of course, the obverse effigy.

Designers:
Obverse: Dora de Pédery-Hunt
Reverse: W.H.J. Blakemore

Physical and chemical specifications:
Denomination: $5. $10.
Weight: (grams) 8.36   16.72
Diameter: 21.59   26.92

Case of Issue: Two-coin clam style case.

Modellers:
Obverse: Dora de Pédery-Hunt
Reverse: Cosme Saffioti

Composition: .900 gold, .100 copper
Edge: Reeded
Die Axis: ↑↑

Date	Description	Issue Price	Mintage	PR-65
1912-2002	$5.00	–	–	250.00
1912-2002	$10.00	–	–	500.00
1912-2002	Set, 2 coins	749.95	1998	750.00

CANADIAN WILDLIFE SERIES
PROOF PLATINUM SETS 1990 - 1994

POLAR BEARS PLATINUM SET 1990. In 1990 the Royal Canadian Mint entered the luxury market for high quality collector coins. Canada's "Monarch of the North" has been transferred from the sparkling Arctic environment by Robert Bateman to the gleaming surface of pure platinum coins.

Designers:
Obverse: Dora de Pédery-Hunt
Reverse: Robert Bateman

Modellers:
Obverse: Dora de Pédery-Hunt
Reverse: $300 - Terry Smith
$150 - William Woodruff
$ 75 - Ago Aarand
$ 30 - Sheldon Beveridge

Physical and chemical specifications:
Denomination: $300 $150 $75 $30
Weight: (oz)   1.000 .500 .250 .100
Diameter: (mm) 30.0 25.0 20.0 16.0
Thickness: (mm) 2.6, 2.12, 1.65, 1.08

Composition: .9995 platinum
Edge: Reeded
Die Axis: ↑↑

Case of Issue: Walnut case with a black suede four hole insert, encapsulated, COA.

Date	Description	Issue Price	Mintage	PR-65
1990	4-coin set	1,990.00	2,629	2,000.

SNOWY OWLS PLATINUM SET 1992. This is the second set in the series of proof platinum coins dedicated to Canadian wildlife.

Designers:
Obverse: Dora de Pédery-Hunt;
Reverse: Glen Loates
Specifications: Same as 1990
Case of Issue: Same as 1990

Modellers:
Obverse: Dora de Pédery-Hunt
Reverse: $300 - Sheldon Beveridge
$150 - Ago Aarand
$ 75 - Terry Smith
$ 30 - William Woodruff

Date	Description	Issue Price	Mintage	PR-65
1991	4-coin set	1,990.00	1,164	2,000.

CANADIAN WILDLIFE SERIES (cont.)

COUGARS PLATINUM SET 1992. This is the third set in the series of proof platinum coins dedicated to Canadian wildlife.

Designers:
Obverse: Dora de Pédery-Hunt
Reverse: George McLean
Specifications: Same as 1990
Case of Issue: Same as 1990

Modellers:
Obverse: Dora de Pédery-Hunt
Reverse: $300 - Ago Aaran, Cosme Saffioti
$150 - Susan Taylor
$ 75 - Sheldon Beveridge
$ 30 - Ago Aarand

Date	Description	Issue Price	Mintage	PR-65
1992	4-coin set	1,955.00	1,081	2,000.

ARCTIC FOXES PLATINUM SET 1993. This is the fourth set in the series of proof platinum coins dedicated to Canadian wildlife.

Designers:
Obverse: Dora de Pédery-Hunt
Reverse: Claude D'Angelo
Specifications: Same as 1990
Case of Issue: Same as 1990

Modellers:
Obverse: Dora de Pédery-Hunt
Reverse: $300 - Susan Taylor
$150 - Sheldon Beveridge
$ 75 - Ago Aarand
$ 30 - Ago Aarand

Date	Description	Issue Price	Mintage	PR-65
1993	4-coin set	1,955.00	1,033	2,000.

CANADIAN WILDLIFE SERIES (cont.)

SEA OTTERS PLATINUM SET 1994. This is the fifth and last set in the series of proof platinum coins dedicated to Canadian wildlife.

Designers:
Obverse: Dora de Pédery-Hunt
Reverse: Ron S. Parker
Specifications: Same as 1990
Case of Issue: Same as 1990,
except burgundy case

Modellers:
Obverse: Dora de Pédery-Hunt
Reverse: $300 - Sheldon Beveridge
$150 - William Woodruff
$ 75 - Terry Smith
$ 30 - Susan Taylor

Date	Description	Issue Price	Mintage	PR-65
1994	4-coin set	1,995.00	766	2,400.

ENDANGERED WILDLIFE SERIES
PROOF PLATINUM SETS 1995 - 2002

CANADA LYNX PLATINUM SET 1995. This is the first set in the series of proof platinum coins commemorating Canada's endangered wildlife.

Designers:
Obverse: Dora de Pédery-Hunt
Reverse: Michael Dumas
Specifications: Same as 1990
Case of Issue:
1/10 oz coin: Leather display case, encapsulated coin
½ oz coin: mahogany case, encapsulated coin
Set, 4 coins: mahogany case, inside green satin, coins individually encapsulated

Modellers:
Obverse: Dora de Pédery-Hunt
Reverse: $300 - Susan Taylor
$150 - Cosme Saffioti
$ 75 - Stanley Witten
$ 30 - Ago Aarand

Date	Description	Issue Price	Mintage	PR-65
1995	30 Dollars	179.95	620	150.
1995	150 Dollars	599.95	226	575.
1995	4-coin set	1,950.00	682	2,100.

ENDANGERED WILDLIFE SERIES (cont.)

PEREGRINE FALCON PLATINUM SET 1996. This is the second set in the series of proof plainum coins commemorating Canada's endangered wildlife.

Designers:	**Modellers:**
Obverse: Dora de Pédery-Hunt	Obverse: Dora de Pédery-Hunt
Reverse: Dwayne Harty	Reverse: $300 - Sheldon Beveridge
Specifications: Same as 1990	$150 - Stanley Witten
Case of Issue: Same as 1995	$ 75 - Cosme Saffioti
	$ 30 - Ago Aarand

Date	Description	Issue Price	Mintage	PR-65
1996	30 Dollars	179.95	910	160.
1996	150 Dollars	599.95	196	575.
1996	4-coins set	2,095.95	675	2,100.

WOOD BISON PLATINUM SET 1997. This is the third set in the series of proof platinum coins commemorating Canada's endangered wildlife.

Designers:	**Modellers:**
Obverse: Dora de Pédery-Hunt	Obverse: Dora de Pédery-Hunt
Reverse: Chris Bacon	Reverse: $300 - Sheldon Beveridge
Specifications: Same as 1990	$150 - William Woodruff
Case of Issue: Same as 1995	$ 75 - Stanley Witten
	$ 30 - Ago Aarand

Date	Description	Issue Price	Mintage	PR-65
1997	30 Dollars	179.95	469	150.
1997	150 Dollars	599.95	116	575.
1997	4-coin set	1,950.00	413	2,100.

ENDANGERED WILDLIFE SERIES (cont.)

GREY WOLF PLATINUM SET 1998. This is the forth set in the series of proof platinum coins commemorating Canada's endangered wildlife.

Designers:
Obverse: Dora de Pédery-Hunt
Reverse: Kerr Burnett

Specifications: Same as 1990
Case of Issue: Same as 1995

Modellers:
Obverse: Dora de Pédery-Hunt
Reverse: $300 - Sheldon Beveridge
$150 - Cosme Saffioti
$ 75 - William Woodruff
$ 30 - Ago Aarand, José Osio

Date	Description	Issue Price	Mintage	PR-65
1998	30 Dollars	179.95	664	150.
1998	150 Dollars	599.95	194	575.
1998	4-coin set	2,095.00	661	2,100.

MUSKOX PLATINUM SET 1999. This is the fifth set in the series of proof platinum coins commemorating Canada's endangered wildlife.

Designers:
Obverse: Dora de Pédery-Hunt
Reverse: Mark Hobson

Specifications: Same as 1990
Case of Issue: Same as 1995

Modellers:
Obverse: Dora de Pédery-Hunt
Reverse: $300 - William Woodruff
$150 - Stanley Witten
$ 75 - Cosme Saffioti
$ 30 - Sheldon Beveridge

Date	Description	Issue Price	Mintage	PR-65
1999	30 Dollars	179.95	999	180.
1999	4-coin set	2,095.95	495	2,100.

ENDANGERED WILDLIFE SERIES (cont.)

PRONGHORN PLATINUM SET 2000. This is the sixth set in the series of proof platinum coins commemorating Canada's endangered wildlife.

Designers:		Modellers:	
Obverse:	Dora de Pédery Hunt	Obverse:	Dora de Pédery Hunt
Reverse:	Mark Hobson	Reverse:	$300 - José Osio
			$150 - Susan Taylor
Specifications:	Same as 1990		$ 75 - Stanley Witten
Case of Issue:	Same as 1995		$ 30 - William Woodruff

Date	Description	Issue Price	Mintage	PR-65
2000	4 coin set	$2,095.95	599	2,100.

HARLEQUIN DUCK PLATINUM SET 2001. This is the seventh set in the series of proof platinum coins commemorating Canada's endangered wildlife.

Designers:		Modellers:	
Obverse:	Dora de Pédery Hunt	Obverse:	Dora de Pédery Hunt
Reverse:	Cosme Saffioti, Susan Taylor	Reverse:	$300 - Stan Witten
			$150 - Susan Taylor
Specifications:	Same as 1990		$ 75 - Cosme Saffioti
Case of Issue:	Same as 1995		$ 30 - Susan Taylor

Date	Description	Issue Price	Mintage	PR-65
2001	4 coin set	$2,395.95	448	2,400.

ENDANGERED WILDLIFE SERIES (cont.)

GREAT BLUE HERON PLATINUM SET 2002. This is the eighth set in the series of proof platinum coins commemorating Canada's endangered wildlife.

Designers:
Obverse: Dora de Pédery Hunt
Reverse: John-Luc Grondin

Specifications: Same as 1990
Case of Issue: Same as 1995

Modellers:
Obverse: Dora de Pédery Hunt
Reverse: $300 - Stan Witten
$150 - Susan Taylor
$ 75 - Stan Witten
$ 30 - José Osio

Date	Description	Issue Price	Mintage	PR-65
2002	4 coin set	$2,495.95	344	2,500.

ARCTIC WALRUS PLATINUM SET 2003. This is the ninth set in the series of proof platinum coins commemorating Canada's endangered wildlife.

Photograph not
available
at press time

Designers:
Obverse: Dora de Pédery Hunt
Reverse: John-Luc Grondin

Specifications: Same as 1990
Case of Issue: Same as 1995

Modellers:
Obverse: Dora de Pédery Hunt
Reverse: $300 - N/A
$150 - N/A
$ 75 - N/A
$ 30 - N/A

Date	Description	Issue Price	Mintage	PR-65
2003	4 coin set	N/A	N/A	N/A

MAPLE LEAF BULLION COINS

In 1979 the Canadian Government introduced a gold bullion coin to compete with similar coins issued by other countries (such as the Krugerrand of South Africa). From 1979 to 1981 only the 50 dollar coin (Maple Leaf) in the one troy ounce size was produced. The Maple Leaf during this period was issued with a gold fineness of .999. During November 1982 the range of the Maple Leaf bullion offering was expanded to three sizes. Now included in the offering were the five dollar or 1/10 maple and the ten dollar or 1/4 maple. With the addition of the two fractional Maple Leafs all sizes were upgraded in gold content to .9999 fine. July of 1986 saw the offering range expanded once again to include the 20 dollar or 1/2 maple. All four coins are produced from 24 karat gold and are legal tender coinage of Canada. In 1988 the Royal Canadian Mint, again expanding on their bullion program, introduced five new coins; four platinum (1/10, 1/4, 1/2 and one maple) and one silver (one maple). In 1990 the reverse hub of the one ounce gold Maple Leaf was re-engraved, enhancing veins in the maple leaf design. Other changes included a more slender stem on the maple leaf and wider spacing of the letters in the legend "Fine Gold 1 oz Or Pur." In 1993 the Royal Canadian Mint added to the series of bullion coin by issuing a 1/20 of an ounce ($1.00) size in gold and platinum. Again in 1994 the $2.00 denomination was added to the bullion coin series (1/15 of an ounce) in both platinum and gold. The $2.00 - 1/15 Maple denomination was discontinued in 1995.

1999 marked the 20th anniversary of the Maple Leaf program. To commemorate this event a privy mark was incorporated into the design of the regular issue Maple Leafs. All denominations carried this privy mark.

GOLD MAPLE LEAFS

REGULAR ISSUES

Twenty Dollars

1/2 Maple

Designer and Modeller:
Obverse:
 1979 to 1989: Arnold Machin, Walter Ott
 1990 to Date: Dora de Pédery Hunt
Reverse:
 1979 to 1989: R.C.M. Staff, W. Ott.
 1990 to Date: R.C.M. Staff
Specifications: See below
Edge: Reeded
Die Axis: ↑↑

1999 20th Anniversary
Issue

2000 Millennium Issue

| | Dollar Value and Ounces | | | | | |
Specifications	$1.00 1/20	$2.00 1/15	$5.00 1/10	$10.00 1/4	$20.00 1/2	$50.00 1.0
Fineness (1979-1982)						.999
Fineness (1982 to date)	.9999	.9999	.9999	.9999	.9999	.9999
Weight (grams)	1.555	2.070	3.131	7.797	15.575	31.150
Diameter (mm)	14.1	15.0	16.0	20.0	25.0	30.0
Thickness (mm)	0.92	0.98	1.22	1.70	2.23	2.80

GOLD MAPLE LEAFS (cont.)

MINTAGES: The production (quantity minted) of regular issue maple leaf bullion coins is on a demand basis. As coins are ordered by the distributors they are struck by the Mint.

		Dollar Value and Ounces					
Composition	Date	$1.00 1/20	$2.00 1/15	$5.00 1/10	$10.00 1/4	$20.00 1/2	$50.00 Maple
Gold	1979	N/I	N/I	N/I	N/I	N/I	1,000,000
	1980	N/I	N/I	N/I	N/I	N/I	1,215,000
	1981	N/I	N/I	N/I	N/I	N/I	863,000
	1982	N/I	N/I	184,000	246,000	N/I	883,000
	1983	N/I	N/I	224,000	130,000	N/I	695,000
	1984	N/I	N/I	226,000	355,200	N/I	1,098,000
	1985	N/I	N/I	476,000	607,200	N/I	1,747,500
	1986	N/I	N/I	483,000	879,200	386,400	1,093,500
	1987	N/I	N/I	459,000	376,800	332,800	978,000
	1988	N/I	N/I	412,000	380,000	521,600	800,500
	1989	N/I	N/I	539,000	328,800	259,200	856,000
	1990	N/I	N/I	476,000	253,600	174,400	815,000
	1991	N/I	N/I	322,000	166,400	96,200	290,000
	1992	N/I	N/I	384,000	179,600	116,000	368,900
	1993	37,080	N/I	248,630	158,452	99,492	321,413
	1994	78,860	3,540	313,150	148,792	104,766	180,357
	1995	85,920	N/I	294,890	127,596	103,162	208,729
	1996	56,520	N/I	179,220	89,148	66,246	143,682
	1997	59,720	N/I	188,540	98,104	63,354	478,211
	1998	44,260	N/I	301,940	85,472	65,366	593,704
	1999	62,820	N/I	709,920	98,928	64,760	627,067
	2000	31,280	N/I	52,970	31,688	24,404	86,375
	2001	20,720	N/I	63,470	35,168	26,556	138,878
	2002	17,140	N/I	450,200	42,940	28,706	344,883
	2003	N/A	N/A	N/A	N/A	N/A	N/A
	2004	N/A	N/A	N/A	N/A	N/A	N/A

Note: N/I refers to Not Issued.

PRICING: Buying and selling prices are based on the interday spot price of bullion plus a small percentage premium for the striking and handling. The smaller the unit the larger the percentage premium charged on buying; however, in later selling the premium could very well disappear.

10TH ANNIVERSARY OF THE MAPLE LEAF BULLION COINS 1989. To commemorate the 10th anniversary of the maple leaf bullion coin program in 1989 the Royal Canadian Mint in 1989 issued a series of proof quality silver, gold and platinum coins individually and in sets. The single coins and sets were packaged in solid maple wood presentation cases with brown velvet liners.

Date	Description	Mintage	Issue Price	Market Price
1989	1 ounce maple	6,817	795.00	550.00
1989	3 coin set; 1 ounce gold, platinum and silver	3,966	1,795.00	1,500.00
1989	3 coin set; 1/10 ounce gold and platinum, and one ounce silver	10,000	195.00	250.00
1989	4 coin set; 1, ½, ¼, 1/10 ounce maples	6,998	1,395.00	1,100.00

125TH ANNIVERSARY OF THE R.C.M.P. 1997. In 1997 the Royal Canadian Mint issued a $50.00 gold (1oz .9999 fine) coin with a guaranteed value of U.S. $310.00 good until January 1st, 2000. After this date the coin has traded at the market price of gold bullion.

Designer: Ago Aarand
Composition: Gold (.9999)
Weight: 31.15 grams, 1 oz
Diameter: 30.00 mm
Edge: Plain, 10-sided

Modeller: Stan Witten
Thickness: 3.25 mm
Die Axis:↑↑
Nominal Value: $50.00

Date	Description	Issue Price	Mintage	Price
1997	Musical Ride	$310.00 US Funds until Jan. 1, 2000	12,913	525.00

GOLD MAPLE LEAF PRIVY MARKS 1997-2001. Beginning in 1997, The Royal Canadian Mint began adding privy marks to specific gold maple leaf denominations to commemorate annual events.

$50 1999-2000
Millennium Fireworks

$10 2001
Basle Fair

Date	Denom. - Size	Issue	Privy Mark	Mintage	Price
1997	$5.00; 1/10 oz	Dillion Gage	Family	100,730	60.00
1998	$5.00; 1/10 oz	Dillion Gage	Eagles	51,440	65.00
1999/2000	$50.00; 1 oz	R.C.M	Fireworks	35,679	75.00
2000	$10.00; 1/4 oz	R.C.M.	Expo Hanover	N/A	200.00
2001	$10.00, 1/4 oz	R.C.M.	Baslerstab	750	250.00
2001	$10.00, 1/4 oz	R.C.M.	Viking	880	200.00
2001	5 coin set		Viking	1000	1,500.00

$10 GOLD MAPLE LEAF HOLOGRAM 2001. A distinctive maple leaf design appears as a high resolution dot matrix hologram, which is struck directly into the coin.

Date	Description	Mintage	Issue Price	Market Price
2001	$10.00; ¼ oz ML cased	14,614	195.00	180.00

GOLD MAPLE LEAF HOLOGRAM SETS 1998-2001. The Hologram Maple Leaf sets are made up of five coins: the maple, half maple, quarter maple, tenth maple and twentieth maple, housed in a presentation box similar to those of the proof platinum wildlife series.

Date	Description	Mintage	Issue Price	Market Price
1998	5 coin set	500	1,995.00	3,500.00
1999	5 coin set	500	1,995.00	3,500.00
2000	Not issued	—	—	—
2001	5 coin set	600	1,995.00	3,500.00

PLATINUM MAPLE LEAFS

REGULAR ISSUE

$50.00 Platinum

Designers and Modellers:
Obverse:
1988 to 1989: Arnold Machin,
Walter Ott
1990 to Date: Dora de Pédery Hunt
Dora de Pédery Hunt
Reverse:
1988 to 1989: R.C.M. Staff, W. Ott.
1990 to Date: R.C.M. Staff
Specifications: See below
Edge: Reeded
Die Axis: ↑↑

| | Dollar Value and Ounces | | | | | |
| | $1.00 | $2.00 | $5.00 | $10.00 | $20.00 | $50.00 |
Specifications	1/20	1/15	1/10	1/4	1/2	Maple
Fineness	.9995	.9995	.9995	.9995	.9995	.9995
Weight (grams)	1.555	2.070	3.131	7.797	15.575	31.150
Diameter (mm)	14.10	15.0	16.00	20.00	25.00	30.00
Thickness (mm)	0.92	0.94	1.01	1.50	2.02	2.52

MINTAGES: The production of maple leafs is on an order basis, unlike the production of coinage for circulation where the Mint will anticipate the number of coins required to fulfill the needs of the economy. Maple leafs will not be struck unless they are ordered.

| | | Dollar Value and Ounces | | | | | |
| | | $1.00 | $2.00 | $5.00 | $10.00 | $20.00 | $50.00 |
Composition	Date	1/20	1/15	1 /10	1/4	1/2	Maple
Platinum	1988	N/I	N/I	46,000	87,200	23,600	26,000
	1989	N/I	N/I	18,000	3,200	4,800	10,000
	1990	N/I	N/I	9,000	1,600	2,600	31,900
	1991	N/I	N/I	13,000	7,200	5,600	31,900
	1992	N/I	N/I	16,000	11,600	12,800	40,500
	1993	2,120	N/I	14,020	8,048	6,022	17,666
	1994	4,260	1,625	19,190	9,456	6,710	36,245
	1995	460	N/I	8,940	6,524	6,308	25,829
	1996	1,640	N/I	8,820	6,160	5,490	62,273
	1997	1,340	N/I	7,050	4,552	3,990	25,480
	1998	2,000	N/I	5,710	3,816	5,486	10,403
	1999	4,000	N/I	4,080	2,092	788	3,248

Note: 1. N/I refers to Not Issued.
2. No single value platinum bullion coins have been issued since 1999.

PRICING: Buying and selling prices are based on the interday spot price of bullion plus a small percentage premium for the striking and handling. The smaller the unit the larger the percentage premium charged on buying, however, in later selling the premium could very well disappear.

10TH ANNIVERSARY OF MAPLE LEAF BULLION COINS 1989. The four-coin proof platinum set was issued to commemorate the 10th anniversary of the first maple leaf coins issued in 1979.

Date	Description	Mintage	Issue Price	Market Price
1989	4 coin set; 1, ½, ¼, 1/10 ounce maple	1,999	1,995.	2,000.

PLATINUM POLAR BEAR ISSUES OF 1999. In 1999 The Royal Canadian Mint issued a special set of platinum Maple Leafs, at the request of a distributor, MTB Bank. They are legal tender coins issued in five denominations with the same specifications as the regular platinum issues but with a polar bear reverse design. The reverse design is a modification of the two dollar polar bear reverse.

Date	Description	Mintage	Issue Price	Market Price
1999	$1.00 - 1/20 oz	1999	N/A	75.
1999	$5.00 - 1/10 oz	1999	N/A	150.
1999	$10.00 - 1/4 oz	999	N/A	350.
1999	$20.00 - 1/2 oz	299	N/A	1,000.
1999	$50.00 - 1 oz	1999	N/A	1,200.
1999	Set, 5 coins	(299)	N/A	2,500.

PLATINUM MAPLE LEAF PROOF HOLOGRAM FIVE-COIN SET 2002. In this set the disctinctive maple leaf appears as a high-resolution dot matrix hologram which has been struck directly onto each of the five coins. The five coins, one ounce, one-half ounce, one-quarter ounce, one-tenth ounce, and one-twentieth ounce are struck with the same specifications and denominations as the regular issues of 1988-1999, see previous page.

Case of Issue: Mahogany box, COA

Date	Description	Mintage	Issue Price	Market Price
2002	Five coin hologram set	500	2,895.95	3,000.

SILVER MAPLE LEAFS

REGULAR ISSUES

The first silver one ounce maple leaf was issued in 1988. The design is a continuation of that used for gold maples. The finish on the maple leaf $5.00 coins is brilliant relief on parallel background.

Designer and Modeller:
Obverse: 1979 to 1989: Arnold Machin, Walter Ott
1990 to date: Dora de Pédery Hunt
Reverse: 1979 to 1989: Royal Canadian Mint,
Walter Ott
1990 to Date: Royal Canadian Mint Staff
Composition: Silver (.9999) **Weight:** 31.15 grams, 1 oz
Diameter: 38.00 mm **Thickness:** 3.21 mm
Edge: Reeded **Die Axis:** ↑↑
Nominal Value: $5.00

Date	Mintage	Price
1988	1,062,000	20.00
1989	3,332,200	16.00
1990	1,708,800	16.00
1991	644,300	16.00
1992	343,800	16.00
1993	1,133,900	16.00
1994	889,946	16.00
1995	326,244	20.00
1996	250,445	50.00
1997	100,970	30.00
1998	591,359	14.00
1999	1,229,442	14.00
2000	403,652	12.00
2001	398,563	12.00
2002	576,196	12.00
2003	N/A	12.00

PRICING: Please remember that the above maple leaf prices are linked to the price of silver and can be priced higher, or lower, than prices shown depending on market conditions. Unlike gold and platinum maple leafs, silver leafs do experience a collector demand which will result in price differentials between dates. The demand is a factor of mintages and their distribution during year of issue.

10TH ANNIVERSARY OF THE MAPLE LEAF BULLION COINS 1989. Issued in 1989 in proof condition to commemorate the 10th anniversary of the introduction of the maple leaf in 1979. Specifications for this coin are the same as the regular issue (see page 378).

Case: Clear finish maple wood box; encapsulated coins; COA.

Date	Description	Mintage	Issue Price	Market Price
1989	1 ounce maple	29,999	39.00	40.00

TEN OUNCE SILVER MAPLE LEAF 1998. In 1998 the Royal Canadian Mint issued the 10 ounce Silver Maple Leaf in celebration of the 10th anniversary of the Silver Maple Leaf bullion coin. This coin is the largest legal tender Canadian coin ever produced. The coin is accompanied by a sterling silver plaque of authenticity. This coin is shown smaller than its actual size.

Designer and Modeller:
Obverse: Dora de Pédery-Hunt
    Reverse: Royal Canadian Mint Staff
Composition: Silver (.9999)
Weight: 311.04 grams, 10 oz

Diameter: 65.0 mm
Thickness: 11 mm
Edge: Lettered, 10th Anniversary
    10e Anniversaire
Nominal Value: $5.00

Date	Description	Mintage	Issue Price	Market Price
1998	10 oz maple	13,533	200.00	150.00

$5 SILVER MAPLE LEAFS WITH PRIVY MARKS 1998-2003. Beginning in 1998 the Royal Canadian Mint started a special issue of the $5.00 - 1 oz silver Maple Leafs. Privy marks were added to the reverse, commemorating special events for each year.

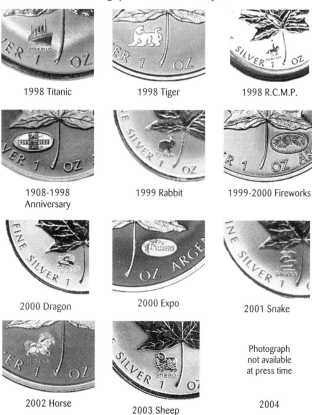

1998 Titanic · 1998 Tiger · 1998 R.C.M.P. · 1908-1998 Anniversary · 1999 Rabbit · 1999-2000 Fireworks · 2000 Dragon · 2000 Expo · 2001 Snake · 2002 Horse · 2003 Sheep · Photograph not available at press time · 2004

Date	Denom - Size	Issuer	Privy Mark	Mintage	Price
1998	$5.00 - 1 oz	Dillon - Gage	Titanic	26,000	60.00
1998	$5.00 - 1 oz	MTB Bank	Tiger	25,000	25.00
1998	$5.00 - 1 oz	Post Office	R.C.M.P.	25,000	50.00
1908 -1998	$5.00 - 1 oz	R.C.M.	90th Anniv.	13,025	25.00
1999	$5.00 - 1 oz	MTB Bank	Rabbit	25,000	25.00
1999-2000	$5.00 - 1 oz	R.C.M.	Fireworks	298,775	15.00
2000	$5.00 - 1 oz	MTB Bank	Dragon	25,000	30.00
2000	$5.00 - 1 oz	R.C.M.	Expo Hanover	N/A	30.00
2001	$5.00 - 1 oz	R.C.M.	Snake	25,000	17.00
2002	$5.00 - 1 oz	R.C.M.	Horse	25,000	17.00
2003	$5.00 - 1 oz	R.C.M.	Sheep	25,000	16.00

Note: The 1998 R.C.M.P. mark was also issued in a special Canada Post presentation book commemorating the 125th anniversary of the force. The presentation book was sold through the Post Office in conjunction with a stamp commemorating the same event.

$5 SILVER MAPLE LEAFS, COLOURIZED, 2001-2004. This four-coin set, depicting the seasons of the year, was first issued in 2001. All specifications are as for the regular issue.

AUTUMN 2001

SPRING 2002

Specifications: As for the regular issue.
Case: Green leatherette case; encapsulated coin; COA

Date	Description	Designer	Mintage	Issue Price	Market Price
2001	$5 / 1 oz, Autumn	Debbie Adams	49,709	34.95	60.00
2002	$5 / 1 oz, Spring		30,000	34.95	40.00
2003	$5 / 1 oz, Summer		N/A	N/A	N/A
2004	$5 / 1 oz, Winter		N/A	N/A	N/A

$5 SILVER MAPLE LEAF HOLOGRAM; "MAPLE OF GOOD FORTUNE." First issued in 2001, the $5 Maple Leaf coin carries a privy mark of Chinese characters, meaning Maple of Good Fortune, or Lucky Maple Leaf, as part of the hologram. The series maintains the traditional bullion finish of a brilliant relief on a frosted background.

Privy Mark 2001

Specifications:	As for the regular issue
Case:	Oval, red velour, clam style; red interior;
	encapsulated coin; COA

Privy Mark 2003

Date	Denom.	Description	Mintage	Issue Price	SP-65
2001	$5/1 oz	Good Fortune	29,817	59.99	100.00
2003	$5/1 oz	Good Fortune	30,000	39.99	45.00

$5 SILVER MAPLE LEAF LOON HOLOGRAM, 15TH ANNIVERSARY OF THE ONE DOLLAR LOON 2002. These maple leaf coins were struck to commemorate the 15th anniversary of the one dollar loon coin issued in 1987. No other coin has caught the imagination of Canadians as the "Loonie."

Specifications:	As for the regular issue
Case:	Black leatherette, clam style case; hunter green interior;
	encapsulated coin; COA

Date	Denom.	Description	Mintage	Issue Price	SP-65
2002	$5	Maple Leaf Loon	30,000	39.95	40.00

$5 SILVER MAPLE LEAF SETS, 2001. Three varieties of silver maples (colourized, hologram and regular) were each combined with the seven proof coins, 1¢ to $2.00 of the 2001 Prestige Set to form the following Premium Proof sets.

Set	Date	Description	Mintage	Price
Set 1	2001	Premium Proof Set, with hologram silver maple leaf, plus 7 coins, 1¢ to $2	3,000	160.00
Set 2	2001	Premium Proof Set, with colourized silver maple leaf, plus 7 coins, 1¢ to $2	Incl. above	90.00
Set 3	2001	Premium Proof Set, with regular silver maple leaf, plus 7 coins, 1¢ to $2	Incl. above	76.00

CHARLTON-ZOELL VARIETY CATALOGUE

After several false starts we have started again, this time we will complete the task. That said here is the grand overall concept. Over the next four or five years, with each successive Standard, starting with the 58th edition, we will add approximately 40 pages on varieties to each catalogue. At the end of the development period we will have a 200-page catalogue of varieties that has been built, priced and researched. Therefore, if a decision is made to separate the varieties section of the Standard, there will be sufficient depth of information for the book to stand alone. To do this we need your help. Over the next few months we will open a variety page on our web site with posting facilities.

Contributors to the Variety Section

Jack Altenburg	Terry Campbell	Patrick Glassford	Joe Kennedy
Ted Bailey	Brian Cornwell	Paul Glover	Marion Krause
Gerald Beaudet	Scott Cornwell	B. Gravestone	Serge Laramee
Paul Bellmore	Morris Furball	Jack Griffin	Ken Potter
	Alain Gallo	Bill Hall	

INTRODUCTION

Since the 5th edition of the Zoel Variety Catalogue in 1970, except for a few good articles in the CNA Journal, very little has been published on varieties in Canada. The complete opposite is true in the United States where dozens of books are in print. Some in their fourth and fifth editions. We are behind in research on minting varieties here in Canada.

Hans Zoell, starting in the early 1960s, was the pioneer of Canadian varieties, but with his retirement and the closing of the Hobby Press in the mid-1970s, variety information ground to a slow crawl. It is with this first 40 pages of the Charlton-Zoell Catalogue that we hope to change this crawl to a walk, then into a trot, and if we are diligent into a run. We will be able to accomplish this if we study the works written by such U.S. notables as E. G. Jewett, Alan Herbert, John A. Wexler, and Bill Fivaz and J.T. Stanton, and carefully adapting their research to Canadian minting varieties, and through this we can make up for lost time.

The main foundation of the U.S. minting varieties is the PDS, three division identification system introduced by Jewett, revised first by Herbert, and refined by him over his five editions of "Official Price Guide to Mint Errors."

The system breaks the minting process down into three basic areas: 1) The planchet, 2) The Die, and 3) The stride. The following pages illustrate a few examples of the over 400 classes that we must eventually cover. It is here, in the following pages, we start with the die and strike divisions.

DIE VARIETIES

II – BROKEN OR DAMAGED HUB VARIETIES: A broken or damaged hub is similar but opposite to its counterpart a broken or damaged die. A broken or damaged die produces raised areas of coin metal on the face of the coin. A broken or damaged hub will produce incused areas on the coin's surface. Remember, the hub design is in relief, the opposite to the die which is incused (see page 387). **Rarity: 3 to 6; Value: $1.00 to $20.00 premium.**

II – CHIPPED CHROME PLATE VARIETIES: Starting in the early 1940s and continuing today all dies produced by the Canadian Mint are chrome plated. Two of the benefits are a smooth surface imparted to the coin, and an increase in the die life. The chrome plating is very thin, therefore if it is chipped or is peeled off, the die is left with a very shallow depression producing a raised relief on the coin's surface (see page 387). **Rarity: 4 to 5; Value: $1.00 premium.**

II – DESIGN EDGE STRIKE VARIETIES: There are four basic methods of lettering or ornamenting the edge of a coin. Two methods are used during the actual striking, and two are proccesses that are applied to the planchet before it is struck. Each mint will have their own style of edge design.

The first method is a steel ring carrying the intended design in relief and the coin is struck in this ring inside a collar. The second method is a set of segmented edge dies which close around the planchet before it is struck. The third method is when the planchet is rolled between a pair of bar dies, each with half of the design or inscription. The fourth method is a slot in a steel block with the design or lettering incused in the slot bottom. The planchet is rolled under the press through the slot (see page 388). **Rarity: 1 to 7; Value: None to $1.00.**

II – DESIGN MODIFICATIONS: Design modifications are minor changes made to a current design to produce a desired result in the design, or the minting process. One main reason for change may be to increase die life. Another may be to improve the overall design asthetics of the coin. Design modification does not belong to the PDS system of classifications (see pages 389-390). **Rarity: 1 to 3; Value: $1.00 to $50.00.**

II – DIE CHIP VARIETIES: Die chips are small irregular raised blobs of metal usually found at the design stress points. They are most often found in the recessed areas of certain letters or numbers. This is because the recessed areas of the letters and numbers on a coin are raised on the die and look like small islands. It does not require much stress before these raised islands of the die start to chip and break off, leaving a raised area on the coin where a recessed area is expected (see page 391). **Rarity: 1 to 2; Value: $1.00 premium**

II – DIE CRACK - DIE BREAK VARIETIES: A die crack may be found anywhere in the die face with no metal missing. The crack may be of any length and in any direction. A die break is a broken area of the die with a missing piece of die metal. Breaks are classified as small, large, rim, and major breaks. Die cracks or breaks may be used as markers (see page 392). **Rarity: 1 to 6; Value: 25-cents to $1.00 premium.**

II – DIE DETERIORATION DOUBLING: Die failure as a result of wear induced by fatigue around the incused letters, or digits of a design element of a die. The doubling usually extends to all sides of the incused elements and may be found on both the obverse and reverse dies. The widening of the letters, digits or design elements is progressive. This form of doubling is often mistaken by the novice for hub doubling. Experts consider this form of doubling damaging to the coin and thus the coin of no premium value except face (see page 393). **Rarity: 1 to 2; Value: 50-cents to $1.00 premium.**

II – DIE OR COLLAR CLASH VARIETIES: When a pair of dies meet with nothing in between to take up the striking force, the dies are free to strike upon one another imparting outlines of the design in the opposite die face. Coins struck from such dies are said to carry clash marks. To classify as a heavy die clash the damage must include a significant portion of the opposite design (see pages 394-395). **Rarity: 3 to 5; Value: $.00 to $50.00 premium.**

II – HUB DOUBLING VARIETIES: In die production a soft steel rod with a shallow conical end is fixed into a hubbing press. A working hub (which was produced from a master die) is placed on top of the die blank, then with extremely high hydraulic pressure the hub is forced into the blank producing a working die. This process may be repeated up to ten times before the design is satisfactorily transferred to the die. The larger the coin the greater the number of pressings required for the transfer. It is in between these many hubbings that doubling occurs. There are eight different hub doubling classes which will be dealt with as the variety book expands. The pricing rule of this variety is that the wider the doubling spread the more the variety will be worth. Hub doubling is commonly known as doubled die (see pages 396-397). **Rarity: 3 to 6; Value: $1.00 to $1,000.00 premium.**

II – OVERPUNCHED DIE VARIETIES: A date or mint mark which is cut, punched or hubbed with the normal style and font size for that date, denomination and series, but is later overpunched with another digit or letter in a different style or font (see page 398). **Rarity: 1 to 7; Value: $1.00 to $500.00 premium.**

II – PITTED OR RUSTED DIE VARIETIES: Pits or rusted areas in the surface of the die result in matching raised points or rough surface areas on the struck coin. Pits may also be the result of holes in the chrome plating due to the improper cleaning of the die before plating. Pits are often used as die markers (see page 398). **Rarity: 3 to 4; Value: No premium value.**

II – POLISHED AND ABRADED DIE VARIETIES: Polished and abraided dies occur when the surface of the die face, including any design, has been altered, removed, ground down, rubbed, scraped, or worn away by the intentional use of an abrasive. The experts consider these coins as damaged and of very little or no value (see pags 399-400). **Rarity: 1; Value: No premium value.**

II – PUNCH ADDITION DIE VARIETIES: A die variety usually found in a colonial mint. The working dies for all Canadian coins from 1908 to the late 1970s were produced at the Royal Mint, London, England, and shipped to Canada at the beginning of each year. If for some reason a design change occurred and the new dies did not arrive on time a device would be added to the previous years dies to distinguish the new year from the previous (see pages 401-402). **Rarity: 1 to 10; Value: Standard value.**

II – PUNCH ADDITION AND SPACING DIE VARIETIES: When the spacing of the punch addition is not placed in the appropriate position but punched in a position other than normal, then another die variety is generated which may be classified by the position it occupies (see pages 403-404). **Rarity: 3 to 5; Value: $1.00 premium.**

II –PUNCH SPACING DIE VARIETIES: Prior to the mid 1970s, at least one or two digits of the date were added to the working die by punching. With a master die being able to produce thousands of working hubs, and these working hubs in a position to produce numerous working dies, it did not make economic sense to seal the use of a master die by completing the date. The addition of letters or digits to a die by punching requires consistency, sometimes lacking in Mint personnel, resulting in spacing differences (see pages 405 to 409). **Rarity: 2 to 5; Value: $1.00 to $10.00 premium.**

II – PUNCH STYLE AND FONT DIE VARIETIES: With a coin design comes the specifications for the type style and fonts to be used on the letters and digits. If for any reason a punch with a change in type style or fonts is later used, a punch style or font die variety is produced (see pages 410-413). **Rarity: 2 to 6; Value: $10.00+ premium.**

II – REPUNCHED DATE AND LETTER VARIETIES: Over the years three different methods have been used in the process of preparing a working die. The earliest being cutting (engaving) a die with hand tools. Following this method was punching, where letters, dates and central designs such as the monarch's bust were themselves made into punches, then punched into a device punch or hub. Today 99.9% of the working dies are made by the hubbing process, with punches still frequently used in making master dies. Early in the 19th century, and continuing to the latter half of the 20th century, letter and digit punches were used extensively on mint marks and dates. Repunching was used to correct mistakes (see pages 410-413). **Rarity: 1 to 7; Value: $1.00+ premium.**

STRIKE VARIETIES

III – MECHANICAL (MACHINE) DOUBLING DAMAGE (MDD): This is the result of a loose die causing die bounce, chatter or die displacement as the die, after the strike, moves sideways or downward across the struck coin before retraction. The sliding action (sideways movement) moves the die into the design leaving a tapered shelf effect (see page 416). **Rarity: 0; Value: No premium value.**

III – MISALIGNED STRIKE VARIETIES: The dies are out of position during the strike. Misalignment takes on two forms; offset and vertical. In offset misalignment either the hammer or the anvil is not centered, resulting in an offset strike from centre of the other die. Vertical misalignment has the hammer die tilted producing a tapered coin (see page 391). **Rarity: 3 to 6; Value: $5.00 to $10.00 premium.**

III – MISMATCHED DIE STRIKE: A coin struck by dies that are not intended to be used as a pair. Dies which do not belong together or would not normally be paired result in mismatched obverse and reverse designs. Mules, which is the common slang term for this variety, are rare in the modern minting process due to very stringent quality controls (see page 417). **Rarity: 5 to 7; Value: $100.00+ premium.**

III – ROTATED DIE STRIKE VARIETIES: All Canadian coins from 1980 on are struck with an upright (medal) axis. Prior to that time, when Canadian coinage was produced in England, an upset (coinage) axis was used. Rotation is measured from the hammer die. In Canada the hammer die is the reverse. When a coin is flipped over, top to bottom, the obverse will be upset. If not, then the degree of rotation is measured. The most collectable is the 180 degree rotation (coinage axis). Rotations less than 10 degrees are not collectable for they may fall within mint tolerances and are considered common (see page 418). **Rarity: 6 to 8; Value: $10.00 to $100.00 premium.**

II – BROKEN OR DAMAGED HUB VARIETIES

NOA SCOTIA ONE CENT 1864
Incomplete "O" in SCOTIA

CANADA ONE CENT 1891
Large Date
Missing serif on "N" in REGINA

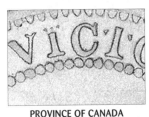

PROVINCE OF CANADA
ONCE CENT 1858
Missing "tops" of VIT in VICTORIA

CANADA TEN CENTS 1881
Missing serifs on "I" in GRATIA

CANADA ONE CENT 1882
Incomplete "O" in VICTORIA

PROVINCE OF CANADA
TWENTY CENTS 1858
Missing top of "T" and "R" in
VICTORIA

II – CHIPPED CHROME PLATE VARIETIES

CANADA ONE CENT 1959

II – DESIGN EDGE STRIKE VARIETIES

Many different collar designs have been used on Canadian coinage. They are plain, lettered, reeded, serrated, interrupted serration and engrailled.

CANADA TWENTY DOLLARS CALGARY OLYMPICS
LETTERED – NON-LETTERED VARIETIES 1988

1985	Speed Skating, lettering
	Speed Skating, no edge lettering
1986	Hockey
	Hockey, no edge lettering
1986	Free Style Skiing, lettering
	Free Style Skiing, no edge lettering
1986	Biathalon, lettering
	Biathalon, no edge letter

CANADA TEN CENTS 1968

Philadelphia Mint
Edge grooves have flat bottoms.

Royal Canadian Mint
Edge groves have V-shaped bottoms.

II – DESIGN MODIFICATIONS

CANADA ONE CENT 1891

Large leaves, Small date – leaves close to beads and vine

Small leaves, Small date – leaves far from beads and vine

CANADA FIVE CENTS 1951

Left: High Relief
Right: A in GRATIA points to a rim denticle

Left: Low Relief
Right: A in GRATIA points between rim denticles

CANADA FIVE CENTS 1953
  The two reverse varieties of Far and Near Maple Leaf are paired with the two obverse varieties of the No Shoulder Fold, Shoulder Fold.

Left: Far maple leaf
Right: No shoulder fold

Left: Near maple leaf
Right: Shoulder fold

II – DESIGN MODIFICATIONS

CANADA TWENTY-FIVE CENTS 1953
The 1953 Large Date is a double variety in that the reverse is married to the No Shoulder Fold obverse, the opposite is true for the Small Date variety.

Small date

Large date

CANADA TWENTY-FIVE CENTS 1978

Canada far from rim

Canada Near rim

CANADA FIFTY CENTS 1978
The jewels in the Queen's crown atop the coat-of-arms were redesigned from square to round.

Square jewels

Round jewels

CANADA FIFTY CENTS 1982
The portrait of Queen Elizabeth was again modified, and the rim beading size was reduced.

Large beads

Small beads

II — DIE CHIP VARIETIES

CANADA ONE CENT 1940

Plugged 4

CANADA ONE CENT 1955

Plugged 9

CANADA FIVE CENTS 1957

Bug tail

CANADA FIVE CENTS 1966

Eyes

CANADA TEN CENTS 1940

Joined 4 and 0

CANADA TEN CENTS 1978

Plugged 8

II – DIE CRACK – DIE BREAK VARIETIES

CANADA FIFTY CENTS 1946
Hoof through "6"

CANADA ONE DOLLARS 1955
A die crack as a marker to confirm the Arnprior variety

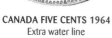

CANADA FIVE CENTS 1964
Extra water line

II – DIE DETERIORATION DOUBLING

CANADA FIVE CENTS 1952

Due to its hardness nickel is a difficult metal to strike. Die ware from the nickel flowing into the letters of the legend results in the ware on the design cavities. Die deterioration doubling is easily recognized by the widening of these cavities.

Doubling on "cents"

Doubling on "Canada"

CANADA FIVE CENTS 1962

Doubling on 1962

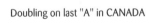

Doubling on last "A" in CANADA

CANADA FIVE CENTS 1979

The two images are not of the same working die, but you can notice the widening of the wearing pattern of die deterioration doubling as the striking procceds.

Doubling on "79"

Doubling on "79"

II – DIE OR COLLAR CLASH VARIETIES

CANADA ONE CENT 1953

Hanging 3

CANADA ONE CENT 1953

Double hanging 3

CANADA ONE CENT 1954

Double hanging 4

CANADA ONE CENT 1961

Hanging 1

CANADA ONE CENT 1962

Triple hanging 2

CANADA ONE CENT 1963

Triple hanging 3

II — DIE OR COLLAR CLASH VARIETIES

CANADA FIVE CENTS 1951

Half moon

CANADA FIVE CENTS 1951

Double Moon

CANADA FIFTY CENTS 1952

Clash in King's ear

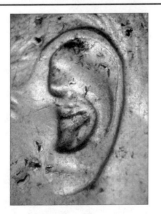

CANADA FIFTY CENTS 1952

Clash in King's ear

II – HUB DOUBLING VARIETIES

CANADA FIFTY CENT 1952
Hub doubling on "HP" of T. H. PAGET.

Doubled "HP"

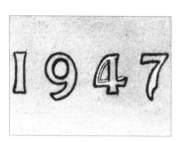

CANADA ONE DOLLAR 1947 POINTED 7

Doubled 4

CANADA ONE DOLLAR 1968
Hub doubling of the water lines in front of the canoe is one of the more classic varieties of this type of variety.

Doubled extra water line

CANADA ONE DOLLAR 1974
This dollar is found with many examples of hub doubling.

Doubled die, double yoke

II – HUB DOUBLING VARIETIES

CANADA ONE DOLLAR 1947 POINTED 7
   As with all examples on this page, the doubling has occurred on the designer's initials.
   This doubling may have been the result of punch doubling.

Doubled "HP"

CANADA ONE DOLLAR 1947 POINTED 7

Tripled "HP"

CANADA ONE DOLLAR 1947 POINTED 7

Quadrupled "HP"

CANADA ONE DOLLAR 1947 MAPLE LEAF

Doubled "HP"

II – OVERPUNCHED DIE VARIETIES

CANADA ONE CENT 1882H
The secondary mint mark is over punched by the primary large H punch

Large H over small H

In this example the secondary narrow H is over punched with the primary wide H punch.

Wide H over narrow H

PROVINCE OF CANADA ONE CENT 1859
The secondary 8 is overpunched with a primary 9 punch.

Wide 9 over 8

CANADA TWENTY-FIVE CENTS 1886
Three years later an 1883 die is overpunched to form an 1886 die (6 over 3).

6 over 3

PITTED OR RUSTED DIE VARIETIES

CANADA TEN CENTS 1956 DOT

II – POLISHED AND ABRADED DIE VARIETIES

CANADA FIFTY CENTS 1950
The first illustration shows the originally issued 50-cent coin, the next two images illustrate different degrees of die resurfacing.

Design in "O"

No design in "O"

No design all around "O"

CANADA FIFTY CENTS 1952

Design between "5" and "2"

No design between "5" and "2"

II – POLISHED AND ABRADED DIE VARIETIES

CANADA FIFTY CENTS 1956

Design to right of "6"

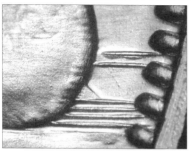

All of the design around the "6" is gone

No design around "6"

CANADA ONE DOLLAR 1968
The regular design is shown (left) before die resurfacing produced the following two varieties.

Island with full waterlines

The Island is almost polished away

Small island, weak waterlines

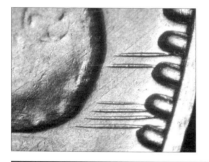

The island has been polished away

No island, weak waterlines

II – PUNCH ADDITION DIE VARIETIES

CANADA ONE CENT 1936 DOT
The series of 1936 Dot coins was produced as interim coinage for 1937.

CANADA TEN CENTS 1936 DOT

CANADA TWENTY-FIVE CENT 1936 DOT

CANADA FIVE CENTS 1947 DOT

CANADA TWENTY-FIVE CENTS 1947 DOT

CANADA ONE DOLLAR 1947 POINTED DOT

II – PUNCH ADDITION DIE VARIETIES

CANADA ONE CENT 1947 MAPLE LEAF
The series of 1947ML coins were struck in 1948.

CANADA FIVE CENTS 1947 MAPLE LEAF

CANADA TEN CENTS 1947 MAPLE LEAF

**CANADA TWENTY-FIVE CENTS
1947 MAPLE LEAF**

CANADA FIFTY CENTS 1947 MAPLE LEAF

Straight 7 variety

CANADA FIFTY CENTS 1947 MAPLE LEAF

Curved 7 variety

CANADA ONE DOLLAR 1947 MAPLE LEAF

II – PUNCH ADDITION AND SPACING DIE VARIETIES

CANADA ONE CENT 1947 MAPLE LEAF
A punch addition results in punch spacing varieties.

Far leaf

Near Leaf

CANADA FIVE CENTS 1947 MAPLE LEAF

High Leaf

Low Leaf

CANADA TEN CENTS 1947 MAPLE LEAF

Attached leaf

Near Leaf

Far Leaf

II — PUNCH ADDITION AND SPACING DIE VARIETIES

CANADA TWENTY FIVE CENTS
1947 MAPLE LEAF

Attached maple leaf

Near maple leaf

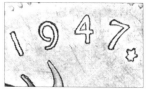

Far maple leaf

II – PUNCH SPACING DIE VARIETIES

NEWFOUNDLAND ONE CENT 1941

The "I" is near to the "4'

The "I" is far from the "4"

NEWFOUNDLAND ONE CENT 1942

The "2" is near to the "4"

The "2" is far to the "4"

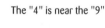

NEWFOUNDLAND FIVE CENTS 1941

The "4" is near the "9"

The "4" is far from the "9"

NEWFOUNDLAND TEN CENTS 1943

The "3" is near to the "4"

The "3" is far from the "4"

II – PUNCH SPACING DIE VARIETIES

CANADA ONE CENT 1888
The last two "8"s are close together

Narrow date

The last two "8"s are far apart

Wide date

CANADA FIVE CENTS 1922
The full date is near the rim, while the last "2" is far from the maple leaf

Near rim

The full date is far from the rim, while the last "2" is near the maple leaf

Far from rim

CANADA FIVE CENTS 1926
Canadian classic example of punch spacing.

Near 6

Far 6

II – PUNCH SPACING DIE VARIETIES

CANADA FIFTY CENTS 1941
"4" and "1" close together

Near

"4" and "1" far apart

Far

CANADA FIFTY CENTS 1943
"4" and "3" close together

Near

"4" and "3" far apart

Far

CANADA FIFTY CENTS 1944
"4" and "4" close together

Near

"4" and "4" far apart

Far

II – PUNCH SPACING DIE VARIETIES

CANADA FIFTY CENTS 1944
The numerals "44" are downward sloping

Low "44"

The numerals "44" are upward sloping

High "44"

CANADA FIFTY CENTS 1945
The "5" is near the "4"

Near 5

The "5" is far from the "4," but also the "5" is a repunched 5

Far 5

CANADA FIFTY CENTS 1945

"5" touches ring   "5" near ring   "5" far from ring

Another series of 1945 punch varieties

II – PUNCH SPACING DIE VARIETIES

CANADA FIFITY CENTS 1946
The "6" is near the "4"

Near "4" and "6"

The "6" is far from the "4"

Far "4" and "6"

CANADA FIFTY CENTS 1947 POINTED 7

The "7" touches the ring

The "7" is far from the ring

ONE DOLLAR 1947

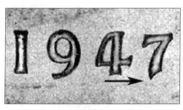

Near 7
The "7" is near the "4"

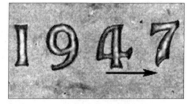

Far 7
The "7" is far from the "4"

II – PUNCH STYLE AND FONT DIE VARIETES

NEWFOUNDLAND ONE CENT 1880
  Thick fonts used, yielding wide digits for a 'wide date' coin, while thin fonts yield a 'narrow date.'

Wide O – Wide fonts yielding thick digits and thus a wide date.

Narrow O – Narrow fonts yielding fine digits and thus a narrow date.

NEWFOUNDLAND TWENTY CENTS 1896

Large 96

Small 96

NEWFOUNDLAND FIFTY CENTS 1899

Wide 99

Narrow 99

II – PUNCH STYLE AND FONT DIE VARIETES

NEW BRUNSWICK ONE CENT 1864
A different type style was used to create the same date.

Tall 6

Short 6

NEW BRUNSWICK FIVE CENTS 1864

Large 6

Small 6

CANADA ONE CENT 1901

Closed 9

Open 9

II − PUNCH STYLE AND FONT DIE VARIETES

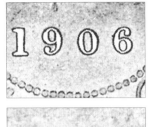

CANADA ONE CENT 1906

Thick date

Thin date

CANADA ONE CENT 1909

Large date

Small date

CANADA FIVE CENTS 1947

Bold date

Thin date

II – PUNCH STYLE AND FONT DIE VARIETES

CANADA TEN CENTS 1980
  Bold type producing a bold date

Bold date

A fine type producing a fine date

Fine date

CANADA TWENTY-FIVE CENTS 1888
  All '8's are wide; whilst the first '8' may be an overdate, the last '8' may be from an broken hub.

Wide 8

Narrow 8

CANADA FIFTY CENTS 1920

Wide 0

Narrow 0

II – REPUNCHED DATE AND LETTER VARIETIES

NEW BRUNSWICK TEN CENTS 1862
A "2" has been punched over an exisiting "2" to the north

Repunched 2

CANADA FIFTY CENTS 1943
A "3" has been punched over an existing "3", to the west

Repunched 3

CANADA FIFTY CENTS 1945
A "5" has been punched over an existing "5", to the west

Repunched 5

CANADA FIFTY CENTS 1947 POINTED 7
A "7" has been punched over an existing "7", to the north

Repunched 7

II — REPUNCHED DATE AND LETTER VARIETIES

CANADA ONE CENT 1859
The "T" in GRATIA, with the primary "T" punched clockwise

"T" in GRATIA secondary T clockwise

CANADA ONE CENT 1859
The "T" in GRATIA, with the primary "T" punched clockwise

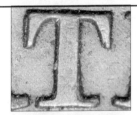

CANADA ONE CENT 1859
The "T" in GRATIA, with the primary "T" punched clockwise

CANADA ONE CENT 1859
The "G" in REGINA, with the primary "G" punched clockwise.

CANADA ONE CENT 1859
The "G" in REGINA, with the primary "G" punched clockwise.

CANADA ONE CENT 1859
The "A" in CANADA, with the last primary "A" punched clockwise.

III – MECHANICAL (MACHINE) DOUBLING DAMAGE (MDD)

CANADA ONE CENT 1962
The shift has rotated the date clockwise

CANADA ONE CENT 1967
The shift has rotated the letter to the west

CANADA FIVE CENTS 1953
The shift in the dies has resulted in the date moving north

CANADA TWENTY-FIVE CENTS 1953
The shift in the dies has the date moving west

CANADA TWENTY-FIVE CENTS 1976
Again, the shift has moved the date to the west resulting in doubling

III — MISMATCHED DIE STRIKE VARIETIES

Dies for the Brilliant Uncirculated Issue
Narrow Ring Obverse

Dies for the Proof Issue
No Ring Reverse

1999 One Dollar Nunavut Mule
Found only in brilliant uncirculated
sets of 1999

II — ROTATED DIE STRIKE VARIETIES

CANADA TEN CENTS 1968
Coinage or upset axis

NEW BRUNSWICK TWENTY FIVE CENTS 1992
Coinage or upset axis

CANADA ONE DOLLAR
CONSTITUTION 1982
Coinage or upset axis

A Course Designed For Canadian Coin Collectors

Have you been bitten by the coin collecting bug? If you're like millions of other people the world over, maybe you have; and just maybe, you find everyday coinage fascinating, that you've decided to collect it. But how exactly should you begin? What should you know before you start to collect the pieces of pocket change which pass through your hands each day?

You probably have a million questions: "What should I collect?" "How should I store my coins?": Where can I meet other collectors like myself?" and "How can I determine the condition of my coins?"

During the past several years, highly talented and knowledgeable team have been developing Canada's first coin collecting correspondence course, for people like you who are new to the hobby as well as for those who have been collecting for some time.

Each of the twelve chapters in the course include a series of fifteen questions, both short answer and multiple choice. Simply read the chapters at your leisure, complete the questions and return them to the CNA/NESA Course Co-ordinator. The course includes more than two hundred pages of material written by many of Canada's renown coin experts. Dozens of supplementary photos are shown as well. Upon completion of the course, you will receive a special "Certificate of Achievement" and three numismatic reference books!

LEARN ALL ABOUT CANADIAN COINS, TOKENS, MEDALS AND PAPER MONEY, FROM A PANEL OF EXPERTS... IN THE PRIVACY AND COMFORT OF YOUR OWN HOME.

(a) Collecting Strategies	(b) Building Your Collection
(c) Storing Your Collection	(d) Grading Coins
(e) The Organized Hobby	(f) "Extinct" Canadian Coins
(g) The "Coining" Process	(h) Canadian Commemorative Coins

...And much, much more. An inexpensive home-study course designed for coin collectors like yourself! Order your course today.

CNA/NESA Numismatic Correspondence Course

Please enroll me in the CNA/NESA Numismatic Correspondence Course. Enclosed is my

cheque, money order or bank draft payable to the Canadian Numismatic Association.

Name: _____

Address:_____

_____

CNA# _____**Phone:** _____

- ❏ CNA Members... $40.00
- ❏ CNA Members... $30.00
  (under 18 yrs of age)

- ❏ Non Members... $60.00
- ❏ Non Members... $40.00
  (Under 18 yrs of age)
  (Includes CNA Membership)

Please forward payment to: The Canadian Numismatic Association
4936 Yonge St., Suite 601, North York, Ontario, Canada M2N 6S3
Tel.: (416) 223-5980 Fax: (416) 223-6782 E-mail: cnainfo@look.ca

420

Application for Membership/ Subscription

Applications for membership/subscription in the Canadian Numismatic Association may be made by any reputable party upon payment of the required dues.

(Check one of each group)
- ❑ New   ❑ Renewal _____   ❑ Reinstatement
- ❑ Regular   ❑ Junior   ❑ Family
- ❑ Corporate   ❑ Life Membership   ·
- ❑ Mr.   ❑ Mrs.   ❑ Ms.   ❑ Club

Name:

Street:

City: Province/State: Postal Code/Zip:

Country:

E-mail address:

Sigature of applicant: Signature of Sponser:

Signature of guardian (if under 18 years of age) Birth date of junior applicant

DUES

Dues shown are in Canadian dollars to Canadian addresses and in U.S. dollars to all other addresses. Payment may be made by money order, bank draft or personal cheque. We regret that we are unable to offer credit card service.

REGULAR –	Canadian and US addresses (18 years of age or over)	$33.00
–	All other addresses (18 years of age or over)	$48.00
JUNIOR –	All addresses	$16.50
	Under 18 must be sponsered by a parent or guardian	
FAMILY –	Husband, wife and children at home, under 18	
–	One journal only	$44.00

ORGANIZATIONS – Clubs, Societies, Libraries, non-profit corporations $33.00

LIFE MEMBERSHIP $595.00

Names and City only of all new members are published in the Journal.

**Please mail application and payment to the
Canadian Numismatic Association,
4936 Yonge St., Suite 601, North York, Ontario, Canada M2N 6S3
Tel.: (416) 223-5980 Fax: (416) 223-6782
E-mail: cnainfo@look.ca**

Application must be complete and accompanied by full dues to be accepted. Please photocopy and mail.